Critical Thinking

Critical Thinking
The Art of Argument

George W. Rainbolt
Georgia State University

Sandra L. Dwyer
Georgia State University

WADSWORTH
CENGAGE Learning™

Australia • Brazil • Japan • Korea • Mexico • Singapore • Spain • United Kingdom • United States

WADSWORTH
CENGAGE Learning™

Critical Thinking: The Art of Argument

George W. Rainbolt
Sandra L. Dwyer

Publisher: Clark Baxter

Senior Sponsoring Editor: Joann Kozyrev

Development Editor: Florence Kilgo

Assistant Editor: Joshua Duncan

Media Editor: Kimberly Apfelbaum

Marketing Manager: Mark T. Haynes

Marketing Coordinator: Josh Hendrick

Marketing Communications Manager:
 Laura Localio

Associate Content Project Manager:
 Sara Abbott

Senior Art Director: Jennifer Wahi

Manufacturing Buyer: Linda Hsu

Senior Rights Acquisition Specialist,
 Text: Katie Huha

Production Service:
 Cadmus Communications

Text Designer: Roy Neuhaus Design

Rights Acquisition Specialist, Image:
 Amanda Groszko

Cover Designer: Jeff Bane, CMB Design

Cover Image: Getty Images

Compositor: KnowledgeWorks Global
 Limited

For product information and technology assistance,
contact us at **Cengage Learning
Customer & Sales Support, 1-800-354-9706**

For permission to use material from this text or product,
submit all requests online at
www.cengage.com/permissions.
Further permissions questions can be emailed to
permissionrequest@cengage.com.

Library of Congress Control Number: 2010932169
ISBN-13: 978-0-495-50157-2
ISBN-10: 0-495-50157-3

Wadsworth
20 Channel Center Street
Boston, MA 02210
USA

Cengage Learning is a leading provider of customized learning solutions with office locations around the globe, including Singapore, the United Kingdom, Australia, Mexico, Brazil and Japan. Locate your local office at **international.cengage.com/ region**

Cengage Learning products are represented in Canada by Nelson Education, Ltd.

For your course and learning solutions, visit **www.cengage.com.**

Purchase any of our products at your local college store or at our preferred online store **www.CengageBrain.com.**

Printed in Canada
1 2 3 4 5 6 7 14 13 12 11 10

Brief Contents

Contents

CHAPTER 2   What Makes a Good Argument?   42

CHAPTER 3 Premises and Conclusions   86

CHAPTER 6   Categorical Arguments   174

CHAPTER 7   Analogical Arguments   228

CHAPTER **8**   Statistical Arguments   258

CHAPTER 10 Moral Arguments   342

The following additional chapters are available for inclusion in custom versions of *Critical Thinking: The Art of Argument:*

Custom Chapter A: Propositional Arguments in a Formal Language

Custom Chapter B: Aristotelian Categorical Arguments

Custom Chapter C: Success in College, More Than Critical Thinking

Custom Chapter D: Critical Thinking Across The Disciplines

Contact your Cengage Learning representative for more information.

Preface

Why *Critical Thinking: The Art of Argument?*

In 2006, we faced the task of choosing the textbook for Phil 1010, Critical Thinking. At Georgia State University, Phil 1010 is a core curriculum course, taken by more than 3,000 students a year, and taught almost exclusively by graduate students. During our textbook search, we identified two challenges that our textbook must meet. First, we needed a book that would help students acquire skills quickly. Georgia State students take Critical Thinking because the course is required. They are under pressure to quickly acquire the skills needed to complete their courses for graduation and they do best if it is clear to them that the course and the required book are helping prepare them for college classes and the rest of their life. Second, we wanted our Critical Thinking instructors, many of whom are in their first year of teaching, to be able to trust the book to explain the fundamentals clearly and accurately so that they do not have to defend oversimplifications and omissions.

In short, we needed a textbook that was **accessible** (easy for students to read and understand), **relevant** to students' lives (both in and out of the classroom), and **rigorous** (did not oversimplify the material).

None of the existing textbooks that we reviewed met all of these criteria, so we wrote *Critical Thinking: The Art of Argument*. Over the course of three years, the book was tested with more than 10,000 students and more than fifty instructors. We revised the book three times in light of classroom feedback, and then, based on reviewer feedback, we revised it further before issuing this first edition. Throughout this process, we focused on maintaining the rigor that has made the text a success at Georgia State. For the four semesters prior to the introduction of the new textbook, 26% of students in Critical Thinking earned an unsatisfactory grade (i.e., a D, a W, or an F), but in the four semesters after the introduction of the new book, only 21.2% of students in the course earned an unsatisfactory grade.

Through this process, we also refined our own understanding of what we meant by "rigor." The right balance needs to be achieved between two extremes: lengthy, complicated explanations and oversimplified, incomplete presentations. "Rigorous" does not mean overly complex and incomprehensible. On the other hand, every teacher has had the experience of presenting a simplified definition or explanation to a class of students, only to have a good student raise a hand and ask, "But what about..." or say "But that doesn't make sense if...." Extensive class testing and several development reviews have helped us craft, test, and clarify explanations and examples to ensure that they are rigorous, relevant, and accessible.

What You Will Find in *Critical Thinking: The Art of Argument*

Critical Thinking: The Art of Argument introduces all major types of arguments. Its focus on accessibility and rigor particularly enhances the presentation of analogical, statistical, and causal arguments. The book's informal, conversational style and relevant, real-life examples from students' lives in class, online, with friends, or at home are proven tools that facilitate comprehension without sacrificing accuracy or thoroughness. In addition, extensive sets of exercises emphasize application over memorization and help meet the goal of offering a complete, approachable presentation of the essentials of critical thinking.

 Critical Thinking: The Art of Argument has unique features to help students learn and help instructors teach.

Consistent Focus on Arguments

Students learn best when they are shown patterns and know what to expect. To provide this consistency, we use an innovative two-part test for a good argument (the true premises test and the proper form test) for all types of arguments. Students sometimes struggle to see the overarching commonalities across the range of arguments found in good reasoning. When we started using our book with the consistent use of the two-part test, students were able to see these patterns clearly and this problem was solved.

Distinctive Semiformal Method for Standardizing Arguments

Students need to focus on argument form in order to grasp the fundamental point that arguments can have a proper formal structure independent of the truth or falsity of their premises. On the other hand, the complexity and abstraction of formal symbolic language intimidates some students. We have adopted an easy-to-understand semiformal method of standardizing arguments. Consider, for example, the case of Affirming the Antecedent (a.k.a. *Modus Ponens*) discussed in Chapter Five. The purely formal approach can be too disconnected from meaning for students to understand:

(1) P ⊃ Q
(2) P
∴
(3) Q

Arguments presented in ordinary language are more comfortable for students:

(1) If Coke has calories, then it provides energy.
(2) Coke has calories.
Therefore,
(3) Coke provides energy.

However, when arguments are presented only in ordinary language, students cannot "see" the argument's logical form. They are often unable to recognize which form the particular example illustrates.

Our semiformal method bridges the student's need for meaning and the requirement to focus on form by using a combination of letters as variables (such as S1 for one statement and S2 for another statement), and common words instead of symbols, like this:

(1) If S1, then S2.
(2) S1.
Therefore,
(3) S2.

Testing of the book revealed that retaining the use of common words for the key parts of arguments (such as "if," "then," and "therefore") allows students to "see" an argument's logical form more easily. The use of S1 and S2 as variables reminds students that affirming the antecedent expresses a relationship between statements. This semiformal method illustrates the concept of logical form while maintaining a visible connection to ordinary speech. The book avoids both extremes: what can be the confusing novelty of purely symbolic standardizations and the inadequate representation of logical form in arguments expressed completely in ordinary language.

Semiformal Method's Unified Focus on Every Argument Form

To further our goal of showing students the commonalities of all arguments, we use the semiformal method of notation to present the logical form for all of the major types of arguments. As an example, look at the treatment of form in Ad Hominem Fallacy (Chapter Two) and Causal Arguments (Chapter Nine).

The Form of the Ad Hominem Fallacy

(1) Person H asserts statement S.
(2) There is something objectionable about Person H.
Therefore,
(3) Statement S is false.

The Form of Causal Arguments

(1) Event E1 is correlated with event E2.
(2) E2 is not the cause of E1.
(3) There is no event E3 that is the cause of E1 and E2.
(4) E1 and E2 are not coincidentally correlated.
Therefore,
(5) E1 is a cause of E2.

This unified focus on form combined with the consistent use of the two-part test for a good argument lead our students to better comprehend the fact that arguments can have a proper formal structure independent of the truth or falsity of their premises.

Informal, Conversational Style of Language

This style facilitates comprehension and makes the content accessible to all students, at all levels and from all backgrounds. For example, we use contractions to make the writing style more accessible and we address the students directly in the second person.

Fallacies in Context

The study of fallacies is only useful when students learn to identify fallacious arguments and to avoid resorting to fallacies in their own arguments. When students study fallacies in a single chapter, for example, they tend to focus on memorizing the names of the fallacies rather than really being able to distinguish a fallacious argument from a good one. To better contrast fallacies with properly formed arguments of the same type, *Critical Thinking: The Art of Argument* introduces each fallacy alongside good arguments of the same type, e.g., causal fallacies are discussed in the chapter on causal arguments, propositional fallacies are in the chapter on propositional arguments, etc.

Exercises Require Application, Not Merely Memorization

Critical thinkers must know how to identify and analyze arguments, not merely define terms. Learning the art of argument requires practice and application—recitation of technical definitions does not contribute to the development of this skill. For this reason, we crafted all of our exercises to avoid mere memorization. We chose exercises like this one:

"Call me Ishmael." This sentence is

(a) a statement.
(b) a question.
(c) a command.
(d) an exclamation.

instead of an exercise that requires memorization like this one:

A statement is

(a) a sentence that makes a claim that can be either true or false.
(b) a sentence that asks for information.
(c) a question or command.
(d) a speech.

Before we started using this book, we found that many students could, for example, spit back the definition of an argument but could not identify one in a passage. In addition to offering invaluable practice, exercises that require application help students overcome this problem.

Unique Pedagogical Aids

- Learning Outcomes. While they are now a key feature of higher education, learning outcomes are rarely explicitly listed for students. Each chapter of *Critical Thinking: The Art of Argument* begins with a list of five practical learning outcomes, specific things students should be able to do after studying the chapter.

- Key Concepts. Points fundamental to a student's success, these concepts are visually enhanced and included in the margin. This presentation helps highlight their importance and facilitates reviewing for exams.

- Habits of a Critical Thinker. Critical thinking is a skill and, like all skills, it requires habits of mind in addition to content knowledge. Special boxes throughout the text point to the habits required to be a good critical thinker. Examples include being inquisitive, being attentive to detail, and being bold.

- Technical Terms. One barrier to college students' learning is the fact that different disciplines use different words for the same thing or the same word for different things. Technical Terms notes throughout the text explain these differences. For example, one Technical Terms note explains different uses of the word "valid."

- Connections. The pages in a book have to be numbered sequentially, 1, 2, 3, etc. But critical thinking is more like a web of topics than a line of topics. The Connections feature shows students the weblike nature of critical thinking by referring them to discussions of related matters elsewhere in the text.

- Guides. These tools are step-by-step instructions that tell students how to perform important tasks. For example, the end of Chapter One presents a guide for finding and standardizing arguments, and this guide is included at the end of relevant chapters, updated with specific comments keyed to each type of argument.

- Reference Guide. Found at the end of the book, the Reference Guide allows students to find material quickly. It contains alphabetical lists of Key Concepts, Guides, Fallacies, and Technical Terms. It also includes all the argument forms discussed in the book.

Additional Resources to *Critical Thinking: The Art of Argument*

Critical Thinking: The Art of Argument is more than a textbook. It is a complete course-delivery package that includes:

- Aplia. This online solution helps students stay on top of their coursework with regularly scheduled homework assignments. Interactive tools and content further increase engagement and comprehension. The Aplia assignments match the language, style, and structure of the textbook, allowing students to apply what they learn in the text directly to their homework.

- PowerPoint presentations for each chapter.

- A test bank of multiple-choice questions that can be used on quizzes and tests.

- Sample essays written by actual college students. While some texts provide sample essays written by professors or found in the news media, none includes texts written by students. Thus, no other text provides students with models they can use when writing their own essays.

- Sample essays written by academics from across the disciplines. These can be used either as prompts for writing assignments or prompts for class discussions.

Acknowledgements

Martin Carrier, Lauren Adamson, Kathryn McClymond, and the University of Bielefeld generously provided me with visiting scholar status and therefore with the time to finish this book. Corbin and Joseph Rainbolt provided helpful distractions and, unbeknownst to them, several examples. Madeline Zavodny read the entire manuscript multiple times and provided voluminous and enlightening comments. She also did more than her share of child care and put up with a grumpy husband. My debts to her are greater than I can say. Bises, Jolie.

GWR

I thank George Rainbolt and Madeline Zavodny for the friendship they showed me when I was ill that helped me continue doing the work I love, including finishing this book. I thank Anne Owens for critiquing and commenting on the manuscript and, above all, for doing it with gentleness and humor that sustained me during chemotherapy.

SLD

We would like to thank the members of the Board of Consultants not only for the fine pieces that are part of the ancillaries but also for their detailed comments.

Laura Paluki Blake, Assistant Director, Cooperative Institutional Research Program (CIRP)
Russell Blyth, Associate Professor of Mathematics, Saint Louis University
Rebecca Bordt, Associate Professor and Chair of Sociology & Anthropology, DePauw University
Gregory Brack, Associate Professor of Counseling and Psychological Services, Georgia State University
Nelson de Jesus, Professor of French, Oberlin College
Nickitas J. Demos, Andrew C. and Eula C. Family Associate Professor of Composition, Georgia State University
Donald Edwards, Regents Professor of Biology, Georgia State University
Paula Eubanks, Associate Professor of Art, Georgia State University
Doug Falen, Assistant Professor of Anthropology, Agnes Scott College
William Fritz, Professor of Geology & Provost and Senior Vice President for Academic Affairs, College of Staten Island, CUNY
Reina Hayaki, Assistant Professor of Philosophy, University of Nebraska
Ted Jelen, Professor of Political Science, University of Nevada Las Vegas

Kathryn McClymond, Associate Professor and Chair of Religious Studies, Georgia State University

Marnie McInnes, Professor of English and Women's Studies & Dean of Academic Life, Depauw University

Laurence Peck, Assistant Professor of Philosophy, Georgia Perimeter College John Schlotterbeck, Professor of History, Depauw University

Paul Wiita, Professor of Physics and Astronomy, Georgia State University

Madeline Zavodny, Professor of Economics, Agnes Scott College

Janice Zinser, Professor of French, Oberlin College

In several cases, the comments were over ten single-spaced pages. As this book ventures to say things about disciplines outside philosophy, the Board saved us from many howlers.

The faculty members of Georgia State University Department of Philosophy wrote many exercises. They gave us many helpful comments, graciously put up with a department chair who often did not give them the attention they deserved, and pitched in to help an absent Coordinator of Graduate Teaching.

Many talented graduate students helped us with suggestions at every stage of the manuscript, as well as helping with the bibliography, permissions log, and index. They include: Joseph Adams, William Baird, Brandi Martinez-Bedard, Ryan Born, Ngoc Bui, Shane Callahan, Nicolas Condom, Theresa Creighton, Timothy Crews-Anderson, Angela Desaulniers, Ian Dunkle, Benjamin Fischer, Jesse Gero, Walter Glazer, Cleo Grimaldi, Andrew Hookom, Maria Montello, Jason Outlaw, Paul Pfeilschiefter, Cindy Phillips, Joy Salvatore, and Tracy Vanwagner.

We also thank Holly Adams, Sarah Alexander, Michael Augustin, J. Aaron Brown, Steve Beighley, Tyson Bittrich, Michael Bolding, Joseph Bullock, Sean Bustard, John Cadenhead, Charles Carmichael, Jeanelle Carda, Grant Christopher, Timothy Clewell, Jason Craig, Stephen Duncan, Keith Fox, Katherine Fulfer, Melissa Garland, Jodi Geever-Ostrowsky, Maria Gourova, Daniel Griffin, Steven Hager, Ian Halloran, Brent Hiatt, Kyle Hirsch, Matthew Hudgens-Haney, Daniel Issler, Lucas Keefer, Eli Kelsey, Katy Kramer, Thomas Kersey, Kathryn Kramer, Richard Latta, Jason Lesandrini, Mary Leukam, James Lorusso, Ryan McWhorter, Katherine Milby, Raleigh Miller, Sherry Morton, Andrew Reagan, John Rivernbark, Bryan Russell, Joseph Slade, Kelly Smith, Kenneth Smith, Anais Stenson, Melissa Strahm, Hugh Thompson, Paul Tulipana, Brad Wissmueller, and Jared Yarsevich.

We also thank the undergraduates who contributed suggestions during testing of the book, including Sarah Bedzk, Jennifer Buchanan, Tibor Zsolt Nagy, David Newey, Mignonette Padmore, and Samantha Vernon.

We thank the following reviewers for their helpful comments, which contributed to improving many aspects of this edition:

Edward Abplanalp, University of Nebraska at Omaha
Rebecca G. Addy, University of Nebraska at Kearney
Jennifer Altenhofel, CSU Bakersfield
Jami Anderson, University of Michigan-Flint
Tim Black, California State University, Northridge
Raymond Brown, Keiser University

Timothy Burns, Loyola Marymount University
Christopher Caldwell, Virginia State University
Barbara Carlson, Clark University
Lee Carter, Glendale Community College
John Casey, Northeastern Illinois University
Sherry Cisler, Arizona State University, West Campus
James Cox, Strayer University
Margaret Crouch, Eastern Michigan University
Michelle Darnell, Fayetteville State University
James Donelan, Franklin Pierce University
L Sidney Fox, California State University Long Beach
Augustine Yaw Frimpong-Mansoh, CSU Bakersfield
John Gibson, University of Louisville
Lawrence Habermehl, American International College
Shahrokh Haghighi, Cal State University, Long Beach
Richard Hall, Fayetteville State University
Courtney Hammond, Cuyamaca College
Steve Hiltz, Southern Methodist University
Ken Hochstetter, College of Southern Nevada
Elaine Hurst, St. Francis College
Benjamin Hutchens, James Madison University
Polycarp Ikuenobe, Kent State University
Barbara King, Chaffey College
David Kite, Champlain College
Rory Kraft, York College of Pennsylvania
Emily Kulbacki, Green River Community College
Emilie Kutash
Michael C. LaBossiere, Florida A&M University
Sunita Lanka, Hartnell College
John Ludes, University of Nevada Las Vegas
Teri Mayfield, Washington State University
Joseph Monast, Modesto Junior College
Anne Morrissey, California State University, Chico
Alan Nichols, Georgia Highlands College
Eric Parkinson, Syracuse University
Andrew Pavelich, University of Houston - Downtown
Nenad Popovic, Southern Methodist University
Francesco Pupa
Joseph Rabbitt, Indiana University-South Bend
Reginald Raymer, University of North Carolina Charlotte
Lou Reich, Cal State University, San Bernardino
Robin Roth, CSU of Dominguez Hills
Gregory Sadler, Fayetteville State University
Steven Schandler, Chapman University
Pat Shade, Rhodes College
Nick Sinigaglia, Moreno Valley College
Taggart Smith, College of Technology, Purdue University,
    West Lafayette campus
John Sullins, Sonoma State University
Weimin Sun, California State University Northridge

Ruth Swissa, Keiser University
William Tell Gifford, Truckee Meadows CC
Jayne Tristan, University of North Carolina at Charlotte
Stuart Vyse
Helmut Wautischer, Sonoma State University
Debra Welkley, California State University Sacramento
Andrew Wible, Muskegon Community College
Hugh Wilder, The College of Charleston
Linda Williams, Kent State University
Nancy M. Williams, Wofford College
Lynn Wilson, Strayer University
Kerry Ybarra, Fresno City College
Marie G. Zaccaria, Georgia Perimeter College

Finally, we thank our editors at Wadsworth, Worth Hawes, Florence Kilgo, and Joann Kozyrev, for most of their late-night suggestions and all of their help with the production process.

George W. Rainbolt
Sandra L. Dwyer
Georgia State University

Introduction: How to Use This Book

Read this.
It will help you get better grades.

This book has some unusual features: learning outcomes, notes, boxes, and guides. Getting to know these features and using them correctly will help you do well in this course.

Learning Outcomes

Learning outcomes are things that your instructor wants you to learn. In this book, they are things you should be able to *do*. (But you'll have to have some knowledge to do them.) Learning outcomes are an ideal place to begin when studying for tests or writing papers. They often are larger tasks that require you to accomplish a series of smaller tasks, and professors often put these sorts of larger tasks on tests and papers.

You'll find a list of learning outcomes at the beginning of each chapter. Here's the learning outcome for this introduction:

After studying the material in this introduction, you should be able to:

Correctly identify and use the learning outcomes, comments, boxes, and guides found in this book.

Key Concept
Key concepts are points that are fundamental to your success in this course and a place for you to begin when you're studying.

Key Concepts

In the margins you will find notes with the title "Key Concept." The feature included here in the margin is an example of a key concept. It tells you that key concepts are especially important.

Habits of a Critical Thinker

Critical thinking is a skill. Most skills require you to know some set of facts and also to have some good habits. A good cook makes it a habit to wash his hands. A good skier makes it a habit to check the weather report. Certain habits are essential to being a good critical thinker and Habits of a Critical Thinker boxes point you to these habits. Here's an example:

Habits of a Critical Thinker

Studying on a Schedule

One habit of critical thinkers who are college students is studying on a schedule. You probably know your schedule of classes, but you might not have put together a schedule for time to study. Students who get good grades usually set and stick to a schedule for study times. If you don't set aside some time to study, other things can fill up your days until you are staring at a bunch of tests with no time to study.

Technical Terms

As people learn more, it becomes impossible for anyone to know everything about every subject. That's why knowledge has been divided into areas, often called "disciplines" or "subjects." Different disciplines use different words for the same thing or the same word for different things. This is a challenge for college students. Technical Terms boxes explain these differences. Here's a Technical Terms note:

Technical Terms: Category Theory

Chapter Six discusses categorical logic. In mathematics, categorical logic is treated as a part of category theory. In a math class, you might hear an instructor talk about the material in Chapter Six as "category theory."

Connections

The pages in a book have to be numbered linearly, 1, 2, 3, etc. But critical thinking is more like a web of topics than a line of topics. Connections comments show you the web-like nature of critical thinking. You will find them where material in one chapter touches on the material in another chapter. Connections notes are in blue. Here's a Connections note:

Connections
The web-like nature of critical thinking is also discussed in Chapter Four.

Guides

Guides are step-by-step instructions that tell you how to perform some important task. See the Guide on Finding and Standardizing Arguments in Chapter One, on page 41.

GUIDE

Finding and Standardizing Arguments

Here's a review of the steps to find and standardize an argument:
1. Look for an attempt to convince.
2. Find the conclusion.
3. Find the premises.
4. Review the following to make sure that you have correctly identified the conclusion and the premises: imperfect indicator words, sentence order, premises and/or conclusion not in declarative form, and unstated premises and/or conclusion.
5. Review the following to make sure that you haven't incorrectly identified something as a premise or a conclusion when in fact it isn't part of an argument: assertions, questions, instructions, descriptions, and explanations.

Reference Guide

The Reference Guide at the end of the book allows you to find material quickly. It contains alphabetical lists of Key Concepts, Guides, Fallacies, and Technical Terms.

Knowing and correctly using the features of this book will help you get a better grade in your class. It will also help you with something more important than a good grade: thinking critically.

Critical Thinking and Arguments

Call me Ishmael. Some years ago—never mind how long precisely—having little or no money in my purse, and nothing particular to interest me on shore, I thought I would sail about a little and see the watery part of the world.

—Herman Melville, *Moby-Dick* (2008, 1)

[The] peculiar evil of silencing the expression of an opinion is that it is robbing the human race, those who dissent from the opinion still more than those who hold it. If the opinion is right, they are deprived of the opportunity of exchanging error for truth. If wrong, they lose what is almost as great a benefit, the clearer perception and livelier impression of truth produced by its collision with error.

—John Stuart Mill, *On Liberty* (1999, 59–60, material omitted and punctuation modernized)

Learning Outcomes

After studying the material in this chapter, you should be able to:

1. Identify arguments.
2. Identify the conclusion and premise(s) of arguments.
3. Distinguish arguments from explanations.
4. Put arguments into standard form.
5. Identify unstated premises and subarguments.

There is no substitute for critical thinking. Critical thinking is the skill of making decisions based on good reasons. Learning to think critically is one of the most valuable skills you can acquire because its reflective, analytical, and evaluative aspects can be brought to bear on any problem or issue. Critical thinking has led people to create ideas and inventions that make life today dramatically better than it was in the past.

When you give reasons for what you believe, you make arguments. In this way critical thinking is linked to arguments. The two passages on the previous page were both written in the middle of the 1800s. The first is quite famous. The second, while less well known, is a central document in the discussion of free speech. The first passage doesn't make an argument. The second passage makes an argument in favor of freedom of speech. In this book, we'll focus on passages like the second one. We'll work on identifying arguments and on determining whether arguments are good or bad.

What Is Critical Thinking?

Suppose that a professor in an economics course asks you to write a paper about whether gas prices will rise or fall over the next six months. How should you decide what you believe? One option would be to flip a coin. Heads, you decide to believe that gas prices will rise. Tails, you decide to believe that gas prices will fall. Another option would be to consult an astrologer and believe what the stars tell you. Neither of these is an example of critical thinking. To use critical thinking skills to write your paper about gas prices, you'd need to look for good reasons to think that gas prices will rise and for good reasons to think that gas prices will fall. Then you'd need to determine which reasons are better. When you provide reasons for believing something, you make an argument.

Here's an argument for the view that gas prices will rise:

> Over the next six months, China will have an increased demand for gas and other petroleum products. So, the price of gas will rise.

Here's an argument for the view that gas prices will fall:

> Over the next six months, Saudi Arabia will increase oil production. So, gas prices will fall.

Unlike someone who flips a coin to decide what to believe about gas prices, someone who considers arguments is beginning to think critically. **Critical thinking** is the skill of correctly evaluating arguments made by others and composing good arguments of your own. Arguments can be about

> **Key Concept**
> **Critical thinking** is the skill of correctly evaluating arguments made by others and composing good arguments of your own.

any subject. For this reason, critical thinking is an important skill. You should use it in every college course you take and throughout the rest of your life.

Many skills other than critical thinking are important. The ability to quickly and correctly multiply is an essential life skill, but it isn't critical thinking. The ability to safely handle equipment in a chemistry lab is essential for doing well in chemistry classes, but it isn't a critical thinking skill; neither are reading, writing, study, artistic, interpersonal, or time management skills.

Critical thinking isn't knowing facts. Knowing facts is important in all college courses. You won't do well in history if you think that the United States has existed for 5 million years. You won't do well in accounting if you don't know a debit from a credit. Knowing facts is also vital outside of class. Lots of people have lost lots of money because they didn't know important facts about their investments. For centuries, lack of knowledge about germs caused countless deaths. But you can fail a course and make serious mistakes in life even when you know lots of facts. If you can't think critically, the facts you know are just floating around in your head. You must use critical thinking skills to understand facts, to put them into context, and to see how they're connected to each other.

Habits of a Critical Thinker

Self-Reflection

If you look back at the Key Concept note above, you'll see that the skill of critical thinking includes composing good arguments of your own. Finding the strengths and flaws in the arguments made by others is usually easier than making arguments of your own. Good critical thinkers compose their own arguments, subject them to critical analysis, and use what they've learned from this critical analysis to compose new and better arguments.

Evaluating your own arguments is part of being self-reflective. Good critical thinkers know their own thoughts. They stop and ask themselves, "What am I thinking?" They evaluate their own arguments. You don't know your own thoughts unless you think about them!

Self-reflective thinkers think about where their thoughts come from. Did someone else put this thought into my head? If so, does that person have anything to gain from my having this thought? Am I prone to these sorts of thoughts even though I shouldn't be? A self-reflective person might discover that she tends to see the downside of things. If she is aware of that bias, she has the opportunity to combat it.

Self-reflective thinkers think about what they are doing with their thoughts. Am I thinking about an argument, am I wishing, am I hoping, am I dreaming? Just as a self-reflective thinker is aware of what the sources of her thoughts tend to be, she is aware of what she tends to do with her thoughts. Am I really arguing with someone, trying to annoy someone, or showing off? Am I using arguments to hide from a difficult discussion?

What Is an Argument?

An **argument** is an attempt to provide reasons for thinking that some belief is true. All arguments have two parts. The first part is the reasons, and the second part is the belief that those reasons are intended to support. The reasons are the **premises** and the belief being supported is the **conclusion**. Look back at our first argument about rising and falling gas prices. The premise is:

(1) Over the next six months, China will have an increased demand for gas and other petroleum products.

The conclusion is:

(2) Over the next six months, the price of gas will rise.

The premise provides a reason for thinking that the conclusion is true.

In this book, an argument is an attempt to provide reasons for thinking that some belief is true. When you hear someone say, "I had an argument with my husband last night," the word "argument" refers to a verbal fight. This text isn't using "argument" that way.

Statements

Premises and conclusions are both statements. A **statement** is a sentence that makes a claim that can be either true or false. Every argument is composed of two or more statements. The **conclusion** is the statement that the argument is intended to support. The **premises** are the statements that are intended to support the conclusion. In other words, conclusions are statements that are support*ed*, and premises are statements that are support*ing*.

Conclusion

Premise — Premise

Premise — Premise

Premise — Premise

Dave Newman/
iStockphoto.com

Key Concept
An **argument** is an attempt to provide reasons for thinking that some belief is true. The reasons are the **premises** and the belief being supported is the **conclusion**.

Key Concept
A **statement** is a sentence that makes a claim that can be either true or false. The **conclusion** is the statement that the argument is intended to support. The **premises** are the statements that are intended to support the conclusion.

Premises support conclusions.

© Cengage Learning

The solar system.

Premises and conclusions must be statements, and every statement is either true or false. A sentence that is neither true nor false can't be a statement and can't be part of a well-formed argument. Here are four sentences:

1. Read the chapter about the planets in our solar system.
2. There are at least eight planets in our solar system.
3. There are at least twenty planets in our solar system.
4. How many planets are in our solar system?

Sentence 1 gives an instruction. It's a perfectly good sentence. But because it gives an instruction, it can't be true and it can't be false. Sentence 4 is a question. Questions can't be true and they can't be false. Questions and instructions aren't statements. Sentences 2 and 3 are declarative sentences. Sentence 2 is true. Sentence 3 is false. Sentences 2 and 3 are both statements.

If an argument includes sentences that aren't statements, then it isn't a well-formed argument. But people often use non-declarative sentences in a way that indicates they want to make an argument. In these cases, the sentences can be restated as declarative sentences.

Connections

Later in this chapter, you'll see how to paraphrase non-declarative sentences into statements.

Technical Term: Truth-Value

In some fields you'll find discussions of the "truth-value" of a statement. This is a technical way of indicating whether a statement is true or false. "The truth-value of this statement is T" is another way of saying that the statement is true. "The truth-value of this statement is F" is another way of saying that the statement is false. In advanced courses, you may come across discussions in which you'll consider truth-values besides "true" and "false."

Statements and Sentences

Don't confuse statements with sentences. Whether a string of words is a sentence is determined by rules of grammar. Whether a string of words is a statement is determined by whether it makes a claim that can be true or false.

As just noted, only one kind of sentence, a declarative sentence, can be true or false.

One sentence can contain two or more statements. Here's an example of one sentence that contains two statements:

(a) Because so much of modern medicine depends on chemistry, it is essential that students who intend to enter the health professions have some understanding of basic chemistry. (Bettelheim 2007, 2)

It contains this statement:

Much of modern medicine depends on chemistry.

and this one too:

It is essential that students who intend to enter the health professions have some understanding of basic chemistry.

The first statement is a premise, and the second statement is a conclusion. You must distinguish sentences from statements to be able to discern premises and conclusions. If you thought that sentence (a) was a single statement, you wouldn't be able to see that it's an argument.

Two or more sentences may contain only one statement. For example, authors sometimes repeat a central point. The following passage contains eight declarative sentences but only seven statements.

Weather influences our everyday activities, our jobs, and our health and comfort. There are few other aspects of our physical environment that affect our lives more than the phenomena we collectively call the weather. On January 25, 2000, North Carolina and nearby states experienced a record-breaking winter storm. In September of that year, Hurricane Floyd brought flooding rains, damaging winds, and rough seas to a large portion of the Atlantic Seaboard. More than 2.5 million people evacuated their homes. These memorable weather events serve to illustrate the fact that the United States has the greatest variety of weather of any country in the world. *Weather clearly influences our lives a great deal.* So there is a need for increased awareness and understanding of our atmosphere and its behavior. (Lutgens 2004, 4; italics added and material omitted)

> **Key Concept**
> One sentence can contain two or more statements. Two or more sentences may contain only one statement.

Critical Thinkers

Rosalind Franklin

Photo Researchers

The importance of critical thinking in chemistry is vividly illustrated in the life and work of the English chemist **Rosalind Franklin** (1920–1958). If she hadn't died of ovarian cancer, she would have won the Nobel Prize in conjunction with James Watson and Francis Crick for their work on discovering the structure of DNA. (Nobel Prizes are not awarded posthumously.) Franklin's work contributed to our understanding of the molecular structure of DNA, RNA, viruses, coal, and graphite. You can see Franklin's paper on DNA, in the journal *Nature* (1953), at http://www.nature.com/nature/dna50/archive.html.

The two sentences in italics make the same statement. In looking for arguments, you can't simply count the sentences to find the statements.

Technical Terms: Arguments, Claims, Statements, Propositions

Statements are also called "propositions." Some textbooks use the term "claim" to refer to arguments and statements. Other books use "claim" to refer to the conclusion of an argument.

EXERCISE 1.1

A. Which of the following sentences would ~~not~~ typically express a statement? Explain why.

The answers for starred exercises can be found at the end of the book.

1. Oxygen is an element.
2. "Why do fools fall in love?" (Title of a song by Frankie Lymon & the Teenagers)*
3. The earth revolves around the sun.
*4. The moon revolves around the sun.
5. "Stop in the name of love." (Title of a song by Diana Ross and the Supremes)†
6. Eat five portions of vegetables every day. *imperative*
7. Comets are made of frozen gases and dust. *Statement*
*8. Pure oxygen rarely occurs naturally on Earth. *Statement*
9. How long do you think it will rain? *Question*
10. Go Tigers! *imperative*
11. Many children use a blanket as a comfort device. *Statement*
*12. I hate broccoli! *Explaination*
13. How many times have I told you to clean your room? *Question*
14. "[The] peculiar evil of silencing the expression of an opinion is that it is robbing the human race, those who dissent from the opinion still more than those who hold it." (Mill 1999, 59–60, material omitted and punctuation modernized) *Statement*
15. "Call me Ishmael." (Melville 2008, 1) *Command, Imperative*

B. (a) For each sentence, indicate whether it makes a statement or not. (b) For each sentence that isn't a statement, describe what it does.

Jack: Let's go up the hill.

Jill: That's a bad idea.

Jack: Why?

Jill: It's a very steep hill.

Jack: I don't care about that.

*Frankie Lymon & the Teenagers. "Why do fools fall in love?" Why Do Fools Fall in Love and Other Hits. Rhino Flashback, 2003 [1956]. CD

†Diana Ross and the Supremes. "Stop in the name of love." Diana Ross and the Supremes—The Ultimate Collection. Motown, 1997 [1965]. CD

Jill: But I've a heart condition.

Jack: I don't care about that either.

Jill: Well, I see that you're a heartless human being.

Jack: To the contrary, I've a very healthy heart.

Jill: But you don't care at all about my heart.

Jack: If you have a heart condition, you should get a good cardiologist to care for it.

Jill: You're making stupid jokes about my heart condition. Are you some kind of jerk or what?

C. How many statements are found in each of the following sentences?

   1. Stefan (walked to the store) (bought a newspaper) and (then went to a café) (to read it.)
   2. Mercury is composed mostly of hot gases. 1 Statement
   3. How many times must I play the fool? question 0
   *4. You break it, you bought it. 2
   5. The internet and cell phones have revolutionized the way people communicate. 2
   6. *Back to Black* (Title of an Amy Winehouse album.)* title
   7. Would you like soup or salad with that? question 0
   *8. He'll have either soup or salad. 2
   9. "[A]sk not what your country can do for you—ask what you can do for your country." (Kennedy 1961) imparative
   10. "The Cherokees believed that they had a sacred duty to avenge the deaths of fallen comrades, and so war parties formed quickly following a death." (Perdue 2005, 3) 2
   11. "One of the striking differences between a cat and a lie is that a cat has only nine lives." (Twain 1999, 30) 1
   *12. "While I know myself as a creation of God, I am also obligated to realize and remember that everyone else and everything else are also God's creation." (Angelou 1994, 34) 3
   13. "[W]hile government should not be in the business of limiting speech, an institution [such as a university] should have the freedom to restrict the speech of anyone at any time who utilizes resources within the jurisdiction of [the] institution." (Shermer 2000, 13)
   14. "There is good reason why it is considered important to be able to listen to another person, why we have to listen—for we do not have to learn to interrupt which comes naturally." (Yakubinsky 1997, 249)
   15. "It does not matter whether a man prospers as an individual: if his country is destroyed, he is lost with it; but if he meets with misfortune, he is far safer in a fortunate [country] than he would be otherwise." (Thucydides 1993, 52–53)

D. Which of the following sentences are ~~not~~ likely to be the premise of any argument? Explain.

   1. Many people in the United States own a car.
   2. Freedom is the most important value.
   3. Hang-gliding is more dangerous than walking on a beach.

*Winehouse, Amy. Back to Black. Republic, 2007. CD

*4. "Give me liberty or give me death." (Henry 1999, 232)

5. Democracy is the best form of government.

6. Communism was an evil system. Conclusion

7. Evil will win if good people don't fight against it. Conclusion

*8. *Back to Black* (Title of an Amy Winehouse album.) title

9. Abortion should be legal. Conclusion

10. Abortion should be illegal. Conclusion

11. How far until the next exit? question

*12. Everyone should take an economics course. Conclusion

13. "It is considered important to be able to listen to another person." (Yakubinsky 1997, 249) Primise

14. "[G]overnment should not be in the business of limiting speech." (Shermer 2000, 13) Conclusion

15. "The Cherokees believed that they had a sacred duty to avenge the deaths of fallen comrades." (Perdue 2005, 3) Primise

E. Which of the following sentences are ~~not~~ likely to be the conclusion of an argument? Explain.

1. Al Gore was the real winner in the presidential election of 2000.

2. The economic policies of George W. Bush helped the country.

3. Thomas Jefferson was the best American President in history.

*4. Bill Clinton lied many times to the American public.

5. Please don't say bad things about any President of the United States.

6. Grass is usually green.

7. Many people like ice cream. Conclusion

*8. How many times have you tried to reboot this computer? question

9. Elementary students should learn a foreign language. Conclusion

10. You should invest in exchange-traded funds. Conclusion

11. You really should watch the Super Bowl tonight. Conclusion

*12. "Call me Ishmael." (Melville 2008, 1) Command

13. "It is considered important to be able to listen to another person." (Yakubinsky 1997, 249) Primise

14. "[G]overnment should not be in the business of limiting speech." (Shermer 2000, 13) Conclusion

15. "The Cherokees believed that they had a sacred duty to avenge the deaths of fallen comrades." (Perdue 2005, 3) explanation

Why Think Critically?

In our gas price example, why is it better to consider arguments instead of flipping a coin or consulting an astrologer? It would be faster to flip a coin, and it might be more fun to visit an astrologer. The answer is that, if there's a good argument for a belief, that belief is more likely to be true. Good arguments give you evidence for the truth of the conclusion. If you carefully examine the arguments concerning gas prices and base your belief about gas prices on those arguments, you're more likely to have a true belief about gas prices than if you flip a coin or consult an astrologer.

Having true beliefs is better than having false beliefs. Perhaps the least interesting reason that true beliefs are better than false ones is that you'll get better grades. If you're taking a geology course and you have false beliefs about the rock formations you're studying, you probably won't do well on your geology tests. When you reveal false beliefs on an exam, your instructor will give you a lower grade and your college career could be on the rocks!

Another reason why you're better off with true beliefs is that false beliefs are often expensive. We hope that you didn't have many false beliefs about the college you chose to attend because if you did, you're probably unhappy at that college. If you are so unhappy that you decide to transfer, it will cost you time and money.

But the best reason to have true beliefs is that you want to understand the world you live in. A person who has lots of false beliefs loses touch with reality.

Key Concept
Good arguments give you evidence for the truth of the conclusion.

Conclusion — Can you argue with it?

Finding Arguments

Here's the bottom line when it comes to finding arguments: you must find a set of statements (the premises) that someone claims support another statement (the conclusion). One reason critical thinking is the *art* of argument is that finding arguments isn't a mechanical process. It isn't like finding the answer to a long division problem. But some guidelines and indicator words can help.

The First Three Steps

When you're trying to determine whether a text contains an argument, follow these three steps. Students often make the mistake of skipping the first step. Don't fall into that trap.

Step 1. Look for an Attempt to Convince

As you read or listen to someone, ask yourself whether the author/speaker wants to *convince* you that something is true. If so, you have a good indication that there's an argument. People only try to convince other people of things that the other people don't already believe. You've probably never seen an argument for the view that grass is green. Arguments are responses to disagreement. When people disagree they'll often try to convince each other to change their minds.

Step 2. Find the Conclusion

The next step is to look for a conclusion. Look for the author's main point. That will be the argument's conclusion. Conclusions are usually easier to find than premises, and finding the conclusion will help you find premises.

Some words are commonly used to point to conclusions. We've listed some below.

Conclusion Indicator Words

so	therefore	thus	hence
consequently	then	accordingly	proves that
as a result	for these reasons	it follows that	we infer that
implies that	means that	which entails that	we can show
accordingly	indicates that	in fact	in short
it is clear that	it is likely that	shows that	suggests that
the point is	it must be that	serves to show that	in conclusion
demonstrates	as a consequence	so we see that	is evidence that

Step 3. Find the Premises

Key Concept
The first three steps for finding arguments.

After finding the conclusion, ask yourself *why* the arguer believes that conclusion. Statements answering that question will be the premises of the argument. Here are some words that often point to premises:

Premise Indicator Words

since	because	for	as
based on	follows from	as shown by	inasmuch as
as indicated by	reason	may be inferred from	derived from
given that	on account of	due to	suppose that
for the reason	seeing that	is clear from	insofar as
assuming that	on the grounds that	granted that	owing to

Habits of a Critical Thinker

Curiosity

Critical thinkers are intellectually curious. As a critical thinker, you want to have true beliefs and seek out good arguments to decide what to believe. Rather than passively receiving beliefs that happen to come your way, you wonder about things, seek out interesting problems, and attempt to find arguments about those problems. Of course, no one is curious about everything. (Some are curious about the history of baseball and others aren't.) But a critical thinker is curious about many different things, enjoys examining arguments, and wants to learn new things.

EXERCISE 1.2

A. In the discussion between Jack and Jill in Exercise 1.1 B, find all the arguments, and identify the premises and conclusion of each argument.

B. In each of the following passages: (a) determine whether or not an argument is present, (b) if an argument is present, identify the premises and the conclusion.

1. Exchange-traded funds result in lower capital gains and so in lower taxes. For this reason, they should be considered by investors in higher tax brackets.

[handwritten annotations: "Premise" pointing to the first sentence; "Conclusion" pointing to the second sentence]

2. *(Premise)* (Every time you hang out with him, you feel miserable.) (So you shouldn't go out with him.) *conclusion*

3. *(Premise)* (I've seen 1,000 swans, and all of them are white.) (Therefore, most swans are white.) *conclusion*

*4. Given that (gas prices will rise) *Premise* and (the housing market will continue to slump,) *Premise* the (United States will surely fall into a recession next year.) *conclusion*

5. *(Premise)* (Due to higher carbon-dioxide emissions) and (increased atmospheric particulates,) *Premise* (global temperatures will rise over the coming century.) *conclusion*

6. *(Premise)* (If you eat too much,) (you'll gain weight.) *conclusion*

7. You say that (all famous philosophers are men.) *conclusion* But look at (Mary Wollenstonecraft— *Premise* she's a famous philosopher) (so some famous philosophers are women.) *conclusion*

*8. (I bet that he's at Starbucks *Premise* because I've seen him there most days at about this time.) *conclusion*

9. The survey was given to 146 thirteen-year-olds selected at random from the list of thirteen-year-old students enrolled at West Junior High School. *No Arguement (statement)*

10. Why don't you try the tai nam? You'll like it. It's my favorite kind of Vietnamese noodles. *Statement*

11. "[A]sk not what your country can do for you—ask what you can do for your country." (Kennedy 1961) *imperative/Exsortation*

*12. "One of the striking differences between a cat and a lie is that a cat has only nine lives." (Twain 1999, 30)

13. "The Cherokees believed that they had a sacred duty to avenge the deaths of fallen comrades, and so war parties formed quickly following a death." (Perdue 2005, 3)

14. "It was the best of times, it was the worst of times, it was the age of wisdom, it was the age of foolishness, it was the epoch of belief, it was the epoch of incredulity, it was the season of Light, it was the season of Darkness, it was the spring of hope, it was the winter of despair, we had everything before us, we had nothing before us, we were all going direct to Heaven, we were all going direct the other way. There were a king with a large jaw and a queen with a plain face, on the throne of England; there were a king with a large jaw and a queen with a fair face, on the throne of France. In both countries it was clearer than crystal to the lords of the State, that things in general were settled for ever. It was the year of Our Lord one thousand seven hundred and seventy-five." (Dickens 1922, 1, material omitted) *Discription/Not an arguement*

15. "Although I believe that [a] table is 'really' of the same color all over, the parts that reflect the light look much brighter than the other parts, and some parts look white because of the reflected light. I know that, if I move, the parts that reflect light will be different, so that the apparent distribution of colours on the table will change. It follows that if several people are looking at the table at the same moment, no two of them will see exactly the same distribution of colours, because no two can see it from exactly the same point of view, and any change in the point of view makes some change in the way the light is reflected." (Russell 1912, 8–9)

C. Redo the questions in Exercises 1.1 D and E in light of the fact that arguments are responses to disagreement. Remember that conclusions tend to be statements about which people disagree and premises tend to be statements about which people agree.

Complicating Factors

The three simple steps discussed above are too simple. You need to know about some complications.

Indicator Words Are Imperfect Guides

The first complication is that someone can write an argument using no indicator words and someone can use indicator words without making an argument. Look again at this argument:

> Over the next six months, China will have an increased demand for gas and other petroleum products. So, the price of gas will rise.

indicator word

"So" is the only indicator word in this passage. Here's the argument rewritten without this word:

> Over the next six months, China will have an increased demand for gas and other petroleum products. The price of gas will certainly rise.

Arguments that contain no indicator words aren't that common. But they do exist, and you need to watch out for them.

Passages that aren't arguments are frequently filled with indicator words. Here's a perfectly appropriate use of "since" that isn't an argument:

> My car has been in the shop since last Tuesday!

Here's an example of "because" occurring outside an argument:

> My car has been in the shop since last Tuesday because the mechanic keeps breaking it!

In this example, the person with the car in the shop isn't trying to convince us that her car is in the shop. This person is only explaining why the car has been in the shop for so long.

Sentence Order

The second complicating factor is that the order in which sentences and statements are made by the arguer doesn't determine whether a statement is a premise or a conclusion. People often speak or write in the order in which things occur to them or in an order that they take to be an effective style. In fact, passages in which the premises are listed first and the conclusion is listed last aren't that common.

Conclusions and Premises Not in Declarative Form

The third complicating factor is that some statements aren't in declarative form. As we saw above,

> only statements can be parts of an argument,
> not all sentences are statements, and
> well-formed arguments contain only declarative sentences.

But people can use sentences that aren't declarative to assert statements. Let's look at an argument that contains statements not in declarative form. To understand it, you'll need some background information.

In the late 1800s, Captain Albert Dreyfus, a Jewish officer in the French army, was accused of passing secret documents to the Germans. He was convicted and sentenced to a long prison term. Investigations by Colonel Picquart revealed that the documents were actually passed to the Germans by another officer, Major Esterhazy. A key piece of evidence indicating Esterhazy's guilt was a telegram. Picquart's investigations also revealed that several high-ranking French generals knew that Dreyfus was innocent. These generals were prejudiced against Jews and afraid of admitting that the army had made a mistake when it brought charges against Dreyfus. They conducted an elaborate cover-up that included falsely accusing Jewish people of making payments to Dreyfus and producing fake documents that were secretly shown to the judges in Dreyfus' trial. (This is a simplified description of the Dreyfus affair.)

The Dreyfus affair became a political scandal, and Emile Zola published a letter to the President of the French Republic entitled *J'accuse!* (*I Accuse!*), in which he argued that Picquart was correct and that Dreyfus was innocent. Many of his arguments were made with non-declarative sentences. Here's one of them.

> (a) Some have gone as far as to claim that Picquart was a forger, that he forged the telegram to ruin Esterhazy. (b) But, good God, why? (c) For what reason? (d) Give me a motive. (e) Was he too paid by the Jews? (Zola 1898, 1, translated by the authors of this book)

We've added the letters (a)–(e) to help refer to the sentences Zola wrote. His point, his conclusion, is clear. He wants to convince you that Picquart didn't forge the telegram that's evidence against Esterhazy. But sentences (b), (c), and (e) are interrogatives (questions), and sentence (d) is an imperative (an order). Although Zola used three interrogatives and an imperative, his point can be made with declarative sentences.

> (1) Picquart had no reason to forge the telegram to ruin Esterhazy.
>
> Therefore,
>
> (2) Picquart didn't forge the telegram.

Critical Thinkers

Emile Zola

Emile Zola (1840–1902) was the author of many works, including a twenty-volume set of novels about the life and troubles of five generations of two French families. These novels trace many problems caused by the Industrial Revolution, but the *J'accuse!* letter did more to ignite public argument about justice, religious persecution, and their relation to the state than any of his novels. Zola was convicted of libel for the letter. Both Dreyfus and Zola were pardoned (but not acquitted!). Many think that Zola's letter led to the French laws that separated church and state. You can get inexpensive editions of Zola's works, including *The Human Beast, The Three Cities Trilogy, The Fat and the Thin*, and more.

EXERCISE 1.3

A. In each of the following passages: (a) determine whether or not an argument is present, (b) if an argument is present, identify the premises and the conclusion.

1. Don't go out with him! Every time you hang out with him, you feel miserable.

2. How can anyone support gun control? Look at all the lives that have been saved because someone had a gun. And then there's the economic benefits of gun sales. Do you want people who make guns to lose their jobs?

3. The car slid off the road because the road was wet and the car's tires were improperly inflated.

*4. The war in Iraq was a serious mistake.

5. Why don't people save for retirement? I'm puzzled by this. Perhaps they fail to understand how long they're likely to live. Or perhaps they think they'll earn more money later in life. Another possibility is that it seems too complicated to save.

6. Murata has more experience and better communication skills than Johnson. We should hire Murata.

7. In 2010, a survey of 1,000 college students found that 87% of them preferred instant messaging to email. The vast majority of college students prefer instant messaging to email.

*8. "Under the statute criminalizing the manufacture and distribution of cocaine, 21 U. S. C. §841, and the relevant Federal Sentencing Guidelines, a drug trafficker dealing in crack cocaine is subject to the same sentence as one dealing in 100 times more powder cocaine. Petitioner Kimbrough pleaded guilty to four offenses: conspiracy to distribute crack and powder; possession with intent to distribute more than 50 grams of crack; possession with intent to distribute powder; and possession of a firearm in furtherance of a drug-trafficking offense." (*Kimbrough* 2007, 1)

9. "As America's youth have grown fatter and the number with adult diabetes continues to rise, there is one obvious way to help. Public schools should stop selling students so much unhealthy food." (*New York Times* "Junking Fat Foods in Schools" 2007, A26)

10. "The idea that the law is what the words that constitute it mean is of course too simple. Most words are open to multiple interpretations. To say that laws are what their words mean would be to leave the meaning of most laws unacceptably ambiguous." (Scalia 1997, vii)

11. "[R]acism is not merely an attitude or set of beliefs; it also sustains or proposes to establish a *racial order*, a permanent group hierarchy." (Frederickson 2002, 6, material omitted)

*12. "[W]hile government should not be in the business of limiting speech, an institution [such as a university] should have the freedom to restrict the speech of anyone at any time who utilizes resources within the jurisdiction of [the] institution." (Shermer 2000, 13)

13. "It is a stark reality that the black communities are becoming more and more economically depressed. In June 1966, the Bureau of Labor Statistics reported on the deteriorated condition of black people in this country. In 1948, the jobless rate of non-white males between the ages of fourteen and nineteen was 7.6 percent. In 1965 [it] was 22.6 percent. The corresponding figures for unemployed white male teenagers were 8.3 percent in 1948 and 11.8 percent in 1965." (Ture 1967, 18–19)

14. The following passage is about one species of male earwig, a winged insect with two penises:

> "Writing in the *Journal of Morphology*, Yoshitaka Kamimura describes his investigations of the private life of the doubly endowed male of the earwig species *Labidura riparia*. He shows that this earwig has a strong preference for its right penis: nearly 90% of field-collected and laboratory-reared males hold their intromittent organs [i.e., their penises] in the 'right-ready' state (right side extended backwards, ready to mate) when not mating, as well as when *in flagrante delicto*. Curiously, the earwig's two penises are morphologically indistinguishable and fully functional. They connect to equivalent testes, and individuals with an injured or experimentally ablated right penis readily revert to using the left one. This right-ready asymmetry is therefore largely—if not entirely—behavioural [i.e., the asymmetry is not determined by differences in the penises and how well they work]." (Palmer 2006, 690–691)

15. "During the first World War, I believed implicitly all the Allied propaganda against Germany and fully accepted the alleged sole war guilt of Germany. I was not awakened to a consciousness of the error of my ways until the publication of the striking articles on the truth about 1914 by Professor Sidney B. Fay which were printed in the leading American historical journal, *American Historical Review*, in 1920–1921." (Barnes 1972, 2, material omitted)

Unstated Premises and Unstated Conclusions

The fourth complicating factor is that sometimes conclusions and premises aren't stated at all! Look back at the quote from Zola. He doesn't state his conclusion. The interrogatives and imperatives are Zola's way of expressing the premise of his argument. But he never says that Picquart didn't forge the telegram. Instead he says:

(a) Some have gone as far as to claim that Picquart was a forger, that he forged the telegram to ruin Esterhazy.

He doesn't directly express his conclusion. An **unstated conclusion** occurs when the author doesn't explicitly state the argument's conclusion.

Unstated conclusions are fairly common. You should suspect that a conclusion is unstated when you find that someone is trying to convince you that some view is true or false but she never explicitly states the view. The author will often do what Zola did and make it clear that she disagrees with something that another person said. Unstated conclusions don't usually cause much trouble. If you ask yourself whether the author is trying to convince you of something, you should be able to determine whether a passage contains an unstated conclusion or doesn't contain an argument at all.

Unstated premises are more difficult. An **unstated premise** occurs when an author (1) believes that a statement is true, (2) intends for this statement to be a premise of an argument, but (3) doesn't include any sentence (declarative or non-declarative) that asserts the statement. You usually can't ask the author if she believes that a certain statement is true and if she intends for this statement to be part of her argument. That can make it hard to determine if a premise is unstated.

Key Concept
An **unstated conclusion** occurs when the author doesn't explicitly state the argument's conclusion.

Key Concept
The three characteristics of an **unstated premise**.

Technical Term: Enthymeme

Arguments with an unstated premise or an unstated conclusion are enthymemes.

Suppose that you found the following in a reading for a class:

> As part of their study, Dr. Frederick's research group is considering giving the drug miconazole to a group of children. But they shouldn't do this because miconazole always has serious side effects that harm children. It causes vomiting, bloody stools, and severe abdominal cramping.

Let's call this argument "argument A." The author's conclusion and one premise are clear.

(A1) Miconazole harms children by causing vomiting, bloody stools, and severe abdominal cramping.

Therefore,

(A3) Dr. Frederick's research group should not give miconazole to a group of children.

This argument is missing a step. A1 by itself doesn't support A3. Here's the missing premise:

(A2) People should not do things that harm children.

Is it likely that the author of argument A believes that A2 is true? Is it likely that the author intends for A2 to be part of the argument? The answer to both questions is "yes." A2 is something that almost everyone believes. The author probably thought that A2 was so obvious that it didn't need to be stated. A2 is also a necessary logical link between A1 and A3. It would be appropriate to attribute an unstated premise, A2, to the author of this argument.

Look at this argument:

> A review of laws regulating gun ownership and use in Britain reveals that those laws are much more restrictive than the laws regulating gun ownership and use found in most U.S. jurisdictions. The number of deaths and injuries per capita involving guns is much lower in Britain than in the United States. It seems clear that more restrictive laws would reduce deaths and injuries in the United States.

Let's call this "argument B." It has two stated premises and a conclusion.

(B1) Laws regulating gun ownership and use in Britain are much more restrictive than the laws regulating gun ownership and use found in most U.S. jurisdictions.

(B2) The number of deaths and injuries per capita involving guns is much lower in Britain than in the United States.

Therefore,

(B4) More restrictive laws regulating gun ownership and use would reduce deaths and injuries in the United States.

You might think that this argument is missing a step. It might be this premise:

(B3) There are no other differences between Britain and the United States that can explain the lower rate of deaths and injuries involving guns in Britain.

Is it likely that the author intends for B3 to be part of the argument? B3 is a controversial statement. Some people believe B3 is true. Others believe it's false. The author of argument B was probably not assuming that everyone would agree that B3 is true. The author probably failed to notice that B3 was a needed step in the argument. It wouldn't be appropriate to attribute B3 to this author as an unstated premise.

Here are two guidelines for finding unstated premises:

1. An unstated premise must be a logically necessary step between the premises and the conclusion. *Not always logically*

2. An unstated premise must be something that the author and almost everyone else thinks is true.

winnable argument

One way of considering the matter of unstated premises is to imagine yourself asking the author: Did you intend this statement as an unstated premise in your argument? Then imagine what you think the author's response would be. If it would be: "Of course! Everyone knows *that's* true," the statement is probably an unstated premise. If it would be: "Hmm, I hadn't thought of that," the statement is probably not an unstated premise.

EXERCISE 1.4

A. Each of the following arguments may contain an unstated premise and/or an unstated conclusion. If one is present, identify the unstated premise and/or the unstated conclusion.

1. Households that have guns are significantly more likely to have deaths due to suicide. Therefore, people shouldn't keep guns in their homes.

2. Households that have guns are significantly less likely to be victims of crime. Therefore, people should keep guns in their homes. *People should have guns at home to not become victims*

3. A single-payer health care system would raise costs. A single-payer health care system would reduce the quality of care. A single-payer health care system is un-American. [Note: A single-payer health care system is one in which one agency, usually the government, functions either as the sole insurance company or the sole provider of health care.]

*4. France and Germany have single-payer health care systems. They spend less on health care than the United States, have a longer life expectancy, and have lower infant mortality rates. It's clear what the United States should do.

5. Either Willa took Bio 101 or Chem 101. And she didn't take both. I think she took Chem 101.

6. She graduated, so she must have completed her academic residency requirements.

7. China's economy is likely to explode over the next ten years. They're making the transition from an agrarian society to an industrial society, and previous societies that went through this transition saw stunning economic progress.

*8. Well, the precipitate isn't calcium. It must be sodium.

9. "The 2008 presidential election has fundamentally shifted, but it hasn't been because of events in Iowa and New Hampshire. It's because of events everywhere else. In Washington, the National Intelligence Estimate was released, suggesting the next president will not face an imminent nuclear showdown with Iran. In Iraq, the surge and tribal revolts produce increasing stability. In Pakistan, the streets have not exploded. In the Middle East, the Arabs and Palestinians stumble toward some sort of peace process. In Venezuela, a referendum set President Hugo Chávez back on his heels. The world still has its problems, but it no longer seems to be building toward some larger crisis. The atmosphere of fear and conflict has at least temporarily abated. With the change in conditions, the election of 2008 is beginning to feel like a postwar election." (Brooks 2007, A33)

10. "I don't know anybody who likes to lose money, but as an investor it's something that simply has to be accepted, because only with risk comes excess return." (Sonders 2007)

11. **Romeo**: Let's elope.

    Juliet: Are you crazy?

    Romeo: What's the problem?

    Juliet: Our families are the problem, Einstein. They'd kill us for eloping.

    Romeo: Einstein doesn't get born for another couple of centuries. Kindly restrict your remarks to this century, please.

    Juliet: Well, our families would kill us in this century. Is that good enough for you?

    Romeo: Very persuasive.

*12. Fossils of amphibians have been found in Antarctica. This shows that the world as a whole must have been much warmer in the past than it is today.

13. "[S]ince the early 1990s, astronomers have found several objects of comparable size to Pluto in an outer region of the Solar System called the Kuiper Belt. Some astronomers have long argued that Pluto would be better categorised alongside this population of small, icy worlds. The critical blow for Pluto came with the discovery three years ago of an object currently designated 2003 UB313. After being measured with the Hubble Space Telescope, it was shown to be some 3,000 km (1,864 miles) in diameter: it is bigger than Pluto. 2003 UB313 will now join Pluto in the [new] category [of dwarf planet], along with the biggest asteroid in the Solar System, Ceres." (BBC 2006)

14. The following passage is from the travel journals of an Englishman who was visiting France in 1787.

    "The palace of Versailles, one of the objects of which report had given me the greatest expectation, is not in the least striking. I view it without emotion: the impression it makes is nothing. What can compensate for the want of unity? From whatever point viewed, it appears as an assemblage of buildings; a splendid quarter of a town, but not a fine edifice." (Dawson 1967, 8)

15. "The post-war consumer group has market strength due to its size and affluence. This is a group where 70 percent of its members are in full- or part-time employment. Previous studies have found that mature women continue to be fashion conscious. Furthermore, [mature women who responded to our survey] were interested in the activity of clothes shopping, but became frustrated by high-street retailers' lack of attention to this sector of the market. An increasing number of fashion retailers are trying to target the younger market, which is in decline. At the same time, the opportunity exists to satisfy the affluent mature market which seeks specific design details in garments. Independent retailers or department stores are supplying these clothes." (Birtwistle 2005, 462, material omitted)

Things That Are Not Arguments

Finding arguments is easier if you're aware of things that aren't arguments: assertions, descriptions, questions, instructions, and explanations.

Know

Assertions

A single statement can't be an argument. It could be an important and true statement. It could be part of an argument. But a single statement can't be an argument because an argument must have at least two statements, a premise and a conclusion.

Connections

If one statement is both a premise and the conclusion in the same argument, the argument commits the fallacy of begging the question. Chapter Two discusses this fallacy.

If you said

(a) Everyone should take a philosophy class.

you'd have made an assertion, not an argument. If you added

Philosophy helps your critical thinking skills and your ability to figure out the structure of complex issues.

then the statement (a) would become a conclusion of an argument. If, instead, you were to have added

So, Paul should take a philosophy course this semester.

then statement (a) would be a premise in an argument. Many passages are lists of assertions that don't form an argument. Descriptions are examples of assertions.

Descriptions

A description is intended to give the reader a mental image of something. You can describe physical things, activities, feelings, sounds, emotions, and tastes. Descriptions can be beautiful, true, and important. But they can't be arguments. Here's a beautiful description from Charlotte Bronte's *Jane Eyre*.

Decanting a liquid from a solid.

Two wax candles stood lighted on the table, and two on the mantelpiece. Half reclined on a couch appeared Mr. Rochester, his foot supported by the cushion; he was looking at Adele and the dog: the fire shone full on his face. I knew my traveller with his broad and jetty eyebrows; his square forehead, made squarer by the horizontal sweep of his black hair. I recognised his decisive nose, more remarkable for character than beauty; his full nostrils; his grim mouth, chin, and jaw—yes, all three were very grim, and no mistake. His shape, now divested of cloak, I perceived harmonised in squareness with his physiognomy: I suppose it was a good figure in the athletic sense of the term—broad chested and thin flanked, though neither tall nor graceful. (Bronte 1908, 115, material omitted)

Questions and Instructions

Above you saw that because questions and instructions are neither true nor false, they can't be statements. That means that they can't be arguments, or even parts of arguments. But as you saw in the Zola example, sometimes the correct interpretation of a passage is that the author is making an argument even though the sentences aren't in declarative form.

Explanations

There are two different kinds of explanations: explanations of how to do something and explanations of why something is true. As an example of how to do something, here's an explanation of how to decant a liquid from a solid.

> Prepare, clean, and dry (1) a container with a small spout, (2) an empty container, and (3) a stirring rod. Pour the liquid-solid mixture into the container with a small spout. If you are decanting more than you can comfortably hold up at one time, do the decanting in batches. Place the stirring rod one to three centimeters above the empty container. Take the container with the liquid-solid mixture and hold it so that the spout rests gently against the stirring rod. Slowly tilt the container with the liquid-solid mixture so that liquid slowly swirls down the stirring rod into the empty container. The stirring rod should stay at the spout of the container so that it keeps any of the solid particles from going into the container with the liquid. Do not attempt to remove all the liquid from the liquid-solid mixture.

Explanations of how to do something are rarely confused with arguments. But explanations of why something is true are often confused with arguments. From this point on "explanation" will refer *only* to explanations of why something is true.

Explanations are often confused with arguments because they're similar in several ways. They both use declarative statements. In an explanation, the statement of what's to be explained is the **explanandum**. The statements that do the explaining are the **explanans**. The explanandum is often mistaken for the conclusion of an argument, and the explanans are often mistaken for premises. They both use the same indicator words. The premise indicator words can be used to indicate explanans and the conclusion indicator words can be used to indicate explananda. They're both concerned with truth. But they're concerned with truth in different ways. An argument is an attempt to *show that* some statement is true. An explanation is an attempt to tell someone *why* a statement is true. An explanation assumes that we all agree that the explanandum is true. An argument assumes that someone doesn't agree that the conclusion is true. Look back at the two statements about the car being in the shop since last Tuesday. (Page 16) Both are examples of explanations.

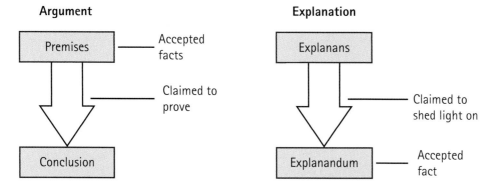

It's also hard to distinguish arguments from explanations because people argue about explanations. One famous case of this concerns the extinction of the dinosaurs. Here's a review of this debate from the web pages of the University of California at Berkeley's Museum of Paleontology:

> Two main camps exist in paleontology today, each having a different view of what killed the dinosaurs. The major sides of the schism can be broken down into "intrinsic gradualists" and "extrinsic catastrophists."
>
> ### The "Intrinsic Gradualists"
> Those scientists falling into this category believe that the ultimate cause of the extinction was intrinsic, meaning of an Earthly nature, and gradual, taking some time to occur (several million years). Two main hypotheses exist today.
>
> 1. Volcanism: We are quite certain that [at] the end of the Cretaceous period there was increased volcanic activity. Over a period of several million years, this increased volcanism could have created enough dust and soot to block out sunlight; producing the climatic change. In India during the Late Cretaceous, huge volcanic eruptions were spewing forth floods of lava.
> 2. Plate Tectonics: Major changes in the organization of the continental plates (continental drift) were occurring. The oceans were receding from the land. A less mild climate would have been the result, and this would have taken a long time.
>
> Note that these two above hypotheses are inextricably tied together; volcanism can't occur without the action of plate tectonics, and vice versa. If the extinction was intrinsic and gradual, both processes probably played a role.

The "Extrinsic Catastrophists"

This side of the controversy holds that the ultimate cause of the extinction was extrinsic, meaning of an extraterrestrial nature, and catastrophic, meaning fairly sudden and punctuated. The main hypothesis was proposed in 1980 by (among others) Luis and Walter Alvarez of the University of California at Berkeley.

The Alvarez Hypothesis: The original hypothesis is the basis for several subsequent variations on the theme that a large extraterrestrial object collided with the Earth, its impact throwing up enough dust to cause the climatic change. (Hutchinson 2006, material omitted)*

Intrinsic gradualists and extrinsic catastrophists are both proposing an explanation of why the dinosaurs are extinct. They don't disagree about whether dinosaurs are extinct. The disagreement occurs because people defend two different proposed explanations. They each provide arguments to support their preferred explanation of the extinction of the dinosaurs. Extrinsic catastrophists might make the following argument:

(1) The extinction of the dinosaurs was swift.
(2) Volcanism and plate tectonics can't explain the swiftness of the extinction of the dinosaurs.
Therefore,
(3) Intrinsic gradualism is false.

Intrinsic gradualists might make the following argument:

(1) If a large extraterrestrial object had collided with the Earth, it would have left a large crater.
(2) There's no such crater.
Therefore,
(3) Extrinsic catastrophism is false.

The two sides in this debate are arguing about explanations. The texts you might read about this issue intersperse arguments and explanations. This makes it difficult to distinguish the arguments from the explanations. The key point to keep in mind is the presence or absence of agreement. If there's no disagreement as to whether a statement is true, that statement probably isn't the conclusion of an argument. If there's disagreement as to whether a statement is true, it's probably the conclusion of an argument.

Habits of a Critical Thinker

Intellectual Courage

Critical thinkers aren't afraid to question their own beliefs and the beliefs of others. It might require intellectual courage for you to consider debates about the extinction of the dinosaurs, vegetarianism, or the existence of God. Your family and friends might have strong views about these issues and you might worry about the loss of their support if you were to come to have different views. It might feel safer just to avoid these issues. A critical thinker has the courage to take these risks and seek the truth even when the truth is uncomfortable.

*Hutchinson, John. "What Killed the Dinosaurs?" 1994. DinoBuzz: Current Topics Concerning Dinosaurs <http://www.ucmp.berkeley.edu/diapsids/extinctheory.html> 3 Oct. 2006. Copyright 1994–2006 by the Regents of the University of California, all rights reserved.

EXERCISE 1.5

A. Find the arguments in the discussions below. Identify the premises and the conclusion of each argument.

    *1. Jack and Jill

        Jack: Let's climb up that beanstalk.

        Jill: Stupid idea.

        Jack: Why?

        Jill: Don't you know that there's a mean giant at the top of the beanstalk?

        Jack: No way!!! Where'd you hear that?

        Jill: I read about it in a book.

        Jack: What did it say in the book?

        Jill: There was some moron named "Jack" who climbed up a beanstalk and came face to face with a giant. The giant went after him, and Jack had to scramble down the beanstalk to save his life.

        Jack: That's a totally different Jack.

        Jill: Yeah, but it might be the same beanstalk!!

        Jack: I hadn't thought of that. Let's get out of here!!!

    2. Two emergency room physicians, Dr. Diagnosis (Dr. D) and Dr. Misdiagnosis (Dr. M).

        Dr. M: The patient is having a heart attack. We must immediately open the blocked arteries.

        Dr. D: Don't do that. The patient is not having a heart attack. It's simply indigestion.

        Dr. M: But the patient is having severe chest pain, and there's a history of heart attacks in his family.

        Dr. D: Indeed. But look closely at the receipt that fell out of his pocket. And then inspect his hands.

        Dr. M: What are you talking about?

        Dr. D: It's a receipt from Joe's Greasy Fried Chicken Shack, and it shows that he ordered five portions of Super-Duper Deep Fat Totally Greasy chicken wings. And his hands have enough grease on them to lubricate every car in California.

B. Determine whether each of the following passages contains: an argument, an assertion, a question, a command, or a description. If the passage contains an argument, identify the premises and conclusion.

    1. Look, we need to take I-285 instead of I-75. At this time of day I-75 is always a mess, and I read in the newspaper this morning that they were repaving part of I-75 today.

    2. The patient presents with fever, sweating, and a cough but claims that she has no pain in the throat or the ears.

    3. Your car is pulling right, but the tires look ok. I think one of your tie rods is bent.

    *4. "Get thee to a nunnery!" (Shakespeare, *Hamlet*, Act 3, Sc. 1)

    5. "Oh! you gods, why do you make us love your goodly gifts, and snatch them straight away?" (Shakespeare, *Pericles*, Act 3, Sc. 1)

    6. "Your mother was a hamster and your father smelt of elderberries!" (*Monty Python and the Holy Grail* 1975)

7. "It is often said that brown sugar is a healthier option than white sugar. In reality, brown sugar is most often ordinary table sugar that is turned brown by the reintroduction of molasses. Normally molasses is separated and removed when sugar is created. Because of its molasses content, brown sugar does contain certain minerals. But these minerals are present in only minuscule amounts. Nutritionally, brown sugar and white sugar are not much different." (O'Connor 2007, D5, material omitted)

*8. "[A]ll genuine political theories presuppose man to be evil. This can be easily documented in the works of every specific political thinker." (Schmitt 1996, 61, material omitted)

9. The following passage is about the Spanish conquest of the Aztecs. It speaks of the Aztec emperor, Moctezuma, the Spanish conquistador, Cortes, and the legendary Aztec god-King, Queutzalcoatl, who had been driven from his throne and had vowed to return some day.

   "Moctezuma was said to believe that Cortes was Queutzalcoatl. There is no reason to doubt the good faith of the authors of these accounts: it is clear that they believed this version. Nonetheless, the same may not have been true of Moctezuma and his relations. The Spaniards appeared for the first time in 1517, whereas Queutzalcoatl was supposed to have returned in a One-Reed year of the Aztec calendar in 1519." (Todorov 1995, 22–23, material omitted)

10. "In a few days Mr. Bingley returned Mr. Bennet's visit, and sat about ten minutes with him in his library. He had entertained hopes of being admitted to a sight of the young ladies, of whose beauty he had heard much; but he saw only the father. The ladies were somewhat more fortunate, for they had the advantage of ascertaining from an upper window that he wore a blue coat, and rode a black horse." (Austen 1981, 7)

11. "In perpetrating a revolution, there are two requirements: someone or something to revolt against, and someone to actually show up to do the revolting. Dress is usually casual and both parties may be flexible about the time and place. In the Chinese revolution of 1650 neither party showed up, and the deposit on the hall was forfeited." (Allen 1991, 69, material omitted)

*12. "Dreams are not to be likened to the unregulated sounds that rise from a musical instrument struck by the blow of some external force instead of by a player's hand, they are not meaningless; they are not absurd. On the contrary, they are psychical [mental] phenomena of complete validity—fulfillments of wishes." (Freud 1969, 155, material omitted)

13. "The growth and intensification of serfdom was a major tendency in Russian history. [A]t the end of the nineteenth century thirty-four million people out of a population of thirty-six millions were reckoned as serfs." (Chamberlain 1965, 5, material omitted)

14. Background information: Amphibians are cold-blooded. They draw all the heat they need to live from their environment.

   "New fossilized remains of an amphibian which roamed the Earth more than 245 million years ago have been discovered in Antarctica, suggesting that its [climate] during much of the Triassic, the epoch when dinosaurs and the first primitive mammals emerged, was remarkably warm. The 60-cm (24-inch) piece of skull was dug out from thick sandstone at Fremouw Peak in the Transantarctic Mountains, just six degrees away from the South Pole. The mixed team of European-American paleontologists has assessed the creature as a Parotosuchus, a 2-m (6.5-ft)-long giant crocodile-like predator (but it was rather related to modern salamanders) that lived 40 million years before the first dinosaurs appeared, inhabiting lakes and rivers." (Anitei 2007)

15. The following passage is about a study conducted by the anthropologist Bronoslaw Malinowski.

"Malinowski's famous study of Melanesian sexual beliefs and practices provides evidence that sexual jealousy really does have a genetic rather than a purely cultural explanation. The tribe that he studied did not believe in physiological paternity; they thought the only function of sexual intercourse was to enlarge the vagina so that spirits could implant the fetus in the womb. Nevertheless, men were as jealous as in societies in which the male role in procreation is understood." (Posner 1992, 97–98, material omitted)

C. Determine whether each of the following passages contains an argument, an explanation, or neither an argument nor an explanation. If it contains an argument, identify the premises and the conclusion. If it contains an explanation, identify the explanans and explanandum.

1. We should decrease class sizes in our elementary schools. Students do better when classes are smaller.

2. He's getting fat and it's easy to see why. He never exercises, he has donuts for breakfast every morning, and hamburgers for dinner every night.

3. The drop in his grades wasn't caused by the divorce of his parents, because that occurred before he was two. There must be some other cause of the problem.

*4. You can see from the deformation of the right foot that it was broken and healed very badly. This dinosaur could barely walk. That's why she died.

5. Thirty-seven times sixty-four is 2,428.

6. "Help!"

7. "You might be surprised to learn that when you turn your car, your front wheels are not pointing in the same direction. For a car to turn smoothly, each wheel must follow a different circle. Since the inside wheel is following a circle with a smaller radius, it is actually making a tighter turn than the outside wheel." (Howstuffworks.com 2007)

*8. "The Cherokees believed that they had a sacred duty to avenge the deaths of fallen comrades, and so war parties formed quickly following a death." (Perdue 2005, 3)

9. "Stocks fell yesterday, led by financial services stocks, on concerns that the economy's expansion will erode [due to] troubles in the mortgage industry." (*New York Times*, "Financial Shares Lead Market Lower," 2007, C13)

10. The following passage comes from a nineteenth century decision of the U.S. Supreme Court. The case involved a dispute in which the state of Georgia sought to impose its laws on the Cherokee tribe.
    "If it be true that the Cherokee nation has rights, this is not the tribunal in which those rights are to be asserted. If it be true that wrongs have been inflicted, and that still greater are to be apprehended, this is not the tribunal which can redress the past or prevent the future." (*Cherokee Nation* 1831, 20)

11. Why don't humans have fur? Because fur is a great place to be a bug. Fur helps keep an animal warm but it is also a breeding ground for ticks, lice, and other parasites. Think about all the fleas on a dog. Humans did not need fur for warmth because they can build shelters, use fire, and make clothes. So humans with less fur gradually replaced those with more, in a classic example of Darwin's natural selection.

*12. "Historians have noted the Protestant origins of many of the early scientists. The Puritan preachers insisted that the universe was law-abiding. The [Protestant] Reverend George Hakewill published [a book] in 1627 [that] argued that scientific observation was more important than traditional authority. It was man's duty to study the universe and find out its laws." (Hill 1966, 92)

13. The following passage comes from an address of Martin Luther King, Jr. In it, he speaks to other clergyman about the war in Vietnam.

"I knew that America would never invest the necessary funds or energies in rehabilitation of its poor so long as adventures like Vietnam continued to draw men and skills and money like some demonic destructive suction tube. So I was increasingly compelled to see the war as an enemy of the poor and to attack it as such." (King 1991, 232–233)

14. "There is good reason why it is considered important to be able to listen to another person, why we have to listen—for we do not have to learn to interrupt which comes naturally. Interrupting is generally considered impolite. Here indispensable social norms not rooted in the organism's natural inclinations are motivated and determined by propriety and politeness." (Yakubinsky 1997, 249, material omitted)

15. The Pope has the power to excommunicate any member of the Catholic Church. Excommunication expels a person from the Church, and, according to Roman Catholic belief, there is no salvation outside of the Church. Following is an excerpt from the Papal announcement excommunicating Martin Luther.

"Our decrees which follow are passed against Martin and others who follow him in the obstinacy of his depraved and damnable purpose, as also against those who defend and protect him with a military bodyguard, and do not fear to support him with their own resources or in any other way. On all these we decree the sentences of excommunication, of anathema, of privation of dignitaries, honors and property on them and their descendants and these and the other sentences, censures, and punishments which are inflicted by canon law on heretics we decree to have fallen on all of these men to their damnation." (Rupp 1970, 65, material omitted)

D. Constructing arguments. Read the following passages and then, in each case, construct two arguments that support opposing explanations.

1. "In recent years, researchers have discovered tantalizing evidence that antidepressants combat depression by promoting neurogenesis, the growth of new neurons in the brain. The evidence derives from several striking observations. One is that stressed monkeys grow fewer new cells in the hippocampus region of the brain than their healthy counterparts do. Secondly, most depression treatments, from drugs such as Prozac to a type of powerful magnetic stimulation, increase new neuron growth by up to 75 percent in rodents.

"And in the most telling study to date, scientists from Columbia University and Yale University directed radiation at the hippocampi of mice to prevent neurogenesis. When given fluoxetine, also known as Prozac, the mice exhibited none of the behavioral changes normally associated with the drug. If neurogenesis is required to kick depression, as the result suggested, maybe its loss sends the mind into a tailspin. 'It's a very appealing idea,' comments Eric Nestler of the University of Texas Southwestern Medical Center at Dallas. 'It provides a mechanism to explain why many cases of depression are chronic and progressive.' It would also explain why Prozac takes a few weeks to exert its effects. The growth of neurons from stem cells takes a few weeks as well.

"But the details nag at some researchers. Fritz Henn of Brookhaven National Laboratory says he was captivated by the idea early on. 'I thought it was a good target for a final common pathway' underlying all forms of depression. But when Henn and his colleagues randomly shocked the feet of mice—a treatment that is known to erode neurogenesis—not all of the animals became depressed. 'That experiment made me leery,' he says. When neurogenesis is abridged by other means, such as irradiation, the animals do not all go on to show signs of depression." (Minkel 2006)

2. "A recent scientific theory is known as "string theory." It says that everything is made of incredibly tiny loops of energy that vibrate in ten or eleven dimensions. These tiny loops, or strings, can explain all of the four basic physical forces: gravity, electromagnetism, and the strong and weak nuclear forces. No other theory can explain all of the forces. But a startling discovery had led some scientists to reject string theory. In 1998 astronomers discovered that all of the galaxies in the universe are flying away from one another at an accelerating rate. This contradicted the prevailing view that the galaxies are flying away from one another but at a slower and slower rate. A previously unknown form of energy was needed to explain the discovery, which scientists called "dark energy."

An explanation of the problem that dark energy poses for string theory and the response of string theorists are given in the passage below. Read the passage and then, based on the information contained in it, construct two arguments, one that could be given by an anti-string theorist and another that could be given by a string theorist.

"Simple calculations suggested this energy should be enormous [but in fact the energy is much smaller]. Ideally, string theory should account for why dark energy is so much weaker than it could be. The only explanation string theory proponents have come up with is an unpalatable one to many physicists: assume that string theory is capable of describing [a large] number of different universes, each with its own dark energy, and note that one of those universes is bound to look like ours. Skeptics see the landscape as an abandonment of centuries-old scientific practice, in which a successful theory is one that ultimately describes only one universe: the one we see around us. In their eyes, string theorists are in the undesirable position of having to change the rules of science to make their theory work." (Minkel 2006, material omitted)

Putting Arguments into Standard Form

Because arguments can be hard to follow, it's useful to put them into standard form. To put an argument into standard form you:

✗ 1. put all the statements into declarative sentences and replace all pronouns with nouns;

2. insert any unstated premises and any unstated conclusion;

3. number each statement;

4. place the premises before their conclusion; and

5. indicate conclusions with the word "therefore."

Here's an example of the format of the standardization of a simple argument:

✗ (1) This is the first premise.
(2) This is the second premise.
[3] This is the third premise.
Therefore,
(4) This is the conclusion.

Let's agree to put brackets ([ ]) around the numbers of unstated premises and conclusions. Premise [3] above is unstated.

Suppose you came across the following passage in an editorial from a business magazine you were studying in a Finance course.

Where is the stock market headed? Some think we are in the middle of a sustained bull market. My view is that stock market prices will go down this coming quarter because if interest rates go up, stock market prices will go down, and the Federal Reserve has indicated that interest rates will rise.

Key Concept
How to standardize arguments.

will need to Know

Following the first of the three steps for finding arguments you begin by looking for an attempt to convince. The word "because" is a premise indicator. The phrase "my view" is another sign that the passage contains a point that's controversial. You also rely on your background knowledge that people frequently disagree about whether stock prices will rise or fall. This passage contains an argument.

Conclusion is alway controversial

The second step is to find the conclusion. The main point of this passage is the statement that stock market prices will go down this coming quarter. You need to put this conclusion into a declarative sentence.

(C) Stock market prices will fall this coming quarter.

The third step is to find the premises. Two of them are clear.

(P) If interest rates rise, stock market prices will fall.
(P) Interest rates will rise.

Your first draft of a standardization of this argument might look like this:

(1) If interest rates rise, stock market prices will fall.
(2) Interest rates will rise.
Therefore,
(3) Stock market prices will fall this coming quarter.

Standardizing isn't rearranging the phrases you find in a text. When you standardize, you should edit the phrases you find to make the argument clearer. Here's another way that critical thinking is an art, not a mechanical process. In this example, the author uses the phrases "will go down" and "will rise." The standardization changes "will go down" to "will fall" to make the contrast between rising and falling prices clearer. You temporarily assign "(C)" to the conclusion. You can't put a number in place of the "(C)" yet because you don't yet know how many premises there'll be. For this same reason you temporarily assign "(P)" to each premise. You have to read and reread the passage. You have to carefully note the relationships between the various sentences in the passage.

This standardization omits material. The two sentences

Where is the stock market headed?

and

Some think we are in the middle of a sustained bull market.

FSM (Fictitious Stock Market) Index, Apr. 2009–Jan. 2010

An imaginary sample of a stock graph.

aren't in the standardization. They're omitted because they aren't part of the argument. The first sentence is a question used to introduce the topic, and the second sentence sets up the argument by pointing to views that the author doesn't share.

What about the phrase "the Federal Reserve has indicated that"? What is the function of this phrase? It supports the view that interest rates will rise. You've discovered that this passage contains two arguments. The one you've just discovered can be standardized like this:

(1) The Federal Reserve has indicated that interest rates will rise.
Therefore,
(2) Interest rates will rise.

The conclusion of this argument is the first premise of the other argument in the passage. You can put the standardizations together like this:

(1) The Federal Reserve has indicated that interest rates will rise.
Therefore,
(2) Interest rates will rise.
(3) If interest rates rise, stock market prices will fall.
Therefore,
(4) Stock market prices will fall this coming quarter.

The passage contains two arguments. The first argument has (1) as its premise and (2) as its conclusion. The second argument has (2) and (3) as its premises and (4) as its conclusion. Statement (2) is the conclusion of one argument *and* a premise in another argument. When the conclusion of one argument is the premise of another argument, the two arguments are **linked arguments**. Arguments that are used to support premises of the **main** argument are called **subarguments**. In the example above, the argument composed of statements (1) and (2) is a subargument. The argument composed of statements (2), (3), and (4) is the main argument. Any number of arguments could be linked together. For example, the author of the argument above might have presented a subargument for (1) and a subargument for (3). In that case there would have been four linked arguments (the main argument and three subarguments).

> **Key Concept**
> When the conclusion of one argument is the premise of another argument, the two arguments are **linked arguments**.

> **Key Concept**
> Arguments that are used to support premises of the **main** argument are called **subarguments**.

Technical Terms: Complex Arguments, Simple Arguments

Linked arguments are sometimes called "complex arguments." Unlinked arguments are sometimes called "simple arguments."

Here's an example of the format of the standardization of an argument that contains subarguments:

(1) This is the first premise of the first subargument.
(2) This is the second premise of the first subargument.
Therefore,
(3) This is the conclusion of the first subargument and the first premise of the main argument.

(4) This is the first premise of the second subargument.
Therefore,
(5) This is the conclusion of the second subargument and the second premise of the main argument.

Therefore,
(6) This is the conclusion of the main argument.

This example has two subarguments and a main argument. The first subargument has two premises, (1) and (2), and its conclusion is (3). The second subargument has one premise, (4), and its conclusion is (5). The main argument has two premises, (3) and (5), and its conclusion is (6). Let's agree to put blank lines between arguments to help you see the main argument and the subarguments.

Here's an example of linked arguments. One popular theory of management is the stockholder theory. This theory holds that the only job of Chief Executive Officers (CEOs) of publicly traded corporations is to maximize value for *stock*holders. R. Edward Freeman (1997) argues against the stockholder theory. He thinks that CEOs should take into account anyone who is a *stake*holder of their corporation. Here's a standardization of his main argument:

(1) Stakeholders include any groups who are vital to the success of the corporation.
(2) Stockholders, employees, and customers are vital to the success of the corporation.
Therefore,
(3) Stockholders, employees, and customers are stakeholders.

(4) Corporations have a responsibility to all stakeholders.
(5) The job of the CEO is to act on behalf of the corporation.
Therefore,
(6) The job of the CEO is to take all stakeholders into account when making decisions on behalf of the corporation.

Statements (1), (2), and (3) form a subargument. Statements (3), (4), (5), and (6) form the main argument. Freeman knows that stockholder theorists are likely to reject premise (4), and he uses linked arguments to defend this premise.

Freeman attempts to support (4) by pointing to the laws which address the interests of the groups named in premise (3). Here's a standardization of two arguments Freeman uses to defend premise (4):

(P) There are labor laws that give employees the right to unionize.
(P) There are civil rights and equal pay laws that put constraints on hiring practices.
Therefore,
(C) Some laws support the interests of employees against corporations.
(P) There are laws that hold manufacturing corporations liable for damage by their products even when they have exercised all care in production and even when the product was misused by the customer.
Therefore,
(C) Some laws support the interests of customers against corporations.

You can combine the conclusions of the above two subarguments to get:

(P) Some laws support the interests of employees against corporations.
(P) Some laws support the interests of customers against corporations.
Therefore
(C) Some laws support the interests of employees and customers against corporations.

You can put all the arguments together like this:

(1) Stakeholders include any groups who are vital to the success of the corporation.

(2) Owners, employees, and customers are vital to the success of the corporation.

Therefore,

(3) Owners, employees, and customers are stakeholders.

(4) There are labor laws that give employees the right to unionize.

(5) There are civil rights and equal pay laws that put constraints on hiring practices.

Therefore,

(6) Some laws support the interests of employees against corporations.

(7) There are laws that hold manufacturing corporations liable for damage by their products even when they have exercised all care in production and even when the product was misused by the customer.

Therefore,

(8) Some laws support the interests of customers against corporations.

Therefore,

(9) Some laws support the interests of employees and customers against corporations. (From premises (6) and (8).)

Therefore,

(10) Corporations have a responsibility to all stakeholders.

(11) The job of the CEO is to act on behalf of the corporation.

Therefore,

(12) The job of the CEO is to take all stakeholders into account when making decisions on behalf of the corporation.

Freeman's main conclusion, (12), is supported by premises (3), (10), and (11). He uses five subarguments to defend these premises. Premises (1) and (2) support (3). Statements (4) and (5) support (6), and statement (7) supports (8). Statements (6) and (8) are then used to support (9), and (9) is used to support (10). This argument has a pretty complex structure. (And, believe it or not, we have simplified Freeman's argument!)

Let's look at the passage from John Stuart Mill's *On Liberty* that you saw at the beginning of this chapter.

> [The] peculiar evil of silencing the expression of an opinion is that it is robbing the human race, those who dissent from the opinion still more than those who hold it. If the opinion is right, they are deprived of the opportunity of exchanging error for truth. If wrong, they lose, what is almost as great a benefit, the clearer perception and livelier impression of truth produced by its collision with error.

Once again, you follow the three first steps outlined above. The first step is to look for an attempt to convince. Mill is arguing for freedom of speech. He's trying to convince you that silencing the expression of an opinion is evil. This makes your second step (find the conclusion) easy. His conclusion is:

(C) No one should silence the expression of an opinion.

The third step is to find the premises. The structure of the premises in this passage is complex. Mill divides the matter into two cases: when the silenced opinion is true ("right") and when the silenced is false ("wrong"). One premise is:

(P) If someone suppresses a true opinion, people who don't know this opinion lose the opportunity to learn it.

and another is

(P) If someone suppresses a false opinion, people who know the truth lose the opportunity to gain a greater appreciation of the truth by comparing it to a false opinion.

We've rewritten Mill's words to make them clearer. For example, we've replaced his "if wrong" with "if someone suppresses a false opinion." You improve clarity by replacing the pronouns in the original text with the noun or noun phrase to which the pronoun refers. Making these sorts of changes to Mill's wording gives you this first draft of a standardization of Mill's argument:

(P) If someone suppresses a true opinion, people who don't know this opinion lose the opportunity to learn it.
(P) If someone suppresses a false opinion, people who know the truth lose the opportunity to gain a greater appreciation of the truth by comparing it to a false opinion.
Therefore,
(C) No one should silence the expression of an opinion.

As you review this, you might notice a missing step. What if an opinion isn't true or false? Mill assumes that:

[P] All opinions are either true or false.

This is a classic case of an unstated premise. If you were to ask Mill, "Are all opinions either true or false?" he'd respond "Of course." Here's the final standardization of the argument:

[1] All opinions are either true or false.
(2) If someone suppresses a true opinion, people who don't know this opinion lose the opportunity to learn it.
(3) If someone suppresses a false opinion, people who know the truth lose the opportunity to gain a greater appreciation of the truth by comparing it to a false opinion.
Therefore,
(4) No one should silence the expression of an opinion.

Any argument can be correctly standardized in different ways. If the word "opinion" in the standardization of Mill's argument above were replaced with the word "view," that would be an equally good standardization. You could move and renumber premise [1] to be premise [3] without changing the quality of the standardization. But some ways of standardizing an argument are much better than others. A standardization of Mill's argument that omitted premise (2) would be seriously flawed. If you made a mistake and thought that this sentence

If wrong, they lose, what is almost as great a benefit, the clearer perception and livelier impression of truth produced by its collision with error.

was the conclusion of Mill's argument, you would produce a poor standardization.

EXERCISE 1.6

A. Find all the arguments in the discussions in Exercise 1.5 A and put them into standard form.

B. For each passage in Exercises 1.5 B, C, and D, determine which contains an argument(s), and put the argument into standard form.

C. Determine whether each of the following passages contains an argument(s). If the passage contains an argument or arguments, put it/them into standard form.

1. Don't cry. Your toy dinosaur's around here somewhere. You were playing with it in the kitchen less than an hour ago, and you haven't been out of the house since then. We'll find it.

2. I got angry. Then I told him, "Listen, I don't want kumquats! I want oranges!"

3. If he goes to work, he'll get very sick. But he won't go to work, so I don't think that he'll get sick.

*4. Why do you want to make me feel so bad?

5. Napoleon either lost at Waterloo or at Austerlitz. There's a statue in honor of his victory at Austerlitz, so he must have lost at Waterloo.

6. "[There is some red dirt on your shoe.] Just opposite the Seymour Street Post Office they have taken up the pavement and thrown up some earth, which lies in such a way that it is difficult to avoid treading in it in entering. The earth is of this peculiar reddish tint which is found, as far as I know, nowhere else in the neighborhood. [You must have been to the post office.]" (Doyle 1890, 12)

7. "Many people have the reasoning faculty, but no one uses it in religious matters. The best minds will tell you that when a man has begotten a child he is morally bound to tenderly care for it, protect it from hurt, shield it from disease, clothe it, feed it, bear with its waywardness, lay no hand upon it save in kindness and for its own good, and never in any case inflict upon it a wanton cruelty. God's treatment of his earthly children, every day and every night, is the exact opposite of all that, yet those best minds warmly justify these crimes, condone them, excuse them, and indignantly refuse to regard them as crimes at all, when *he* commits them. (Twain 2007, 380–381, material omitted)

*8. "Early in the morning of March 10, 2003, after a raucous party that lasted into the small hours, a groggy and hungover 20-year-old named Ryan Holle lent his Chevrolet Metro to a friend. That decision, prosecutors later said, was tantamount to murder. The friend used the car to drive three men to the Pensacola home of a marijuana dealer, aiming to steal a safe. The burglary turned violent, and one of the men killed the dealer's 18-year-old daughter by beating her head in with a shotgun he found in the home. Mr. Holle was a mile and a half away, but that did not matter. He was convicted of murder under a distinctively American legal doctrine that makes accomplices as liable as the actual killer for murders committed during felonies like burglaries, rapes, and robberies." (Liptak 2007, A1)

9. [Peter Singer] thinks that the suffering of non-human animals is as morally important as our own suffering. [He] claims that there are no morally relevant differences between some non-human animals and some severely mentally impaired human beings. [I]f the reflective, communicative, emotional, or social abilities of such impaired humans [are] not any greater than that of a pig or a primate, then we must treat [all] these beings in similar ways." (Feinberg 2002, 546, material omitted)

10. The following passage was written by an economist, and it concerns the question of whether the United States could produce more goods than it is currently producing.

    "[T]he U.S. economy currently holds very little excess capacity. The official data show that capacity utilization in manufacturing now stands at 82.4 percent up from a cyclical low of 73.9. Although these figures suggest ample excess capacity, the impression is misleading. Most U.S. manufacturing excess capacity resides in obsolete or noncompetitive plants and equipment." (Kaufman 2007, 24)

11. The following comes from a speech made by Malcolm X in 1964.

    "1964 threatens to be the most explosive year America has ever witnessed. Why? It's also a political year. The year when all of the white political crooks will be back in your and my community with their false promises, building up our hopes for a letdown, with their trickery and their treachery. [I]t can only lead to one thing: an explosion." (Breitman 1965, 25, material omitted)

*12. "My pulse is throbbing like a war drum. I want to slaughter something—give pain, give death to what, I do not know. But the piece ends. The men of the orchestra wipe their lips and rest their fingers. I creep slowly to the veneer we call civilization with the last tone and find the white friend sitting motionless in his seat, smoking calmly.

    " 'Good music they have here,' he remarks, drumming the table with his fingertips.

    "Music. The great blobs of purple and red emotion have not touched him. He has only heard what I felt. He is far away and I see him dimly across the ocean and the continent that have fallen between us. He is so pale with his whiteness and I am *so* colored." (Hurston 2000, 116)

13. "The study was undertaken to investigate the effect of sesame oil in hypertensive patients. Thirty-two male and 18 female patients aged 35 to 60 years old were supplied sesame oil and instructed to use it as the only edible oil for 45 days. Blood pressure, anthropometry, lipid profile, lipid peroxidation, and enzymic and non-enzymic antioxidants were measured at baseline and after 45 days of sesame oil substitution. Substitution of sesame oil brought down systolic and diastolic blood pressure to normal. The same patients were asked to withdraw sesame oil consumption for another 45 days, and the measurements were repeated at the end of the withdrawal period. Withdrawal of sesame oil substitution brought back the initial blood pressure values. The results suggested that sesame oil as edible oil lowered blood pressure, decreased lipid peroxidation, and increased antioxidant status in hypertensive patients." (Sankar 2006, 19, material omitted)

14. "Several years have now elapsed since I first became aware that I had accepted, even from my youth, many false opinions for true, and that consequently what I afterward based on such principles was highly doubtful; and from that time I was convinced of the necessity of undertaking once in my life to rid myself of all the opinions I had adopted, and of commencing anew the work of building from the foundation, if I desired to establish a firm and abiding superstructure in the sciences. But as this enterprise appeared to me to be one of great magnitude, I waited until I had attained an age so mature as to leave me no hope that at any stage of life more advanced I should be better able to execute my design. On this account, I have delayed so long that I should henceforth consider I was doing wrong were I still to consume in deliberation any of the time that now remains for action. Today, then, since I have opportunely freed my mind from all cares [and am happily disturbed by no passions], and since I am in the secure possession of leisure in a peaceable retirement, I will at length apply myself earnestly and freely to the general overthrow of all my former opinions." (Descartes 1913, 21)

15. "Under federal law, the maximum prison term for a felon convicted of possessing a firearm is ordinarily 10 years. If the offender's prior criminal record includes at least three convictions for 'violent felon[ies,' federal law] mandates a minimum term of 15 years. [However,] Congress amended [the law] in 1986 to exclude from qualification for enhanced sentencing 'any conviction which has been expunged, or set aside or for which a person has been pardoned or has had civil rights [i.e., rights to vote, hold office, and serve on a jury] restored.'

"[Mr.] Logan pleaded guilty to being a felon in possession of a firearm and received a 15-year sentence, the mandatory minimum under ACCA. In imposing this sentence, the court took account of three Wisconsin misdemeanor battery convictions, none of them revoking any of Logan's civil rights. Logan challenged his sentence on the ground that his state-court convictions fell within [the] 'civil rights restored' exemption [added in 1986]. Rights retained, Logan [claimed], should be treated the same as rights revoked but later restored.

"The exemption [added in the 1986] does not cover the case of an offender who retained civil rights at all times. The ordinary meaning of the word 'restored'—giving back something that has been taken away—does not include retention of something never lost. Moreover, the context in which 'restored' appears in [the text of the law] counsels adherence to the word's ordinary meaning. In [the text of the law] the words 'civil rights restored' appear in the company of 'expunged,' 'set aside,' and 'pardoned.' Each of those terms describes a measure by which the government relieves an offender of some or all of the consequences of his conviction." (*Logan* 2007, 1, material omitted)

Diagramming Arguments

One can take a standardized argument and make a kind of picture that represents the structure of the argument. These pictures are **argument diagrams**. Let's look again at this standardization:

(1) The Federal Reserve has indicated that interest rates will rise.
Therefore,
(2) Interest rates will rise.

(3) If interest rates rise, stock market prices will fall.
Therefore,
(4) Stock market prices will fall this coming quarter.

Here's the diagram of these arguments.

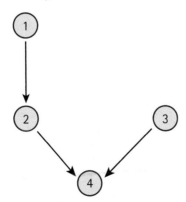

In a diagram, each statement is represented by a number in a circle. A line of inference from a premise to the conclusion is represented by a line with an arrow pointing to the conclusion. A conclusion is touched by the point of an arrow. In a set of linked arguments like this one, the diagram will always include more than one conclusion and at least one circle will have an arrow pointing to it and an arrow pointing away from it.

Key Concept
One can take a standardized argument and make a kind of picture that represents the structure of the argument. These pictures are **argument diagrams**.

EXERCISE 1.7

A. Diagram the other arguments that are standardized in this chapter.

***B.** Diagram the arguments you standardized in Exercise 1.6.

Chapter Summary

Critical thinking is the skill of correctly evaluating the arguments made by others and composing good arguments of your own. A person thinks critically when she bases her beliefs on good arguments.

An argument is an attempt to provide reasons for thinking that some belief is true. The reasons are premises, and the belief the reasons are intended to support is the conclusion. Both premises and conclusions are statements. But not all statements are parts of an argument. For an argument to be present, there must be an attempt to convince. Indicator words are helpful but imperfect guides. Some arguments present premises and conclusions in non-declarative forms. Some arguments have unstated premises and/or conclusions. Some passages contain two or more arguments linked together, called "subarguments" and the "main argument." Recognizing these complications will help you distinguish arguments from groups of statements that aren't arguments, such as descriptions and explanations.

It can be hard to distinguish arguments from explanations. Explanations and arguments use many of the same indicator words. Ultimately, the difference between the two is based on whether there's an attempt to convince. If there's no disagreement about the truth of a statement, there's usually no argument for that statement.

Arguments can be standardized in order to clarify them. In a standardization, premises and conclusions are numbered. Premises and subarguments are listed first. The word "therefore" is used to indicate each conclusion. Blank lines are used to indicate the difference between a subargument and a main argument. Brackets are used to indicate unstated premises and conclusions. Diagramming is a second method of clarifying the relations between arguments and subarguments. Arrows and lines graphically depict the relations between the premises, conclusions, and sub- and main arguments.

GUIDE

Finding and Standardizing Arguments

Here's a review of the steps to find and standardize an argument:

1. Look for an attempt to convince.
2. Find the conclusion.
3. Find the premises.
4. Review the following to make sure that you have correctly identified the conclusion and the premises: imperfect indicator words, sentence order, premises and/or conclusion not in declarative form, and unstated premises and/or conclusion.
5. Review the following to make sure that you haven't incorrectly identified something as a premise or a conclusion when in fact it isn't part of an argument: assertions, questions, instructions, descriptions, and explanations.
6. Rewrite the premises and the conclusion as declarative sentences. Make sure that each premise and the conclusion is a grammatically correct declarative sentence. Rewrite the premises and conclusion as necessary to make them clearer, but don't change the meaning of the passage. Remove pronouns from the sentences and replace them with nouns or noun phrases.
7. Review any phrases you have omitted to be sure that they aren't premises or a conclusion.
8. Number the premises and the conclusion. Put [ ] around the number of an unstated premise or conclusion. Place premises before their conclusion and insert "Therefore," between the premises and the conclusion. Use blank lines to indicate subarguments.
9. Compare your standardization to the original passage to make sure that you haven't omitted any arguments found in the passage and to be sure that you have correctly identified the premises and the conclusion.

2

What Makes a Good Argument?

[The Catholic Church] holds that it is not admissible to ordain women to the priesthood for very fundamental reasons. These reasons include: the example recorded in the Sacred Scriptures of Christ choosing his Apostles only from among men; the constant practice of the Church, which has imitated Christ in choosing only men; and her living teaching authority which has consistently held that the exclusion of women from the priesthood is in accordance with God's plan for his Church.

—Pope Paul VI, "Response to the Letter of His Grace the Most Reverend Dr. F.D. Coggan, Archbishop of Canterbury, concerning the Ordination of Women to the Priesthood" (1976, 599)

Learning Outcomes

After studying the material in this chapter, you should be able to:

1. Produce examples of each of the following kinds of arguments: arguments that pass the true premises test, arguments that fail the true premises test, arguments that pass the proper form test, and arguments that fail the proper form test.

2. Produce examples of deductive and inductive arguments.

3. Produce examples to illustrate the difference between a valid argument and a sound argument as well as the difference between a strong argument and a cogent argument.

4. Produce examples to illustrate the differences between relevant premises and irrelevant premises.

5. Use the true premises test and the proper form test to evaluate simple arguments.

Critical thinkers choose beliefs based on good arguments. But what is a good argument? Is Pope Paul's argument on the previous page a good argument? After studying the material in this chapter, you should be able to tell.

Determining whether an argument is a good argument is a complex matter. The rest of this book will be devoted to distinguishing good arguments from bad ones. As you will see in later chapters, there are different kinds of arguments and they have to be evaluated in different ways. But all good arguments share some common features. These features are the focus of this chapter.

The Two Characteristics of a Good Argument

All good arguments share two characteristics:

1. The argument's premises are <u>true.</u>
2. The argument has a proper form.

These characteristics can be used as tests for determining whether an argument is a good argument. First, check to see if the argument's premises are true. Second, check to see if the argument has a proper form. Let's call the first test the "true premises test" and the second test the "proper form test." If an argument passes both tests, it's a good argument.

Key Concept
The two characteristics of a good argument.

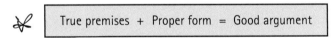

| True premises + Proper form = Good argument |

Here's a good argument about the philosopher Socrates:

(1) Socrates was a human being.
(2) All human beings are mortal.
Therefore,
(3) Socrates was mortal.

Both premises are true: Socrates was a human being, and all human beings are mortal. The argument has a proper form: the truth of these two premises is a good reason to think that the conclusion is true.

An argument is bad when it fails one or both of the tests. Here's an argument that fails the true premises test:

(1) The authors of this textbook have seen at least 40,000 fish and all of them had two fins.
Therefore,
(2) All fish have two fins.

The premise of this argument is false. We've probably seen at least 40,000 fish in our lives. We've been to many fish markets and several aquariums. But most of the fish we've seen have had more than two fins.

This argument passes the proper form test. Pretend that it was true that we'd seen more than 40,000 fish and all of them had two fins. In that case, we'd have good grounds for thinking that all fish had two fins. *If* the premises were true, they would provide a good reason to think that the conclusion was true. This illustrates an important point about the proper form test: when performing **the proper form test**, you *assume* or *pretend* that all the premises are true.

Here's an argument that fails the proper form test:

(1) All roses are plants.
(2) All roses have thorns.
Therefore,
(3) All plants have thorns.

This argument passes the true premises test. Roses are plants and they've got thorns. But the fact that one kind of plant has thorns doesn't mean that all plants have thorns.

Here's an example of an argument that fails both tests:

(1) All roses are plants.
(2) All roses eat meat.
Therefore,
(3) All plants eat meat.

The second premise is false. Roses don't eat meat. The argument fails the true premises test.

Now let's see if this argument passes the proper form test. Your first step is to assume or pretend that both premises are true. In this case, the first premise really is true but you have to pretend that the second premise is true. You pretend that roses eat meat. But when you assume that roses are plants and pretend that roses eat meat, you see that the two premises don't provide good grounds for the conclusion. Even if it were true that roses were plants and that roses ate meat, this wouldn't demonstrate that all plants eat meat. This argument fails the proper form test.

Now you can see another reason why critical thinking is the *art* of argument. The mastery of any art, any skill, takes practice. Talent, a desire to know, loving family members, and other kinds of luck all help, but without regular practice no one would excel at any art. To master the art of argument, you need to practice pretending that premises are true even when you know they aren't.

A bad argument can have a true conclusion. Suppose that a person makes the following silly argument:

(1) Over the next six months, my sister will drive more than she has in the past six months.
Therefore,
(2) Over the next six months, the price of gas will rise.

Let's assume that, over the next six months, gas prices rise. (2) turns out to be true. That doesn't mean that (1) and (2) form a good argument. The person

Key Concept
When performing the proper form test, you *assume* or *pretend* that all the premises are true.

who made this argument just got lucky. The conclusion of the argument happened to be true, even though the premise of the argument doesn't provide a good reason for the conclusion.

We've written as if passing or failing the true premises test and the proper form test was like passing or failing a course that had only two possible grades: P for passing and F for failing. In reality, the true premises test and proper form test are like grades on a 0–100 scale. There are many passing scores (you can pass with a 93, an 85, or a 72) and many failing scores (you can fail with a 50, a 33, or a 22). Some passing arguments are better than other passing arguments, and some failing arguments are worse than other failing arguments. An argument's final grade will depend on its score on both tests. (You shouldn't try to actually assign grades to arguments. This is just an illustrative analogy.)

EXERCISE 2.1

A. Which of the following arguments pass the true premises test? Which pass the proper form test? Explain.

1. (1) Oxygen is an element essential for life on Earth as we know it.
Therefore,
(2) If oxygen were to vanish from the Earth's atmosphere, life as we know it would cease.

2. (1) All birds can fly. *Premise are not true*
(2) Penguins are birds.
Therefore,
(3) Penguins can fly.

3. (1) All cars are blue. *Premises are not true. Bad form*
(2) All pigs have wings.
Therefore,
(3) All buses have three wheels.

*4. (1) Elephants are mammals. *True Premises*
(2) Dogs are mammals.
Therefore, *Bad form argument*
(3) Elephants are dogs.

5. (1) Many types of plastic can be recycled. *True Premise, + lack proper form*
(2) Many types of glass can be recycled.
Therefore, *Bad Argument Bad form*
(3) Many types of paper can be recycled.

6. (1) Julia Roberts is either a man or a woman.
(2) Julia Roberts is a man.
Therefore,
(3) Julia Roberts isn't a woman.

7. (1) Everyone likes pizza.
   (2) Everyone who likes pizza buys it regularly.
   Therefore,
   (3) Pizza sales will rise over the next six months.

*8. (1) If you drop wood into water, it floats unless it's held underwater by a heavy object.
   (2) Trees are made of wood.
   Therefore,
   (3) When trees fall into water, they float unless they're held underwater by a heavy object.

9. (1) The discovery of antibiotics increased life expectancy.
   (2) Antibiotics have no effect on viruses.
   Therefore,
   (3) There must be some causes of reduced life expectancy besides viruses.

10. (1) All cars have three wheels.
   (2) Everything with three wheels is blue.
   Therefore,
   (3) All cars are blue.

11. (1) If you walk on the lines in the sidewalk, you will be eaten by bears.
   (2) Sometime in the next week, someone will walk on the lines in the sidewalk.
   Therefore,
   (3) Sometime in the next week, someone will be eaten by bears.

*12. (1) I have seen 4,000 houses, and every last one of them was purple.
   Therefore,
   (2) All houses are purple.

13. (1) I have seen 4,000 ducks, and every last one of them had webbed feet.
   Therefore,
   (2) All ducks have webbed feet.

14. (1) Many people like candy.
   (2) Many people like cats.
   Therefore,
   (3) Many people like going to the movies.

15. (1) If you walk to the store, you will get a latté.
   (2) You did not get a latté.
   Therefore,
   (3) You did not walk to the store.

B. Use the examples in 2.1 A above as models for these exercises.

1. Compose an argument that fails *only* the true premises test.
2. Compose an argument that fails *only* the proper form test.
3. Compose an argument that fails *both* the true premises test and the proper form test.
4. Compose an argument that fails *neither* the true premises test *nor* the proper form test.

True Premises

When is a premise true? Truth has puzzled scholars for centuries. Fortunately we can focus on a simple theory of truth. A statement is true when what it says about the world is accurate. A statement is false when what it says about the world is inaccurate. The statement

> All roses are plants.

is true because what it says about the world is accurate. Roses are in fact plants. The statement

> All roses eat meat.

is false because what it says about the world isn't accurate. Roses don't eat meat.
Statements are attempts to describe the world. When a statement succeeds in correctly describing the world, it's true. When it fails to correctly describe the world, it's false.

Connections

Chapter One notes that all statements are either true or false.

Audience

All arguments have an audience. The **audience** of an argument is the group that the person making the argument wishes to convince. A premise can be true even though no one in the audience knows that it's true. Look at this statement about transfatty acids, an ingredient found in some processed foods.

> Transfatty acids contribute to heart disease.

Suppose that someone said this in 1965. At that time, no one knew whether this statement was true. It wasn't until the 1990s that scientists learned that this statement is true. Suppose that in 1965 someone offered the following argument:

(1) Transfatty acids contribute to heart disease.
(2) Children should not be given foods that contribute to heart disease. Therefore,
(3) Children should not be given foods that contain transfatty acids.

Is this a good argument? Let's assume that the second premise is true. Then this argument is a good argument. Even in 1965, the premises were true and they provided good grounds for the conclusion. But in 1965 no one in the audience for this argument knew that premise (1) was true. This means that in 1965 no one knew that this was a good argument. It was only in the 1990s that premise (1) was shown to be true and therefore people came to see that the argument above is a good argument. Because a premise can be true even though no one knows that it's true, an argument can be a good argument even though no one knows that it's a good argument.

Key Concept
A statement is true when what it says about the world is accurate.

Key Concept
The **audience** of an argument is the group that the person making the argument wishes to convince.

Asteroid belts.

Suppose that you were writing an essay in an astronomy class. Your class is studying our solar system. In such a class, the statement

There is a belt of asteroids between Mars and Jupiter.

might be a statement that everyone in the class knows. On the other hand, if you were in a psychology class, this same statement might be one that fewer people know. When you're composing your own arguments, you should use premises that your audience knows.

Critical Thinkers

Carolyn Spellman Shoemaker

Astronomer **Carolyn Spellman Shoemaker** (1929–still star-gazing) has discovered 800 asteroids as well as discovering more comets than any other astronomer (32 as of 2002). She studied history and political science in college but decided to study the stars, beginning in 1980 at the Palomar Observatory in San Diego, California. She was research professor of astronomy at Northern Arizona University. Her best-known work is in developing photographic techniques for the detection of fast-moving asteroids. Her most significant discovery, made with her husband, planetary geologist Eugene, and fellow astronomer David Levy, was of the Comet Shoemaker-Levy 9, which collided with Jupiter in 1994.

EXERCISE 2.2

A. For each of the following statements, indicate an audience that is likely to know that the statement is true and an audience that isn't likely to know that the statement is true.

1. In 1900, William I was the Emperor of Germany. *fact*
2. Each water molecule contains two atoms of hydrogen and one atom of oxygen.
3. In 2007, Dina Bowman published an article in *The Journal of Sociology*.
*4. Between 1997 and 2007, standardized testing became more common in American elementary schools.
5. Football is a popular American sport.
6. The famous philosopher René Descartes was born in France and died in Sweden.
7. Two plus two equals four.
*8. The two tests for a good argument are the true premises test and the proper form test.
9. Hyat Custovic is 5'6" tall.
10. All matter exhibits wave-like properties. (This is a version of the de Broglie hypothesis, a fundamental theory of physics.)
11. The speed of a computer processor of a given price doubles approximately every two years. (This statement is often called "Moore's Law.")
*12. "Buy land—they aren't making any more of it." (This statement has been attributed to many people, including Will Rogers and Mark Twain.)
13. "Outside of a dog, a book is a man's best friend. Inside of a dog, it is too dark to read." (Attributed to Groucho Marx. Source unknown) This quote contains two statements.
14. The U.S. Census occurs every ten years.
15. "TRPML3 is a member of the TRPML subfamily of the transient receptor potential cation channel superfamily." (Kim 2007, 36138)

B. List five things that you know that your instructor is unlikely to know. Then do the same thing for one of your best friends.

The Problem of Ignorance

The **problem of ignorance** is that you don't know everything. The problem makes it hard to answer this question: When can you assume a premise? If you had complete knowledge, you could assume a premise when it was true and not assume it when it was false. But because of the problem of ignorance, this strategy won't work.

Another effect of the problem of ignorance is that sometimes you don't know what you don't know. Think about that last sentence for a moment. Sometimes you think that you know something but you don't. You might remember being sure of something only to discover that you were wrong.

On the other hand, sometimes you do know what you don't know. For example, because you read it in a reputable newspaper, you might know that the President of France was taken to the hospital. But you might not have read any news of his condition since then. In this case, you know what you don't know. You know that you aren't up-to-date on the President's medical condition.

Habits of a Critical Thinker

Recognizing Your Own Ignorance

No one knows everything. Do you know all the following: how the screen on your cell phone works? why electricity doesn't pass through plastic? all about the U.S. tax code? You may not like to admit that you don't know something. But a problem doesn't go away if you refuse to acknowledge it. Until you acknowledge your ignorance, you can't work to reduce it.

When you don't have knowledge, the best course of action is simply to admit it. If you don't have enough knowledge to tell whether a premise in an argument is true or false, you should admit that. When evaluating arguments, be prepared to admit that you can't completely carry out the true premises test. When someone asks you a question, you should remember that "I don't know" is always a possible response. In fact, it may be the most frequent correct answer to questions. Don't be afraid to say, "I don't know." Admission of your ignorance usually isn't an admission of failure. It shows that you have a correct appreciation of your own ignorance.

It takes practice to recognize your own ignorance. It's often hard to admit that you don't know something. But you'll get better at it with practice. This is another part of the art of argument.

There's no complete cure for ignorance, but you can do things that reduce your ignorance. First, you can avoid basing your beliefs on arguments with improper forms. Basing your beliefs on an argument with an improper form usually increases your ignorance. Second, as just noted in the Habits of a Critical Thinker box above, you can recognize your ignorance. Third, you can follow some guidelines that minimize the chance that you'll assume false premises.

Connections

Chapter Three discusses some guidelines for assuming premises.

Habits of a Critical Thinker

Not Jumping to Conclusions

It's easy to jump to conclusions, especially to conclusions that are critical of others. Suppose that a student at a university located in the middle of the downtown of a major metropolitan area writes a letter to the editor of the student newspaper complaining about the lack of parking. The student writing the letter asserts that the university administration is a bunch of idiots for not recognizing this problem and building more parking decks. The letter contains no evidence that the author has done any research on the issue. Research might have revealed: how the ratio of parking spots to students at the university compares to the ratio at other universities, the cost of acquiring land in the center of a large city, what else might be done with the large sums of money it would take to construct a parking deck, and other reasons why the university hasn't built more parking decks. But our imaginary student didn't look into this. He jumped to a conclusion. Remember the problem of ignorance and evaluate arguments only after you've done adequate research and carefully considered everything you know about the situation.

EXERCISE 2.3

A. Write five questions to indicate five things that you don't know that you wish you knew.

B. List five things that you know that you don't know.

C. Briefly describe three actual cases in your life in which you thought that you knew something but it turned out that you didn't know what you thought you knew.

Proper Form

An argument has a proper form when

If the premises were true, they would provide support for the conclusion.

Proper form is a matter of the logical relationship between the premises and the conclusion, of the *logical form* of the argument. What is the logical form of an argument? To answer this question, let's begin with the notion of what a form is.

You've used variables in your math classes. A variable represents a number, but it can represent any number. Think about the mathematical formula

$$2x = x + x$$

This tells you that two times any number is equal to that number added to itself. You can put any number in place of the "*x*."

2 times 2 equals 4, and 2 plus 2 also equals 4

$$2 \times 2 = 2 + 2$$

2 times 10 equals 20, and 10 plus 10 also equals 20

$$2 \times 10 = 10 + 10$$

Why is $2x = x + x$ called a "*formula*"? Because it's a form, a shape, of a mathematical equation. This formula expresses a relationship between $2x$ and $x + x$ and holds no matter what value you put in for x.

Logical form is like mathematical form. Logical form expresses a relationship that holds between the premises and the conclusion. This relationship holds even if the subject discussed in the premises changes. Let's look at the argument about fish mentioned above.

(1) The authors of this textbook have seen at least 40,000 fish and all of them had two fins.
Therefore,
(2) All fish have two fins.

Let's follow the mathematical model and use variables that stand for parts of this argument.

(1) The authors of this textbook have seen at least 40,000 *x* and all of them had *y*.
Therefore,
(2) All *x* have *y*.

> **Key Concept**
> An argument has a proper form when: *if* the premises were true, they would provide support for the conclusion.

Using variables reveals the logical form of the argument. If you put in "fish" for "*x*" and "two fins" for "*y*," the premise of this argument is false. But if you put in "gills" for "*y*" instead of "fins," then you have this argument.

(1) The authors of this textbook have seen at least 40,000 fish and all of them had gills.
Therefore,
(2) All fish have gills.

Now the premise is true and the argument passes both the true premises test and the proper form test. *Only the gills argument passes the true premises test. Both the fins argument and the gills argument pass the proper form test.*

Let's look again at the argument about roses. It fails the proper form test.

(1) All roses are plants.
(2) All roses have thorns.
Therefore,
(3) All plants have thorns.

This argument is about groups of things. Roses, plants, and things with thorns are all groups. Let's use "G1" to stand for the group "roses," "G2" to stand for the group "plants," and "G3" to stand for the group "things with thorns." You can then put this argument into the following form:

(a) (1) All G1 are G2.
(2) All G1 are G3.
Therefore,
(3) All G2 are G3.

Here's another argument with form (a):

(1) All Germans are Americans.
(2) All Germans are people with large feet.
Therefore,
(3) All Americans are people with large feet.

In this case G1 = Germans, G2 = Americans, and G3 = people with large feet. This argument fails the true premises test. It also fails the proper form test. It has the same form as the argument about roses, which also fails the proper form test. Any argument that has form (a) fails the proper form test. Form (a) is an improper form.

The notion of logical form is so important that you should look at another example.

(1) If Anne goes to the café, she will get a latté.
(2) Anne will go to the café.
Therefore,
(3) Anne will get a latté.

Does this argument pass the true premises test? You don't know. You don't know who Anne is. You don't know whether she likes lattés. Here's another argument with the same form.

(1) (If Bill Clinton became President of the United States,) he received more electoral votes than his opponent.

[handwritten: If S1]   *[handwritten: Then S2]*   *[handwritten: S2]*

(2) Bill Clinton became President of the United States.
Therefore,
(3) Bill Clinton received more electoral votes than his opponent.   *[handwritten: S2]*

This argument passes the true premises test. You have one argument that may or may not pass the true premises test and one that does pass the true premises test. But both arguments have the same logical form. In this case, the logical form of the argument refers to statements. Let's use S1 and S2 as variables. Here's the logical form of the two arguments above:

(b) (1) If S1, then S2.
(2) S1.
Therefore,
(3) S2.

In the first argument with form (b), the variables are used as follows:

S1 = Anne goes to the café.
S2 = Anne gets a latté.

In the second argument with form (b), the variables are used like this:

S1 = Bill Clinton became President of the United States.
S2 = Bill Clinton received more electoral votes than his opponent.

Form (b) is a proper form. Both the Anne argument and the Bill Clinton argument pass the proper form test. But the Anne argument fails the true premises test, while the Bill Clinton argument passes the true premises test.

EXERCISE 2.4

A. Call the following argument forms A, B, C, and D.

A (1) All G1 are G2.
(2) All G1 are G3.
Therefore,
(3) All G2 are G3.   *[handwritten: lack form]*

B (1) All G1 are G2.
(1) All G2 are G3.
Therefore,
(3) All G1 are G3

C (1) If S1, then S2.
(2) S1.
Therefore,
(3) S2.

D (1) If S1, then S2.
(2) S2.
Therefore,
(3) S1.

Identify the form of each argument. In some cases, the form of the argument is neither A, B, C, nor D. In that case, indicate "other form."

1. (1) All dogs are mammals.
(2) All mammals are things with hair.
Therefore,
(3) All dogs are things with hair.

2. (1) If that's a car, then I'm a donkey.
   (2) I'm a donkey.
   Therefore,
   (3) That's a car.

3. (1) All children are humans.
   (2) All humans are mammals.
   Therefore,
   (3) All children are mammals.

*4. (1) All men are humans.
   (2) All men are under eighteen years of age.
   Therefore,
   (3) All women are under eighteen years of age.

5. (1) If you throw a match on that gas, it will burn.
   (2) You will throw a match on that gas.
   Therefore,
   (3) It will burn.

6. (1) All houses are made of wood.
   (2) All houses are made of stone.
   Therefore,
   (3) Everything made of wood is made of stone.

7. (1) If he gets in trouble, he'll call his Mom.
   (2) He won't get in trouble.
   Therefore,
   (3) He won't call his Mom.

*8. (1) Some computers are PCs.
   (2) All PCs aren't Macintoshes.
   Therefore,
   (3) Some computers aren't Macintoshes.

9. (1) She's either at the grocery store or at the mall.
   (2) She isn't at the mall.
   Therefore,
   (3) She's at the grocery store.

10. (1) All cows are pigs.
    (2) All pigs are ducks.
    Therefore,
    (3) All cows are ducks.

11. (1) George is a human.
    (2) All humans are mammals.
    Therefore,
    (3) George is a mammal.

*12. (1) If you jump from the Empire State Building, you will die.
    (2) You will jump from the Empire State Building.
    Therefore,
    (3) You will die.

13. (1) If you are human, you will die.
(2) You will die.
Therefore,
(3) You are human.

14. (1) All pigs are things that have wings.
(2) All pigs are things that love country music.
Therefore,
(3) All things that have wings are things that love country music.

15. (1) Cell phones have replaced many cameras.
(2) Cameras all use film.
Therefore,
(3) Cell phones all use film.

Deductive and Inductive Arguments

Arguments have two types of forms, deductive and inductive. A **deductive** argument claims that the truth of the premises shows that the conclusion *must* be true. An **inductive** argument claims that the truth of the premises shows that the conclusion is *likely* to be true.

Technical Terms: Deduction and Induction

Some disciplines define deductive and inductive arguments in terms of the generality and specificity of the statements. In these fields, deduction is said to be from general to specific and inductive from specific to general. "Deduction" is sometimes used to refer generally to the process of reasoning. In other cases, "deduction" is used to refer to the act of taking something away from something else. You've probably heard of tax deductions.

In some cases, the phrase "inductive arguments" is used to refer to what this book calls "statistical arguments." Chapter Eight discusses this type of argument. In mathematics, one type of proof is called "mathematical induction." In a proof by mathematical induction the demonstration of the validity of a law concerning all the positive integers is provided by proving that the law holds for the integer 1 and that if it holds for an arbitrarily chosen positive integer k, it must hold for the integer k + 1. Mathematical induction is an example of deductive reasoning. "Induction" can also refer to a ceremony to officially install a person in some position, the process by which an electrical conductor becomes electrified, the movement of a mixture of air and gas from the carburetor of a car into the piston chamber of the car's engine, and to a process that embryonic cells undergo as they become the various different kinds of cells found in an adult organism.

Deductive Forms

The argument above about Anne and her lattés is a deductive argument. Pretend that you know that it's true that

(1) If Anne goes to the café, Anne will get a latté.

Pretend that you also know that it's true that

(2) Anne will go to the café.

In that case, it's *certain* that

(3) Anne will get a latté.

If Anne didn't get a latté, you know that one of the premises is false. Either she didn't go to the café or it isn't true that if Anne goes to the café, she'll get a latté. This argument has a proper deductive form. Any argument with the form:

(b) (1) If S1, then S2.
     (2) S1.
     Therefore,
     (3) S2.

is a deductive argument with a proper form.

Here's another proper deductive form:

(1) Either S1 or S2.
(2) Not S2.
Therefore,
(3) S1.

Here's an example of an argument with this form:

(1) Either Margaret is outside or she is in the kitchen.
(2) Margaret is not in the kitchen.
Therefore,
(3) Margaret is outside.

As with the argument about Anne and her latté, you don't know whether the premises of this argument are true or false because you don't know who Margaret is or what she is doing. But you do know that this argument has a proper deductive form. As you look at this form, you'll see that, no matter what you put in for S1 and S2, if both premises were true, the conclusion would have to be true.

You've already seen some arguments with improper deductive forms. Remember the argument about roses.

(1) All roses are plants.
(2) All roses have thorns.
Therefore,
(3) All plants have thorns.

The form of this argument looks like this:

(a) (1) All G1 are G2.
     (2) All G1 are G3.
     Therefore,
     (3) All G2 are G3.

As you saw above, the truth of the premises of an argument with this form doesn't guarantee that the conclusion is true.

Inductive Forms

Let's look at some inductive argument forms. The arguments concerning fish discussed above are inductive arguments. To see the form of these arguments, let's use "X" to refer to things and "F" to refer to features of those things.

(1) The authors of this textbook have seen at least 40,000 X and all of them had F.
Therefore,
(2) All X have F.

Think about this example of the above form:

(1) The authors of this textbook have seen at least 40,000 swans and all of them were white.
Therefore,
(2) All swans are white.

Forty thousand swans is a lot of swans. If someone had seen 40,000 swans and all of them were white, that person would have good reason to think that all swans were white. But good reason isn't certainty. It would still be possible that there's a black swan out there. In arguments with this form, the truth of the premise doesn't guarantee the truth of the conclusion. But this argument has a proper inductive form.

Here's an example of an improper inductive form:

(1) The authors of this textbook have seen at least 4 X and all of them had F.
Therefore,
(2) All X have F.

If we've seen only four swans, that isn't enough evidence to draw a conclusion about the color of all swans.

Critical Thinkers

John Latham

National Portrait Gallery, London

John Latham (1740–1837), a British naturalist, has been called the "grandfather" of Australian ornithology. He discovered and named many Australian birds, including the emu. Latham might be best known for having first described, in 1790, a large waterbird that was, in fact, a black swan (*Cygnus atratus*). It had been assumed by European naturalists that all swans were white.

Here's another inductive argument form. It concerns events. Let's use "E" to refer to events.

(1) Many times in the past, when E1 occurred, E2 usually occurred shortly thereafter.
Therefore,
(2) In the future, if E1 occurs, E2 will probably occur shortly thereafter.

This form is found in the following argument regarding how to start a car.

(1) Many times in the past, when people have turned the key in their car's ignition, it has almost always started the car.
Therefore,
(2) In the future, if you turn the key in a car's ignition, it will probably start the car.

This argument has a proper inductive form, but the truth of the premises doesn't show that the conclusion *must* be true. Even the most reliable car will fail to start every now and then. But turning the key in the ignition is a good way to start a car. Given the inductive evidence you have, it would be weird for you to try to start your car by bouncing up and down in the seat.

Here's an improper inductive argument form:

(1) Yesterday, when E1 occurred, E2 occurred shortly thereafter.
Therefore,
(2) In the future, if E1 occurs, E2 will probably occur shortly thereafter.

And here's an example of an argument with this form:

(1) Yesterday, I had a ham sandwich for lunch, and when I got back to the office my boss told me that I was getting a raise.
Therefore,
(2) Tomorrow, if I have a ham sandwich for lunch, I'll get another raise.

This argument fails the proper form test. That something happened one time in the past isn't a good reason to think that it will happen again in the future.

Connections

Deductive arguments can be divided into at least two groups: propositional and categorical. Chapter Five focuses on propositional arguments. Chapter Six considers categorical arguments. Inductive arguments can be divided into at least three groups: analogical, statistical, and causal. Chaper Seven discusses analogical arguments, Chapter Eight looks at statistical arguments, and Chapter Nine considers causal arguments.

Thus far, this book has been using the words "good argument," "bad argument," "proper form," and "improper form." But more specific words are used in philosophy, logic, and math courses. A deductive argument that passes the proper form test is called a "valid" argument. A deductive argument that fails the proper form test is called an "invalid" argument. An inductive argument that passes the proper form test is called a "strong" argument. An inductive argument that fails the proper form test is called a "weak" argument.

Because all deductive arguments claim that if the premises are true then the conclusion must be true, they're all either valid or invalid. An argument can't be almost valid or somewhat valid. Deductive validity is not a matter of degree. But inductive arguments claim that whenever all the premises are true, the conclusion is likely to also be true. Thus, inductive arguments can be stronger or weaker. You evaluate the form of inductive arguments in degrees of likelihood: from extremely weak (premises offer not much evidence at all) through degrees of probable strength to high degrees of strength to almost certain (premises offer extremely good evidence). Inductive strength is a matter of degree.

Philosophers and logicians have given special names for deductive arguments that pass both tests of a good argument and for inductive arguments that pass both tests of a good argument. A valid deductive argument that also has all true premises is called a "sound" argument. A strong inductive argument that has all true premises is called a "cogent" argument.

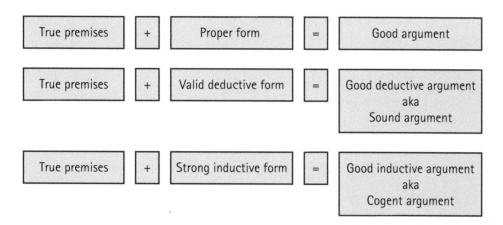

GUIDE
Terms Used in Logic, Philosophy, and Math to Refer to Good and Bad Arguments

		Deductive	Inductive
All True Premises?	Yes	No Name	No Name
	No	No Name	No Name
Proper Form?	Yes	Valid	Strong
	No	Invalid	Weak
Proper Form AND All True Premises?	Yes	Sound	Cogent
	No	Unsound	Not Cogent

Technical Terms: Valid, Strong, Sound, Cogent

The terms "valid," "strong," "sound," and "cogent" are used in many different ways. In many cases, "valid" means "legally recognized." Your driver's license may be valid or invalid. In other cases, it means "meeting certain conditions." If your bank requires that your ATM PIN be six characters and you attempt to enter a PIN with five, you may get a message that says: "Invalid PIN." "Strong" often refers to physical strength. "Sound" often refers to what you hear and "cogent" is often used to indicate that reasoning is good.

Technical Terms: Test Validity, Content Validity, Criterion Validity, Construct Validity, and Reliability

A great deal of research in social sciences concerns the analysis of tests and testing procedures. Test analysts frequently use the terms "test validity," "content validity," "criterion validity," "construct validity," and "reliability." Social scientists and educational researchers use the word "valid" in a way that is different from the logical concept of validity used in this text.

A valid test is a test that is an accurate and useful measure of what it seeks to measure. If you were looking to hire an accountant and you gave all the applicants a test to determine their knowledge of cake-baking procedures, your test wouldn't be valid. Its results wouldn't be a useful measure of the applicants' abilities as accountants. Test validity is usually broken down into content validity, criterion validity, and construct validity.

Tests are often constructed with questions, each of which is called a "test item." Each test item is designed to test a certain skill or knowledge of a certain thing. Well-constructed test items will test only that specific skill or item of knowledge. When all test items are well constructed, the test is said to have content validity.

Tests are sometimes designed to act as predictors of future performance of some kind. For example, the ACT and SAT tests are intended to indicate which students will do well in college. If subsequent research shows a test is a good predictor of what it was designed to predict, that test is said to have criterion validity.

Every test is constructed on the basis of a theory about what's being tested. When a test is constructed so that it matches its underlying theory, it has construct validity.

The validity of a test is often discussed in conjunction with its reliability. Reliable tests have similar outcomes when they're administered multiple times. If groups of test-takers take several forms of a test in different places at different times with similar results, the test is said to be reliable. A reliable test is one that gives consistent results. A reliable test can be invalid. If you developed a reliable test of our potential accountants' cake-baking abilities, the test would give the same result if an applicant took it over and over again. On the other hand, an unreliable test can't be valid. If a test gives inconsistent results, it can't be an accurate measure of what it seeks to measure.

EXERCISE 2.5

A. In each of the following passages, determine whether or not an argument is present. If an argument is present, state whether it is inductive or deductive and explain your answer.

1. If that's a cow, then I'm a goat. Oh, it's a cow! I guess I'm a goat!

2. I called Joi and she said that she was at the library. So, I bet she's at the library.

3. The syllabus said that the paper had to cite three sources. You only cited one. Be careful! You won't get the grade you want.

*4. Francis had pepperoni and mushrooms on her pizza. It follows that she had pepperoni on her pizza.

5. That was a good talk. I had never considered the way that one's emotions can affect one's moral judgments. And the speaker was very clear, too.

6. Where is Bret? He's either in class or in the rec center. He isn't here in class, so he must be in the rec center.

7. Take one capsule orally three times a day for ten days. Finish all this medication unless otherwise directed by your physician.

*8. My son started talking when he was two years old. This makes it obvious that all children start speaking at that age.

9. Socrates was a human being. All human beings are mortal. Therefore, Socrates was mortal.

10. "Real people begin their lives as helpless infants, and remain in a state of extreme, asymmetrical dependency for anywhere from ten to twenty years. At the other end of life, those who are lucky enough to live on into old age are likely to encounter another period of extreme dependency which may itself continue in some form for as much as twenty years." (Nussbaum 2006, 69–70, material omitted)

11. "I reasoned thus with myself: I am wiser than this man, for neither of us appears to know anything great and good; but he fancies he knows something, although he knows nothing; whereas I, as I do not know anything, so I do not fancy I do. In this trifling particular, then, I appear to be wiser than he, because I do not fancy I know what I do not know." (Plato 1897, 19)

*12. In *On the Heavens* (Book II, Section 14) the ancient Greek philosopher Aristotle discussed the shape of the Earth. Here is a paraphrase of his claims.

The earth is either flat or spherical. If the earth is flat, it does not project a circular shadow on the moon during a lunar eclipse. If the earth is round, it projects a circular shadow on the moon during a lunar eclipse. The Earth projects a circular shadow on the moon during a lunar eclipse. The earth is spherical.

13. In 1628, the English medical doctor William Harvey (1578–1657) published *Exercitatio Anatomica de Motu Cordis et Sanguinis in Animalibus* (An Anatomical Exercise on the Motion of the Heart and Blood in Animals). Harvey demonstrated that the blood is not produced by the liver, as everyone until then had thought, but rather circulates through the body. Harvey proposed a number of arguments to support the conclusion that the blood circulates. Look at the following paraphrase of Harvey's work:

Every time the heart pumps 1/6 of an ounce of blood goes through it and the heart beats 1000 times every half hour. So, the heart pumps 540 pounds of blood in a day. The blood is either produced by the liver or it circulates. But if the blood is produced by the liver, the liver would have to produce 540 pounds of blood in a day, which it does not do. From this we can see that blood circulates.

14. "Santiago Ramón y Cajal was born in May 1852 in the village of Petilla, in the region of Aragon in northeast Spain. His father was at that time the village surgeon (later on, in 1870, his father was appointed as Professor of Dissection at the University of Zaragoza). Cajal was a rebellious teenager, and his father apprenticed him for a while to a shoemaker and to a barber. Cajal, however, had decided to become an artist. His passion for drawing, his sensitivity to visual esthetics and his talent in converting visual images into drawings remained the hallmarks of his future scientific activity. Finally enrolled in the medical school at Zaragoza, as a young student, Cajal, seized by a "graphic

mania," was very fond of philosophy and gymnastics, restless, energetic, shy and solitary. He graduated in medicine at the University of Zaragoza in 1873. Shortly after his degree he was drafted into the army and dispatched to Cuba, at that time under Spanish rule, as a medical officer. Cajal returned to Spain very sick (he had contracted malaria in Cuba, and then tuberculosis), and at the end of 1875 he started his academic career as "Auxiliary Professor" of Anatomy at the University of Zaragoza." (nobelprize.org 2007) [Santiago Ramón y Cajal won the 1906 Nobel Prize in Medicine.]

   15. "For Kant, human dignity and our moral capacity are radically separate from the natural world. [T]he idea that we are at bottom split beings, both rational persons and animal dwellers in the world of nature, never ceases to influence Kant's way of thinking. What's wrong with the split? Quite a lot. First, it ignores the fact that our dignity just is the dignity of a certain sort of animal. Second, the split wrongly denies that animality itself can have a dignity. Third, it makes us think of the core of ourselves as self-sufficient, not in need of the gifts of fortune. Fourth, it makes us think of ourselves as a-temporal. We forget that the usual human life cycle brings with it periods of extreme dependency." (Nussbaum 2002,188–189, material omitted)

B. For each of the following conclusions, construct (a) a deductive argument that passes the proper form test and (b) an inductive argument that passes the proper form text. Your argument doesn't have to pass the true premises test.

   1. The moon is made of green cheese.
   2. Martha Stewart is a good cook.
   3. It often rains in the Amazon jungle.
   *4. Most people prefer to eat in the company of other people.
   5. You should buy a new computer.
   6. My computer is gray.
   7. It is 5:42 PM.
   *8. My mother is a hamster.
   9. The Atlanta Braves are a good baseball team.
   10. I like Coldplay.

C. For the exercises in part A above, standardize the argument if one is present.

D. At the beginning of this chapter, you encountered the following argument as an example of an argument that passes the proper form test:

(1) Socrates was a human being.
(2) All human beings are mortal.
Therefore,
(3) Socrates was mortal.

   a. Is this argument deductive or inductive argument?
   b. Think about the nature of the evidence you have for premise (2). Is this relevant to your deciding whether this argument is deductive or inductive?
   c. Create a linked argument by constructing a subargument that supports premise (2).

E. The following argument doesn't pass the proper form test. Demonstrate this clearly by using variables to illustrate its form and then constructing a more obviously invalid argument with the same form by substituting new phrases for those variables.

(1) Residents of the 4th Congressional District of our state will not be affected by the upcoming tax hike.

(2) Residents who do not earn more than the minimum wage will not be affected by the upcoming tax hike.

Therefore,

(3) Residents of the 4th Congressional District of our state do not earn more than the minimum wage.

Relevance

Relevance is an essential part of the proper form test. Premises are **relevant** to the conclusion when the truth of the premises provides some evidence that the conclusion is true. Premises are **irrelevant** when the truth of the premises provides no evidence that the conclusion is true. When an argument has a proper form, its premises are relevant to the conclusion. When an argument has an improper form, its premises are irrelevant to the conclusion.

> **Key Concept**
>
> Premises are **relevant** to the conclusion when the truth of the premises provides <u>some evidence</u> that the conclusion is true. Premises are **irrelevant** when the truth of the premises provides <u>no evidence</u> that the conclusion is true.

Technical Term: *Non Sequitur*

An argument that contains a premise or premises that are irrelevant to the conclusion is sometimes said to contain a "*non sequitur.*" "*Non sequitur*" is Latin for "it doesn't follow."

Suppose you're studying with a friend and talking about topics to focus on for a geology test. The test covers the first five chapters of the textbook. You suggest studying sedimentary rocks because this topic is covered in Chapter Four. You're making the following argument:

(1) The test covers Chapters 1–5.
(2) The topic of sedimentary rocks is in Chapter 4.
Therefore,
(3) We should study sedimentary rocks.

Suppose your friend responds that he doesn't want to study sedimentary rocks because his brother thinks that sedimentary rocks are boring. Your friend is making the following argument:

(1) My brother thinks that sedimentary rocks are boring.
Therefore,
(2) We shouldn't study sedimentary rocks.

This premise is irrelevant to the conclusion. Whether or not this premise is true, it doesn't provide a good reason to believe the conclusion.

Relevance is a matter of degree. The premise of an argument can be more or less relevant to its conclusion. The more support a premise provides for a conclusion, the more relevant it is to the conclusion. Remember the metaphor of the grading of a test. A completely irrelevant premise gets a very low grade (maybe a 0). A premise that provides almost certain proof of a conclusion gets a high passing grade (perhaps a 95), while a premise that provides only a bit of support for a conclusion just barely earns a passing grade (say a 63).

EXERCISE 2.6

A. For each of the following pairs of statements, indicate whether the first statement is relevant or irrelevant to the second statement.

   1. Krystal's losing weight. Krystal's on a diet.
   2. Luke's a cruel and unfeeling person. Luke's views about water conservation are false.
   3. Danica got good grades in art and music courses. Danica would be a good airline pilot.
  *4. Oosh failed his College Algebra course. Oosh won't graduate on time.
   5. Wireless mice are more comfortable because they don't have a cord attached. Wireless mice will last longer than corded mice.
   6. The pipes are rusted, and the roof needs to be replaced. The house is in bad shape.
   7. On the SAT, Arica's scores ranked in the bottom 25th percentile. Arica's likely to be a very nice person.
  *8. Many country music fans hate NASCAR Sprint Cup Racing. Many country music fans hate NASCAR Camping World Truck Racing.
   9. The moon's made of green cheese. The moon is edible.
  10. On Monday, the Federal Reserve announced plans to lend $60 billion to banks. Inflation is likely to fall over the next six months.
  11. Children from single-parent families tend to have lower academic achievement in high school. Children from single-parent families tend to have lower incomes.
 *12. Today Coca-Cola reported that case sales fell 2% in the first quarter of 2005. Coca-Cola profits fell in the first quarter of 2005.
  13. Researchers have trained chimpanzees to understand words spoken by humans and found that they can understand simple commands. Chimpanzees may someday speak with humans.
  14. "[O]ffspring [of self-fertilizing plants] carry only the genes of their single parent and do not maintain enough variation for evolutionary flexibility in the face of environmental change." "[S]elf-fertilization is a poor strategy for long-term survival." (Gould 1992, 20, material omitted)
  15. Background: A pluton is a large mass of rock (tens to hundreds of kilometers across), usually roughly circular, that was produced when magma rose from the center of the Earth but cooled and solidified before breaking through the surface. When it cools, it turns into granite.
      "A prominent positive magnetic anomaly spans the 100 km distance between Prince Edward Island and Cape Breton Island in the southern Gulf of St. Lawrence. Analysis of the magnetic anomaly led to the interpretation that it is produced by four separate, approximately circular, source bodies aligned along the northwesterly trend of the anomaly.

Seismic data, physical property measurements, and magnetic and gravity anomalies were used to further investigate the anomaly sources through forward modeling techniques."

Statement 1: "The four source bodies have densities and magnetic susceptibilities compatible with granitic compositions."

Statement 2: "[The] bodies are interpreted as plutons emplaced along the boundary between Ganderian composite terranes to the north and the Ganderian Brookville–Bras d'Or terrane to the south." (Cook 2007, 1551, material omitted)

B. One place where people offer arguments to influence the beliefs of others is in court. Attorneys attempt to persuade juries of the guilt or innocence of people charged with a crime. The relevance of each piece of evidence is important. The following argument was made by Counselor Smart, for the conclusion that the defendant, Shifty McRogue, is guilty of robbing a local bank. For each premise, decide whether it's relevant or irrelevant to the conclusion. Give reasons for your answers.

(1) Several witnesses have confirmed that the defendant has been in desperate need of money ever since he lost his job at the cracker factory.

(2) And McRogue has the profile of a criminal, anyway, since we know he has established a prior criminal record: he served thirty days in jail just last year for driving under the influence.

(3) Moreover, I have an expert witness, Dr. Quack, the famous phrenologist, who will testify that McRogue has a predisposition to rob banks.

(4) In fact, if found guilty, this would be the defendant's third conviction; under the state's "three strikes" legislation, he would automatically serve the maximum sentence for his crime.

(5) Ever since his release from jail, McRogue has been seen regularly in the company of Max Cheatem, an ex-convict who himself served time for armed robbery.

(6) Two weeks ago, Max Cheatem lent McRogue his blue two-door Ford—a car of the same make, model, and color as the getaway vehicle used in the robbery.

(7) And finally, the bank was held up by an assailant carrying a .22 pistol; three days before the robbery, the defendant purchased a .22 pistol.

Therefore,

(8) McRogue is guilty of robbing the bank.

Dependent and Independent Premises ✗

Premises can be relevant in two ways. Let's look at two arguments. The first, which you saw in Chapter One, concerns employment law.

(1) There are labor laws that give employees the right to unionize.

(2) There are civil rights and equal pay laws that put constraints on hiring practices.

Therefore,

(3) Some laws support the interests of employees against corporations.

The second is the argument above about studying for a test.

(1) The test covers Chapters 1–5.

(2) The topic of sedimentary rocks is in Chapter 4.

Therefore,

(3) We should study sedimentary rocks.

In the first argument, if you remove either of the premises, the other still provides some support for the conclusion. The conclusion is that there are "some laws" that support employees. The premises are two examples of such laws. Removing one of the premises would do nothing more than reduce the number of examples. In this case, each premise supports the conclusion independently of the others. (1) and (2) are examples of independent premises. An **independent premise** is a premise that's intended to provide some support for the argument's conclusion even when the rest of the argument's premises are removed.

The premises in the argument about studying for the geology test are dependent premises. A **dependent premise** is a premise that's intended to provide support for the argument's conclusion only when combined with another premise in the argument. Premise (1) by itself doesn't provide any support for (3).

(1) The test covers Chapters 1–5.
Therefore,
(3) We should study sedimentary rocks.

Premise (1) doesn't provide support for (3) unless it's combined with a premise about the contents of Chapters 1–5. The same is true of premise (2).

(2) The topic of sedimentary rocks is in Chapter 4.
Therefore,
(3) We should study sedimentary rocks.

But together (1) and (2) are relevant to (3).

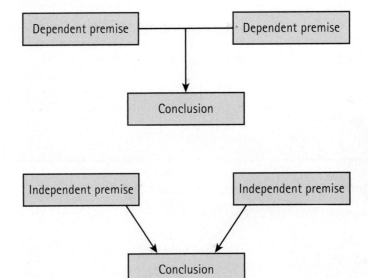

The difference between independent and dependent premises is important when you evaluate arguments because it means that you can't just look at premises individually to determine whether they're relevant to the conclusion. It might be that you're examining an argument with dependent premises. In that case, if you look at each premise individually you could mistakenly conclude that the premises were irrelevant to the conclusion

> **Key Concept**
> An **independent premise** is a premise that's intended to provide some support for the argument's conclusion even when the rest of the argument's premises are removed. A **dependent premise** is a premise that's intended to provide support for the argument's conclusion *only* when combined with another premise in the argument.
>
> *Can't support the conclusion on its own.*

and therefore that the argument failed the proper form test. When you think about the relevance of premises, you have to take two steps. First, look at each premise by itself and see if it's relevant to the conclusion. When you do this, you're checking for the relevance of independent premises. Second, look at the premises as a group. When you do this, you're checking for the relevance of dependent premises.

Technical Terms: Dependent and Independent Premises

In some cases, authors use "dependent premise" to refer to a premise that's true only if another premise in the argument is true. The truth of the dependent premise depends on the truth of the other premise in the sense that if the other premise is false, so is the dependent premise. In this sense, an independent premise is a premise whose truth isn't logically related to the truth or falsity of the other premises in the argument.

Technical Term: Convergent Argument

An argument that's composed exclusively of independent premises is sometimes called a "convergent argument."

EXERCISE 2.7

A. In each of the following passages, determine whether or not an argument is present. If an argument is present, standardize the argument. Determine whether the premises are relevant to the conclusion. If they're relevant, determine whether they're independent premises or dependent premises.

1. Socrates was a human being. All human beings are mortal. Therefore, Socrates was mortal.

2. Transfatty acids contribute to heart disease. Children shouldn't be given foods that contribute to heart disease. Therefore, children shouldn't be given foods that contain transfatty acids.

3. Julia Roberts is either a man or a woman. Julia Roberts is a man. Therefore, Julia Roberts isn't a woman.

*4. If you walk on the lines in the sidewalk, you'll be eaten by bears. Sometime in the next week, someone will walk on the lines in the sidewalk. Therefore, sometime in the next week, someone will be eaten by bears.

5. All cows are pigs. All pigs are ducks. Therefore, all cows are ducks.

6. Reza didn't have a bump on his head. If he'd fallen, he'd have a bump on his head. He didn't fall.

7. The coffee cup was still warm. The newspaper was open on the dinning room table. The microwave was heating up a frozen dinner. The killer couldn't have gone far!

*8. Many people think that air pollution is a serious problem. And vehicle emissions are a significant cause of air pollution. So it's clear that most people support laws requiring a reduction in the emissions produced by cars.

9. I walked down the street through the cold, crisp air. A front had come through, and the city air, usually so full of city smells, had a hint of the countryside in it. The smell of the horses pulling the carriages in Central Park added to the country-feel of the day.

10. The first survey indicated that 26% of likely voters favor Senator Smith. A second survey, taken a week later, found that 23% of likely voters favored him. It seems that Smith is likely to get about 25% of the vote in the primary.

11. The Toyota has better gas mileage than the Honda. The Toyota costs less and has a better repair record. I'd say you should buy the Toyota.

*12. "Segregation of white and colored children in public schools has a detrimental effect upon the colored children. The impact is greater when it has the sanction of the law; for the policy of separating the races is usually interpreted as denoting the inferiority of the negro group. A sense of inferiority affects the motivation of a child to learn. Segregation with the sanction of law, therefore, has a tendency to [retard] the educational and mental development of negro children and to deprive them of some of the benefits they would receive in a racial[ly] integrated school system." (*Brown v. Board of Education* 1954, 495)

13. "Sarah, a woman of twenty-five, lively and engaging at the time of the first interview, is intelligent, humorous, and sad as she describes her experiences of self-defeat. [Her self-defeat is an unwanted pregnancy.] Pregnant again by the same man and confronting a second abortion, she sees the hopelessness of the relationship." (Gilligan 1982, 116)

14. "[The Catholic Church] holds that it is not admissible to ordain women to the priesthood, for very fundamental reasons. These reasons include: the example recorded in the Sacred Scriptures of Christ choosing his Apostles only from among men; the constant practice of the Church, which has imitated Christ in choosing only men; and her living teaching authority which has consistently held that the exclusion of women from the priesthood is in accordance with God's plan for his Church." (Pope Paul VI 1976)

15. "Atheists have solid reasons not to believe. We don't need a divine being to explain the natural world, and don't know why we should trust claims about humankind's divine origins because they are in religious texts. Give *2001: A Space Odyssey* a thousand years and who knows what might happen." (Porter 2007, A34)

B. Return to the passages found in Exercise 2.6 A. If the passage contains an argument, indicate whether the premises of the argument are relevant and, if they are, whether they're dependent premises or dependent premises.

C. Read the following conversation between the famous detective Sherlock Holmes and his friend Dr. Watson, from Sir Arthur Conan Doyle's novel *The Sign of the Four.*

"[Holmes leaned] back luxuriously in his armchair, and sending up thick blue wreaths from his pipe, [and said: "I see] that you have been to the Wigmore Street Post-Office this morning [and] that when there you dispatched a telegram."

"Right!" said [Watson]. "Right on both points! But I confess that I don't see how you arrived at it. It was a sudden impulse upon my part, and I have mentioned it to no one."

"It is simplicity itself," [Holmes] remarked, chuckling at my surprise,—"so absurdly simple that an explanation is superfluous. Observation tells me that you have a little reddish [dirt] adhering to your instep. Just opposite the [Wigmore] Street Office they have taken up the pavement and thrown up some earth which lies in such a way that it is difficult to avoid treading in it in entering. The earth is of this peculiar reddish tint which is found, as far as I know, nowhere else in the neighborhood."

"How, then, did you deduce the telegram?"

"Why, of course I knew that you had not written a letter, since I sat opposite to you all morning. I see also in your open desk there that you have a sheet of stamps and a thick bundle of post-cards. What could you go into the post-office for, then, but to send a [telegram]? Eliminate all other factors, and the one which remains must be the truth." (Doyle 1890, 12–13, material omitted)

Holm**es** presents two arguments in this passage.

a. Standardize each of them.
b. Determine whether they are inductive or deductive.
c. Determine whether the premises are relevant to the conclusion.
d. Assume that Sherlock Holmes' fictional world is real and evaluate Holmes' arguments using the true premises and proper form tests.

Arguing about Arguments

When you claim that someone is making a bad argument, you're either constructing an argument to show that someone else's argument fails the true premises test or constructing an argument to show that the other person's argument fails the proper form test. Suppose that one person makes an argument and then another person argues that this argument fails the true premises test and/or fails the proper form test. In many cases, the first person will argue that the second person's argument against the first person's argument is a bad argument. (Now there's a weird sentence. Better read it again.) This can lead to an "argumentative tennis match" as the two people arguing make arguments for and against the various parts of their opponent's arguments. Argumentative tennis matches are complex but exciting, and participating in these tennis matches is an excellent way to improve your critical thinking skills.

Let's imagine an argumentative tennis match between Al (who doesn't believe in God) and Theresa (who does). Al offers the following argument:

(1) There is evil in the world.
(2) An all-good, all-knowing, and all-powerful God would not allow evil to exist.
Therefore,
(3) There is no all-good, all-knowing, and all-powerful God.

Theresa can respond in two ways. She can offer a **counter argument**, an argument that draws a conclusion opposed to Al's argument. For example, Theresa could respond with the following argument:

(1) Some people have had mystical religious experiences.
(2) When people have mystical religious experiences, they are experiencing God.
Therefore,
(3) Some people have experienced God.

(4) If someone has experienced something, that thing exists.
Therefore,
(5) God exists.

Theresa's response is a counter argument because it doesn't attempt to show that Al's argument fails either of the two tests for a good argument. Instead, she offers an argument for a conclusion opposed to Al's.

> **Key Concept**
> A **counter argument** is an argument that draws a conclusion opposed to another argument.

I understand your point of view + but I think something

Key Concept
A **refutation argument** is an argument whose conclusion is that another argument fails the true premises or proper form test.

Theresa's other option is to offer a **refutation argument**, an argument whose conclusion is that another argument fails the true premises or proper form test. Here's an example of a refutation argument that Theresa might make:

(1) It is important that humans be able to choose between doing good and doing evil.
Therefore,
(2) It is important that people be allowed to do evil things.
Therefore,
(3) An all-good, all-knowing, and all-powerful God would allow some evil to exist.

The conclusion of this argument is the opposite of premise (2) of Al's argument. Theresa has presented a refutation argument intended to show that Al's argument fails the true premises test. Whether Theresa offers a counter argument or a refutation argument, she has shot the argumentative tennis ball back to Al's side of the net. It's his turn to respond with either a counter argument or a refutation argument.

As you watch an argumentative tennis match, you need to keep track of where the ball is. You need to keep track of whether someone is presenting an original argument, a counter argument, or a refutation argument. In theory this process of argument, counter argument, and refutation argument could continue forever. In practice the match stops either because one side is convinced to change beliefs or because the arguers run out of time.

EXERCISE 2.8

A. In Exercise 2.7 A, develop (a) a counter argument and (b) a refutation for each of the passages that contains an argument.

B. Evaluate each of your counter arguments and each of your refutation arguments using the true premises and proper form tests.

Fallacies and Relevance

Key Concept
Fallacies are bad arguments that are so common that they've been given a name.

Fallacies are bad arguments that are so common that they've been given a name. Bad arguments that have been named as a fallacy occur frequently because they look like good arguments. Some people use fallacies without noticing that they're bad arguments. Other people deliberately use fallacies when they're unable to provide good arguments. These people want to convince people to change their beliefs, but they don't have a good argument. Instead, they use a fallacious argument and hope that the people they're trying to convince won't notice.

You'll find discussions of fallacies throughout this book. This section discusses six fallacies that involve relevance: the Easy Target Fallacy, Appeal to

Popularity, Appeal to Novelty or Tradition, *Ad Hominem*, Appeal to Ignorance, and Begging the Question.

Fallacy: Easy Target

The Easy Target Fallacy occurs in three steps. First, someone makes an inaccurate claim about the views held by someone else. Second, the person argues that the inaccurately described view is false. Finally, the person asserts that this argument shows that the accurate view is false. The most common cases of this fallacy occur when someone presents an exaggerated version of someone else's view. When someone presents his opponent's views in an exaggerated way, he (distorts) his opponent's claims. He's offering an argument that's irrelevant to the issue at hand, but by misdescribing his opponent's view, his argument might deceive others into thinking he has countered the opponent's view. This fallacy is called the "Easy Target Fallacy" because when it occurs someone creates a view that's an easier target to attack than their opponent's actual view.

> **Key Concept**
> The three steps of the
> **Easy Target Fallacy**.

[handwritten margin notes: distorts his opponent's claim. attack something that is not the real issue. 1) make inaccurate claim 2)]

Here's the form of an Easy Target Fallacy. "S" is a variable that refers to statements.

(1) S2, a distorted version of S1, is false.
Therefore,
(2) S1 is false.

Technical Term: Straw Man Fallacy

The Easy Target Fallacy is often called the "Straw Man Fallacy."

Suppose that Catherine asserts that school lunches should be made with less fat and less sugar. William responds to Catherine as follows:

> I can't believe that you favor the government deciding what people eat! If the government decided what people could eat, we wouldn't be able to have a hot dog at the ball park or buttery popcorn at the movies. I want my hot dog, with chili please, and extra butter on my popcorn when I go to the movies!

William has committed the Easy Target Fallacy. He has chosen a target that's easier to attack than Catherine's actual view. Catherine didn't assert that the government should decide what people eat. She asserted that there should be less fat and sugar in school lunches. Here's a standardization of William's argument:

(1) If the government decided what people could eat, we wouldn't be able to have a hot dog at the ball park or buttery popcorn at the movies.
(2) We should be able to have a hot dog at the ball park and buttery popcorn at the movies.
Therefore,
(3) The government shouldn't decide what people can eat.

Therefore,
(4) School lunches shouldn't be made with less fat and less sugar.

Premise (3) of William's argument is irrelevant to (4).

Habits of a Critical Thinker

Giving Opposing Views Their Due

Someone who commits the Easy Target Fallacy needs to focus on giving opposing views their due. Considering views that aren't in accord with your own beliefs can be difficult to do. But if you dismiss a view without giving it the consideration it deserves, you'll never know whether the view is true.

Fallacy: Appeal to Popularity

Key Concept

The fallacy of **Appeal to Popularity** occurs when someone argues that a view is true on the grounds that it's popular.

The fallacy of **Appeal to Popularity** occurs when someone argues that a view is true on the grounds that it's popular. Here's the form of this fallacy:

(1) Most people approve of or believe S.
Therefore,
(2) S is true.

[handwritten: most people think this, most think this then it is true.]

The fact that most people approve or believe something doesn't mean that it's true. Before the introduction of telescopes, many people believed that there were only five planets in the solar system. This doesn't mean there really were only five planets in the solar system. Suppose that Rachael and Van are discussing the question of whether extra sensory perception (ESP) exists. If Rachael offered the following argument:

(1) Most people think that ESP exists.
Therefore,
(2) ESP exists.

she'd have committed the fallacy of Appeal to Popularity. (1) is not sufficiently relevant to (2).

Technical Term: *Argumentum Ad Populum*, Bandwagon Fallacy

For many centuries, the discussion of logic and critical thinking occurred in Latin. Therefore, most fallacies were originally named in Latin. These Latin names are still used. The Latin name for an Appeal to Popularity is "*Argumentum Ad Populum*." It's also called the "Bandwagon Fallacy."

Debra Lau Whelan wrote an article entitled "13,000 Kids Can't Be Wrong." Here's the beginning of the article:

Whether it's learning proper research skills, locating quality Web sites, or getting better test scores, an overwhelming number of kids think media specialists are essential to learning, according to a new study by professors Ross Todd and Carol Kuhlthau of Rutgers University's Center for International Scholarship in School Libraries. Student Learning Through Ohio School Libraries reveals that 99.4 percent of students in grades 3 to 12 believe school libraries and their services help them become better learners. (Whelan 2004, 46)

This passage and the article's title indicate that Whelan is making the following argument:

[handwritten: Bad argument Can use an example]

(1) 99.4 percent of students in grades 3 to 12 believe school libraries and
      their services help them become better learners.
Therefore,
(2) School libraries and their services help students become better learners.

The fact that 99.4% of students believe that something is true doesn't indicate that it's true. Elementary and high-school students have little information about the benefits and costs of school libraries. Thirteen thousand kids could be wrong.

Fallacy: Appeal to Novelty or Tradition

The fallacy of **Appeal to Novelty or Tradition** occurs when someone argues that a statement is true because people have either believed it for a short time (novelty) or for a long time (tradition). Here's the form of the fallacy:

(1) S has been believed by people for a short/long time.
Therefore,
(2) S is true.

In discussing how to organize the catalog of a university, someone might argue: *Tradition*

(1) We have always organized the sections of the catalog by academic
      department, not by major.
Therefore,
(2) We should continue to organize the sections of the catalog by
      academic department, not by major.

Don't use

This person has committed the fallacy of Appeal to <u>Tradition</u>. On the other hand, someone might argue: *Novelty*

for Et'

(1) We have never organized the sections of the catalog by academic
      department.
Therefore,
(2) We should organize the sections of the catalog by academic department.

This person has committed the fallacy of Appeal to <u>Novelty</u>. They've argued that something should be done only because it's new and different.

   Appeal to Novelty and Appeal to Tradition make the same mistake. Both reason from the claim about *how long* people have believed a view to a claim about the truth of a view. How long people have believed something is irrelevant to its truth. The fact that for hundreds of years many people believed that the Earth was flat doesn't mean that it was.

> ### Technical Terms: *Argumentum Ad Novitatem, Argumentum Ad Antiquitatem*
> The Latin name for the Appeal to Novelty is "*Argumentum Ad Novitatem.*" The Latin name for the Appeal to Tradition is "*Argumentum Ad Antiquitatem.*"

At the beginning of this chapter, you saw the following quote.

[The Catholic Church] holds that it is not admissible to ordain women to the priesthood for very fundamental reasons. These reasons include: the

Key Concept
The fallacy of **Appeal to Novelty or Tradition** occurs when someone argues that a statement is true because people have either believed it for a short time (novelty) or believed it for a long time (tradition).

*Novelty
believed for a
short time*

*Tradition
believed for a
long time.*

example recorded in the Sacred Scriptures of Christ choosing his Apostles only from among men; the constant practice of the Church, which has imitated Christ in choosing only men; and her living teaching authority which has consistently held that the exclusion of women from the priesthood is in accordance with God's plan for his Church.

Pope Paul argues that women shouldn't be allowed to be priests. He makes two arguments for his view. The first is a Biblical argument concerning the actions of Christ. It doesn't commit the fallacy of Appeal to Tradition. His second argument can be standardized as follows:

(1) The constant practice of the Church has been to exclude women from the priesthood.
(2) The Church has consistently held that women should be excluded from the priesthood.
Therefore,
(3) Women should continue to be excluded from the priesthood.

This argument commits the fallacy of Appeal to Tradition. Rather than use the word "tradition" he uses the phrase "constant practice" and "consistently." But the Pope is arguing that because some practice has been done for a long time, it should continue.

EXERCISE 2.9

A. Each of the following passages may contain one of the following fallacies: Easy Target, Appeal to Popularity, Appeal to Novelty, or Appeal to Tradition. Determine whether one of these four fallacies is present and, if so, which fallacy it is.

1. Munstermeister is North Rhine-Westphalia's best selling beer! And North Rhine-Westphalia is Germany's most populous province. You should enjoy Munstermeister too!

2. Budweiser is the best selling beer in the world. So it must be the best beer in the world.

3. The Reinheitsgebot law about what ingredients could be used in beer governed Germany's beer production from 1516 to 1987. And look how good German beer is. Germany should reinstate the Reinheitsgebot.

*4. New Munstermeister Brat is Germany's first beer with the flavor of bratwurst brewed right in! You should try Munstermeister Brat today!

5. **Angela**: "I think that you shouldn't have any more beer. You've had two and you have to drive home."

   Danielle: "I can't believe that you think you should always decide what I eat and drink! It's a free country and I'm going to eat and drink what I want!"

6. "Mamas, Don't Let Your Babies Grow Up to Be Cowboys." (Title of a Willie Nelson (2003) song)

7. Scientists at Very Cool University observed 12,456 gastropod mollusks (also known as snails and slugs) and noticed that 12,367 had two pairs of tentacles on their head. The remaining mollusks appeared to have lost one or more tentacles due to injury. They concluded that all gastropod mollusks have two pairs of tentacles.

*8. As we consider whether or not to move from paper add–drop forms to an online add–drop process, we need to remember that we've used paper add–drop forms for a long time. An online process might not work well for our university.

9. **Eric**: "If we move to the online add–drop process, students who do not have access to the internet will have trouble adding and dropping courses. We don't want that. So we shouldn't use an online add–drop policy."

   Samantha: "I think that most students nowadays have easy access to the internet. Most of my friends can surf on their cell phones. And the paper forms are a pain. I think online adds and drops is a great idea."

10. Everyone thinks that the Earth is round. So why do you persist in saying that it's flat?

11. **Amanda**: "I think it is important for the United States to remain in Iraq. If we don't, oil supplies to the West could be threatened."

   Luke: "How can you say that the United States should invade a country every time we think that there is a problem with oil supplies? We need to work to conserve energy at home, not send in the military to take it from others."

*12. **Martha**: "You need to put sage in the stuffing for your turkey."

   Gareth: "Why do you say that?"

   Martha: "Well, my mother always put sage in her stuffing."

13. "Give me liberty or give me death!" Patrick Henry (Henry 1999, 232)

14. The iPad is a revolutionary mobile tablet computer. [Assume that this is stated as a part of an argument for the conclusion that you should buy an iPad.]

15. "Congress ordered [the Census Bureau] to study the common-sense idea of counting inmates at their homes rather than at prison. [The B]ureau responded with an obtuse and evasive report that supports the bad old status quo. The report [suggests] the change [desired by Congress] might require the costly and invasive procedure of interviewing every inmate." (*The New York Times*, "Counting Noses in Prison" 2006) [The argument in this passage is attributed to the Census Bureau by *The New York Times*.]

B. Construct a fallacious appeal to tradition and a fallacious appeal to novelty in support of the following conclusions.

   1. Astrological signs have an influence on a person's destiny.
   2. Everyone should get a college education.
   3. You should get married.
   *4. The earth is flat.
   5. Dwight Yoakam is a great country singer.

C. Discuss whether there are any fallacies in the following quote. Here's some background information. The U.S. government keeps a stock of oil set aside for emergency, the "Strategic Petroleum Reserve" (SPR). After the attacks of September 11, 2001, President Bush directed that the amount of oil in the SPR be increased. The government gradually started buying oil and adding it to the SPR. In the presidential campaign of 2004, these purchases became an issue because the price of gas rose sharply. The Democratic candidate for President, Senator John Kerry, argued that the government should stop buying oil because its price was too high and because the purchases by the government were driving up prices. *The Washington Post* then reported President Bush's response to Senator Kerry's proposal.

"On May 19, Bush was asked about a plan by his Democratic opponent, Sen. John F. Kerry (Mass.), to halt shipments that are replenishing emergency petroleum reserves. Bush replied by saying we should not empty the reserves—something nobody in a responsible position has proposed. "The idea of emptying the Strategic Petroleum Reserve would put America in a dangerous position in the war on terror," Bush said." (Milbank 2004, A21)

Fallacy: *Ad Hominem*

Key Concept
A person commits the *Ad Hominem* Fallacy when he attacks a person instead of arguing against the view the person asserts.

A person commits the ***Ad Hominem* Fallacy** when he attacks a person instead of arguing against the view the person asserts. It has the following form:

(1) H asserts statement S.
(2) There is something objectionable about Person H.
Therefore,
(3) Statement S is false.
or
(3′) H's arguments for S are bad arguments.

"H" refers to human beings. This form is an improper form. The premises say nothing at all about S except that H asserted it. The fact that there's something objectionable about a person is irrelevant to the question of whether what a person says is true or whether that person has made a good argument.

People can perceive others to be objectionable for many reasons. In the past, it was quite common for a view to be rejected because the person who asserted the view was thought to be objectionable because of race, sex, religious beliefs, ethnicity, age, or social position. Even today, such cases of the *Ad Hominem* Fallacy are all too common.

Here's an example of the *Ad Hominem* Fallacy. Craig Crawford wrote a review of a book by Frank Rich. Rich's book was entitled *The Greatest Story Ever Sold: The Decline and Fall of Truth from 9/11 to Katrina*. In it, Rich argues that the administration of President George W. Bush used "deception, misinformation, and propaganda" to mislead the American people into supporting the war in Iraq and re-electing Bush. Crawford believes that Rich uses *ad hominem* attacks.

The occasional *ad hominem* asides—referring to Mr. Bush as a "glad-handing salesman," a "spoiled brat" and a "rich kid who used his father's connections to escape Vietnam"—will delight the Bush haters among Mr. Rich's fan base, but tend to undermine the often eloquent conclusions that he draws from his own raw material. (Crawford 2006, E2)

Crawford is correct. Rich has committed the *Ad Hominem* Fallacy. Referring to Bush as a "glad-handing salesman" or a "spoiled brat" has no relevance to Bush's arguments in defense of his actions.

Technical Terms: *Argumentum Ad Hominem, Argumentum Ad Personam*

The phrase "*ad hominem*" comes from the Latin name for the *Ad Hominem* Fallacy, "*Argumentum Ad Hominem.*" While this book avoids using the Latin names of fallacies, it uses the Latin name for this fallacy because its Latin name is common. The Latin phrase "*Argumentum Ad Personam*" is sometimes used to refer to an *ad hominem* argument.

The **Fallacy of Guilt by Association** is a form of the *Ad Hominem* Fallacy. It occurs when people are attacked based on their association with a person, group, or view that's considered objectionable.

In the typical case, someone asserts that another person's view must be false because some objectionable group of people also hold the view. If you asserted that a view is false because it was held by the Communists, you'd be committing the Fallacy of Guilt by Association.

Here's an example from a radio broadcast by Rush Limbaugh as reported on his web page. As background information, Ayman al-Zawahiri is a leader of Al-Qaeda, the group that organized the attacks on the World Trade Center and the Pentagon on September 11, 2001. The issue under consideration here is whether sending additional troops to Iraq will enable that country to have a stable and peaceful society.

> LIMBAUGH: Ayman al-Zawahiri [is] taunting Bush, "Come on, what do you mean 20,000? Give us 50, give us a hundred thousand to kill, you're going to lose 'em anyway." Who does this sound like, by the way? Ayman al-Zawahiri, "Send us 20,000, give us 50, why not another hundred? They'll be defeated anyway." We have heard this somewhere before.
>
> KERRY: You can put a hundred thousand troops in, and you can up the casualties, up the stakes, increase the violence, and not get a resolution.
>
> LIMBAUGH: Yes! It was John Kerry, ladies and gentlemen, who served in Vietnam. [H]e, once again, is on the same page with Al-Qaeda. John Kerry and the Democrats, whether they know it or not, their instincts lead them to say things that end up being parroted and repeated by Al-Qaeda as though Al-Qaeda are Democrat allies. (Limbaugh 2007, material omitted)

John Kerry, the Democratic candidate for President of the United States in 2004, is quoted as asserting that sending additional troops to Iraq wouldn't have a positive effect. Limbaugh didn't offer any good arguments in support of the view that Kerry's assertion was false. Rather than present a good argument, Limbaugh made an *ad hominem* attack of the guilt by association form. He attacked Kerry and the Democrats by associating them with Al-Qaeda.

Comments about a person are not always examples of the *Ad Hominem* Fallacy. Look again at the form of the *Ad Hominem* Fallacy. Both premises are about a person. The first asserts that a person made a statement and the second asserts that the person has some objectionable feature. But the conclusion of the argument is not about a person. It's about a statement. On the other hand, conclusions aren't always about statements. Sometimes an argument draws a conclusion about a person. You

Key Concept
The **Fallacy of Guilt by Association** is a form of the *Ad Hominem* Fallacy. It occurs when people are attacked based on their association with a person, group, or view that's considered objectionable.

might argue that a person is dishonest. You might argue that a person isn't a good person for a job. When the conclusion of an argument is about a person (not a statement) premises about that person may be relevant. If he were attempting to defend the conclusion that Bush is a flawed person or that you shouldn't vote for Bush, Rich's claims that Bush is a "glad-handing salesman" and a "spoiled brat" wouldn't be examples of the *Ad Hominem* Fallacy.

Fallacy: Appeal to Ignorance

Someone commits the fallacy of **Appeal to Ignorance** when he claims that a statement is true because it hasn't been shown to be false.

(1) It has not been shown that S is false.
Therefore,
(2) S is true.

In an Appeal to Ignorance the evidence being offered in the premises is actually the lack of evidence. Premise (1) doesn't provide a good reason to believe (2).

Suppose that Brittany and Travis are talking about Samantha, a friend who has moved to another town. They're discussing whether Samantha has bought a new car. Travis might make the following argument:

> Well, what's to say that she didn't buy a new car? After all, she could have bought a new car. I think she got a new car.

Travis has committed the fallacy of Appeal to Ignorance. He has reasoned from a claim that he doesn't know that Samantha didn't buy a new car to the claim that she bought a new car. The following would also be an example of the same fallacy:

> Well, what's to say that she bought a new car? After all, she didn't have to buy a new car. I don't think she got a new car.

In this case, Travis has reasoned from his lack of knowledge that Samantha has bought a new car to the claim that she didn't buy a new car. The appropriate conclusion that Travis and Brittany should draw from their lack of evidence about Samantha's car is that they don't know whether she has bought a new car.

Technical Term: *Argumentum Ad Ignorantiam*, Argument from Ignorance
___

The Latin name for the fallacy of Appeal to Ignorance is "*Argumentum Ad Ignorantiam*." The Fallacy of Appeal to Ignorance is sometimes called the fallacy of "Argument from Ignorance."

Fallacy: Begging the Question

This chapter ends with a fallacy that's an exception to the rule that every bad argument fails the true premises tests and/or the proper form test. The fallacy of **Begging the Question** occurs when a premise of an argument asserts the conclusion of the argument. The classic example of Begging the Question concerns the following argument for the existence of God.

(1) God wrote the Bible.
Therefore,
(2) Everything said in the Bible is true.

(3) The Bible asserts that God exists.
Therefore,
(4) God exists.

This argument begs the question because the argument's conclusion is asserted in the first premise. Premise (1) asserts that God wrote the Bible. If God wrote the Bible, God exists, which is the conclusion of the argument.

The form of an argument that begs the question is shockingly simple.

(1) S.
Therefore,
(2) S.

Remember that "S" is a variable that stands for statements. In the case of begging the question, a premise *is* the conclusion! Continuing with the existence of God example, the simplest form of Begging the Question would be:

(1) God exists.
Therefore,
(2) God exists.

Put this way, an argument that begs the question wouldn't fool anyone. Those who beg the question generally add additional premises and subarguments to hide the fact that the conclusion of the argument is contained in one of the premises. This occurred in the argument for the existence of God at the beginning of this section. The two additional premises and the subargument served to conceal the assertion of the conclusion in premise (1).

Technical Term: *Petitio Principii*, Begging the Question

The Latin name for Begging the Question is *"Petitio Principii."*

Recently, the phrase "begging the question" has come to be used to refer to a question that naturally comes to mind. For example, in a radio interview on the war in Iraq someone might assert that travel is difficult in a certain region because terrorist attacks have increased. The interviewer might then say: "That begs the question of why the attacks have increased." When you hear the phrase "beg the question" you'll need to examine the context to determine which of these two uses of the phrase is being employed.

The problem with arguments that beg the question is that they aren't arguments at all. Every argument has two parts, at least one premise and one conclusion. Look back at the form of an argument that begs the question. It contains only one statement. An argument that begs the question isn't an argument but an assertion disguised to look like an argument. This explains why "arguments" that beg the question don't fail either the true premises test or the proper form test. They fail a more basic test, the test of what it takes to be an argument. An argument has to have at least two statements, but an "argument" that begs the question only has one.

Connections

Chapter One discusses the two parts of every argument, premises and conclusions.

EXERCISE 2.10

A. Each of the following passages may contain one of the following fallacies: *Ad Hominem*, Appeal to Ignorance, Begging the Question, Easy Target, Appeal to Popularity, Appeal to Novelty/Appeal to Tradition. Determine whether one of these six fallacies is present and, if so, which fallacy is present.

   1. I think that the oysters made me sick. After all, no one has shown me that they didn't make me sick.

   2. Every morning for the past ten years I've had raisin bran for breakfast. I must keep having it.

   3. If you don't start believing in this mission, you'll spend the next ten years in the brig.

   *4. My opponent has committed adultery. He cheated on his taxes. He hired an illegal alien as a nanny. His views on tax reform simply can't be trusted.

   5. Where is that package? Hmm, the time before last, a package fell off the porch and into the bushes. I better check there.

   6. "And I wonder, still I wonder, who'll stop the rain?" (Lyrics from *"Who'll Stop the Rain?"* Creedence Clearwater Revival 1976)

   7. When an abortion occurs, one person, the pregnant woman, has killed an innocent person without any justification. If someone kills an innocent person without justification, they've committed murder. Therefore, abortion is a type of murder.

   *8. The chest pains indicate that he either has heart problems or acid reflux. The EKG shows no heart problems, so he must have acid reflux.

   9. Taxation is government theft of property. And theft is illegal! So taxation must be illegal as well.

   10. Congressman Eskandari's tax proposal doesn't deserve serious consideration. After all, Eskandari has been a Congressman for fourteen years and everyone knows what that means—that he has never met a tax plan he didn't like.

   11. People buy more Budweiser than milk. Budweiser must be a great beer.

   *12. "Mr. and Mrs. Dursley, of number four, Privet Drive, were proud to say that they were perfectly normal, thank you very much. They were the last people you'd expect to be involved in anything strange or mysterious, because they just didn't hold with such nonsense." (Rowling 1997, 7)

   13. "Who says I am not under the special protection of God?" (Often attributed to Adolf Hitler, but source is undocumented)

   14. Senator Joseph McCarthy argued that those named on a list of people were Communists. Regarding one person on his list, he stated: "I do not have much information on this [person] except the general statement of the agency that there is nothing in the files to disprove his Communist connections." (Rover 1996, 132)

   15. "In *that* direction," the Cat said, waving its right paw round, "lives a Hatter: and in *that* direction," waving the other paw, "lives a March Hare. Visit either you like: they're both mad."

   "But I don't want to go among mad people," Alice remarked.

   "Oh, you can't help that," said the Cat: "we're all mad here. I'm mad. You're mad."

   "How do you know I'm mad?" said Alice.

   "You must be," said the Cat, "or you wouldn't have come here."

   Alice didn't think that proved it at all.

   (Carroll 1982, 64)

B. The problem of skepticism is a famous philosophical puzzle. It begins with a simple question. How do you know that your car, your friends, the chair in which you are sitting, and the entire universe exists? Before you answer, read the following story.

"It all began that cold Wednesday night. I was sitting alone in my office watching the rain come down on the deserted streets outside, when the phone rang. It was Harry's wife, and she sounded terrified. They had been having a late supper alone in their apartment when suddenly the front door came crashing in and six hooded men burst into the room. The men were armed and they made Harry and Anne lie face down on the floor while they went through Harry's pockets. When they found his driver's license one of them carefully scrutinized Harry's face, comparing it with the official photograph and then muttered, "It's him all right." The leader of the intruders produced a hypodermic needle and injected Harry with something that made him lose consciousness almost immediately. For some reason they only tied and gagged Anne. Two of the men left the room and returned with a stretcher and white coats. They put Harry on the stretcher, donned the white coats, and trundled him out of the apartment, leaving Anne lying on the floor. She managed to squirm to the window in time to see them put Harry in an ambulance and drive away."

"By the time she called me, Anne was coming apart at the seams. It had taken her several hours to get out of her bonds, and then she called the police. To her consternation, instead of uniformed officers, two plain clothes officials arrived and, without even looking over the scene, they proceeded to tell her that there was nothing they could do and if she knew what was good for her she would keep her mouth shut. If she raised a fuss they would put out the word that she was a psycho and she would never see her husband again."

"Not knowing what else to do, Anne called me. She had the presence of mind to note down the number of the ambulance, and I had no great difficulty tracing it to a private clinic at the outskirts of town. When I arrived at the clinic I was surprised to find it locked up like a fortress. There were guards at the gate and it was surrounded by a massive wall. My commando training stood me in good stead as I negotiated the 20-foot wall, avoided the barbed wire, and silenced the guard dogs on the other side. The ground floor windows were all barred, but I managed to wriggle up a drainpipe and get in through a second story window that someone had left ajar. I found myself in a laboratory. Hearing muffled sounds next door I peeked through the keyhole and saw what appeared to be a complete operating room and a surgical team laboring over Harry. He was covered with a sheet from the neck down and they seemed to be connecting tubes and wires to him. I stifled a gasp when I realized that they had removed the top of Harry's skull. To my considerable consternation, one of the surgeons reached into the open top of Harry's head and eased his brain out, placing it in a stainless steel bowl. The tubes and wires I had noted earlier were connected to the now disembodied brain. The surgeons carried the bloody mass carefully to some kind of tank and lowered it in. My first thought was that I had stumbled on a covey of futuristic Satanists who got their kicks from vivisection. My second thought was that Harry was an insurance agent. Maybe this was their way of getting even for the increases in their malpractice insurance rates. If they did this every Wednesday night, their rates were no higher than they should be!"

"My speculations were interrupted when the lights suddenly came on in my darkened hidey hole and I found myself looking up at the scariest group of medical men I had ever seen. They manhandled me into the next room and strapped me down on an operating table. I thought, "Oh, oh, I'm in for it now!" The doctors huddled at the other end of the room, but I couldn't turn my head far enough to see what they were doing. They were mumbling among themselves, probably deciding my fate. A door opened and I heard a woman's voice. The deferential manner assumed by the medical malpractitioners made it obvious who was boss. I strained to see this mysterious woman, but she hovered just out of my view. Then, to my astonishment, she walked up and stood over me and I realized it was my secretary, Margot. I began to wish I had given her that Christmas bonus after all."

"It was Margot, but it was a different Margot than I had ever seen. She was wallowing in the heady wine of authority as she bent over me. "Well, Mike, you thought you were so smart, tracking Harry here to the clinic," she said. "It was all a trick to get you here. You saw what happened to Harry. He's not really dead, you know. These gentlemen are the premier neuroscientists in the world today. They have developed a surgical procedure whereby they remove the brain from the body but keep it alive in a vat of nutrient. The Food and Drug Administration wouldn't approve the procedure, but we'll show them. You see all the wires going to Harry's brain? They connect him up with a powerful computer. The computer monitors the output of his motor cortex and provides input to the sensory cortex in such a way that everything appears perfectly normal to Harry. It produces a fictitious mental life that merges perfectly into his past life so that he is unaware that anything has happened to him. He thinks he is shaving right now and getting ready to go to the office and stick it to another neurosurgeon. But actually, he's just a brain in a vat."

"Once we have our procedure perfected we're going after the head of the Food and Drug Administration, but we needed some experimental subjects first. Harry was easy. In order to really test our computer program we need someone who leads a more interesting and varied life—someone like you!" I was starting to squirm. The surgeons had drawn around me and were looking on with malevolent gleams in their eyes. But Margot gazed down at me and murmured in that incredible voice, "I'll bet you think we're going to operate on you and remove your brain just like we removed Harry's, don't you? But you have nothing to worry about. We're not going to remove your brain. We already did—three months ago!"

"With that they let me go. I found my way back to my office in a daze. For some reason, I haven't told anybody about this. I can't make up my mind. I am racked by the suspicion that I am really a brain in a vat and all this I see around me is just a figment of a computer. After all, how could I tell? If the computer program really works, no matter what I do, everything will seem normal. Maybe nothing I see is real. It's driving me crazy. (Pollock 1986, 1–3, material omitted)"

"Suppose that you were Mike, the detective in this story. How could you determine whether Margot was telling the truth or not? How could you tell whether you are a brain in a body or a brain in a vat? Here are two arguments you might try."

a. (1) I see that I have a body (that is, hands, feet, arms, etc.).

Therefore,

(2) I am not a brain in a vat.

b. (1) I think that I see that I have a body.

Therefore,

(2) I am not a brain in a vat.

Does either of these arguments beg the question? Why or why not? Evaluate both of these arguments using the true premises and proper form tests.

Chapter Summary

Good arguments have true premises and a proper form. Bad arguments have false premises and/or an improper form.

The true premises test is limited by the argument's audience. What's an uncontroversial premise for one audience might not be known to another audience.

An argument with a proper form is an argument in which the truth of the premises provides support for the truth of the conclusion. An argument with one or more false premises can still have a proper form. Putting arguments into the various logical forms allows you to see whether the argument passes the proper form test.

Arguments can be divided into two types. Deductive arguments claim that the premises of the argument guarantee the truth of the conclusion. Inductive arguments claim that the premises provide some support for, but no guarantee of, the truth of the conclusion.

When applying the proper form test, you must check the relevance of the premises to the conclusion. Premises can be relevant (they provide evidence for the conclusion) or irrelevant (they provide no evidence for the conclusion). In some arguments each premise is individually relevant to the conclusion. These are independent premises. In other arguments the premises are only relevant when combined with the other premises. These are dependent premises. To test for relevance requires first looking at the premises individually and then looking at them as a group.

Fallacies are bad arguments that are so common that they've been given a name. They usually have some feature that makes them appear to be good arguments.

The fallacies of relevance are arguments that fail the proper form test because their premises are irrelevant to the conclusion. *Ad Hominem*, Appeal to Ignorance, Begging the Question, Easy Target, Appeal to Popularity, Appeal to Novelty, or Appeal to Tradition are all fallacies of relevance.

An argument that begs the question isn't really an argument but an assertion disguised to look like an argument.

GUIDE

Finding, Standardizing, and Evaluating Arguments

Here's a review of the steps to take to find, standardize, and evaluate an argument. Steps 1–9 below are copied from the Guide for Finding and Standardizing Arguments found in Chapter One. These steps are repeated here so that you have one handy place to see all the steps. As this book discusses the various types of arguments in later chapters, it will present different versions of this guide for each of type of argument.

Finding Arguments

1. Look for an attempt to convince.
2. Find the conclusion.
3. Find the premises.
4. Review the following to make sure that you've correctly identified the conclusion and the premises: imperfect indicator words, sentence order, premises and/or conclusion not in declarative form, unstated premises, and/or conclusion.

5. Review the following to make sure that you haven't incorrectly identified something as a premise or a conclusion when in fact it isn't part of an argument: assertions, questions, instructions, descriptions, and explanations.

Standardizing Arguments

6. Rewrite the premises and the conclusion as declarative sentences. Make sure that each premise and the conclusion is a grammatically correct declarative sentence. Rewrite the premises and conclusion as necessary to make them clearer but don't change the meaning of the passage. Remove pronouns from the sentences and replace them with the nouns or noun phrases to which they refer.

7. Review any phrases you've omitted to be sure that they aren't premises or a conclusion.

8. Number the premises and the conclusion. Put [ ] around the number of an unstated premise or conclusion. Place the premises before their conclusion and insert "Therefore," between the premises and the conclusion. Use blank lines to indicate subarguments.

9. Compare your standardization to the original passage to make sure that you haven't omitted any arguments found in the passage and to be sure that you've correctly identified the premises and the conclusion.

Evaluating Arguments: The True Premises Test

10. Check to see whether the premises are accurate descriptions of the world.

11. Consider whether the premises are appropriate for the argument's audience.

12. Review the premises to be sure they are reasonable.

Evaluating Arguments: The Proper Form Test

13. Determine whether the argument is a deductive argument or an inductive argument.

14. Determine whether the premises are relevant to the conclusion. Look at each premise individually to see whether the truth of the premise provides some evidence for the truth of the conclusion. Look at the premises as a group to see whether the truth of all of them provides some evidence for the truth of the conclusion.

Evaluating Arguments: Checking for Fallacies

15. Compare the argument to the list of fallacies on page 410 to see whether the argument commits any of the fallacies.

3

Premises and Conclusions

Nanuwak had a difficult time processing the salmon with the ground-slate knife. Not long into the fish cutting, the [stone] blade showed several chips at the cutting surface. At the start she found that the stone knife cut the flesh more easily than the salmon's skin. Eventually she was sawing at the flesh and using "lots of muscle" to cut it.

—Lisa Frink, Brian Hoffman, and Robert Shaw, "Ulu Knife Use in Western Alaska: A Comparative Ethnoarchaeological Study" (2003, 119)

Learning Outcomes

After studying the material in this chapter, you should be able to:

1. Recognize and correctly evaluate empirical premises.
2. Recognize and correctly evaluate testimonial premises.
3. Recognize and correctly evaluate definitional premises.
4. Recognize and correctly evaluate statements by experts.
5. Correctly determine the strength and scope of conclusions.

The passage on the previous page is from an article about how Eskimos use stone knives. If these statements were premises, would they pass the true premises test? Are they premises that you should assume, or should you look for a subargument? Assuming premises must be done carefully. Premises should be assumed only when they're likely to be true. This chapter will explore some guidelines for deciding whether a premise is likely to be true. It will also examine some details about conclusions and point out some things that make some conclusions more difficult to support.

Three Kinds of Premises

No matter what premise you put in an argument, someone can ask you why you think that premise is true. To answer that question, you can make a subargument. But someone can ask you why you think the premises of your subargument are true. You can then make more subarguments. In principle, you could go on forever. But you won't live forever so you can't go on providing subarguments. You must offer some premises without supporting them. These premises are assumed premises. When can you assume a premise? It depends on what kind of premise it is. Three kinds of statements are often used as premises: empirical statements, definitional statements, and statements by experts. In each case, some guidelines will help you determine when these statements are likely to be true and therefore may be assumed.

Empirical Statements

Definition of Empirical Statements

Empirical statements are statements that report what people observe through their senses. When you observe with your senses you're getting *direct* empirical evidence. When you get reports of observations from other people or from instruments, you're getting *indirect* empirical evidence. Suppose that you're working in the library and a friend comes in and tells you that it has started to rain. If she is telling the truth, your friend has direct empirical knowledge of the rain and you have indirect empirical knowledge of the rain. If you saw the rain on TV, that would be another kind of indirect empirical knowledge. Indirect empirical experience comes in two kinds: reports of observations of others (such as your friend) and observations that you make with the aid of instruments (such as the TV).

> *direct - I felt it*
> *indirect - some one else gave me the info*

Key Concept
Empirical statements are statements that report what people observe through their senses.

> *Presentation of Truth 2*

Technical Terms: Empirical Knowledge, Empirical Theories

Empirical knowledge is any knowledge acquired, either directly or indirectly, through observation. Empirical theories are theories about things you can observe.

A moving crane.

Here are some examples of empirical *direct +* statements: *indirect empirical*

1. Triangular shapes are the most stable form for constructing the large moving cranes used in the construction of buildings.
2. Grass turns purple when mowed by an unwilling teenager.
3. In 2006, more than 1 million smokers stopped smoking for at least one day.
4. René Descartes was living in China when he invented analytic geometry.
5. More world championships have been won by the New York Yankees than by any other baseball team.
6. Cell phones regularly explode.

what is likely to be true.

The odd numbered statements are true and the even numbered statements are false, but all six statements are empirical statements. Statements 1, 3, and 5 are uncontroversial empirical statements. Because they're likely to be true, uncontroversial empirical statements may be assumed to pass the true premises test. Don't confuse uncontroversial empirical statements with statements you know to be true. Even if you didn't know that statements 1, 3, or 5 above are true, they're all plausible and easily verifiable empirical statements. They may be assumed to be true.

Statements 2, 4, and 6 are uncontroversially false empirical statements. Uncontroversially false empirical statements can be rejected without argument. You might think that you'd never find an uncontroversially false empirical statement in an argument. After all, why would anyone put an uncontroversially false premise into an argument? But sometimes people decide too quickly or make simple mental errors. You might hear someone say:

Everyone knows that two plus two equals four.

You might think that this empirical statement is uncontroversially true. But think for a moment. People don't learn to add until they're four or five years old. That means that lots of people don't know that two plus two equals four. This statement isn't uncontroversially true, it's uncontroversially false! It fails the true premises test.

Lisa Frink and her team of researchers were studying the adoption of metal knives by Eskimos in Alaska. Before contact with Europeans, Eskimos used stone knives made of ground-slate. Then they started using metal knives. Frink wondered if metal knives were more efficient than slate knives. To test this, the researchers made some slate knives and asked some Eskimos to use them to cut up salmon. Here's an image of the traditional knives that the Eskimos used. These knives are called "ulus."

Key Concept
Uncontroversially true empirical statements may be assumed to pass the true premises test.

One of the Eskimos who tested the knives was Mary Nanuwak. Here's part of the quote you saw at the beginning of this chapter. The letters are added for clarity.

(a) Not long into the fish cutting, the [stone] blade showed several chips at the cutting surface. (b) At the start she found that the stone knife cut the flesh more easily than the salmon's skin. (c) Eventually she was sawing at the flesh and using "lots of muscle" to cut it. (Frink 2003, 119)

Ulu knife.

Sentences (a), (b), and (c) are empirical statements. Statement (a) is a direct observation by Nanuwak and Frink. Sentences (b) and (c) state direct empirical experience of Nanuwak and indirect empirical experiences of Frink. All three of them are uncontroversial. You can assume that they pass the true premises test. If someone were to state:

Stone ulus aren't good knives.

that wouldn't be an empirical statement. It's an evaluation.

Connections

Chapter Ten will say more about evaluative (moral) statements.

Habits of a Critical Thinker

Avoiding Self-Deception and Rationalization

One thing you can observe is yourself. When you say "I'm tired," you have made an empirical statement about yourself. You can make incorrect empirical statements about yourself. When you do that, you could be deceiving yourself.

Self-deception prevents you from being a good critical thinker. It keeps you from accurately evaluating your own beliefs. Believing fictions about oneself can be reassuring or fun. But discovering your actual strengths and weakness through honest self-evaluation puts you in a better position to make good decisions.

Rationalization is a common form of self-deception. When you rationalize, you present yourself with a bad argument that's plausible enough to fool you into thinking that you have good reasons for doing what you want to do.

You might want to go out over the weekend. You know that midterms are next week and you've got a biochemistry test. But you think to yourself: "Face it. I'm not going to pass that test anyway. I may as well have some fun." Your argument might be standardized like this:

(1) I am going to fail my biochemistry test.
(2) If I am going to fail a test, there's no point in studying.
(3) If there is no point in studying, I might as well go to a party.
Therefore,
(4) I should go to a party.

This argument fails the true premises test. Premise (1) is almost certainly false. Whether you fail the biochemistry test depends, in part, on whether you study for it. Teachers don't give tests that students will necessarily fail. You know this, but you really want to go out over the weekend. If you argue yourself out of studying, you have fallen prey to rationalization.

Testimonial Empirical Statements

Remember the two types of indirect empirical statements: statements that are the reports of what others have experienced and statements about observations made using instruments. The reports of what others have experienced are **testimonial statements**. Your friend's statement that it has started to rain is (from your perspective) an example of testimony. (From her perspective, it's a direct empirical statement.)

When are testimonial premises likely to be true? When should you assume testimonial premises? Two important criteria help us answer these questions: plausibility and reliability.

Suppose that, instead of telling you that it has started to rain, your friend rushes in and says: "Space aliens are landing outside the library!" Your friend's claim isn't plausible. It doesn't fit with your background knowledge (such as that aliens don't usually land on Earth). It wouldn't be appropriate for you to use your friend's statement as an assumed premise in an argument. Testimonial statements should only be used as assumed premises when they're *plausible*.

Let's return to the original case. Your friend comes in and tells you that it has started to rain. Unless your college is in a desert, this claim is plausible. However, what if your friend has developed a habit of telling you that it's raining even when it isn't raining? This has become a running joke. In that case, you shouldn't use your friend's testimony as an assumed premise. The problem in this case isn't plausibility but reliability. Testimonial statements should only be used as assumed premises if the person making the statement is *reliable*. A person is reliable when her past testimonial statements have been true. A plausible statement made by a reliable individual may be assumed to pass the true premises test.

When considering reliability, you must think about whether people can accurately report their own experiences. Some people have better memories than others. Some people are less distracted by traumatic incidents than others. Some people are more truthful than others. One of the authors of this book found to her surprise that she wasn't always a reliable witness. When asked to report what happened one morning, she said that she'd seen a police car chasing a brown truck and that this brown truck crashed into a telephone pole. Then she found herself getting up from the ground with no memory of being thrown down. News footage later showed a white truck crashing into a brown car, which crashed into the telephone pole. The intensity of the experience affected her perception or memory. What she thought she saw didn't cohere with other evidence. If you know that the testimony you were intending to report came from people undergoing traumatic experiences, you shouldn't use that testimony as an assumed premise.

Plausibility and reliability show that your knowledge of whether a testimonial statement is likely to be true turns on your background knowledge. You have background knowledge about aliens (including the knowledge that they haven't landed recently in your city) which makes your friend's claim implausible. In the case of your friend's running joke, you're also relying on the background knowledge that your friend is unreliable about rain. Knowing how to apply background knowledge is another part of the art of argument. Knowing which facts to consider, for what audience, and in what context, are things that you can only learn with practice. The more times you make a judgment about accepting someone's testimony, the more you'll develop a feel for what is plausible and how reliable someone is.

Critical Thinkers

Marsha Coleman-Adebayo

Courtesy of Marsha Coleman-Adebayo

Whistleblowers are employees who, based on their own empirical observations, report illegal or unethical conduct that harms the public. They offer prime examples of how empirical testimonial evidence in arguments can have life-saving or life-threatening consequences. **Marsha Coleman-Adebayo,** member of the Board of Directors of the National Whistleblowers Center, became a whistleblower when she was senior policy analyst for the United States Environmental Protection Agency (EPA). Coleman-Adebayo discovered that a U.S. company mining vanadium was generating toxic waste, poisoning workers, and harming the environment. Coleman-Adebayo made that information public.

She suffered retaliation and death threats due to her testimony. Her experience and the courage she exhibited led to the Notification of Federal Employees Anti-Discrimination and Retaliation Act (called the "NO FEAR Act"). President George W. Bush signed the bill into law in 2002. It requires federal agencies to protect whistleblowers.

EXERCISE 3.1

A. Determine which of the following are empirical statements.

1. Blue is the most popular color.
2. Red is the color of grass.
3. According to the American Heart Association, "Coronary heart disease is America's No. 1 killer."
*4. According to the American Association of Fried Food Lovers, high cholesterol makes us healthy.
5. Cats and dogs make good pets.
6. My roommate says that I snore.
7. My roommate says that there are humans on Mars.
*8. There are plenty of spiders around.
9. Spiders are arachnids, which are animals that have eight legs.
10. According to Dr. Who, an independent psychologist in Macon, GA, everyone should eat 30 large pizzas per day.
11. Spiders are very often poisonous.

*12. The items on the desk are pens.

13. Pens are writing instruments made with ink inside a tube.

14. According to the International Society of Astronomers, Pluto is a dwarf planet.

15. According to what is seen through the Hubble telescope, Pluto is smaller than some asteroids.

B. If each of the following were premises in an argument, which of them could be assumed to pass the true premises test because they are uncontroversially true empirical statements?

1. Blue is the most popular color.

2. Red is the color of grass.

3. According to the American Heart Association, "Coronary heart disease is America's No. 1 killer."

*4. According to the American Association of Fried Food Lovers, high cholesterol makes us healthy.

5. Cats and dogs make good pets.

6. My roommate says that I snore.

7. My roommate says that there are humans on Mars.

*8. There are plenty of spiders around.

9. Spiders are arachnids, which are animals that have eight legs.

10. "Abra Kadabra," said Houdini, as he unlocked the chains on his arms.

11. Spiders are very often poisonous.

*12. Does your watch have a second hand?

13. Your phone must be pretty old since it doesn't have an alarm clock function.

14. Hooray!

15. According to a renowned psychologist, women are from Venus, and men are from Mars.

C. Determine whether the following statements are testimonial statements.

1. The doctor said that she saw a broken bone on the x-ray.

2. According to the thermometer, it is five degrees Celsius.

3. The witness claimed that the driver of the car didn't brake before hitting the pedestrian.

*4. The food critic reported that the potatoes were salty.

5. My roommate says that there are humans on Mars.

6. Spiders are arachnids, which are animals that have eight legs.

7. "Abra Kadabra," said Houdini, as he unlocked the chains on his arms.

*8. Spiders are very often poisonous.

9. Does your watch have a second hand?

10. Your phone must be pretty old since it doesn't have an alarm clock function.

11. My roommate says she saw a mouse in the dining hall last night.

*12. My roommate claims says that there are invisible winged horses in the dining hall.

13. According to the American Heart Association, "Coronary heart disease is America's No. 1 killer."

14. According to the International Society of Astronomers, Pluto is a dwarf planet.

15. According to what is seen through the Hubble telescope, Pluto is smaller than some asteroids.

D. Look in your textbooks for your other courses. Provide (a) two examples of uncontroversially true empirical statements and (b) two examples of testimonial statements.

E. Determine whether the numbered statements are empirical statements. These statements are from an article on autism in the journal *Molecular Psychiatry*.

"[1] Autism/autistic disorder (MIM 209850) is a development disorder characterized by three classes of symptoms including impairments in communication and reciprocal social interactions, and repetitive or stereotyped behaviors and interests. [2] Twin studies have indicated that genetic factors play an important role in the etiology of autism as the concordance rate for monozygotic twins is much higher than that of dizygotic twins. [3] In addition, family studies indicate that the recurrence to siblings, estimated from the multiple studies at 1–3%, is profoundly higher than the risk to the general population, which has been estimated at ~0.5–2/1000. [4] The mode of inheritance of autism appears complex and latent-class analyses suggest that 3–10 genes may underlie the disorder, although analysis of one genome-wide linkage has been used to suggest that at least 10 and as many as 100 genes underlie the disorder." (Buxbaum 2004, 144, material omitted)

F. Explain whether and why the empirical statements in the following passage would make good premises.

"[1] "The rhesus macaque is the unsung hero of the maternity ward. [2] In 1940, Nobel laureate Karl Landsteiner and his student Alexander Weiner discovered in this monkey a blood protein they called the Rh (for Rhesus) factor. [3] Researchers soon found the Rh factor in some but not all humans and realized that a mother could react immunologically against the factor in her fetus. [4] Now a simple test and a vaccine prevent that reaction—and resulting mental retardation or even death in about 20,000 U.S. newborns a year." (Pennisi 2007, 216)

Definitional Statements

What's the difference between an empirical statement and a definitional statement? Let's compare some examples of each.

1. Empirical statement: Triangular shapes are the most stable form for constructing large moving cranes used in construction.
   Definitional statement: A triangle is a three-sided polygon.

2. Empirical statement: Mark followed a recipe to make this cake.
   Definitional statement: A recipe is a set of directions for making or preparing food.

3. Empirical statement: More world championships have been won by the New York Yankees than by any other baseball team.
   Definitional statement: A home run is a hit in baseball that allows the batter to touch all the bases and score a run.

Key Concept
A **definitional statement** is a report about how a word is used.

The second statement in each pair is a **definitional statement**, a report about how a word is used. An empirical statement is a report of an observation. It wouldn't be useful to consult a dictionary when trying to determine the truth of the first statement in each pair above. Even if you looked up each word in the first statement, it wouldn't give the sort of information required to know whether triangular shapes are in fact best for insuring strength of a construction crane. In order to know which geometrical shapes make the best cranes, empirical investigation is needed.

The definition

A triangle is a three-sided polygon.

Key Concept
Uncontroversial definitional statements may be assumed to pass the true premises test.

is uncontroversial. It presents an accurate report of how people use the word "triangle." Like uncontroversial empirical statements, uncontroversial definitional statements may be assumed to pass the true premises test because they're likely to be true. While dictionaries can't resolve issues surrounding controversial terms, if used properly they're your best first step in trying to decide whether a definitional statement is true.

Frink's article about Eskimo knife use contains a good example of an uncontroversial definitional statement.

This study deals with salmon butchering using a traditional semilunar knife known as the ulu. (Frink 2003, 116)

In this sentence Frink defines an ulu as a traditional semilunar knife. There's no reason to doubt this uncontroversial definitional statement.

Here's an uncontroversially false definitional statement:

If something has the genetic code of the species *homo sapiens*, it's a human being.

This is a definition of "human being." You might think that it's true. But think for a moment. Recall from your high school biology classes that the genetic code of every living thing is present in every cell of that thing. And recall that every hair that falls from your head contains many cells from your body. Each of the cells has the genetic code of the species *homo sapiens*. But a strand of your hair isn't filled with thousands of human beings. This definition is uncontroversially false and fails the true premises test.

Connections

Chapter Four will say more about definitions. This chapter discusses only one type of definition, dictionary definitions.

EXERCISE 3.2

A. Determine which of the following are definitions.

1. Blue is the most popular color.
2. Red is the color of grass.
3. SCUBA means self-contained underwater body apparatus.
*4. According to the American Association of Fried Food Lovers, high cholesterol makes us healthy.
5. Cats and dogs make good pets.
6. My roommate says that I snore.
7. My roommate says that there are humans on Mars.
*8. There are plenty of spiders around.
9. Spiders are arachnids, which are animals that have eight legs.
10. According to Dr. Who, an independent psychologist in Macon, GA, everyone should eat 30 large pizzas per day.
11. Spiders are very often poisonous.
*12. The items on the desk are pens.
13. Pens are writing instruments made with ink inside a tube.
14. According to the International Society of Astronomers, Pluto is a dwarf planet.
15. According to what is seen through the Hubble telescope, Pluto is smaller than some asteroids.

B. If each of the following were premises in an argument, which of them could be assumed to pass the true premises test because they are uncontroversially true definitional statements?

1. Blue is the most popular color.
2. Green is the color of grass.
3. According to the American Heart Association, "Coronary heart disease is America's No. 1 killer."
*4. According to the American Association of Fried Food Lovers, high cholesterol makes us healthy.
5. Cats and dogs make good pets.
6. My roommate says that I snore.
7. My roommate says that there are humans on Mars.
*8. There are plenty of spiders around.
9. Spiders are arachnids, which are animals that have eight legs.
10. According to Dr. Nous, an independent psychologist in Macon, GA, everyone should eat 30 large pizzas per day.
11. Spiders are very often poisonous.
*12. According to my dictionary, SCUBA means self-contained underwater body apparatus.

13. Your phone must be pretty old since it doesn't have an alarm clock function.

14. "Abra Kadabra," said Houdini, as he unlocked the chains on his arms.

15. According to a renowned psychologist, women are from Venus, and men are from Mars.

C. Find two examples of uncontroversially true definitions in textbooks from your other courses.

D. For items 1–6 individually and items 7–10 in the paragraph below, determine whether each of the following is an empirical statement or a definitional statement. Of the empirical statements, which are testimonial? Then indicate which of the statements would make good premises and why.

1. Sometimes the sun appears to be about a hundred yards off.

2. My roommate said that the sun was so bright today that it appeared to be about a hundred yards away.

3. The sun is a star that provides light and heat to the planets in this solar system.

*4. According to my dictionary, a star is a heavenly body capable of core fusion.

5. A planet is a heavenly body not capable of core fusion, said Gibor Basri, an astronomer at the University of California at Berkeley.

6. According to the results of a Google search, Gibor Basri received a BS in Physics from Stanford University in 1973, and a PhD in Astrophysics from the University of Colorado, Boulder in 1979.

[7] "Reflecting on infectious conditions, it appears that disease burden, rapid change in disease incidence (suggesting preventability), and public concern about risk are three essential characteristics that define a public-health disorder. [8] By any one of several criteria, diabetes is associated with a very high burden to individuals with the disease, as well as to society in general. [9] Further, there is convincing and increasing evidence that primary, secondary, and tertiary prevention strategies are effective in reducing the disease burden associated with diabetes. [10] Yet most would still consider diabetes primarily to be a clinical disease. In part, this perception is based on the fact that, in association with aging and a possible strong family history, diabetes and its complications may appear inevitable to many. Further, much of the burden associated with diabetes is insidious, coming on gradually only after a considerable number of years. Thus, the burden associated with diabetes has not dramatically increased in the past few months or years; it has been here for some time and is increasing steadily." (Vinicor 1994, 22)

E. Determine whether the numbered statements are definitions.

"[1] Autism/autistic disorder (MIM 209850) is a development disorder characterized by three classes of symptoms including impairments in communication and reciprocal social interactions, and repetitive or stereotyped behaviors and interests. [2] Twin studies have indicated that genetic factors play an important role in the etiology of autism as the concordance rate for monozygotic twins is much higher than that of dizygotic twins. [3] In addition, family studies indicate that the recurrence to siblings, estimated from the multiple studies at 1–3%, is profoundly higher than the risk to the general population, which has been estimated at ~0.5–2/1000. [4] The mode of inheritance of autism appears complex and latent-class analyses suggest that 3–10 genes may underlie the disorder, although analysis of one genome-wide linkage analysis has been used to suggest that at least 10 and as many as 100 genes underlie the disorder." (Buxbaum 2004, 144, material omitted)

F. Determine whether each of the following is an empirical statement, a testimonial premise, or a definition. Indicate which of the statements would make good premises.

1. "Cry9C is one of several so-called Bt proteins, but it is more heat stable and harder for humans to digest than its kin qualities that are typical of such allergens as peanuts." (Kaiser 2000, 1867)*

2. "The term basketry refers to woven textiles created manually without a frame or loom." (Berman 2000, 422)

3. "We observed 29 instances of wicker (FIG. 12), constituting 11.24% of the basketry weaves." (Berman 2000, 427)

*4. "[O]ne of the best recent works, Wang Lixin's *Meiguo chuanjiaoshi yu wan Qing Zhongguo xiandaihua* (*American Missionaries and the Modernization of China in the Late Qing*), argues that American missionaries, rather than being tools of cultural or other imperialism, were actually engaged in 'cultural exchange,' making a significant contribution to China's modernization in the late Qing period." (Dunch 2002, 316)

5. "Powerful storms have caused mass mortality of at least 10 Caribbean mangrove forests during the past 50 years." (Cahoon 2003, 1094)

Statements by Experts

The faculty in the Department of Religious Studies know a lot about Islam but less about classical music. The faculty in the Department of Music know a lot about classical music but less about Islam. The faculty of a college is a collection of experts. **Experts** are people who have specialized knowledge about a particular field. Many experts work outside of college. The authors of this book would never dream of attempting to fix the transmissions of their cars. We know a lot about critical thinking but not much about transmissions, marketing, plumbing, the cell structure of plants, insurance, how children learn to read, and many other subjects.

Key Concept Experts are people who have specialized knowledge about a particular field.

Technical Term: Authority

Another name for an expert is an authority.

Some statements made by experts may be used as assumed premises. But appropriately assuming statements made by experts is a difficult matter. Because the use of the statements of experts is so common, this book will spend quite a bit of time laying out some guidelines for their use. You should use five criteria to determine whether a statement by an expert may be used as an assumed premise: appropriate credentials, reliability, lack of bias, appropriate area of expertise, and expert consensus. A statement made by an expert that passes all of these <u>five criteria</u> may be assumed to pass the true premises test.

Key Concept A statement made by an expert that passes all five of these criteria may be assumed to pass the true premises test: appropriate credentials, reliability, lack of bias, appropriate area of expertise, and expert consensus.

*Jocelyn Kaiser, Panel Urges Further Study of Biotech Corn. Science, Volume 290, no. 5498 (December 8, 2000): 1867. Copyright © 2000 American Association for the Advancement of Science. All rights reserved.

Appropriate Credentials

Anyone can say that she's an expert. Credentials are the evidence that a person provides to show that she really is an expert. The most common sort of credential is an *academic degree*. Having a degree in a particular field is evidence that a person is an expert in that field. However, a person can lie about her degrees or go on the internet and buy a degree from a fake university. You may need to do some research to verify that the institution awarding the degree is a real university. This can be a bit more challenging than it sounds because the web pages of fake universities can look quite nice. But when you dig down into them you'll find very short lists of faculty, odd course names, or unusual information about the university's address.

In addition to academic degrees, positions, publications, grants, awards, and honors are important credentials. *Positions* are the jobs an expert has had. The jobs that provide credentials are extremely varied. Being a professor is a job that provides a credential. Many jobs in the business world indicate a level of expertise. The Chairman of the Board of Governors of the United States Federal Reserve is Ben Bernanke. (The Federal Reserve system is the central banking system of the United States.) That Mr. Bernanke is Chairman of the Board of Governors of the United States Federal Reserve is one of his credentials. It indicates that he's an expert about central banking.

Especially for academic experts, *publications* and *grants* are important credentials. Professors write papers and send them to journals in the hope that they'll be published. The journals receive many more papers than they can print. They use a board of editors to select the best of them. The same is true of books. Professors also apply for grants. Boards of reviewers select some of these applications for funding. Someone who has been published or has earned a grant has an important credential.

Awards and *honors* are also important credentials. For example, the title of "Associate of the Society of Actuaries" is awarded to actuaries who pass a certain number of tests. Actuaries help businesses manage risk. For example, actuaries help determine your car insurance premiums. The Society of Actuaries is a professional group for actuaries. The title "Associate of the Society of Actuaries" indicates that a person has achieved a level of expertise in helping businesses manage risks.

Reliability

Reliability isn't about the expert's knowledge. It's about the expert's history of telling the truth. The question of the reliability of an expert is essentially the same as the question of the reliability of your friend's statements about rain. As with your friend, if you know that an expert has made many false statements in the past, the expert's current statements shouldn't be assumed as premises.

Lack of Bias

An expert is biased when that expert has some reason to make statements that aren't true. The most common causes of bias have to do with money. For example, if experts are being paid by a company whose profits will be affected by the truth or falsity of what the experts say, you should be hesitant to use the statements of these experts as assumed premises. On the other hand, you can't dismiss experts' views only because the experts are being paid. The key is to consider whether the way the experts are paid will influence their views. Suppose that your instructor is being paid an annual salary. This payment method is unlikely to influence the grades she gives. On the other hand, suppose that your instructor was paid for every student who passed the class. In that case, it would be reasonable to suspect that the instructor's grades could be biased.

Another common source of bias is a political or ideological viewpoint. An expert might strongly believe in a cause. The expert might cite evidence in a slanted way in order to further the cause. Statements made by such an expert shouldn't be used as assumed premises.

Don't confuse bias with interest. Almost all experts are interested in the field they study. A physicist who has spent her whole life trying to determine whether quarks are the smallest particles in the universe finds this question extremely interesting. Her experiments may yield evidence that quarks are the smallest or that they're not, or her results may be inconclusive. The physicist wants to know what the smallest particle is but has no stake in what that particle turns out to be.

Bias can be hard to eliminate. Suppose that you're also a physicist and the physicist studying quarks is your friend. You're one of the few experts on quarks and you've been chosen to be on a panel that will decide how grant money for the study of quarks will be distributed. Because one of the applicants is your friend, you're biased. If you're one of a small number of experts on quarks it may not be possible to remove you from the panel making the grant decisions. In that case, it would be essential that you reveal that you're friends with one of the applicants. When you do this, you're making your bias transparent. A **transparent bias** is a bias that's known to those evaluating the arguments of the person who's biased. On the other hand, a bias that isn't transparent is a **hidden bias**.

The American Enterprise Institute (AEI) is associated with conservative causes. It publishes studies on economic, social, and foreign policy issues. It makes no attempt to hide its perspective. The following is easily found on its web pages:

> AEI's purposes are to defend the principles and improve the institutions of American freedom and democratic capitalism—limited government, private enterprise, individual liberty and responsibility, vigilant and effective defense and foreign policies, political accountability, and open debate. Its work is addressed to government officials and legislators, teachers and students, business executives, professionals, journalists, and all citizens interested in a serious understanding of government policy, the economy, and important social and political developments. (AEI 2006)

People For the American Way (PFAW) is associated with liberal causes. It works in areas broadly similar to the AEI. Its perspective is similarly open.

> People For the American Way is an energetic advocate for the values and institutions that sustain a diverse democratic society. Many of these are now threatened by the influence of the radical right and its allies who have risen to positions of political power. Our most fundamental rights and freedoms—and even our basic constitutional framework—are

Key Concept
A **transparent bias** is a bias that's known to those evaluating the arguments of the person who's biased. On the other hand, a bias that isn't transparent is a **hidden bias**.

at risk. People For the American Way works in close collaboration with other leading national and state progressive organizations to mobilize Americans at this defining moment in our history. (PFAW 2006)

The AEI and the PFAW are transparently biased.

Hidden biases are much more problematic than transparent biases. In general, if an expert's biases are transparent *and* the other conditions for the assumption of a premise based on expertise have been met, you may use that expert's statements as assumed premises. When it comes to biases, the condition of expert consensus (which is discussed below) is particularly important. If both the AEI and the PFAW were to assert the same statement, this statement could be appropriately used as an assumed premise.

It's hard to know your own biases. Tyler might be biased against people who are overweight. He might unconsciously assume that the arguments made by overweight people are worse than those made by those who aren't overweight. Suppose that Tyler is a manager who supervises a large group of people and that he makes decisions about how his company should use its employees. Tyler's two associate managers favor different uses, and each presents Tyler with arguments for their view. One of the associate managers is overweight. Tyler might incorrectly find that the arguments made by the overweight associate manager are weaker than those made by the other associate manager.

Appropriate Area of Expertise

A statement by an expert should only be used as an assumed premise if the statement falls within the expert's area of expertise. Suppose that one of the authors of this textbook said:

Transmission fluid is usually green.

It wouldn't be appropriate to use this statement as an assumed premise because we aren't experts about automotive mechanics. On the other hand,

Critical Thinkers

Mahzarin Banaji, Anthony Greenwald, Brian Nosek

Mahzarin Banaji, Anthony Greenwald, and **Brian Nosek** have developed a test that they believe reveals people's hidden biases. They call it the Implicit Association Test (IAT). If you go to implicit.harvard. edu/implicit, you can see their results and even take their tests to see whether, according to these researchers, you have unconscious biases.

given the expertise of the authors of this book, it would be appropriate for you to use our statement that

Human rights are one kind of moral rights.

as an assumed premise.

Fallacy: Inappropriate Expertise

Famous athletes who know a great deal about their sports are frequently seen making statements about cars, shampoo, motor oil, mortgages, and many other things. None of these statements should be used as an assumed premise. An argument that contains a premise that's assumed on the basis of expertise but is about an issue outside an expert's area of expertise commits the fallacy of **Inappropriate Expertise**.

Albert Einstein has become a misused expert. In addition to his groundbreaking work in physics, he became known during World War II because of a letter he wrote to President Roosevelt about atomic experiments being carried out by Nazi scientists in Germany. Because Einstein's knowledge helped spur the United States to concentrate more intensely on its own atomic program, many thought that Einstein helped bring the war to a quicker end. For the rest of Einstein's life and even after his death, his name was constantly associated with genius. Reporters asked his opinion on everything from breakfast cereal to political candidates, a host of things that were irrelevant to his expert knowledge of physics.

Key Concept
An argument that contains a premise that's assumed on the basis of expertise but is about an issue outside an expert's area of expertise commits the fallacy of **Inappropriate Expertise**.

Technical Term: Appeal to an Inappropriate Authority, *Argumentum ad Verecundiam*

The fallacy of Inappropriate Expertise is also called the fallacy of Appeal to an Inappropriate Authority. The Latin name for this fallacy is *Argumentum ad Verecundiam.*

Expert Consensus

If experts disagree about the truth of a statement, you shouldn't use that statement as an assumed premise. Disagreement between experts is an opportunity for critical thinking. You should examine the arguments of the disagreeing experts. Now that you're becoming familiar with what makes a good argument, you're in a better position to critically evaluate the arguments made by experts.

Habits of a Critical Thinker

Resourcefulness

The task of deciding whether an argument passes the true premises test can be daunting. You need to check to see whether an empirical statement is uncontroversial, examine testimonial statements, consider whether a statement is an appropriate use of definition, and consider the criteria for the evaluation of statements by experts. Doing these things requires you to be resourceful. A resourceful person figures out many different ways to get the job done. And evaluating premises requires you to do many different things. For example, to determine whether a person is an appropriate expert you may need to do more than a simple web search. You might have to interview people or check court records. You might have to examine other works by this person. A good critical thinker is resourceful, figuring out the best way to evaluate premises.

Students often forget to check for disagreement between experts. If you only examine the view of one expert, it's impossible for you to determine whether the view you're reading is held by many experts or is the subject of intense debate. Before you use a statement of an expert as an assumed premise, you should check at least two experts.

GUIDE

Proper Citation of Experts

When you use an assumed premise on the grounds that it was made by an expert, you must cite the expert. Citations serve two functions. First, they show where your assumed premise came from so others can check it for themselves. Second, they give proper credit to experts for the work they've done. When you get an idea from an expert but don't cite it, you're asserting that you came up with the idea yourself. Failure to cite experts is theft of ideas. It's plagiarism.

How to Cite

Citations come in many formats. The rules for capitalization, punctuation, etc. vary dramatically from discipline to discipline. To illustrate this, let's look at one article cited in two different formats. Here's an example of what's often called "science format."

> Carnevale, G. (2006). A new snake mackerel from the Miocene of Algeria. *Palaeontology* 49, 391–403.

Here's an example of the same article cited in what's often called "Chicago style."

> 1. Giorgio Carnevale, "A New Snake Mackerel From the Miocene of Algeria," *Palaeontology* 49 (2006): 391–403.

The second format is called "Chicago style" because it comes from *The Chicago Manual of Style*. This book tells academics how to cite the hundreds of different materials that they may need to cite. Science format and Chicago style are only two of many different formats.

In addition to using different formats, different rules govern the placement of citations. In science format, a reference to the article above would be made by putting

> (Carnevale 2006)

into the text of the article at the place at which the author wishes to refer to Carnevale's article. In Chicago style, there would be a "1" in the text and then the material above would either appear at the bottom of the page or at the end of the chapter or book. The "1" in the text would be in superscript; like this: [1].

You'll use different citation formats for different classes. You should consult with your instructor regarding the proper citation format for that class. When you've chosen a major, you should buy a good citation guide for that discipline. Any faculty member in your major discipline should be able to point you to the standard citation reference work for her discipline.

What You Need to Cite

You must cite all uses of others' ideas. This means that *whenever* you use an expert's ideas, you need to cite that expert. If you use the words of others, you've used their ideas and must provide a citation. But you can use other people's ideas without using their words, and when you do that you still must provide a citation. It doesn't matter whether you use the words the expert wrote. You must always give credit where credit is due.

Premises and the Internet

The internet is a powerful tool for researching premises. Like all powerful tools, the internet can be misused. Think about empirical statements. Finding information about them used to require a trip to the library or at least reading from the thick volumes of an encyclopedia. Now you can go on the internet. But there's one big problem when you compare the internet to a library or an encyclopedia. Anyone can post anything to the internet. There's very little quality control, and much of what's on the web is false.

Here's an example from the web page english.pravda.ru. This web site claims to be the English language version of a web successor to the Russian newspaper *Pravda*, which was the official newspaper of the Communist party in Soviet Russia. (The authors of this textbook have been unable to verify these claims.)

> If aliens visited the Earth, their traces would be unusual, preternatural and having no scientific explanation. There have been plenty of such artifacts.
>
> In the Libyan desert mysterious glassy formations—tektites—were found. Radioactive isotopes were detected in the tektites. They prove that the tektites came into being as a result of strong radioactive emanation not earlier than one million years ago. The Earth was formed not millions, but billions of years ago, and tektites appeared on the formed planet. There were many attempts to give the explanation to these mysterious formations. There was a version that they appeared after a comet collided with the Earth, but no version was able to explain many peculiar features of tektites, such as their concentration on some areas of the surface of the Earth. (*Pravda* 2006)

These statements aren't uncontroversial empirical statements. They aren't definitions. No expert is identified. You can't check for appropriate credentials, reliability, lack of bias, or appropriate area of expertise. None of these claims should be used as an assumed premise.

Tektites.

The internet has also made researching the credentials of people who say that they're experts easier and more dangerous. People who want others to think that they're an expert actuary could quickly create a web site for a fake group, the Association of Actuaries, and claim to be the President of this Association. You can't assume that the credentials you find on the web are accurate.

What can you do about these problems with the internet? Parts of the internet are subject to quality control, and you need to restrict your research to those parts. Because you're a college student, the most important kind of organization that controls a portion of the web is your college. Universities work hard to see that the information in their web pages is accurate. University libraries review internet resources and give students access to reliable resources. Your library and its librarians are one of your best resources for navigating the internet.

A Common Mistake

What does it mean when you don't have a good reason to assume a premise? Students sometimes jump from the claim that

A statement shouldn't be used as an assumed premise.

to the claim that

The statement is false.

Don't make this mistake. Even if a statement shouldn't be used as an assumed premise, that doesn't mean that the statement is false. It only means that the statement shouldn't be assumed to be true, that you should seek a subargument for the premise. When it comes to beliefs about the truth or falsity of a statement you have at least three options.

1. You can believe that the statement is true.
2. You can believe that the statement is false.
3. You can believe that you don't know whether the statement is true or false.

People often overlook option 3.

Connections

Chapter Two notes that "I don't know" is often the correct answer to a question.

EXERCISE 3.3

A. Identify the expert appealed to in each of the following passages and then identify the claims made by the expert. Determine whether each of the claims can be assumed to pass the true premises test.

1. "'The organic market has grown and so has the temptation for organic fraud,' said Robynn Shrader, chief executive officer for the NCGA (National Cooperative Grocers Association). Our program will add a very critical safety checkpoint in the supply chain that will empower retailers and provide peace of mind for organic consumers." (Smith 2007, 3, material omitted)

2. "Any employee who is convicted of unlawful manufacture, distribution, sale, use or possession of a controlled substance or other illegal or dangerous drug, or who admits guilt of any such offense in a court proceeding, shall be suspended for not less than two months or dismissed after compliance with procedural requirements." (*Safety Net* 2006, 15)

3. From a brochure announcing the publication of a book for an introduction to philosophy course: "[This] is an outstanding book on all fronts. The top-notch introductory essays and extensive glossary make the book extremely user-friendly from the student's perspective." (Stanley 2006)

*4. "Roger Penrose (1989, 1994) has argued that creative mathematicians do not think in a mechanistic way, but that they often have a kind of insight into the Platonic realm which exists independently from us [though] modesty forbids him saying it of himself. [Roger Penrose] has enjoyed some of the most profound mathematical experiences of recent times. If he has nothing more than a mere hunch that he is glimpsing into the Platonic realm, that in itself is something for us all to ponder." (Brown 1999, 78, material omitted)

5. "A liberal arts education is associated with an increase in humanitarianism and a sense of civic responsibility, a greater interest in and more liberal attitudes toward a variety of social and political issues, and greater regard for civil rights and higher levels of tolerance related to social, racial, and ethnic diversity." (Henderson-King 2000, 142–143, material omitted)

6. "Policymakers that are accountable to the public should be more responsive to civil society organisations since they are reliant on the public for re-election and organized interests represent citizen interests." (Mahoney 2007, 338)

7. "Emotion must be included in a discussion of body intelligence because it is one of the means by which our bodies communicate knowledge to conscious awareness." (Norris 2001, 113)

*8. "Since communication can take place directly through the body, the body can be intentionally used to transmit information." (Norris 2001, 116)

9. Suppose a representative of Bayer were to propose the following argument to support the conclusion that aspirin, or acetylsalicylic acid, is an effective cure against the common cold:

   (1) 95% of aspirin users are of the opinion that aspirin is an effective remedy against the common cold.

   Therefore,

   (2) Aspirin is an effective remedy against the common cold.

10. "According to Bourdieu (1977), schools perpetuate inequality by rewarding the culture (i.e., behavior, habits, tastes, lifestyles, and attitudes) of the dominant class." (Ross 1999, 447)

11. "Raphael (1996a, 2000) argued that as welfare recipients are pushed to move into the labor market, their dependence on the state may be eliminated, but it is replaced by increased dependence on abusive partners." (Scott 2002, 881)

*12. "In his survey of Arab cities during the Ottoman period, Andre Raymond states, 'The number of caravanserais serves as a definitive index of the amount of economic activity in a city.' According to Raymond, the urban khan governs the level of whole-sale trade in an exclusive fashion, thereby serving as an absolute indicator of the amount of large-scale commercial activity in a given city." (Um 2003, 180–181, material omitted)

13. "The main motivation for this paper stems from the observation that in the 1980s and 1990s firms invested heavily in downsizing. Recent examples are National Westminster bank, AT&T, IBM and Scott Paper. As documented by Audretsch (1995: p. 27), Cameron (1994b), The Economist (1996a), Sampson (1995) and Kets de Vries and Balazs (1997), the mass firings that followed from this downsizing to a great extent involved middle managers." (Boone 2000, 581)

14. "Five volunteers watching the republican presidential debate in Miami, in December 2007, were wearing electrode-studded headsets that track electrical activity in the brain. When presidential candidate Mitt Romney said he was the only candidate to have got-ten the problem of healthcare solved, "there was a pronounced shift in activity in their prefrontal lobes. 'They liked what they were hearing,' said Brad Feldman, an analyst with EmSence Corp., the company that conducted the test to monitor voters' brains." (Alter 2007, W1)

15. " 'People say one thing in a focus group and do another thing in the voting booth' says Alex Lundry, research director for TargetPoint, a campaign strategy consultancy." (Alter 2007, W6)

B. Determine whether each of the following would be a good premise and why or why not. Explicitly use the guidelines discussed above. To do some of these exercises, you will need to find and consult the citations page of this book.

1. There are at least five planets visible to the naked eye.

2. "The subprime mortgage crisis has been a financial disaster for much of Wall Street" wrote Kate Kelley, reporter for the *Wall Street Journal*. (Kelley 2007, A1)

3. According to my neighbor who watched the nightly news last night, the subprime mort-gage crisis has been a financial disaster.

*4. Kate Kelly, of the *Wall Street Journal* reported that "Mr. Blankfein is set to be paid close to $70 million this year, according to one person familiar with the matter." (Kelley 2007, A1)

5. You probably decided whether to accept #4 as a premise based on the credentials of re-porter Kate Kelly. But should Kate Kelly accept the claim about Blankfein's salary, based on the testimony of "one person familiar with the matter"?

6. Use the material from Exercise 3.3 A.14 above.

7. Use the material from Exercise 3.3 A.15 above.

*8. "The term basketry refers to woven textiles created manually without a frame or loom." (Berman 2000, 422)

9. "We observed 29 instances of wicker (FIG. 12), constituting 11.24% of the basketry weaves." (Berman 2000, 427)

10. "[O]ne of the best recent works, Wang Lixin's *Meiguo chuanjiaoshi yu wan Qing Zhong-guo xiandaihua* (*American Missionaries and the Modernization of China in the Late Qing*), argues that American missionaries, rather than being tools of cultural or other imperialism, were actually engaged in 'cultural exchange,' making a significant contribution to China's modernization in the late Qing period." (Dunch 2002, 316)

11. "Powerful storms have caused mass mortality of at least 10 Caribbean mangrove forests during the past 50 years." (Cahoon 2003, 1094)

*12. "A liberal arts education is associated with an increase in humanitarianism and a sense of civic responsibility, a greater interest in and more liberal attitudes toward a variety of social and political issues and greater regard for civil rights and higher levels of tolerance related to social, racial, and ethnic diversity." (Henderson-King 2000, 142, material omitted)

13. "The landscape, when considered through a contemporary aesthetic lens, is already a cultural 'sculptural' form marked and transformed through thousands of years of human activity." (Tilley 2000, 36)

14. George Clooney, well-known celebrity for his roles on television and the big screen, spoke to the United Nations in 2006, asking the UN to help the people in Darfur who were suffering due to group conflicts. (Note: To determine this, you will need to do some research about George Clooney and his knowledge of Darfur.)

15. In the United States, most lawyers specialize in a particular area of the law because it is nearly impossible to have specialized knowledge about all different areas of the law. Suppose that Mr. Smith becomes a member of the state bar of New York. He works exclusively as a criminal defense attorney and comes to be recognized as an expert in criminal law. Now suppose that a reporter interviews Mr. Smith about one of his famous criminal defense cases and that at the end of the interview the reporter asks Mr. Smith who will prevail in a high profile case in which a recording company is suing a celebrity musician for breach of contract (a matter of contract law). The celebrity claims the contract cannot be enforced because the record company didn't give sufficient consideration for its bargain. Mr. Smith, never shy about offering his opinion, states that the contract shouldn't be enforced because no consideration was given in his view. Can Mr. Smith's statement about the musician's contract case be used as assumed premise?

C. Evaluate the credentials of the authors of this book.

  1. Look at the front of this book to find our names and the name of the university where we work.

  2. Then search the web to determine our positions, degrees, publications, and awards.

D. Identify the four empirical statements and two definitions in the following passage.

  "Most of us grew up with the conventional definition of a planet as a body that orbits a star, shines by reflecting the star's light and is larger than an asteroid. Although the definition may not have been very precise, it clearly categorized the bodies we knew at the time. In the 1990s, however, a remarkable series of discoveries made it untenable. Beyond the orbit of Neptune, astronomers found hundreds of icy worlds, some quite large, occupying a doughnut-shaped region called the Kuiper belt. Around scores of other stars, they found other planets, many of whose orbits look nothing like those in our solar system. They discovered brown dwarfs, which blur the distinction between planet and star. And they found planet-like objects drifting alone in the darkness of interstellar space. These findings ignited a debate about what a planet really is and led to the decision last August by the International Astronomical Union (IAU), astronomers' main professional society, to define a planet as an object that orbits a star, is large enough to have settled into a round shape and, crucially, "has cleared the neighborhood around its orbit." Controversially, the new definition removes Pluto from the list of planets." (Soter 2007, 34)

E. "Less than a decade ago, the biggest problem in global health seemed to be the lack of resources available to combat the multiple scourges ravaging the world's poor and sick. Today, thanks to a recent extraordinary and unprecedented rise in public and private giving, more money is being directed toward pressing health challenges than ever before. But because the efforts this money is paying for are largely uncoordinated and directed mostly at specific high-profile diseases—rather than at public health in general—there is a grave danger that the current age of generosity could not only fall short of expectations but actually make things worse on the ground. (Garrett 2007, 14)

Imagine that someone makes the following argument, relying on and quoting some of Garrett's claims. Evaluate the premises of this argument.

(1) "Less than a decade ago, the biggest problem in global health seemed to be the lack of resources available to combat the multiple scourges ravaging the world's poor and sick."

(2) "Today, thanks to a recent extraordinary and unprecedented rise in public and private giving, more money is being directed toward pressing health challenges than ever before."

Therefore,

(3) Experts in global health believe we are making progress on the problem of global health.

Conclusions

Two features are crucial to assessing the conclusions of arguments: strength and scope.

Strength of Conclusions

A conclusion can be stated with more or less strength. Let's suppose that all of the following statements are offered as conclusions:

(a) It's just possible that inflation will rise next year.
(b) Inflation may rise next year.
(c) There is a good chance that inflation will rise next year.
(d) Inflation is likely to rise next year.
(e) Inflation is very likely to rise next year.
(f) It's certain that inflation will rise next year.

Each of these sentences expresses the same statement.

(A) Inflation will rise next year.

But (a) through (f) express (A) with varying degrees of strength. Statement (a) expresses (A) weakly. Statement (f) expresses (A) with a great deal of strength. These statements use only some of the ways that you can indicate the strength of a conclusion. Words such as "might," "could," "should," "probably," "definitely," and many others can be used to indicate the strength of a conclusion. The **strength of a conclusion** refers to the degree of certainty that the author of an argument attributes to the conclusion.

As conclusions get stronger they require more evidence to support them. If your conclusion is (a), it wouldn't take that much evidence. But it would require a lot of evidence to show that (f) is true. In fact, you probably couldn't provide enough evidence to show that (f) is true.

> **Technical Terms: Strength of Arguments and Strength of Conclusions**
>
> Logicians use the word "strength" to refer both to good inductive arguments and to conclusions. This leads to confusing sentences such as: "We have a strong argument for a weak conclusion." However, this double usage of the word "strength" is so common that this textbook adopts it. When you see the words "strong" or "weak" discussed in the context of arguments, you need to read carefully to see whether the words refer to the argument or to the conclusion.

Scope of Conclusions

Some conclusions are about groups of things. When a conclusion is about a group of things, the conclusion will have a scope. Look at the following statements:

(a) There is at least one person who is taller than the authors of this book.
(b) Some people are taller than the authors of this book.
(c) Quite a few people are taller than the authors of this book.
(d) About half of all people are taller than the authors of this book.
(e) Most people are taller than the authors of this book.
(f) Everyone is taller than the authors of this book.

Statement (a) is true and (f) is false. Statement (a) has narrower scope. Statement (f) has broader scope. In fact, (a) has the narrowest possible scope and (f) has the broadest possible scope. **Scope refers to the percentage of a group in a conclusion that's claimed to have a particular feature.** The broader the scope of a conclusion, the better the argument in support of that conclusion needs to be. It wouldn't take much of an argument to defend (a). It would take an extremely good argument to show that (f) is true.

Key Concept

The **strength of a conclusion** refers to the degree of certainty that the author of an argument attributes to the conclusion.

how strongly the person state

Key Concept

Scope refers to the percentage of a group in a conclusion that's claimed to have a particular feature.

If a conclusion refers to more than one group, it will have more than one scope. Look at the statement:

(g) Most trees are taller than some houses.

This statement refers to two groups, trees and houses. Its scope with respect to trees is broader than its scope with respect to houses.

In addition to a conclusion having multiple scopes, it can have ambiguous scope. Look at the statement:

(h) People are taller than the authors of this book.

Is this statement asserting (a), (f), or something in between? It makes a big difference, and you can't answer this question because this statement has ambiguous scope.

When you're evaluating arguments, you should note the strength and the scope of the conclusion. The stronger the conclusion and the broader its scope, the better an argument will have to be in order to provide a good reason to believe the conclusion. Very strong conclusions and very broad conclusions should attract your attention. While you can defend strong and broad conclusions, it's often difficult to do so.

EXERCISE 3.4

A. Arrange the following statements from weakest to strongest.

1. It will probably rain tomorrow.

2. It is almost certain to rain tomorrow.

3. It may rain tomorrow.

4. It will rain tomorrow.

5. It is nearly impossible that it will rain tomorrow.

B. For each of the following, determine whether the scope and strength of the conclusion is warranted.

1. I have known five members of the Green party and all have been from France. Ralph Nader and Cynthia McKinney are members of the Green party, so they too are most likely from France.

[handwritten: not justified]

2. The great physician Dr. Dominose of Harvard University has done extensive research on nutritional needs. He has found that if a man weighs more than 500 pounds, that man would require as much protein as would be found in 30 pizzas in order to sustain himself. It is thus clear that everyone should eat 30 pizzas per day.

[handwritten: not justified]

3. In early 2009, there were several cases of the disease SARS reported by the Chinese government. Clearly, by 2011, there will be a SARS epidemic of tremendous proportions.

*4. "Usually, girls who become cheerleaders in middle school are already part of the in-group (e.g., Preps) at school; thus, a congruity exists between peer groups and the social status of an activity." (Bettis 2003, 130)

5. "Any war between the two Chinas [the People's Republic of China and Taiwan] could easily involve the United States. Under the 1979 Taiwan Relations Act, official U.S. law stipulates that the United States would view any conflict over Taiwan with 'grave concern.' The 1995–96 Taiwan Strait crisis showed that the United States does not take its interest in Taiwan's security lightly." (O'Hanlon 2000, 42)

6. I have visited three condominium communities and each had monthly assessments of $300 or more. I shouldn't buy a condo since I don't want to spend that much on assessments.

7. Tom Cruise is a scientologist. So is John Travolta. It seems that all movie stars are scientologists.

*8. "Its high content of alpha linolenic acids has made the ancient flax seed become our modern miracle food. Alpha linolenic acid is a type of plant-derived omega 3 fatty acid, similar to those found in fish such as salmon. Benefits of flax seed include lowering total cholesterol and LDL cholesterol (the Bad cholesterol) levels. [F]lax seed may also help lower blood triglyceride and blood pressure. It may also keep platelets from becoming sticky therefore reducing the risk of a heart attack. Aside from alpha linolenic acid, flax seed is rich in lignan. Lignan is a type of phytoestrogen (antioxidant) and also provides fiber. Research reveals that lignan in flax seed shows a lot of promise in fighting disease—including a possible role in cancer prevention, especially breast cancer. Moderately include flax seed in your diet." (Tsang 2009, material omitted)

9. Anyone processing photographic films and papers that use silver nitrate is familiar with the pungent aroma of chemical developers. I've worked with it and known hundreds of others who have, and we all agree it's a bad smell. I've never met anyone who disagreed. Likely, anyone you meet will also think the smell is bad.

10. Fifty percent of marriages end in divorce. Hence, it is certain that your marriage will end in divorce.

11. "Although dependencies on violent men may have preexisted welfare reform and exist for some women who have never had to rely on welfare, they could be exacerbated by changes in the welfare regulations." (Scott 2002, 892, material omitted)

*12. "The upper stories of the house, inhabited and used collectively by the family, could be securely closed off from the lower level by a door at the top of the stairs. It is possible that this upper door, rather than the front entrance to the house, acted as the true threshold to the domestic space. Today the current inhabitants enter and leave via the front door, which is kept unlocked and open. They lock only the upper door, which is unornamented and smaller, but seems to fulfill a more central function as a social boundary." (Um 2003, 185)

C. For the next two exercises, think about the following argument:

(1) Bipeds are two-footed animals.

Therefore,

(2) George Bush is a biped.

1. Explain why the premise doesn't support the conclusion by itself.

2. Provide the premise that is needed to support the conclusion.

3. Explain in your own words why stronger conclusions require stronger arguments.

*4. Give an example that illustrates that stronger conclusions require stronger arguments.

For the next two exercises, think about the following argument:

"In *Born to Rebel*, F. Sulloway (1996) argued that, throughout history, later-borns have been more likely than first-borns to challenge the status quo. The authors tested Sulloway's hypothesis among a group of U.S. college students who had participated in civil disobedience as part of a labor dispute. The authors predicted that there would be a higher percentage of later-borns among those who had been arrested than among a group of their friends who had not participated in civil disobedience or among a control group of students drawn from classes at the college. The findings, in fact, revealed a significant relationship between the number of times the students had been arrested and birth order."

In stating the results of their study, Zweignhaft and Von Ammon noted, "When we examined the number of times the participants had been arrested (none, one, or more than one) in terms of their birth orders (first-borns, including only children, and later-borns), we found that 24 of the 56 (43%) who had not been arrested were later-borns, that 6 of the 12 (50%) who had been arrested once were later-borns, and that all 5 (100%) of those who had been arrested more than once were later-borns." (Zweigenhaft 2000, 624)

5. Given the findings of the study, what is the strongest conclusion that can be supported?

    (a) The study shows that it is possible that there is a relationship between birth order and the likelihood someone has been arrested.

    (b) The study shows that it is likely that there is a relationship between birth order and the likelihood someone has been arrested.

    (c) The study shows that there is certainly a relationship between birth order and the likelihood someone has been arrested.

6. Which of the following statements is best supported by the evidence?

    (a) In the study, some later-borns had been arrested.

    (b) In the study, most later-borns had been arrested.

    (c) In the study, all later-borns had been arrested.

For the next two exercises, look at the following argument:

"Women who take fish oil supplements while pregnant may improve the hand-eye coordination of their children, according to a small Australian study. In a trial published online Dec. 21 in The Archives of Disease in Childhood: Fetal and Neonatal Edition, scientists divided 98 women into two groups. Beginning at 20 weeks of pregnancy continuing until the women gave birth, the first group took a daily dose of four grams of fish oil, while the second group took four grams of olive oil each day. Neither the mothers nor the researchers knew which supplement the women had received until the study ended. The researchers examined 72 children born to women who completed the study when the children were 2½ years old. In tests of locomotor ability, speech and hearing, vocabulary and practical reasoning, the children whose mothers were given fish oil during pregnancy scored slightly higher, but the differences were not statistically significant. However, after controlling for maternal age, birth weight, breast-feeding and other factors, the children of the women who took fish oil were significantly better at hand-eye coordination than those of the women who took the olive oil supplement. The authors acknowledged that their sample was small, and that they could not exclude the possibility that the result was due to chance. Still, children who received prenatal fish oil did consistently perform better on all measures of development. "These preliminary data indicate that supplementation with a relatively high-dose fish oil during the last 20 weeks of pregnancy is not only safe," the authors concluded, "but also seems to have potential beneficial effects that need to be explored further." (Bakalar 2007, F6)

7. Given the findings of the study, what is the strongest conclusion that can be supported?

    (a) The study shows that it is possible that prenatal exposure to fish oil improves a child's hand-eye coordination.

(b) The study shows that it is very probable that prenatal exposure to fish oil improves a child's hand-eye coordination.

(c) The study shows with certainty that prenatal exposure to fish oil improves a child's hand-eye coordination.

*8. From the information provided in the passage above, what should you say about the scope of the findings?

(a) Some children who had prenatal exposure to fish oil had better hand-eye coordination than those without prenatal exposure to fish oil.

(b) Most children who had prenatal exposure to fish oil had better hand-eye coordination than those without prenatal exposure to fish oil.

(c) All children who had prenatal exposure to fish oil had better hand-eye coordination than those without prenatal exposure to fish oil.

(d) Given the information in the passage, the scope cannot be properly assessed.

For the next two exercises, look at the following argument:

"A new study of Sumatran orangutans in Indonesia suggests that ancient apes may have developed upright walking while still living in the trees—well before human ancestors, known as hominids, ever descended to the ground. The study authors spent many hours observing Sumatran orangutans as they moved about the canopy of their rain forest home in Gunung Leuser National Park. The critically endangered animals—which number about 7,300 in the wild—live nearly their whole lives aloft. On sturdier branches the orangutans use all four limbs. But on thinner branches in search of fruit, the apes move on two legs and use their arms for balance. "When they are on the very fine stuff, they are using bipedalism," said study co-author Robin Crompton of the University of Liverpool in England. "It shows that bipedalism can be adaptive in the trees," Crompton said. "People have suspected that it evolved in the trees, but no one has been able to see a sensible reason why it should happen." The researchers think they've uncovered that sensible reason: Upright bipedalism in human ancestors was quite likely an adaptation to moving and feeding on ripe fruit in the peripheries of trees, they say." (Handwerk 2007, material omitted)

9. Which statement best describes the strongest conclusion about bipedalism in humans that one could draw from the study reported in this passage?

(a) It is just possible that in human ancestors, bipedalism started in trees.

(b) In the ancestors of humans, bipedalism may have started in trees.

(c) It is certain that in the ancestors of humans, bipedalism started in trees.

10. Which statement best describes the strongest conclusion about bipedalism in orangutans that one could draw from the study reported in the passage above?

(a) It is possible that upright bipedalism in orangutans helps these animals get access to food.

(b) It is likely that upright bipedalism in orangutans helps these animals get access to food.

(c) It is certain that upright bipedalism in orangutans helps these animals get access to food.

For the next two exercises, look at the following argument:

"Individuals aged 15 to 26 years were randomly sampled within households and households within media markets. Markets were systematically selected from the top 75 media markets, representing 79% of the U.S. population. The baseline refusal rate was 24%. Sample sizes per wave were 1872, 1173, 787, and 588. Data on alcohol advertising expenditures on television, radio, billboards, and newspapers were collected. Youth who saw more alcohol advertisements on average drank more (each additional advertisement seen increased the number of drinks consumed by 1% [event rate ratio, 1.01; 95% confidence interval, 1.01–1.02]). Youth in markets with greater alcohol advertising expenditures drank more (each additional dollar spent per capita raised the number of drinks consumed by 3% [event rate ratio, 1.03; 95% confidence interval, 1.01–1.05]). Examining only youth younger than the legal drinking age of 21 years, alcohol advertisement exposure and expenditures still related to drinking. Youth in markets with more alcohol advertisements showed increases in drinking levels into their late 20s, but drinking plateaued in the early 20s for youth in markets with fewer advertisements. Control variables included age, gender, ethnicity, high school or college enrollment, and alcohol sales. Conclusion. Alcohol advertising contributes to increased drinking among youth." (Snyder 2006, 18, material omitted)

11. From the information provided in the passage, the scope of the conclusion, "alcohol advertising contributes to increased drinking among youth," is ambiguous. Given the information provided, which of the following statements do you think one could safely conclude?

    (a) All youth exposed to alcohol advertising drink more than all youth not exposed.

    (b) Some youth exposed to alcohol advertising drink more than some youth not exposed.

*12. Is it possible to show that statement (a) above is true? Why or why?

For the next two exercises, look at the following argument:

"Nexavar, a drug currently on the U.S. market to treat kidney cancer, was shown to "significantly" extend survival in patients with liver cancer. A study of 602 patients showed those receiving Nexavar had a median overall survival of 10.7 months compared to 7.9 months among patients taking placebo. About half the patients received Nexavar while the other half received placebo, or a fake treatment. Patients in the study had advanced liver cancer that could not be cured by surgery. Researchers said the survival difference translates into a significant 44% survival advantage for patients in the Nexavar group compared to those in the placebo group." (Dooren 2007, D1, material omitted)

13. The conclusion provided in the excerpt above has an ambiguous scope. Given the information provided, which of the following statements do you think one could safely conclude?

    (a) Among individuals with liver cancer who participated in the study, a few patients taking Nexavar live longer than a few patients who take a placebo.

    (b) Among individuals with liver cancer who participated in the study, many patients taking Nexavar live longer than some patients who take a placebo.

14. Now think about the strength of the conclusion, which is also ambiguous: "Nexavar, a drug currently on the U.S. market to treat kidney cancer, was shown to 'significantly' extend survival in patients with liver cancer." Which of the following statements do you think best describes how strongly the author likely intends the conclusion to be?

    (a) It is just possible that Nexavar can extend the life of those with liver cancer.

    (b) Nexavar may extend the life of those with liver cancer.

    (c) It is very likely that Nexavar can extend the life of those with liver cancer.

    (d) It is certain that Nexavar can extend the life of those with liver cancer.

For the next exercise think about the following argument:

"In the U.S., certain health conditions are readily accepted as 'public-health disorders,' and others continue to be primarily viewed as 'clinical diseases.' Reflecting on infectious conditions, it appears that disease burden, rapid change in disease incidence (suggesting preventability), and public concern about risk are three essential characteristics that define a public-health disorder. By any one of several criteria, diabetes is associated with a very high burden to individuals with the disease, as well as to society in general. Further, there is convincing and increasing evidence that primary, secondary, and tertiary prevention strategies are effective in reducing the disease burden associated with diabetes. Yet most would still consider diabetes primarily to be a clinical disease. In part, this perception is based on the fact that, in association with aging and a possible strong family history, diabetes and its complications may appear inevitable to many. Further, much of the burden associated with diabetes is insidious, coming on gradually only after a considerable number of years. Thus, the burden associated with diabetes has not dramatically increased in the past few months or years; it has been here for some time and is increasing steadily. Finally, our understanding of public concern is only now being systematically investigated. Factors that galvanize the public to demand societal or governmental action are quite complex and very different from those elements that convince the scientist/expert to request 'public-health responses.' Legitimate and important public-health dimensions associated with diabetes complement the critical role of clinical care. To effectively establish these public-health perspectives, public concern must be incorporated into efforts to define the burden of diabetes and our extant ability to prevent and thereby reduce this burden." (Vinicor 1994, 22)

15. What is the strongest conclusion one should draw from the argument above?

(a) Diabetes must be treated as a public health issue and not a clinical disease.

(b) Diabetes probably would be better treated as a public health issue instead of a clinical disease.

(c) Diabetes should continue to be treated as a clinical matter because physicians and the public don't agree on the conditions required for something to be called a public health matter.

Chapter Summary

Some premises have to be assumed. Three main sources for assumed premises are uncontroversially true empirical statements, uncontroversially true definitional statements, and appropriate statements by experts. Some empirical statements are based on observations directly from our own senses. Others are based on indirect observations through the use of instruments (such as telescopes and microscopes) or on the reports of the observations made by others. Indirect observations based on the reports of others are testimonial empirical statements.

They may be assumed if they are plausibile and the person making the report is reliable. Statements made by experts may be assumed to pass the true premises tests when the experts have appropriate credentials, are reliable, unbiased, have an appropriate area of expertise, and there is expert consensus about the statement.

When reviewing arguments, you should note the strength and the scope of the conclusions. Arguments with weak and narrow conclusions are more likely to be good arguments than arguments with stronger and broader conclusions.

4 Language

It is a truth universally acknowledged, that a single man in possession of a good fortune, must be in want of a wife.

However little known the feelings or views of such a man may be on his first entering a neighbourhood, this truth is so well fixed in the minds of the surrounding families, that he is considered the rightful property of some one or other of their daughters.

"My dear Mr. Bennet," said his lady to him one day, "have you heard that Netherfield Park is let at last?"

Mr. Bennet replied that he had not.

"But it is," returned she; "for Mrs. Long has just been here, and she told me all about it."

Mr. Bennet made no answer.

"Do you not want to know who has taken it?" cried his wife impatiently.

"You want to tell me, and I have no objection to hearing it."

This was invitation enough.

—Jane Austen, *Pride and Prejudice* (2008, 3)

Learning Outcomes

After studying the material in this chapter, you should be able to:

1. Understand why language is important to the evaluation of arguments.

2. Identify and evaluate definitions.

3. Understand the importance of clear language.

4. Recognize and avoid ambiguity and vagueness.

5. Understand the links between language and emotion.

The passage on the previous page contains an argument. But it may be hard for you to find it because *Pride and Prejudice* was written in the early 1800s and you aren't used to the language. Understanding language is vital because all arguments are presented and evaluated in a language.

Identifying Definitions

The conclusion of Mrs. Bennet's argument is "Netherfield Park is let at last." What's Netherfield Park? And what does it mean to "let" it? If you don't know the answers to these questions, you can't evaluate Mrs. Bennet's argument. Only by reading *Pride and Prejudice* can you discover that Netherfield Park is a mansion. If you look in a dictionary, you'll discover that a definition of "let" is "to become rented." Mrs. Bennet's conclusion is that the mansion at Netherfield Park has finally been rented.

If you don't understand the language of a passage, you can't do the true premises test because you don't know whether the statement is true or false. If you don't understand the language of a passage, you can't do the proper form test because you can't tell whether the premises support the conclusion. One key to understanding the language of a passage is to know the meaning of its words. A **definition** is a statement giving the meaning of a word. Good definitions are essential because they help you understand statements, and understanding statements is required to do the true premises and proper form tests.

Key Concept
A **definition** is a statement giving the meaning of a word.

Extension and Intension

This textbook focuses on definitions for nouns and verbs. Nouns and verbs are **class terms**, terms that refer to a group of things. The word "mansion" is a noun that refers to mansions, a class of objects. The word "let" is a verb that refers to renting, a class of actions. Every definition of a class term indicates the word's extensional meaning and its intensional meaning. The **extension** of a class term is the collection of things in its class. Take the class term "planet." The extension of "planet" is: Mercury, Venus, Earth, Mars, Jupiter, etc. To be complete, this list would have to be really long because it would have to include every planet, including those orbiting stars other than our Sun.

Key Concept
Nouns and verbs are **class terms**, terms that refer to a group of things.

Key Concept
The **extension** of a class term is the collection of things in its class.

The **intension** of a class term is the collection of features that all of the members of the class have in common. The intension of "planet" is:

an object that does not produce its own light and revolves around a star.

Key Concept
The **intension** of a class term is the collection of features that all of the members of the class have in common.

Technical Term: Intensional

Students sometimes confuse the word "intensional" with the word "intentional." "Intentional" refers to an action that is done on purpose. You can say: "He intentionally drove his car into the telephone post." Although the two words look alike, "intensional" has nothing to do with "intentional."

The extension and the intension of a word inform each other. On the one hand, if you know that Mercury, Venus, and Mars are planets, you can tell something about the intension of the word by looking at the features that Mercury, Venus, and Mars share. On the other hand, in order to explain why Mercury belongs in the class of planets, you must know something about the intension of "planet."

The extension of "let" is all the cases in which someone has rented something. The intension of "let" is "to take and use for a limited period of time under an agreement to pay for this use."

GUIDE

Definitions and Quotation Marks

In standard American English, you put double quotation marks (" ") around a word to indicate that you are talking about the word itself and not about the thing for which the word stands. You should write

"Tree" has one syllable and four letters.

but

A tree fell on my car.

Technical Terms: Denotation, Connotation

The word "denotation" is sometimes used to refer to extension. The word "connotation" is sometimes used to refer to intension. In other cases, "denotation" is used to refer to the explicit meaning of a word, and "connotation" is used to refer to things associated with a word. Using words this way, the denotation of "apple" is the fleshy rounded red, yellow, or green edible fruit of a tree of the rose family. The connotation of "apple" includes health ("an apple a day keeps the doctor away") and sin (Genesis 3:2–6). Because "denotation" and "connotation" have two possible meanings, we'll use "extension" and "intension."

EXERCISE 4.1

A. For each of the following words, describe its extension and its intension. You may use a dictionary to complete this exercise. However, if you do so, be sure to cite the dictionary you're using.

   1. Dog
   2. Car
   3. Skipping
   *4. Writing
   5. Music

    6. Stipulate

    7. Benzene

  *8. Universalism

    9. Feminist

  10. Clarity

  11. Precision

*12. Courage

  13. Perfection

  14. Wisdom

  15. Justice

B. Determine whether the following passages contain a definition. If it contains a definition, indicate its extension and its intension.

    1. Winder Hall is made of stone.

    2. What's a flash memory stick? It's a flash memory data storage device integrated with a universal serial bus (USB) interface.

    3. Parents are mothers and fathers.

  *4. A roof is the cover of a building.

    5. A cup is an open, usually bowl-shaped, drinking vessel.

    6. A building is a house, an office, or a factory.

    7. It's cold and windy today.

  *8. As used in this document, a "professor" is an assistant professor, an associate professor, or a full professor.

    9. My calculator is dead.

  10. In French, children are *enfants*.

  11. A Coke? It's a carbonated soft drink.

*12. Many people like mushrooms.

  13. Caleb: What's that, Daddy?

    Daddy: It's a lawn mower, a machine that cuts grass.

  14. "An act of clemency is an official act by a [legal] executive that removes all or some of the actual or possible punitive consequences of a criminal conviction." (Moore 1989, 4, material omitted)

  15. "[A] society is a cooperative venture for mutual advantage." (Rawls 1971, 4, material omitted)

Genus and Species

Most definitions follow the genus/species format. A definition with a genus/species format defines a word by indicating (a) the genus (a group of which the thing being defined is a member) and (b) the species (the feature or features that set the particular thing to be defined apart from the other things in the group).

Key Concept
The parts of a definition with a genus/species format.

Look at this definition of "airplane":

An airplane is a vehicle that flies through the air.

The word being defined is "airplane," the genus is "vehicle," and the species is "flies through the air." "Vehicle" is the genus because a vehicle is a group of things and airplanes are one of the things in this group. "Flying through the air" is the species because it's the feature that sets airplanes apart from other vehicles. In this definition

An igloo is a dwelling made of packed snow or ice.

"igloo" is the word being defined, "dwelling" is the genus, and the species is "being made of packed snow or ice."

Compare the following definitions:

(a) A vehicle is an object used to transport people or objects.
(b) An airplane is a vehicle that flies through the air.
(c) A dog is a mammal that chases vehicles.

In (a), "vehicle" is the word being defined. In (b), "vehicle" is the genus, and in the (humorous) definition (c), "vehicle" is part of the species. Don't fall into the trap of thinking that a particular word (such as "vehicle") is either always a genus or always a species. Whether a word is a genus or a species isn't a permanent fact about that word. It's a matter of how the word is used in a particular definition.

Don't assume that the species must refer to one simple sort of thing. The species of a definition can be a complex list of things. Here's a definition of "flu":

Flu is a disease caused by one of many viruses that infect the respiratory tract and produce: fever (usually 100°F to 103°F in adults and often even higher in children), coughing, a sore throat, a stuffy nose, headache, muscle aches, and extreme fatigue.

The genus of this definition is "disease," and that's pretty simple, but the species is complex:

caused by one of many viruses that infect the respiratory tract and produce: fever (usually 100°F to 103°F in adults and often even higher in children), coughing, a sore throat, a stuffy nose, headache, muscle aches, and extreme fatigue.

Many different viruses cause the flu. You can have the flu and not have all the symptoms listed above. One person might not get a cough, another person might not get muscle aches, etc. The definition of "flu" has to have a complex species.

Technical Term: Genus and Difference

"Genus and difference" is another name for genus and species.

Dictionary Definitions

Two kinds of definitions need a special look: dictionary definitions and technical definitions. They're the most common kinds of definitions.

Flu Virus*

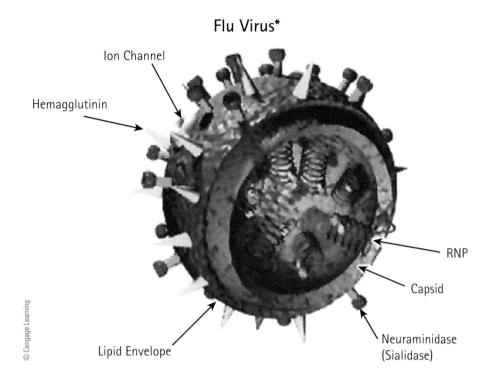

Ion Channel

Hemagglutinin

RNP

Capsid

Neuraminidase
(Sialidase)

Lipid Envelope

© Cengage Learning

Dictionary definitions are definitions that state the common usage of words. If the word being defined is a class term, dictionary definitions usually pick out the extension and intension of the word. Dictionaries generally use the genus/species format. Suppose you're reading a book and come across the word "kite," but it doesn't make sense to you because the topic makes it clear that they're not talking about the things you flew on the end of a long string when you were a kid. You check a dictionary and it says:

> Kite, any of various small hawks with long narrow wings and a forked tail.

You probably didn't know about this usage of "kite." (Can you find the genus and the species? Can you pick out its extension and its intension? See the answers at the bottom of the page.)

Key Concept
Dictionary definitions are definitions that state the common usage of words.

Technical Terms: Lexical Definition, Reportive Definition

"Lexical definition" and "reportive definition" are other names for dictionary definitions.

---

*National Institutes of Health, part of the United States Department of Health and Human Services.

The genus is "small hawks" and the species is "having long narrow wings and forked tail." Its extension would be a list of all the kites in the world. The intension is "a small hawk with long narrow wings and forked tail."

> ### GUIDE
>
> ### Dictionaries
>
> Dictionaries are an important resource for evaluating arguments. Dictionaries are also essential for reading plays, speaking a foreign language, reading a description of a painting, understanding your college catalog, and any other task that involves language.
>
> Dictionaries usually present information about the etymology (the roots and previous meanings) of words. Words change meaning over time. Two hundred years ago the word "corn" referred to the plant most Americans now call "wheat." If you didn't know this, you might well be confused by some passage written in the 1800s. A dictionary would reveal this older meaning of "corn."
>
> Some dictionaries are more comprehensive than others. *The Oxford English Dictionary* (OED) attempts to present all English words from their first recorded use to their contemporary meanings. The OED is composed of twenty volumes and 22,000 pages. A student dictionary is usually intended for high-school students. A collegiate dictionary is usually appropriate for college students.
>
> In addition to standard dictionaries, many specialized dictionaries are available. These include dictionaries for children, Scrabble players, crossword puzzlers, and aficionados of every sort. Most relevant to this book are the specialized dictionaries used in academic, medical, legal, and other professional fields. Specialized dictionaries can be stand-alone works. They can also be parts of technical guides, desk references, field manuals, encyclopedias, and handbooks. They provide definitions for key technical terms of a discipline or profession. Examples include: *Taber's Cyclopedia of Medical Terms, Black's Law Dictionary, Concise Chemical and Technical Dictionary, Technical Manual of Classical Ballet, Technical Dictionary of the Shoe Industry, English–German,* and *Technical Dictionary of Data Processing, Computers, Office Machines in English, German, French, and Russian.* Specialized dictionaries can help you understand your course material. University libraries often provide access to online editions of specialized dictionaries.
>
> Using dictionaries is another part of the art of argument. Making standard and specialized dictionaries part of your life will broaden and deepen your intellectual skills. That will help you become a better critical thinker.

EXERCISE 4.2

A. Determine whether the following passages contain a definition. If it contains a definition, indicate its extension and its intension. If the definition is in genus/species format, indicate the genus and the species.

1. A computer is a machine used for processing words and numbers.
2. A cat is a carnivorous mammal long domesticated as a pet and for catching rats and mice.
3. Tableware is forks, knives, and spoons.
*4. What's that? It's a computer.

5. How much wood could a woodchuck chuck if a woodchuck could chuck wood?

6. "The Sun's yearly path around the celestial sphere is called the ecliptic." (Chaisson 2005, 29, material omitted)

7. The moons of Jupiter are the four small points of light that Galileo saw when he was the first person to look at Jupiter through a telescope. (This passage was written by the authors of this book from information provided in Chaisson 2005.)

*8. "The mutual gravitational attraction between the Sun and the planets is responsible for the observed planetary orbits." (Chaisson 2005, 54, material omitted)

9. "Cartographers have been at work since the days of the early Egyptians, but it is only in the last half century that their technology has advanced beyond simple manual drawing on a piece of paper." (McKnight 2005, 41, material omitted)

10. "Orthophoto maps are multicolored, distortion-free photographic image maps." (McKnight 2005, 45)

11. Orthophoto maps are maps used to show topographic details of areas with very low relief, such as marshlands. (This passage was written by the authors of this book from information provided in McKnight 2005.)

*12. "Matter is anything that occupies space, displays a property known as *mass*, and possesses inertia." (Petrucci 2005, 4)

13. A base is a substance that, when prepared as a solution, makes phenol red become yellow. (This passage was written by the authors of this book from information provided in Petrucci 2005.)

14. Iodine is the element that, at room temperature, is a violet-black solid, has a melting point of 114°C, and a boiling point of 184°C. (This passage was written by the authors of this book from information provided in Petrucci 2005)

15. A furtum is a "thing which has been stolen." (Nolan 1990, 676)

Technical Definitions

A **technical definition** gives a word a meaning that doesn't match common usage. Technical definitions refer to something that's important for those working in a particular field. A **technical term** is a word with a technical definition.

Some philosophers needed a quick way to refer to beings that have the right to life. They decided to use the word "person." When you find the word "person" in an article by one of these philosophers, it may refer to any beings that have a right to life. If such a philosopher thought that gorillas have a right to life, he might say:

Gorillas are persons.

If you don't know the philosophers' technical definition of "person," this statement might confuse you.

In construction, "rebar" refers to a steel rod with ridges that's used to reinforce concrete. "Rebar" isn't a word that has common usage. Most people never use this word. But those in construction need a word to refer to this

Key Concept
A **technical definition** gives a word a meaning that doesn't match common usage.

Key Concept
A **technical term** is a word with a technical definition.

type of steel rod, so they invented the word "rebar." ("Rebar" is an abbreviation of "reinforcing bar.")

Technical terms are used in every discipline. Learning to recognize technical definitions and remembering their meanings is indispensable for success in college. You've spent a lot of time studying technical definitions when you've studied for tests.

Here's a passage from a chemistry article:

> Melting points were measured by a Kofler micromelting point apparatus and the results were uncorrected. IR spectra were recorded on a Bruker Vector 22 spectrometer in KBr with absorption in cm^{-1}. H NMR spectra were determined on a Bruker AC 400 spectrometer as $CDCl_3$ solutions. Chemical shifts (δ) are expressed in ppm downfield from the internal standard tetramethylsilane, and coupling constants (J) are given in Hz. (Fan 2005, 19)

You may not understand the complete meaning of this passage. (We don't.) It's filled with technical terms.

Numerous clues help you find technical terms. Authors sometimes put them in special type such as **bold**, underlined, or *italic*. You've probably noticed by now that the authors of this book put a technical term in a special note in the margins. But such clues aren't always present, and even if they are provided they'll only be given the first time the technical term is used.

As noted above, if you don't understand a word, your first step should be to look it up in a standard dictionary. However, technical terms usually aren't in standard dictionaries. If the word you don't know isn't in a standard dictionary, that's a clue that it's a technical term. You should check a specialized dictionary. If the word you don't know is in a standard dictionary, but the meaning indicated there doesn't make sense in the context in which you find it, that's another clue that it's a technical term. Again, you should check a specialized dictionary.

Here are three important facts about technical terms.

(1) One technical term can be used in two fields with different meanings.

"Crystallized" is used in the field of biology to describe any physical mass organized in a structurally uniform manner. This same word is used in English courses to describe a previously incoherent idea that has been made coherent.

(2) Two different technical terms can be used in two different fields to refer to the same thing.

"Taxonomy" and "ontology" are used in different fields to refer to the same thing. Both are used to mean a method of organizing and classifying a large number of types of entities.

(3) Technical terms can be used in one or more fields in a way completely different from the common use of the same word.

The example of "person" above illustrates this point. If you read a sentence and it looks like a perfectly ordinary word isn't being used to mean what you think it means, it could be a technical term. When this happens, a standard dictionary may be misleading. It reports the common usage of a word, not its technical usage. You need to check a specialized dictionary.

Technical Term: Stipulative Definition

Another name for a technical definition is "stipulative definition."

Why do people use technical definitions? One reason is convenience. Chapter Nine discusses causal arguments. Causes are relationships between events and/or states of affairs. We will need to refer to events and/or states of affairs many times. It would be annoying to repeat the phrase "events and/or states of affairs" over and over. We will technically define "event" to refer to events and/or states of affairs. Using this one short word is more convenient. We will turn "event" into a technical term.

Acronyms are another example of technical definitions used for convenience. **Acronyms** are words formed by the initial letters of all the main words in a phrase. The word "GPA" is an acronym for "grade point average," "NATO" is an acronym for "North Atlantic Treaty Organization," and "US" is an acronym for "United States."

Another reason for the use of technical definitions is that new things need names. Common usage can't supply the name of a new thing. In the late 1930s people developed self-contained underwater breathing apparatuses. For a while, this name was abbreviated to the acronym "SCUBA." As SCUBA gear stopped being a new thing, the word "SCUBA" stopped being an acronym, entered common usage and is now written like this, "scuba."

Another reason for the use of technical definitions is that people need a precise word. Think about the word "dead." The dictionary definition includes meanings such as (1) no longer alive, (2) unresponsive, (3) weary and worn-out, (4) inanimate, and (5) no longer in existence or use. Health insurance companies aren't legally required to pay for healthcare once a patient is dead. Suppose that a person is in the hospital. His brain stops working but his heart and lungs continue to work for another two days. Even after the heart and lungs stop working, some cells in his body will continue to be alive for a while. When does the insurance company's obligation to pay end? When the brain stops working? When the heart stops? When the lungs stop working? When the last cell in the person's body dies? The dictionary definitions of "dead" aren't precise enough. The insurance company needs a technical definition. The insurance contract might include language such as:

> In this contract, "dead person" refers to a person whose brain, heart, and lungs have ceased to function.

This allows the contract to clearly indicate when payments by the insurance company will stop.

Technical Term: Precising Definition

A technical definition that's used because of a need for precision is sometimes called a "precising definition."

Sometimes a researcher needs a definition that's more precise than common usage because the researcher needs a word to be used in a theory. Recall the definition of "planet" discussed above.

A planet is a body that does not produce its own light and orbits a star.

Key Concept

Acronyms are words formed by the initial letters of all the main words in a phrase.

"Star" was defined this way:

A star is a body that produces its own light.

Recently, with the development of new technologies and more powerful telescopes, scientists discovered objects in space that don't fit into the extensions of these definitions. They discovered that sometimes a planet breaks out of orbit from around a star and goes wandering off into space. This sort of object doesn't fall into the extension of "planet" as defined above because it's not orbiting a star. This sort of object doesn't fall into the extension of "star" as defined above because it doesn't produce its own light. Another problem with the definitions above was caused by the discovery that some objects don't yet produce their own light but will in the future, and other objects don't now produce their own light but did in the past. (You could call these things "proto-stars" and "dead stars.") Astronomers needed a more precise technical definition of "planet" and "star." The following is a paraphrase of a technical definition of "planet" proposed by astronomer Gibor Basri:

A spherical object never capable of core fusion, which is formed in orbit around an object in which core fusion occurs at some time. (Basri 2003)

"Core fusion" refers to a star's ability to generate its own light. The descriptive phrase "object in which core fusion occurs" refers to what people ordinarily call a star. Basri's proposal solves the problems noted above. Planets are things that aren't and never were capable of generating their own light and were formed in orbit (as opposed to being in orbit) around an object that is or was capable of generating its own light (that is, a star). You can infer a definition of "star" from his definition of "planet."

A star is a body that will, does, or did produce its own light.

As we write this book, Basri is in the process of submitting his proposal to national and international organizations of astronomers. Perhaps by the time you're reading this book, his proposal will be an officially recognized technical definition.

Critical Thinkers

Gibor Basri

Courtesy of Gibor Basri

Gibor Basri (1951–still searching for planets) has been an astrophysicist for thirty years. He's a professor in the astronomy department at the University of California, Berkeley. Dr. Basri has written nearly 200 publications. One of his most famous areas of research is his work to improve the definition of "planet." You can read about Professor Basri's work in on his webpage: http://astro.berkeley.edu/~basri/

Technical Terms: Other Kinds of Definitions

Functional definitions usually follow the genus-species format and provide the function of the thing being defined as the species of the definition. Operational or behavioral definitions define a word in terms of how a thing is identified or observed. Cluster definitions emphasize that not all of the things in the extension of the word being defined have to have the same features. They may have some (but not all) of the cluster of features identified with the things in the extension.

Suppose you wanted to define the word "tent." "A shelter used by humans for living or camping" is a functional definition. "A thing that looks like a small colored square when viewed from an airplane" is an operational definition. "A shelter that is portable and/or makes for living or camping and/or is made of cloth and/or has a framework of poles and/or was used by Native Americans for living quarters" is a cluster definition. All three of these definitions are in genus-species format.

EXERCISE 4.3

A. Determine whether the following passages contain a definition. If it contains a definition, indicate whether it's a dictionary definition or a technical definition. If it's a technical definition, indicate whether is being used for convenience, a new thing, greater precision, or for a theory. A passage may contain more than one definition.

1. This Dr. Pepper is cold.

2. A magazine is a periodical containing miscellaneous pieces (as articles, stories, poems) and often illustrated.

3. For the purposes of this document, "magazine" refers only to a room in which gunpowder is kept in a fort. Although there are other uses of this word, clarity requires us to focus on one particular use.

*4. ABC is the American Broadcasting Company.

5. A keyboard is an assemblage of systematically arranged keys by which a machine or device is operated.

6. "You don't know about me without you have read a book by the name of *The Adventures of Tom Sawyer*, but that ain't no matter. That book was made by Mr. Mark Twain, and he told the truth, mainly. There was things which he stretched, but mainly he told the truth. That is nothing. I never seen anybody but lied one time or another, without it was Aunt Polly, or the widow, or maybe Mary. Aunt Polly—Tom's Aunt Polly, she is—and Mary, and the Widow Douglas, is all told about in that book, which is mostly a true book; with some stretchers, as I said before." (Twain 2008, 1)

7. "The broader question it explores is how exit options are constructed in social contractarian (SC) arguments that seek to justify a particular division of the social surplus generated by political cooperation." (Fried 2003, 41, material omitted)

*8. "E-mail spam, also known as unsolicited bulk email (UBE) or unsolicited commercial email (UCE), is the practice of sending unwanted email messages, frequently with commercial content, in large quantities to an indiscriminate set of recipients." (Wikipedia "Spam" 2007)

9. "Give me liberty, or give me death!" (Henry 1999, 232)

10. "Active sites are the locations at which catalysis occurs, whether on the surface of a heterogeneous catalyst or an enzyme." (Petrucci 2005, A30)

11. "Punk is musical freedom. It's saying, doing, and playing what you want. In Webster's terms, 'nirvana' means freedom from pain, suffering, and the external world, and that's pretty close to my definition of punk rock." (Kobain 2007)

***12.** "The term 'firearm' means any weapon (including a starter gun) which will or is designed to or may readily be converted to expel a projectile by the action of an explosive." (18 USC 921, material omitted)

13. "income = wages or salary from work and earnings from investments." (Macionis 2006, 478)

14. "Auguste Comte and Karl Marx stand among the giants of sociology." (Macionis 2006, 10)

15. "[Here is] the sense of 'harm' that is used in the harm principle: only setbacks of interests that are wrongs, and wrongs that are setbacks to interest, are to count as harms in the appropriate sense." (Feinberg 1984, 36, material omitted)

Evaluating Definitions

Key Concept
A **good definition** is a definition in which both the extension and the intension are *accurate* and *clear*.

A **good definition** is a definition in which both the extension and the intension are *accurate* and *clear*. In other words, a good definition clearly and correctly tells you the borders of the extension of the word being defined and it also allows you to clearly determine the features that all of the members of this class have in common. Let's look at some factors that need to be considered when evaluating a definition.

Correct Extension

Key Concept
A definition that excludes some members of the class being defined has an extension that's **too narrow**. A definition that includes entities that don't belong to that class has an extension that's **too broad**.

A definition is accurate when it has correct extension and correct intension. What does it mean for a definition to have a correct extension? A definition that excludes some members of the class being defined has an extension that's **too narrow**. A definition that includes entities that don't belong to that class has an extension that's **too broad**. Good definitions are neither too narrow nor too broad.

To understand what it means for a definition to be too broad or too narrow, let's look at three definitions of "human being." One traditional definition of "human being" holds that

(a) Human beings are animals that are toolmakers.

In the 1960s biologist Jane Goodall lived with and studied chimpanzees in their natural habitat. Among other things, she discovered that chimpanzees make and use tools on a regular basis. Her research shows that the definition of human as a toolmaker was too broad. It included species other than the species that was being defined by that criterion. (If you want to know more about Goodall's work, you could read her *The Chimpanzee: The Living Link between 'Man' and 'Beast'* (1992).)

You can graphically represent this case (see the graphic at the top of the next page). Use a circle with a solid border to indicate the extension of "human being." All humans are inside the circle, and all non-humans are outside the circle. Use a circle with a dashed line to indicate the extension of a proposed definition of "human being" as a toolmaker.

Madeline is inside the circle with a solid border because she's a human being. She's inside the circle with the dashed line because she's a toolmaker. A chair is outside the border because a chair isn't a human being. Chimpanzees aren't inside the solid border because they aren't humans, but they're inside the dashed line because they're toolmakers. That the dashed line is outside the solid is a representation of the fact that definition (a) is too broad.

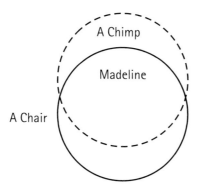

(a) Human beings are animals that are toolmakers.

Suppose someone said that

(b) Human beings are bipedal primate mammals that can speak a language.

Definition (b) is too narrow because some humans (infants, some of the very elderly) can't speak. You can graphically represent this case like this:

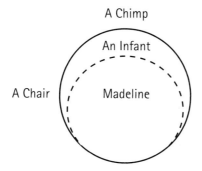

(b) Human beings are bipedal primate mammals that can speak a language.

Madeline is inside both the solid and the dashed circle because she's a human being who can speak a language. A human infant is inside the solid circle and outside the dashed circle. This represents the fact that definition (b) is too narrow.

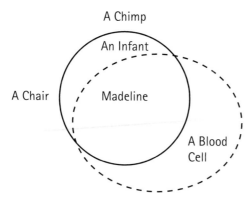

(c) Human beings are things with a perfect genetic code of a *homo sapiens.*

A definition can be too broad and too narrow at the same time. Suppose that someone claimed that

(c) Human beings are things with a perfect genetic code of a *homo sapiens*.

Definition (c) is too broad because it includes any cell from a human body (such as those found in a drop of blood spilled on a counter) that has a perfect genetic code. Recall from your high-school science classes that every cell of an organism contains its genetic code. Definition (c) is also too narrow because it excludes those people who have genetic mutations (as most humans do).

To represent this graphically, let's assume that Madeline has a perfect genetic code of a *homo sapiens* and that the infant doesn't. This means that a drop of Madeline's blood also has a perfect genetic code of a *homo sapiens*. This represents the fact that definition (c) is too broad and too narrow. The graphical representation of an extensionally perfect definition would have the solid line and the dashed line perfectly matched.

Correct Intension

Accurate definitions correctly point to the central features of everything belonging to the word being defined. If a definition points to unimportant or inessential features, the definition is poor. Definitions can fail to accurately indicate the intension of a word in at least three ways: metaphorical language, unnecessary negations, and synonymous language.

Good definitions don't use metaphors. Metaphors occur when someone compares two seemingly unrelated objects in order to point to some likeness between them. Here's an example of metaphor from Shakespeare:

> Life's but a walking shadow, a poor player
> That struts and frets his hour upon the stage
> And then is heard no more: it is a tale
> Told by an idiot, full of sound and fury,
> Signifying nothing. (*Macbeth*, Act 5, Scene 5)

This passage contains three metaphors. It compares life to three things: a shadow, a bad actor, and a tale. But life can't be defined as a kind of shadow, a kind of actor, or a kind of tale.

Life is a tale told by an idiot.

is a poor definition of the word "life." Metaphor is perfectly appropriate in many contexts. Metaphors are often vivid, rich, and fascinating. They offer you insight by suggesting ways to see things that may be hard to describe or define. But they don't clearly indicate the intension of a word.

Technical Term: Figurative Language

Another name for metaphorical language is "figurative language."

Good definitions define without negations. Definitions stated with a negative tell you what a thing isn't. They don't tell you what it is. Suppose someone said:

An apple is not an orange.

This definition doesn't clearly point to the intension of "apple." Mentioning one class to which apples don't belong doesn't eliminate much. Houses, dreams, coffee cups, telephones, and pine trees are also not oranges.

In a few cases a negative definition is appropriate. A scholar may want to focus on all things that lack a certain feature. In that case, a negative definition will be useful. Suppose that students at a university are asked (but not required) to check a box on their admission application that indicates their ethnicity. Some students don't check any box. A researcher might use a technical term, "non-respondent," and define a "non-respondent" as a student who didn't check any box. Given the nature of the admission application, this is an appropriate negative definition.

Good definitions avoid synonyms. Synonyms are two words that have the same meaning. No two words are perfectly synonymous. More or less subtle shades of difference are always present. But some words are close to perfectly synonymous. Think about "sofa" and "couch." The *Oxford English Dictionary* (OED 2008) says that

> a sofa is a long upholstered seat with a back and arms, for two or more people.

It says that

> a couch is a long upholstered piece of furniture for several people.

"Sofa" and "couch" are close to being perfectly synonymous.

You might think that the OED could simply say that

> a sofa is a couch.

Why doesn't the OED define "sofa" this way? Because if you don't know the definition of the synonym, it won't provide any information about the word being defined. Suppose that someone doesn't know what "sofa" means. You tell him that

> "Sofa" means the same thing as "couch."

Your statement is true. "Sofa" and "couch" are close synonyms. But you haven't indicated the intension of "sofa." Unless this person knows the intension of "couch," your definition won't be helpful. The definition of sofa given by the OED indicates the intension of the word. A synonym doesn't.

In a few cases synonymous definitions are acceptable. If the context is translation from one language to another, offering a synonym might be perfectly appropriate. Suppose that in one of your courses the professor says that *malus domestica* don't produce fruit in tropical climates. He's using the Latin scientific name of this plant. But you don't know what a *malus domestica* is. You ask a classmate: "What's a *malus domestica* anyway?" She replies "It's an apple tree." This helps you because you already know the intension of "apple tree." But outside of the context of translation, synonyms are almost always bad definitions.

Persuasive Definitions

Sometimes people put an incorrect extension or intension in a definition in hopes of fooling people. A **persuasive definition** looks like it is stating a dictionary definition but actually gives the words a technical definition to be used in an argument. Suppose that two college students, Wen and Chris, are

Key Concept
The difference between a **persuasive definition** and a dictionary definition.

arguing about whether there should be a military draft. Wen offers the following arguments:

(1) Children are all nothing but fragile, immature, undeveloped, inexperienced, adorable human beings who are 21 years old and younger.

(2) Any civilized country (including the United States) should take measures to protect its children.

(3) U.S. federal law requires male citizens 18 years old to register for the military draft.

(4) Members of the military are the first citizens to be sent to war.

Therefore,

(5) The United States has a government that is deliberately instigating the murder of its own children.

Therefore,

(6) The military draft should be abolished

The first premise of this argument is a definition. Wen's definition of "children" doesn't match common usage so it's a technical definition. But Wen isn't using a technical definition for any of the good reasons you saw earlier in this chapter. Instead he defines "children" to bias the case against the draft. His definition is persuasive. He chooses only features of children that support the conclusion that we shouldn't have a draft. If an argument contains a persuasive definition, it fails the true premises test because a persuasive definition isn't accurate.

If a persuasive definition is a bad technical definition, what's a good one? Because technical definitions are made up by authors for their own use, there is a sense in which a technical definition can't have an incorrect extension or intension. The author is just telling you how he or she is using a term. But a technical definition can be unclear. In that case, it's a bad technical definition. In addition, the case of persuasive definitions shows that technical definitions can be misused.

Connections

Persuasive definitions often use emotionally charged language. Emotionally charged language is discussed later in this chapter.

EXERCISE 4.4

A. Determine whether the following passages contain a definition. If a passage contains a definition, evaluate it using the following factors: broad, narrow, metaphors, negations, synonyms.

1. Red things are those things that have the quality of redness.

2. A vehicle is a means of transporting something.

3. Chicken is the most popular meat in the United States.

*4. To understand a concept is to grasp that concept.

5. Buildings are things that are not natural.

6. Hazing is any activity that singles out first-years or newcomers.

7. A dragon is a mythical serpent or lizard that is monstrous, winged, fire-breathing, and has a crested head and enormous claws.

*8. An economist is a person who knows the price of everything and the value of nothing.

9. "Empirical: Objectively quantifiable observations." (Smith 2007, 6)

10. "The function concept is one of the most important ideas in mathematics" (Barnett 2005, 3)

11. "Formally, statistics is a branch of mathematics that focuses on the organization, analysis, and interpretation of a group of numbers." (Aron 2006, 2)

*12. "Earth is surrounded by a life-giving gaseous envelope called the atmosphere." (Lutgens 2004, 9)

13. "The central concept of deductive logic is the concept of argument form." (Epp 2004, 1)

14. "Men do not want solely the obedience of women, they want their sentiments. All men, except the most brutish, desire to have, in the woman most nearly connected with them, not a forced slave but a willing one. They have therefore put everything in practice to enslave their minds." (Mill 1970, 141, material omitted)

15. "The term 'forfeiture' has been defined legally as the 'loss of some right or property as a penalty for some illegal act.'" (Hyde 1995, 26)

B. In Exercises 4.2 above, you set out the intension of some words. Go back to the intensions you gave in these exercises, formulate them as definitions, and evaluate them. In particular, indicate whether your intensional definitions have correct extension. Are they too broad, too narrow, too broad and too narrow, or neither too broad nor too narrow? If they are too broad, too narrow, or too broad and too narrow, provide examples to show this. Then evaluate the definitions you composed to see if they have metaphors, negations, or synonyms.

Language and Clarity

There's a lot more to language than definitions. One key feature of language is clarity. Even if you know the meanings of all the words in a passage, you may not be able to figure out what a passage means because the words aren't put together clearly. Lack of clarity is one of the most common faults that professors see in student writing.

The first step to writing clearly is to remember to try to write clearly. You talk to people all the time and they almost always know what you mean. You might think that this means that your writing is clear. But writing is different from talking. For one thing, practice makes perfect and you don't practice writing clearly as much as you practice speaking clearly. Also, when you talk you use a lot more than words to make yourself clear. You use gestures, facial expressions, and body language. When you write, all of that goes away. In addition, when you talk, people can easily ask you questions. When someone sits down to read something you've written, you probably won't be there to answer their questions. Finally, when you write (at least for college courses) you're probably writing about things that are new to you. For all these reasons, when you write you need to remember to try to write clearly.

Ambiguity

Ambiguity is one of the most common problems with clarity. A passage is **ambiguous** when it doesn't make clear which of two or more meanings it's intended to have. Suppose that Melissa said:

I put coins in the bank next to the old oak tree.

Does she mean that she buried the coins in the river bank next to a tree? Or does she mean that she put the coins in the safe deposit box of a bank that has an old oak tree beside it? You can't tell. Here's a famous example of ambiguity. In 1967, the Beatles released a song called "Lucy in the Sky with Diamonds" (Beatles 1967).* Here's part of the lyrics:

Picture yourself in a boat on a river,
With tangerine trees and marmalade skies.
Somebody calls you, you answer quite slowly,
A girl with kaleidoscope eyes.

Cellophane flowers of yellow and green,
Towering over your head.
Look for the girl with the sun in her eyes,
And she's gone.

{Refrain}
Lucy in the sky with diamonds.
Lucy in the sky with diamonds.
Lucy in the sky with diamonds.

The capital letters of the title are "LSD," the acronym for a psychedelic drug. Is this song about a woman, Lucy, or a description of the effects of LSD? The song has two meanings. (The psychedelic music illustrates this point.)
In songs and poetry, ambiguity isn't a problem. It can be fun. But when it comes to arguments, ambiguity is a problem. It leads to a fallacy.

 ## Fallacy: Equivocation

The **Fallacy of Equivocation** occurs when an argument trades on ambiguity. This fallacy is committed when one meaning of a word is used in one premise and another meaning of the same word is used in another premise or in the conclusion. Look at the following argument:

(1) Many Democratic candidates run for office.
(2) Republicans claim they believe in democratic ideals.
Therefore,
(3) Republicans should vote for Democrats.

In this argument, the word "democratic" is used in both premises. But it isn't used to mean the same thing in each premise. In the first premise it means

(a) a political party in the United States, not a type of government.

In the second premise it means

(b) a type of government, not a political party.

If someone uses sense (a) in both premises, then premise (1) is true but premise (2) is false, and the argument fails the true premises test. If someone uses sense (b) in both premise, then premises (1) is false and premise (2) is true. The argument still fails the true premises test. If someone uses sense (a) in premise (1) and sense (b) in premise (2), then both premises are true and the argument passes the true premises test. But the argument fails the proper form test. Here's the argument using sense (a) in premise (1) and sense (b) in premise (2):

(1) Many Democratic party candidates run for office.
(2) Republicans claim they believe in a democratic form of government.
Therefore,
(3) Republicans should vote for Democrats.

Once you see that the word "democratic" is used in one sense in the first premise of the argument and in a different sense in the second premise of the argument, you can see that the truth of these premises doesn't support the conclusion.

Technical Term: Equivocating
_____

Someone who commits the Fallacy of Equivocation is equivocating.

Here's another example of this fallacy. Philip Kitcher has noted that you sometimes see the following argument in the debate over whether evolution should be taught in schools (Kitcher 1983. Kitcher's discussion of this issue is much more sophisticated than indicated here.)

(1) We ought not teach theories in school.
(2) Evolution is a theory.
Therefore,
(3) We ought not teach evolution in school.

The word "theory" has two meanings:

(a) the general or abstract principles of a body of fact.
(b) an unproved assumption.

Let's first assume that this argument is using sense (a) in both premises. On sense (a), a theory is a collection of statements of fact. In that case, premise (1) is false, and this argument fails the true premises test. Now let's assume that this argument is using sense (b) in both premises. In that case, premise (2) is false. Evolution isn't an unproven assumption. Many scientists have made many arguments in support of evolution. Those arguments may be flawed, but evolution hasn't been assumed. Once again this argument fails the true premises test. Finally, let's assume that the word "theory" is used in sense (b) in (1) and (a) in (2). Then all the premises are true and the argument passes the true premises test. But now the argument fails the proper form test. You could rewrite it like this:

(1) We ought not teach unproven assumptions in school.
(2) Evolution is a body of fact.
Therefore,
(3) We ought not teach evolution in school.

The truth of (1) and (2) doesn't provide any support for (3). Only arguments that avoid the Fallacy of Equivocation, that use words consistently, can be good arguments.

Improper grammar can lead to ambiguity. When this happens, you have a case of amphiboly. **Amphiboly** occurs when the grammatical structure of the statements in a passage makes it ambiguous. The most common place to find amphiboly is in newspaper headlines and it's often funny.

> Patient at Death's Door—Doctors Pull Him Through
> Teacher Strikes Idle Kids
> Lawyers Give Poor Free Legal Advice
> Juvenile Court to Try Shooting Defendant
> Autos Killing 110 a Day—Let's Resolve to Do Better
> (Thompson 2007)

In each of these cases, the grammatical structure of the headline makes it unclear. Does "Lawyers Give Poor Free Legal Advice" mean that lawyers are giving free legal advice to people who are poor, or does it mean that lawyers aren't charging for poor legal advice?

In student papers, the most common type of amphiboly is ambiguous pronoun reference. **Ambiguous pronoun reference** occurs when pronouns such as "he," "she," "it," "they," "this," and "that" don't refer clearly to one thing. Suppose a friend of yours made the claim that

> Teddie never argues with his father when he's drunk.

As the claim is stated, you don't know who is drunk. Is it Teddie or his father? Amphiboly exists because the word "he" is ambiguous. The sentence is poorly worded, and it's impossible to tell what it means.

Vagueness

A word is **vague** when the boundaries of its extension aren't clear. One example of a vague word is "old." Suppose that someone said

> "Old" is an adjective that refers to a person who is more than forty years old.

This isn't accurate. You don't suddenly become old when you turn forty. Five-year-olds aren't old, and eighty-year-olds are old. But the boundary between young and old isn't clear.

Many words are vague. When does a girl become a woman? When is a person tall? When is it cold outside? In the cases of "girl," "tall," and "cold," borderline

Key Concept
Amphiboly occurs when the grammatical structure of the statements in a passage makes it ambiguous.

Key Concept
Ambiguous pronoun reference occurs when pronouns such as "he," "she," "it," "they," "this," and "that" don't refer clearly to one thing.

Key Concept
A word is **vague** when the boundaries of its extension aren't clear.

Habits of a Critical Thinker

The Principle of Charity

In critical thinking, the principle of charity isn't a principle about giving to the less fortunate. It's a principle about how to deal with ambiguous passages. Suppose that you're reading a text with an ambiguous argument. The author might be making one of two different arguments. One of these two arguments is a better argument than the other. The principle of charity states that you should assume the meaning of the text that makes for a better argument.

cases can't be avoided. Borderline cases are cases which aren't clearly within the extension of the word and not clearly outside the extension of the word.

The dictionary definition of a vague word should capture its vagueness. A dictionary that defined "woman" as a human female who is eighteen or more years old would be failing to capture the common (vague) usage. A good dictionary definition of "woman" should be somewhat vague to capture the vagueness of "woman." "An adult female person" seems good because the word "adult" is roughly as vague as the word "woman."

You can't avoid using vague words and you can't completely remove vagueness. The key is to make sure that an argument doesn't rely on vagueness. Look at this argument:

(1) Tax increases relate to economic growth.
(2) We want to encourage economic growth.
Therefore,
(3) We shouldn't increase taxes.

Let's assume that the second premise of this argument is true. But what about the first premise? Is it true or false? To attempt to answer this question is to fall into the trap of failing to recognize vagueness. When a statement is vague, you can't determine whether it's true or false. You can't determine whether (1) is true or false until you know what "relate" means. "Relate to" might mean many things. It could mean "cause," or it could mean "prevent." (1) might mean

(1a) Tax increases cause economic growth.

or it might mean

(1b) Tax increases prevent economic growth.

Until you know whether the author meant (1a), (1b), or something else, you can't begin the process of determining whether (1) is true. An argument with a vague premise fails the true premises test because you can't know that premise (1) is true.

Here are some words that are often vague. When you see one, you should be alert for the possibility of vagueness being used in an argument.

Vagueness Indicator Words

relates to	involves	connects to	is associated with
is concerned with	relies on	revolves around	

It can be difficult to distinguish vagueness from ambiguity. When you have ambiguity but not vagueness, you have a passage that has two clear meanings but you aren't sure which of the two is being used in a passage. You could represent the situation as two boxes with clearly defined borders.

Ambiguous

Suppose that you read the following in a newspaper: "He saw the President of the United States and the President of General Motors and then talked with the President." This sentence is ambiguous because you don't know whether the third use of "President" in the sentence refers to the President of the United States or the President of General Motors. There isn't much vagueness here because the word "President" isn't very vague.

When you have vagueness but not ambiguity, you have a passage that has one clear meaning but the boundaries of the extension of the vague word aren't clear. You could represent the situation as one box with blurry borders.

Vague

Suppose you read that: "The President's office was painted in a light color." In this context, "light" isn't ambiguous. But it's vague because it's hard to know exactly when a color stops being light and starts being dark.

In some cases, you have both vagueness and ambiguity. You could represent that situation as two boxes with blurry borders.

Ambiguous and Vague

Suppose that you read this: "Taylor is cool." It's ambiguous because it could be saying that Taylor has a problem that could be solved by putting on a sweater or it could be saying that Taylor is a stylish person. It's also vague because the boundaries of being cold and being stylish are both difficult to define.

EXERCISE 4.5

A. Determine whether the following passages contain any ambiguity and/or inappropriate vagueness.

1. I don't know. I guess that she is sort of tall.
2. The key? What key?
3. Give me that mouse!
*4. That car is yellow.
5. The '68 Chevies and the '69 Pontiacs used the same color of yellow.

6. There're lots of branches in the gutter.

7. "Should I turn left?" "Right."

*8. "A leaf obtains CO_2 for photosynthesis from the air; adjustable pores in the epidermis, called stomata, open and close at appropriate times to admit air carrying CO_2." (Audesirk 2005, 116, material omitted)

9. "The dry and barren surface of the moon reminds us of how truly special Earth is—blanketed with green plants, blue oceans, and white clouds." (Audesirk 2005, 1, material omitted)

10. "Infinite. Nothing. Our soul is cast into a body, where it finds number, time, dimension. Thereupon it reasons, and calls this nature, necessity, and believes nothing else." (Pascal 2007, 83)

11. "As long as the utility reigning in moral value judgments is solely the utility of the herd, there can be no morality of 'neighbor love.'" (Nietzsche 2002, 598)

*12. "I'm undaunted in my quest to amuse myself by constantly changing my hair." (This quote is often attributed, without citation, to Hillary Clinton.)

13. "All of us in America want there to be fairness when it comes to justice." (This quote is often attributed, without citation, to George W. Bush.)

14. "It is beyond me to keep secret my international orientation. The state to which I belong as a citizen does not play the least role in my spiritual life. I regard allegiance to a government as a business matter, somewhat like the relationship with a life insurance company." (Einstein 1997, ix)

15. "The word 'harm' is both vague and ambiguous." (Feinberg 1984, 31, material omitted)

Language and Emotion

Many words generate or suppress emotions. "Luxurious" generates positive emotions, and "rotting" generates negative emotions. Words that generate or suppress emotions have an emotional charge. People trying to sell products study the emotional charge of words and try to associate their products with words that have a positive emotional charge. When one of the authors of this book was in high school, home computers were rare. Input devices were primitive. Most computers had just a keyboard. There were no mice. A new input device was introduced. It was called a "scalar input device." It was a small stick of plastic connected to a ball. The ball was set in a box. When you pushed the stick of plastic up, the things on the computer went up, when you pulled the stick of plastic down, the things on the computer went down. From a marketing perspective, "scalar input device" wasn't a good phrase. Many people don't know what "scalar" means, and "input device" has a negative emotional charge. It sounds dull. A new word was invented for the scalar input device. It was renamed a "joystick," a stick of joy. This word has a positive emotional charge. This word has stuck and you may have never heard the phrase "scalar input device."

Habits of a Critical Thinker

Recognizing Bias and Prejudice

When you see emotionally charged language in a passage of writing, you should be alert for bias and prejudice. In bowling, a ball is biased when it tends to roll to the left or right. The ball is biased because it tends to deviate from the course it should follow. Bias in people is similar. A person is biased when something about his personality causes his beliefs to deviate from the course they would take if he followed good arguments. "Prejudice" is a synonym for "bias." Someone who's prejudiced is biased because he has pre-judged an issue. He has reached a conclusion before ("pre") he has fairly examined the arguments about the issue.

Bias is unavoidable. Everyone comes to issues with beliefs that shape how they frame the debate and evaluate the arguments. We all have some irrational emotional reactions and these color our view of things. One of the authors of this book hates being called "sir." He is biased against people who call him "sir," and it takes more effort for him to correctly evaluate the arguments of someone who calls him "sir" simply because he's annoyed by the use of "sir." This same author is biased in favor of people who like baseball.

A crucial step in minimizing the effect of your biases is recognizing them. If a person is aware of his own biases, he's much better equipped to combat them. The effect of unrecognized biases is hard to remove. You can't work to minimize an effect that you don't recognize.

Do you think that the language in this textbook, in your other textbooks, and in your class discussions is dry and dull? If you do, one reason may be that you're used to the emotionally charged language that's common on television and the radio. Marketers, talk-radio hosts, and politicians are masters at using emotionally charged language in place of good arguments. Textbooks and professors don't do that, and this sometimes makes their language seem boring. Textbooks and professors want you to focus on the information and arguments in a book. They want you to be moved by their ideas, not by their language.

Connections

Bias is also discussed in Chapters Three and Eight.

Fallacy: Appeal to Emotions

Key Concept
The **Fallacy of Appeal to Emotions** occurs when someone uses emotionally charged language in place of arguments.

The **Fallacy of Appeal to Emotions** occurs when someone uses emotionally charged language in place of arguments. Various emotions can be used: pity, fear, ridicule, spite, anger, flattery, and many others. One of the authors of this book sits on a committee to hear petitions of students asking for changes in their grades. In this job, he often sees students committing fallacious appeals to pity. A student might write,

> I deserve a B in this class. If I don't get a B, I'll lose my financial aid and have to drop out of college.

Grades are based on performance in a class, not on financial need. The first sentence that this imaginary student wrote could be supported with arguments about his work in class. But no such arguments are provided. The passage only appeals to pity.

Political candidates sometimes use appeals to fear. You might find a politician asserting

> If we don't win the war in Iraq, terrorists will strike the United States again.

One could make an argument to support this claim, but no argument is presented here. This statement asserts that one event (not winning the war in Iraq) would cause another event (a terrorist strike in the United States). To support this claim, the politician must provide a causal argument. If no argument is made, this statement is a fallacious appeal to fear.

Connections

Causal arguments are discussed in Chapter Nine.

Euphemism

Emotionally charged language includes not only words that generate emotions but also words that suppress them. These words are **euphemisms**. "Ethnic cleansing" is a euphemism. In some cases, members of an ethnic majority have engaged in the systematic expulsion, imprisonment, rape, and killing of members of an ethnic minority in order to achieve ethnic homogeneity in a particular region. Announcing that you plan to expel, imprison, rape, and kill people because they belong to a particular ethnic group is likely to cause a strong emotional reaction in people. The phrase "ethnic cleansing" associates these activities with the simple and comforting act of cleaning one's home. In this way it attempts to suppress the emotional reaction that's likely to result from a non-emotionally charged description of the activity.

An administrative assistant is a secretary, someone employed to manage routine work for someone else. Although the word "secretary" once had a positive emotional charge, it gradually lost it and gained a negative charge. The phrase "administrative assistant" was developed to avoid this negative charge. The authors of this textbook think that "administrative assistant" is developing a negative charge. Perhaps a new euphemism will replace it.

Key Concept
Euphemisms are words that suppress emotions.

Rhetorical Devices

In addition to words, the way that a passage is written can have a powerful influence on emotions. **Rhetorical devices** are ways that writing can be made more emotionally powerful. The example of the Dreyfus affair discussed in Chapter One is an example of the power of rhetoric. Here's Zola's argument:

Key Concept
Rhetorical devices are ways that writing can be made more emotionally powerful.

> Some have gone as far as to claim that Picquart was a forger, that he forged the telegram to ruin Esterhazy. But, good God, why? For what reason? Give me a motive. Was he too paid by the Jews?

Here's our standardization of this argument:

(1) Picquart had no reason to forge the telegram to ruin Esterhazy.
Therefore
(2) Picquart did not forge the telegram.

The standardized version of Zola's argument isn't nearly as emotionally powerful as the unstandardized version. Arguments presented in standard form are often less emotionally powerful than arguments presented in non-standard form. One reason you should put arguments into standard form is that it helps you reduce the chance that the emotional power of the language used to present the argument has misled you into thinking that a bad argument is a good argument.

Connections

Chapter One notes that one reason to standardize arguments is that standardization serves to remove much of the emotional charge from a passage.

Scholars have identified many rhetorical devices. Let's look at a few. (The Department of Classics at the University of Kentucky has an extensive list on their web pages: http://www.uky.edu/AS/Classics/rhetoric.html).

Zola's passage makes use of one common rhetorical device, the rhetorical question. **Rhetorical questions** are sentences that have the grammatical form of a question but are intended to persuade with emotion. "What time is it?" is a genuine question. "How can anyone support gun control?" and "But, good God, why?" are rhetorical questions. The key to recognizing rhetorical questions is to see that they expect no answer. In many cases, the arguer is substituting a question for a statement because the arguer has no subargument to support a controversial premise. A rhetorical question is offered instead. Beware of such premise substitutes. They're often a sign that the author of a passage wants to change your beliefs based not on the power of critical thinking but instead on the power of rhetoric. Part of the art of argument is learning to distinguish between (a) a rhetorical device used by an author to get you to focus on an argument (as was the case with Zola) and (b) a rhetorical device used instead of arguments. If you feel tempted to put a rhetorical question in one of your papers, you may be trying to change people's beliefs using the power of rhetoric instead of the power of critical thinking. You need to resist that temptation and insert an argument instead.

Alliteration is another common rhetorical device. It occurs when an author repeats the same sound at the beginning of words. After winning a big battle, Julius Caesar sent a message to Rome: *"Veni Vidi Vici."* ("I came, I saw, I conquered.") This is alliteration in either Latin (the "v" sound at the beginning of each word) or English (the "I" sound at the beginning of each phrase).

Another rhetorical device is **anaphora**. It occurs when someone repeats the same words at the beginning of series of phrases. Winston Churchill was prime minister of Britain when the Nazis attacked France. He gave a speech intended to rally British spirits. He famously said

> Even though large parts of Europe and many old and famous states have fallen or may fall into the grip of Nazi rule, we shall not flag or fail. We shall go on to the end, we shall fight in France, we shall fight on the seas and oceans, we shall fight with growing confidence and growing strength in the air, we shall defend our island, whatever the cost may be, we shall fight on the beaches, we shall fight on the landing grounds, we shall fight in the fields and in the streets, we shall fight in the hills; we shall never surrender. (Churchill 2003, 218)

Key Concept

Rhetorical questions are sentences that have the grammatical form of a question but are intended to persuade with emotion.

Key Concept

Alliteration occurs when an author repeats the same sound at the beginning of words.

Key Concept

Anaphora occurs when someone repeats the same words at the beginning of series of phrases.

The repeated use of "we shall" at the beginning of many phrases is an example of anaphora.

Personification, another rhetorical device, occurs when someone writes as if an inanimate object was a person. Here's an example of personification from the *Bible*:

> Wisdom sings her song in the streets. In the public squares she raises her voice. (Proverbs 1:20)

Key Concept
Personification occurs when someone writes as if an inanimate object was a person.

Wisdom can't sing but a person can. This proverb provokes more emotion because of the use of personification.

This introductory textbook can't provide a full study of rhetorical devices. You might study them in an English class. In a creative writing class, you'll be encouraged to use rhetorical devices to bring out emotional responses. In other classes, you might use rhetorical devices sparingly to spice up your papers. But, in general, you should avoid using rhetorical devices and be wary of writing that uses them.

Critical Thinkers

Jane Austen

© Bettmann/CORBIS

Jane Austen (1775–1817) was an English novelist whose sharp and humorous eye, character portrayals, and critical social commentary have made her work as popular and relevant today as it was in her lifetime. She's widely acknowledged as a master of the English language. Several film and television adaptations have been made of her work. The quote at the beginning of this chapter is from one of her books.

EXERCISE 4.6

A. In each of the following passages, indicate whether emotionally charged language and/or rhetorical devices are used.

1. Textbooks and professors want you to focus on the information and arguments in a book.
2. Is it really possible that someone thinks we should start using roundabouts in the United States? They're a disaster!
3. Put that down right now!
*4. The differently-abled tend to have lower incomes than those who are not differently-abled.
5. By the authority vested in me by the Board of Regents of the State of Very Cool, I pronounce you all graduates of Very Cool University with all the rights, responsibilities, and privileges thereunto appertaining.

6. The box was long and thin. It was slightly damaged on one end, but I couldn't see what was inside.

7. 2 + 2 = 4

*8. Could you tell me where I can find the W.C.?

9. Man, how long until lunch?

10. Stop! You're under arrest!

11. "I have been afraid of putting air in a tire ever since I saw a tractor tire blow up and throw Newt Hardbine's father over the top of the Standard Oil sign. I'm not lying. He got stuck up there. About nineteen people congregated during the time it took for Norman Strick to walk up to the Courthouse and blow the whistle for the volunteer fire department. They eventually did come with the ladder and haul him down, and he wasn't dead but lost his hearing and in many other ways was never the same afterward. They said he overfilled the tire." (Kingsolver 2001, 1)

*12. "My education was dismal. I went to a series of schools for mentally disturbed teachers." (Allen 2001, 89)

13. "Paul D. sits down in the rocking chair and examines the quilt patched in carnival colors. His hands are limp between his knees. There are too many things to feel about this woman. His head hurts. Suddenly he remembers Sixo trying to describe what he felt about the Thirty-Mile Woman. 'She is a friend of my mind. She gather me, man. The pieces I am, she gather them and give them back to me in all the right order. It's good, you know, when you got a woman who is a friend of your mind.' He is staring at the quilt but he is thinking about her wrought-iron back. He wants to put his story next to hers." (Morrison 2001, 314)

14. "I have a dream that one day this nation will rise up and live out the true meaning of its creed: 'We hold these truths to be self-evident, that all men are created equal.' I have a dream that one day on the red hills of Georgia, the sons of former slaves and the sons of former slave owners will be able to sit down together at the table of brotherhood. I have a dream that one day even the state of Mississippi, a state sweltering with the heat of injustice, sweltering with the heat of oppression, will be transformed into an oasis of freedom and justice. I have a dream that my four little children will one day live in a nation where they will not be judged by the color of their skin but by the content of their character." (King 1991, 219)

15. "'What's happening in these filtration camps is unspeakable,' said Holly Cartner, Executive Director of the Europe and Central Asia division of Human Rights Watch. 'We saw the same kind of torture and ill-treatment in filtration camps during the last Chechen war. The Russians must not get away with committing these abuses for a second time.'" (Human Rights Watch 2007)

Chapter Summary

If you don't understand the language of a passage, you can't do the true premises test because you don't know whether the premises are true or false. If you don't understand the language of a passage, you can't do the proper form test because you can't tell whether the premises support the conclusion.

A definition is a statement giving the meaning of a word.

Nouns and verbs are class terms because they refer to a group of things. Every definition of a class term indicates the word's extensional meaning and its intensional meaning. The extension of a class term is the collection of things in this class. The intension of a class term is the collection of features that all of the members of the class have in common.

Most definitions have the genus/species format. They define a word by indicating (a) the genus (a group of which the thing being defined is a member) and (b) the species (the feature or features that set the particular thing to be defined apart from the other things in the group).

Dictionary definitions are definitions that attempt to capture the common usage of a word. Technical definitions attempt to provide a definition for a special context outside of ordinary and common usage. Technical definitions can serve multiple functions: providing convenience, increasing precision, defining new things, and helping present a theory.

Definitions are evaluated by looking at how accurately and clearly they describe the extension and intension of a word. Good definitions avoid metaphors, negations, and synonyms. They are neither too broad nor too narrow.

One key feature of language is clarity. Even if you know the meanings of all the words in a passage, you may not be able to figure out what a passage means because the words aren't put together clearly. A passage is ambiguous when it doesn't make clear which of two or more meanings it's intended to have. The Fallacy of Equivocation occurs when an argument is ambiguous because one meaning of a word is used in one premise and another meaning of the same word is used in another premise or in the conclusion. Amphiboly occurs when the grammatical structure of the statements in a passage makes it ambiguous. Another clarity problem is inappropriate vagueness. A word is vague when the boundaries of its extension aren't clear.

Language often has an emotional charge that can be used to persuade by emotion instead of by critical thinking. The Fallacy of Appeal to Emotions occurs when people attempt to use emotionally charged language in place of arguments. Emotionally charged language sometimes appears in definitions, and when it does the definition is a persuasive definition. Emotionally charged language includes not only words that generate emotions but also words that suppress them. Such words are euphemisms. Rhetorical devices are tools that make writing more emotionally powerful. In argumentative writing, they're dangerous because they can put emotions in place of arguments.

5 Propositional Arguments

[T]here is good hope that death is a blessing, for it is one of two things: either the dead are nothing and have no perception of anything, or it is, as we are told, a change and a relocating for the soul from here to another place. If it is complete lack of perception, like a dreamless sleep, then death would be a great advantage . . . . If death is like this, I say it is an advantage, for all eternity would then seem to be no more than a single night. If, on the other hand, death is a change from here to another place, and what we are told is true and all who have died are there, what greater blessing could there be? [W]hat would you give to keep company with [heroes like] Homer? I am willing to die many times if that is true.

—Socrates, as told by Plato in his *Apology* (1981, 43, material omitted)

Learning Outcomes

After studying the material in this chapter, you should be able to:

1. Identify simple and compound statements.
2. Identify a negation, a disjunction, a conjunction, and a conditional.
3. Distinguish inclusive disjunctions from exclusive disjunctions.
4. Identify the antecedent and the consequent of a conditional.
5. Identify eight propositional argument forms and know which are proper and which are improper.

In Chapter Two you saw that arguments can be classified as either deductive or inductive. Many arguments, such as Socrates' argument on the previous page, are deductive. In this book you'll study the two most common kinds of deductive arguments: propositional arguments and categorical arguments. This chapter discusses propositional arguments and Chapter Six focuses on categorical arguments. In this chapter, you'll look at eight propositional argument forms. One of these forms is found twice in the quote on the previous page. After studying this chapter, you should be able to determine the form of Socrates' arguments and whether they pass the proper form test.

Identifying Propositional Statements

The first key to understanding propositional arguments I believe is to recognize that some statements have statements inside them and other statements don't. Compare the following two statements:

(a)   The Eiffel Tower is in Paris.
(b)   The Eiffel Tower is in Paris, and so is the Arc de Triomphe.

Both (a) and (b) are statements because both are either true or false. In this case, both are true. But (b) is different from (a) because (b) has two statements inside it. They are:

(b1)   The Eiffel Tower is in Paris
(b2)   The Arc de Triomphe is in Paris.

Statements like (a) are simple statements, and statements like (b) are compound statements. A **simple statement** is a statement that doesn't contain any other statement. A **compound statement** is a statement that contains at least one other statement.

Here are some simple statements:

Ceelay's bird can fly.
Most birds can fly.
Birds are the only animals that can fly.
Flying buttresses are arched masonry supports for the walls of buildings.
Flying buttresses bear weight away from the walls of the main structure.

The statements are simple *not* because they're short and *not* because they're about easy-to-understand subjects. They're simple because they make only one claim.

The definition of a compound statement seems a bit odd. How can a compound statement contain only one other statement? Doesn't a compound statement have to contain at least two other statements? The answer is "No" because of compound statements like this one:

(c) The Eiffel Tower isn't in Paris.

Statement (a) is in statement (c). Statement (c) is a compound statement that contains only one other statement. You can see that (a) is contained in (c) by rewriting (c) like this:

(c1) It's not the case that the Eiffel Tower is in Paris.

(c) and (c1) say the same thing, and the exact words of (a) are at the end of (c1).

There are four main types of compound statements: negations, disjunctions, conjunctions, and conditionals.

Negations

Negations are statements that deny another statement. Here are some negations:

There are some birds that can't fly.
It's not the case that all birds can fly.
It's false that all birds can fly.
Birds don't fly.

As these examples show, you can express negations in different ways.

The cassowary is a large flightless bird found in the tropical forests of New Guinea and northeastern Australia. One of the tallest and heaviest living birds, the southern cassowary is smaller than the ostrich and the emu.

javarman, 2010/Used under license from Shutterstock.com

Let's use "S1," "S2," "S3," etc. as variables to stand for statements. A **negation** is a statement that can be put into this form:

Not S1

Key Concept
The form of a **negation**.

Connections

Chapter Two discusses the use of variables.

A negation is true when the statement it contains is false. The statement

(a) The Eiffel Tower isn't in New York.

is true. The statement it contains

(b) The Eiffel Tower is in New York.

is false.

When you're looking for negations, you have to be careful because some statements look like negations but aren't. Think about the statement

(c) Joe is taller than average.

What's the negation of this statement? You might think it's

(d) Joe is shorter than average.

But that isn't correct. There are two different ways for Joe not to be taller than average. He could be shorter than average or he could be average. The correct negation of statement (c) is

(e) Joe isn't taller than average.

The statement that Joe isn't taller than average tells us that Joe is either shorter than average or average.

Compare the statements about Joe's height to the statement that

(f) The light is on.

If the light is on a normal switch (not a dimmer switch), then the negation of this statement is either

(g) The light is off.

or

(h) The light isn't on.

Statements (g) and (h) say the same thing because a light is either on or off. Unlike Joe's case, there's no third possibility. Statements like (c) and (d) are contraries and statements like (f) and (g) are contradictories. When you see a negation, you need to be careful to look for both contradictories and contraries.

As the cases of Joe and the light indicate, when you identify a statement as a contrary or contradictory, you're relying on your background knowledge. You have background knowledge about height and lights that allows you to see that there are two possible ways for Joe not to be taller than average but only one way for a light not to be on.

Key Concept
A negation is true when the statement it contains is false.

Connections

Chapter Six discusses contradictories and contraries in more detail.

Disjunctions

Speaking roughly, disjunctions are compound statements that contain two or more statements joined by an "or." The statements in a disjunction are its disjuncts. To define a disjunction as a compound statement that uses "or" is only *roughly* correct because phrases such as "unless" and "any one of" can also be used to indicate a disjunction.

Here are some disjunctions:

Either Ceelay's bird can fly or it has lost its wings.
Ceelay's bird can fly unless it has lost its wings.
Flying buttresses can have any one of the following functions: support, decoration, or illumination.
Flying buttresses are supportive of buildings, or they're decorative, or they're both.

Key Concept
The form of a
disjunction.

You'll see some complications in a moment, but for now you can say that a **disjunction** is a statement that can be put into the following form:

S1 or S2.

Key Concept
A **disjunction** is true
when at least one of its
disjuncts is true.

S1 and S2 are the disjuncts.

A disjunction is true when at least one of its disjuncts is true. Suppose that you and a friend, Bret, are talking about what another friend, Jaime, had for lunch yesterday. Suppose that Bret says

(a) I bet Jaime had either a bagel sandwich or a hamburger.

This disjunction contains two other statements.

(a1)   Jaime had a bagel sandwich.
(a2)   Jaime had a hamburger.

Let's suppose that you and Bret later discover that Jaime had a bagel sandwich. In that case (a1) is true and (a2) is false. But because (a1) is true, (a) is also true.

A statement may be both a negation and a disjunction. Here's an example:

It's false that Jaime had either a bagel sandwich or a hamburger.

This statement would be true if Jaime had a chicken salad sandwich and false if she had either a bagel sandwich or a hamburger.

Many disjunctions are like (a) in that they have two disjuncts. But in theory an infinite number of disjuncts could be in one disjunction.

Suppose that you wanted to make a disjunction that set out the acceptable forms of identification that you can use when you go to vote in the state of Georgia. In Georgia there are six different forms of acceptable identification. Here's the list from the web site of the Secretary of State of Georgia:

Voters are required to present identification at their polling place prior to casting their ballot. Proper identification shall consist of any one of the following:

(1) A Georgia driver's license which was properly issued by the appropriate state agency;

(2) A valid voter identification card or other valid identification card issued by a branch, department, agency, or entity of the State of Georgia, any other state, or the United States authorized by law to issue personal identification containing a photograph;

(3) A valid United States passport;

(4) A valid employee identification card containing a photograph of the elector and issued by any branch, department, agency, or entity of the United States government, this state, or any county, municipality, board, authority, or other entity of this state;

(5) A valid United States military identification card containing a photograph of the elector;

(6) A valid tribal identification card containing a photograph of the elector

(State of Georgia, 2009)

This long disjunction is claiming that prospective voters must have one of the above forms of identification in order to vote.

Connections

The use of "valid" in (2)–(6) above is different from the use of "valid" when it refers to an argument. See the Technical Terms note on "valid" in Chapter Two.

Surprisingly, the little word "or" has two different meanings. Suppose that your local pizza place isn't a very good pizza place. The menu reads

Toppings: pepperoni, mushrooms

The menu is saying

(a) You can have pepperoni or mushrooms on your pizza.

Suppose that a game show host says to a contestant

(b) You can have what's in this box or what's behind that curtain.

Compare statements (a) and (b). They both use the word "or." But while you can have more than one topping on your pizza, the game show contestant can't have both what's in the box and what's behind the curtain. In (a) "or" means

one or the other (or both)

But in (b) "or" means

one or the other (but not both)

When "or" is used to mean "one or the other (or both)," it's an inclusive disjunction. When "or" is used to mean "one or the other (but not both)," it's an exclusive disjunction. The "or" in the pizza example is inclusive. The "or" in the game show example is exclusive. (Later you'll see that when it comes to the proper form test, the difference between inclusive and exclusive disjunctions makes a big difference.)

Inclusive disjunctions are statements that have this form:

S1 or S2 (or both).

Exclusive disjunctions have this form:

S1 or S2 (but not both).

Speaking precisely, a disjunction is a statement that can be put into one of these two forms. The exclusive form is more common. In fact, outside of a pizza place, inclusive disjunctions are hard to find.

Key Concept
The form of **inclusive disjunctions**. The form of **exclusive disjunctions**.

EXERCISE 5.1

A. Indicate whether the following statements are simple or compound. If it's a compound statement, indicate whether it's a negation and/or a disjunction. If it's a disjunction, indicate whether it's inclusive or exclusive.

1. Josh likes Coke Zero.
2. Dinosaurs are extinct.
3. Joi doesn't like Pepsi.
*4. Francis had milk or juice with breakfast.
5. David is either on the 11th floor or the 12th.
6. It's false to say that everyone likes baseball.
7. "Matter can exist in three states: gas, liquid, and solid." (Bettelheim 2007, 16)
*8. "The rem, which stands for *roentgen equivalent for man*, is a measure of the effect of the radiation when a person absorbs 1 roentgen." (Bettelheim 2007, 77)
9. "All alkali metals are soft enough to be cut with a knife, and their softness increases in going down the column [on the periodic table of elements]." (Bettelheim 2007, 43–44)
10. "Unlike our stairways, the spaces between energy levels in an atom are not equal . . . ." (Bettelheim 2007, 47)
11. "I am not at all tired, my dear, and would much prefer to go out." (Dickens 1904, 47, material omitted)
*12. "I'll wait if you make haste . . . ." (Dickens 1904, 143)
13. "[The] music [of the horse-drawn wagon] changed as the horses came to a stand, and subsided to a gentle tinkling, except when a horse tossed his head or shook himself and sprinkled off a little shower of bell-ringing." (Dickens 1904, 61)
14. "[Harriet Tubman's] name deserves to be handed down to posterity, side by side with the names of Jeanne D'Arc, Grace Darling, and Florence Nightingale, for not one of these women, noble and brave as they were, has shown more courage, and power of endurance, in facing danger and death to relieve human suffering, than this poor black woman, whose story I am endeavoring in a most imperfect way to give You." (Bradford 1897, 4)
15. "You may already know something about the world of research." (Salkind 2006, 1, material omitted)

Conjunctions

Speaking roughly, conjunctions are compound statements that contain two or more statements joined by an "and." The statements in a conjunction are its conjuncts. To define a conjunction as a compound statement that uses "and" is only *roughly* correct because other words (such as "but," "even though," "nevertheless," "although," and "still") can be used to indicate a conjunction. Here are some conjunctions:

Flying buttresses of the
Cathedral of Strasbourg.

Birds fly and insects fly.

Most birds fly, but penguins don't.

Flying buttresses can be supportive even though they may be described as useless.

Conjunctions are usually composed of two conjuncts, although they can have three or more.

Many statements are compound; nevertheless, some are simple.

The moon wasn't full that night; still, someone or something could be seen moving across the lawn.

Speaking strictly, a **conjunction** is a statement that can be put into the following form:

S1 and S2

Let's return to the discussion you and Bret were having about what Jaime had for lunch. But suppose that, instead of the disjunction, Bret says

(a) I bet Jaime had a bagel sandwich and a hamburger.

This conjunction contains the same statements as Bret's disjunction that you saw above.

(a1)   Jaime had a bagel sandwich.
(a2)   Jaime had a hamburger.

Once again, you and Bret later discover that Jaime only had a bagel sandwich. In that case (a2) is false and (a1) is true. But now statement (a) is false. Statement (a) is only true if Jaime was really hungry and had a bagel sandwich and a hamburger. A conjunction is true when all of its conjuncts are true.

You can combine negations, disjunctions, and conjunctions in one statement. Here's an example:

Key Concept
The form of a
conjunction.

Key Concept
A conjunction is true
when all of its conjuncts
are true.

(b) The Eiffel Tower isn't in Paris and Jaime had either a bagel sandwich or a hamburger.

This statement contains three simple statements.

S1 = The Eiffel Tower is in Paris.
S2 = Jaime had a bagel sandwich.
S3 = Jaime had a hamburger.

Here's the form of this statement:

Not S1 and (S2 or S3 (or both))

(Why is this disjunction inclusive? Because Jaime could have had both a bagel sandwich and a hamburger.)

Sometimes "and" is used to indicate that one event caused another. Here's an example. Suppose that Kim says

(a) Rod had six beers and then he had a car accident.

Kim is probably trying to say that Rod's accident was caused by having too much alcohol. Grammatically (a) looks like a conjunction, and you might be tempted to think that (a) can be put into the form of a conjunction.

Wrong: S1 = Rod had six beers.
S2 = Rod had an accident.
S1 and S2.

But "S1 and S2" isn't an appropriate restatement of (a). What Kim's trying to say is

S1 caused S2.

Connections

Chapter Nine discusses causal arguments.

Conditionals

Key Concept
A conditional asserts that *if* one statement in the compound is true, *then* the other statement in the compound is true.

A fourth type of compound statement is a conditional. A conditional asserts that *if* one statement in the compound is true, *then* the other statement in the compound is true. Look at this conditional:

(a) If it rains today, then she'll take the bus.

This statement asserts that if the statement

(a1)   It rains today.

is true, then the statement

(a2)   She'll take the bus.

Key Concept
The "if" statement in a conditional is its **antecedent**, and the "then" statement is its **consequent.**

is true. The "if" statement in a conditional is its **antecedent**, and the "then" statement is its **consequent.** In the example above, (a1) is the antecedent and (a2) is the consequent. Here are some more conditionals:

If birds can fly, they have wings.
If flying buttresses offer support to a building, then they aren't just decorative features.
If you aren't too tired, you'll go to the store.
If your eyes are open, then you're awake unless you're asleep or dead.

In the first of these statements, the antecedent is "Birds can fly" and the consequent is "Birds have wings."

Punctuation helps you identify what type of statement is being made. In the fourth statement in the group above, the comma after "open" and the lack of a comma after "awake" indicate that the statement is a conditional whose consequent contains a disjunction with three disjuncts (you're awake, you're asleep, you're dead).

Strictly speaking, a **conditional** is a statement that can be put into the following form:

> If S1, then S2.

Key Concept
The form of a
conditional.

A conditional asserts that if the antecedent is true, then the consequent is true. This means that if the antecedent is true and the consequent is true, then the conditional is true. When the antecedent of a conditional is true and its consequent is false, the conditional is false. Look at this conditional.

> If it's snowing, then the temperature is below 40 degrees Fahrenheit.

Suppose it's snowing. Then the antecedent is true, the consequent is true, and the conditional is true. (Snow forms only where the temperature is below 32 degrees Fahrenheit, but sometimes it's below 32 up in the atmosphere and above 32 at ground level. The snow doesn't have time to melt before it hits the ground.) But suppose you wanted to show that this conditional is false. How would you do that? You'd have to find a case when it was snowing but the temperature wasn't below 40, a case where the antecedent was true but the consequent was false. To be precise, a conditional is true when its consequent is true or its antecedent is false.

Key Concept
A **conditional** is true
when its consequent is
true or its antecedent is
false.

Conditionals: Some Complications

Conditionals appear in many different ways. This can be complicated and confusing. Let's look at three complications.

Complication 1. You can put the consequent before the antecedent. The following two sentences make the same statement:

> If you aren't too tired, you'll go to the store.
> You'll go to the store, if you aren't too tired.

These examples also show that you can leave the "then" out of the conditional.

Complication 2. You can use "implies that" or "provided that" to make a conditional. The following two sentences make the same statement:

> If all dogs are mammals, then all dogs have hair.
> That all dogs are mammals implies that all dogs have hair.

The following two sentences also make the same statement:

> If she gets a B or better on the final, then she'll pass the course.
> Provided that she gets a B or better on the final, she'll pass the course.

You can also change the order of sentences that use "provided that." The statement

> She'll pass the course, provided that she gets a B or better in the course.

says the same thing as the other two sentences just above.

Complication 3. The phrase "only if" is tricky. This phrase is often used to make a conditional, but students can become confused. Here are the two crucial points to keep in mind.

1. The statement after an "if" is an antecedent.

2. The statement after an "only if" is a consequent.

Let's go back to our snow case but change it a bit.

(a) It's snowing *only if* the temperature is below 40 degrees.

If you think about it carefully, what (a) says is:

(a1) If it's snowing, then the temperature is below 40 degrees.

Statement (a) doesn't say

(b) If the temperature is below 40 degrees, then it's snowing.

You can see that (a) says (a1) and not (b) because (a) and (a1) are true but (b) is false. The temperature often drops below 40 without it snowing.

"Only if" is also tricky because people sometimes use "if" when they mean "if and only if." Suppose that one of your friends says

(c) I'll take you to the grocery store if you help me carry this sofa upstairs.

Your friend is using only the word "if" but she's telling you two things. She's telling you

(c1) If you help me carry this sofa upstairs, then I'll take you to the grocery store.

and she's also telling you

(c2) I'll take you to the grocery store only if you help me carry this sofa upstairs.

Statement (c2) is a bit impolite so people use "if" instead of "if and only if." When you see the word "if," you must look at the context and see whether, in the particular case, "if" means "if and only if." Here's another part of the art of argument. It takes practice to notice cases where people express their claims in polite language that you'll need to rewrite when you standardize their arguments.

Technical Terms: Hypothetical Statements, Implications

Conditionals are also called "hypothetical statements" or "implications." Some textbooks use "conditional" to refer to both conditionals and disjunctions.

GUIDE

Negation, Disjunction, Conjunction, and Conditional Indicator Words

Negation	not, false
Disjunction	or, unless, any one of
Conjunction	and, but, even though, nevertheless, although, still
Conditional	if, . . . then, if, only if,* implies that, provided that

*The statement after an "if" is an antecedent, but the statement after an "only if" is a consequent.

Patricia Blanchette

Patricia Blanchette is Associate Professor of Philosophy at the University of Notre Dame. Her research critically evaluates the role of conceptual analysis and other issues at the intersection of philosophical logic and the philosophy of mathematics. She's the author of many articles including an article on Logical Consequence in the *Blackwell Guide to Philosophical Logic*. She is also author of an article in *The Journal of Philosophy* (1996) about the work of two other logicians ("Frege and Hilbert on Consistency"), which was named one of the ten best articles published in philosophy in 1996.

EXERCISE 5.2

A. Indicate whether the following statements are simple or compound. If it's a compound statement, indicate whether it's a negation, a disjunction, a conjunction, and/or a conditional. If it's a disjunction, indicate whether it's inclusive or exclusive.

   1. Provided that my wife gets home on time, I'll be able to bring my daughter to gymnastics.
   2. I'll have a seltzer with lime.
   3. Taylor is tired and hungry.
   *4. I'll get that for you, but only if you're good.
   5. The sauce was composed of three ingredients: cream, white wine, thyme.
   6. If you step on a crack, you'll break your mother's back.
   7. Don't touch that burner!
   *8. While many people like fennel, others can't stand it.
   9. "No pestilence had ever been so fatal, or so hideous." (Poe 1982, 43)
   10. "Of all the gin joints in all the towns in all the world, she walks into mine." (Said by Humphrey Bogart in the film *Casablanca*; Curtis 1942)
   11. "I am not at all tired, my dear, and would much prefer to go out." (Dickens 1904, 47, material omitted)
   *12. "I'll wait if you make haste." (Dickens 1904, 143, material omitted)
   13. "[The] music [of the horse-drawn wagon] changed as the horses came to a stand, and subsided to a gentle tinkling, except when a horse tossed his head or shook himself and sprinkled off a little shower of bell-ringing." (Dickens 1904, 61)
   14. "No man is an island." (Donne 1839, 575)
   15. "[S]end not to know [f]or whom the bell tolls . . . ." (Donne 1839, 575)

B. Review the books that have been assigned for the courses you're taking this semester or have taken in past semesters. Find two examples of each of the following: simple statements, negations, inclusive disjunctions, exclusive disjunctions, conjunctions, conditionals. Be sure to provide correct citations for your quotes.

C. Determine whether each of the following sentences is a simple statement, a compound statement, or an argument. If it's an argument, indicate the premise(s) and the conclusion. If it's a compound statement, indicate whether it's a negation, a disjunction, a conjunction, and/or a conditional. If it's a disjunction, indicate whether it's inclusive or exclusive.

1. It's raining, so carry an umbrella.

2. When it's raining, people carry umbrellas.

3. Desks are made of wood or metal.

*4. Because wood scratches, metal is a better material for desks.

5. My desk is made of wood.

6. While there are many ways to make phone calls now, including standard land-lines, cell phones, VoIP phones, and satellite phones, there are fewer coin phones than there used to be.

7. The costs of cell phone services have decreased and areas with coverage have increased, so that now there is less reason to ever use a coin phone.

*8. "Elite and non-elite schools may have different cultures that shape lifestyles and habits of drinking, participating in athletic activities, smoking, and other behaviors that ultimately affect health." (Ross 1999, 447)

9. "Because education develops one's ability to gather and interpret information and to solve problems on many levels, it increases one's control over events and outcomes in life." (Ross 1999, 446)

10. "Sensory impressions . . . affect our emotions." (Norris 2001, 114)

11. "Emotion must be included in a discussion of body intelligence because it is one of the means by which our bodies communicate knowledge to conscious awareness." (Norris 2001, 113)

*12. "Policymakers that are accountable to the public should be more responsive to civil society organisations since they are reliant on the public for re-election and organized interests represent citizen interests." (Mahoney 2007, 338)

13. "We have suggested that in addition to serving domestic and ritual purposes, baskets were used as forms of tribute, trade, and gifts in Taino and Lucayan-Tdno economies and that their spatial distribution will help us define and explain the social, political, and cultural dynamics of the northern Antilles during the 15th-century. " (Berman 2000, 431)

14. "[T]he notion of cultural imperialism . . . is an unsatisfactory model for analyzing either cultural interaction in general or the missionary movement in world history in particular." (Dunch 2002, 318)

15. "[I]f the sum of angles in a triangle, ideas of 'normal' human physicality, youth fashions, and medical definitions of death are all products of cultural imperialism, then surely *every* definition is an exercise of power, and *every* change of mind a succumbing to domination." (Dunch 2002, 307)

Evaluating Propositional Arguments

Now that you can identify propositional statements, you're ready to evaluate propositional arguments. Let's look at eight propositional argument forms. There are an infinite number of propositional argument forms. Fortunately, most of them will never be used by anyone. The eight forms discussed in this chapter cover the majority of cases.

Technical Terms: Sentential Logic, Truth-Functional Logic, Syllogism

"Sentential logic" and "truth-functional logic" are other names for propositional logic.

In addition to being the most common forms found in propositional logic, the eight argument forms discussed in this book all have precisely two premises and a conclusion. Deductive arguments with two premises and a conclusion are sometimes called "syllogisms."

Denying a Disjunct

An argument that **denies a disjunct** has one of the following four forms:

1. (1) S1 or S2 (or both).
   (2) Not S1.
   Therefore,
   (3) S2.

2. (1) S1 or S2 (or both).
   (2) Not S2.
   Therefore,
   (3) S1.

3. (1) S1 or S2 (but not both).
   (2) Not S1.
   Therefore,
   (3) S2.

4. (1) S1 or S2 (but not both).
   (2) Not S2.
   Therefore,
   (3) S1.

Key Concept
The four forms of
denying a disjunct.

These forms are proper forms. One premise is a disjunction. The other premise asserts that one of the disjuncts is false. It denies one of the disjuncts. Forms 1 and 3 deny the first disjunct (S1). Forms 2 and 4 deny the second disjunct (S2). Because a disjunction claims that at least one of its disjuncts is true, denying one disjunct means that the other is true.

Suppose that the catalog for your university says

All students must take Math 1113 or higher.

Your friend Irene is enrolled at your university, and so she must take Math 1113 or a math course with a number higher than 1113. Let's call a math course with a number higher than 1113 "a higher-level math course." In that case, the following statement is true:

(a) Irene must take Math 1113 or a higher-level math course (or both).

(This disjunction is inclusive because students can always take extra courses if they want to.) If

S1 = Irene must take Math 1113.
S2 = Irene must take a higher-level math course.

then the form of (a) is

S1 or S2 (or both)

Now suppose that you know that Irene won't take Math 1113. She's planning to graduate after next semester, and Math 1113 isn't offered next semester. You know

Not S1

You can conclude that Irene will take a higher-level math course. You can conclude

S2

You've made an argument that denies a disjunct. Here's the standardization of the argument:

(1) Irene must take Math 1113 or a higher-level math course (or both).
(2) Irene can't take Math 1113
Therefore,
(3) Irene must take a higher-level math course.

This argument has form 1 above and passes the proper form test.

Technical Terms: Disjunctive Syllogism, Alternative Syllogism

"Disjunctive syllogism" and "alternative syllogism" are names sometimes used for an argument that denies the disjunct.

Remember from Chapter Two that there's a technical term for proper deductive argument forms. They're called "valid" forms. Deductive arguments that pass the proper form test are called "valid" arguments, and deductive arguments that fail the proper form test are called "invalid." Because it's common to use "valid" in this way, this book will use this technical term. Just remember that

Key Concept
The distinction between a valid and an invalid argument.

valid argument = a deductive argument that passes the proper form test
invalid argument = a deductive argument that fails the proper form test

And don't forget about the true premises test. Any argument that denies a disjunct is valid (= has a proper form). But not all arguments that are valid pass the true premises test. If either premise of an argument that denies a disjunct is false, the argument isn't a good argument. In Irene's case, you don't know whether the premises of this argument are true. You don't know whether Irene is a real person or just someone made up by the authors of this book.

Fallacy: Affirming an Inclusive Disjunct

Key Concept
The forms of **affirming an inclusive disjunct**.

Here are the two forms of an argument that **affirms an inclusive disjunct**:

1. (1) S1 or S2 (or both).
   (2) S1.
   Therefore,
   (3) Not S2.

2. (1) S1 or S2 (or both).
   (2) S2.
   Therefore,
   (3) Not S1.

These forms are invalid. This form differs from denying a disjunct because it puts the negation in the conclusion instead of the premises.

Habits of a Critical Thinker

Knowing the Power of History

This chapter has a lot of strange-sounding words like "disjunction" and "conditional." Later you'll see that many propositional arguments have names that aren't even in English. They're in Latin. Why all these strange words? It's the power of history.

Take something as simple as driving on the right side of the road. Why do we do that? Have studies shown that it's safer? No, it's the power of history. In the late 1700s, workers in the United States and France started using big wagons pulled by several pairs of horses. To save weight, these wagons didn't have a driver's seat. The drivers used whips on the horses, and most drivers were right-handed and held their whips in their right hand. People who are right-handed mount horses from the left side of the horse. For these reasons, they sat on the left rear horse. Once on the left rear horse, they wanted to drive on the right so that wagons coming the other way would be on their left so that they could look down and make sure that their wagon's wheels didn't hit the oncoming wagon's wheels. That's why they drove on the right side of the road. This practice spread due to conquest and one country's desire to drive on the same side as its neighbors. (For details on right- and left-hand driving, see Peter Kincaid's *The Rule of the Road: An International Guide to History and Practice* (Santa Barbara, CA: Greenwood Press, 1986).)

This example is pretty trivial but history shapes important things like the borders and cultures of countries. A good critical thinker knows that there may not be a good contemporary reason for everything. Some things are the result of history.

A Conestoga wagon had no seat in the front of the wagon. The draft animals were controlled by a teamster who either walked along side the wagon or rode the wheel horse, the animal immediately in front of the wagon on the left side.

The State Museum of Pennsylvania, Pennsylvania Historical and State Commission

Remember your local pizza place that has only two toppings, pepperoni and mushroom. Look at the following argument.

(1) You can have pepperoni or mushrooms on your pizza (or both).
(2) You've ordered pepperoni on your pizza.
Therefore,
(3) You can't order mushrooms on your pizza.

If

S1 = You have pepperoni on your pizza.
S2 = You have mushrooms on your pizza.

You can see that this argument is an example of form 1 of affirming an inclusive disjunct.

This argument says that if you order pepperoni on your pizza, then this guarantees that you won't order mushrooms. But you could have a pepperoni and mushroom pizza, so this argument has an invalid (= improper) form.

Affirming an Exclusive Disjunct

Key Concept
The two forms of
**affirming an exclusive
disjunct**.

While affirming an inclusive disjunct is an invalid form, affirming an exclusive disjunct is a valid form. An argument **affirms an exclusive disjunct** when it has one of the following forms:

1. (1) S1 or S2 (but not both).   2. (1) S1 or S2 (but not both).
    (2) S1.   (2) S2.
    Therefore,   Therefore,
    (3) Not S2.   (3) Not S1.

These forms are valid. The first premise of these forms is the statement of an exclusive disjunction. Let's suppose that there are only two political parties, the Democrats and the Republicans. Then suppose that someone made the following argument:

(1) Either a Democrat or a Republican won the election.
(2) A Democrat won the election.
Therefore,
(3) A Republican didn't win the election.

Elections aren't like pizza. Only one person can win. The "or" in the first premise is an exclusive disjunction. If

S1 = A Democrat won the election.
S2 = A Republican won the election.

You can see that this argument is an example of form 1 of affirming an exclusive disjunct. This form is a valid (= proper) form.

Now you can see why the distinction between inclusive and exclusive disjunction is important. If a disjunction is exclusive, then affirming a disjunct is a valid form. If a disjunction is inclusive, then affirming a disjunct is an invalid form. You need to read carefully to determine which "or" the author is using.

Fallacy: False Dichotomy

Our focus in this chapter is on the proper form test for propositional arguments. But one fallacy involving the true premises test comes up in arguments with disjunctions. The **Fallacy of False Dichotomy** occurs when a premise of an argument with a disjunction is false because there are other alternatives besides the two presented in the premise.

Look at the following argument:

(1) Dwight is either a biology major or a finance major (or both).
(2) Dwight isn't a biology major.
Therefore,
(3) Dwight is a finance major.

This argument is valid (= has a proper form) because it's denying a disjunct. But it fails the true premises test. The first premise is false. At most colleges, students can choose from many different majors. The disjunctive premise is mentioning only two options when there are lots of others. The fact that Dwight isn't a biology major isn't enough to conclude that he's a finance major.

Key Concept
The **Fallacy of False Dichotomy** occurs when a premise of an argument with a disjunction is false because there are other alternatives besides the two presented in the premise.

Technical Terms: False Dilemma, False Alternatives

The Fallacy of False Dichotomy is sometimes called a "False Dilemma" or "The Fallacy of False Alternatives."

EXERCISE 5.3

A. Indicate whether the following passages contain an argument(s). If one or more arguments are present, indicate its form: denying a disjunct, affirming an inclusive disjunct, affirming an exclusive disjunct, or some other form. If a disjunction is present, indicate whether or not it's a false dichotomy.

1. What do you think we should do about this candidate?

2. If you step on a crack, you'll break your mother's back. And you're sure to step on a crack. Your mother's back is toast.

3. That's either Mozart or Bach. It can't be Bach because there's an electric guitar. It must be Mozart.

*4. Where are my keys? They're either in the car or on the table in the kitchen. They aren't in the kitchen, so I'd better check the car.

5. Emily had milk or juice with breakfast, and she always has milk. So she didn't have juice.

6. What should we do tonight? Read Chapter 5 or go to a café?

7. The Catalog says that to graduate you have to take Biology 101 or Chemistry 101. I saw Ceelay's Bio book so I know she took Biology 101. She didn't take Chemistry 101.

*8. The Catalog says that to graduate you have to take Biology 101 or Chemistry 101. Laura didn't take Biology so she must have taken Chemistry.

9. "Either this man is dead or my watch has stopped." (Marx 1937)

10. The following is a comment about who should administer U.S. aid to Pakistan. "The Pakistani authorities have ruled out using foreign nonprofit groups, known as NGOs, shorthand for nongovernmental organizations. But neither do they approve the American choice of private contractors. They [think that] the money [should] go through them." (Perlez 2007, A10)

11. "Officials at Cornell, which operates Arecibo, said that with the repainting, the 44-year-old instrument, the most sensitive radio telescope on the planet, should be good for 30 or 40 more years." (Fountain 2007, D3)

*12. "This is no time for ceremony. The question before the house is one of awful moment to this country. For my own part, I consider it as nothing less than a question of freedom or slavery." (Henry 1901, 2475) Assume that this passage is part of an argument for the conclusion that the American colonies should take up arms against the British.

13. In 1896, Henri Becquerel exposed uranium salts to light for several hours. Afterwards, they gave off light. This is an example of phosphorescence, a process in which a substance absorbs energy and then slowly releases it as light. He then placed the glowing uranium salts on some photographic plates covered in thick paper. Photographic plates are the material then used to take pictures. He observed that if he placed a coin between the uranium salts and the paper-wrapped photographic plate, he could create a photo of the coin. Becquerel was surprised to note that he could still take "photos" of the coins even after the uranium salts had stopped glowing. He concluded that the salts must be giving off some other sort of "light" that was triggering the photographic plate. Becquerel had discovered what we now call radioactivity. (Written by the authors of this book from information found in Bettelheim 2007, 63–64.)

14. "[Holmes leaned] back luxuriously in his armchair, and sending up thick blue wreaths from his pipe, [said: 'I see] that you have been to the Wigmore Street Post-Office this morning [and] that when there you dispatched a telegram.'

    'Right!' said [Watson]. 'Right on both points! But I confess that I don't see how you arrived at it. It was a sudden impulse upon my part, and I have mentioned it to no one.'

    'It is simplicity itself,' [Holmes] remarked, chuckling at my surprise,— 'so absurdly simple that an explanation is superfluous . . . . Observation tells me that you have a little reddish [dirt] adhering to your instep. Just opposite the [Wigmore] Street Office they have taken up the pavement and thrown up some earth which lies in such a way that it is difficult to avoid treading in it in entering. The earth is of this peculiar reddish tint which is found, as far as I know, nowhere else in the neighborhood . . . .'

    'How, then, did you deduce the telegram?'

    'Why, of course I knew that you had not written a letter, since I sat opposite to you all morning. I see also in your open desk there that you have a sheet of stamps and a thick bundle of post-cards. What could you go into the post-office for, then, but to send a [telegram]? Eliminate all other factors, and the one which remains must be the truth.' (Doyle 2004, 10–11)

15. Background information: An alkene is an unsaturated hydrocarbon that contains a carbon–carbon double bond. "The first structure for benzene was proposed by Friedrich August Kekulé in 1872 and consisted of a six-membered ring with alternating single and double bonds, with one hydrogen bonded to each carbon. Although Kekulé's proposal was consistent with many of the chemical properties of benzene, it was contested for years. [. . .] If benzene contains three double bonds, Kekulé's critics asked, why doesn't it undergo reactions typical of alkenes?" (Bettelheim 2007, 359)

Affirming the Antecedent

An argument that affirms the antecedent has one premise that's a conditional and a second premise that affirms the antecedent of the conditional. The conclusion affirms the consequent of the conditional. Here's the form of an argument that **affirms the antecedent**:

(1) If S1, then S2.
(2) S1.
Therefore,
(3) S2.

Key Concept
The form of **affirming the antecedent**.

This is a valid (proper) form. Let's look again at our example about snow.

(1) If it's snowing, then the temperature is below 40 degrees Fahrenheit.
(2) It's snowing.
Therefore,
(3) The temperature is below 40 degrees Fahrenheit.

This argument affirms the antecedent.

Rodrigo Enrique Elizondo-Omaña and three other researchers recently did an experiment to determine whether the pace of a course had any effect on student learning in anatomy courses. (Anatomy is the study of the structure and organs of living things.) The experiment was conducted on two groups of anatomy students who were given an anatomy test before and after they took the course. One group took the course in one-hour class periods over twenty weeks. The other group took the same course in two-hour class periods over nine weeks. The same material was covered, and the same tests were administered. The researchers reasoned that if a difference emerged in the groups' scores, there'd be reason to think that pace was a factor in learning. It turned out that there was a significant difference in scores. The group of students in the twenty-week course scored significantly higher than the group who took the course in nine weeks. Elizondo-Omaña concluded that the pace of a course is an influential factor in how well students learn anatomy in anatomy courses. His argument may be paraphrased as follows:

(1) If there's a significant difference in test scores of groups of students who took the course for different lengths of time, then the pace at which the students took the course must have been a factor in their learning.
(2) There was a significant difference in test scores of groups of students who took the course for different lengths of time.
Therefore,
(3) The pace at which the students took the course must have been a factor in their learning.

Let "S1" stand for the antecedent of the conditional (1), and let "S2" stand for the consequent of this conditional. Elizondo-Omaña's argument affirms the antecedent and so has a valid form. (This argument is a simplified version of Elizondo-Omaña's 2006.)

Technical Term: *Modus Ponens*

Affirming the antecedent is often called by its Latin name, *modus ponens*.

Fallacy: Denying the Antecedent

Suppose that the results of Elizondo-Omaña's study had been different. Suppose that there was no significant difference among the students' group scores. The researchers might then have made the following argument:

(1) If there's a significant difference in test scores of groups of students who took the course for different lengths of time, then the pace at which the students took the course must have been a factor in their learning.
(2) There was *not* a significant difference in test scores of groups of students who took the course for different lengths of time.
Therefore,
(3) The pace at which the students took the course must *not* have been a factor in their learning.

Key Concept

The form of **denying the antecedent**.

Using S1 and S2 as above, this argument has the form of **denying the antecedent**:

(1) If S1, then S2.
(2) Not S1.
Therefore,
(3) Not S2.

This form is invalid. Arguments with this form have one premise that's a conditional and another premise that denies the antecedent of the conditional. The conclusion denies the consequent of the conditional.

In order to understand why this argument form is invalid (improper), remember our example about snow. Suppose that someone were to deny the antecedent like this:

(1) If it's snowing, then the temperature is below 40 degrees Fahrenheit.
(2) It isn't snowing.
Therefore,
(3) The temperature isn't below 40 degrees.

Just because it isn't snowing doesn't show that the temperature is 40 degrees Fahrenheit or higher. Comparing the snow argument and our modified version of Elizondo-Omaña's argument illustrates the value of standardization. Until you standardize the modified version of Elizondo-Omaña's argument, it's hard to see that it's invalid. But once the argument is standardized, you

Critical Thinkers

Rodrigo Enrique Elizondo-Omaña

Rodrigo Enrique Elizondo-Omaña is Professor of Anatomy and Secretary of Educational Research at the School of Medicine, Universidad Autónoma de Nuevo León, Monterrey, Nuevo León, Mexico. In addition to his research on the pace of student learning, Professor Elizondo-Omaña has argued that medical students become better doctors if they learn clinical reasoning skills while gaining the content knowledge of science. See his "The Development of Clinical Reasoning Skills: A Major Objective of the Anatomy Course" (*Anatomical Sciences Education* 1 (2008), pp. 267–268).

Courtesy of Rodrigo Elizondo

can see that it's an example of denying the antecedent. (*Important*: Elizondo-Omaña did not make this bad argument.)

Denying the Consequent

Arguments that **deny the consequent** have this form:

(1) If S1, then S2.
(2) Not S2.
Therefore,
(3) Not S1.

This form is valid. In this form one premise is a conditional. The other premise denies the consequent of that conditional. The conclusion is that the antecedent of the first premise is false. Let's look at our snow example again.

(1) If it's snowing, then the temperature is below 40 degrees Fahrenheit.
(2) The temperature isn't below 40 degrees.
Therefore,
(3) It isn't snowing.

This has a valid (= proper) form. If the premises are true, then the conclusion must be true.

Here's an example from an editorial that Knight Steel and T. Franklin Williams wrote in the *Journal of the American Geriatrics Society*. They're concerned "that so little has been accomplished in the field of geriatric medicine" (Steel 2006, 1142). They're also concerned about the fact that few doctors are being trained as geriatric specialists. They believe that the lack of specialists in geriatrics is the reason that there has been little progress in the field. Paraphrasing part of their reasoning yields the following argument with a valid form:

(1) In order for us to make good progress in the field of geriatric medicine, there needs to be a sufficient number of geriatric specialists trained to conduct research.
(2) There isn't a sufficient number of new geriatric specialists being trained to conduct research.
Therefore,
(3) We aren't making good progress in the field of geriatric medicine.

(This is a simplified version of an argument presented by Steel 2006, 1142.)

Technical Term: *Modus Tollens*

Denying the consequent is often called by its Latin name, *modus tollens*.

Fallacy: Affirming the Consequent

Arguments that **affirm the consequent** have the following form:

(1) If S1, then S2.
(2) S2.
Therefore,
(3) S1.

This form is invalid. In this form one premise is a conditional. The other premise affirms the consequent of the conditional and the conclusion affirms the antecedent of the conditional.

Key Concept
The form of **denying the consequent**.

Key Concept
The form of **affirming the consequent**.

Imagine that the call for more geriatric specialists was answered. Say that in the next five years, a significant number of new doctors trained in that specialty. Would that necessarily solve the problem that occupied Steel and Williams? Think about the following modified version of Steel and Williams' argument:

(1) In order for us to make good progress in the field of geriatric medicine, there needs to be a sufficient number of geriatric specialists trained to conduct research.
(2) There's a sufficient number of new geriatric specialists being trained to conduct research.
Therefore,
(3) We're making good progress in the field of geriatric medicine.

Does this argument have a valid form? Let's look again at our snow example.

(1) If it's snowing, then the temperature is below 40 degrees Fahrenheit.
(2) The temperature is below 40 degrees.
Therefore,
(3) It's snowing.

This argument form is invalid. You've seen days when the temperature was below 40 degrees Fahrenheit but it didn't snow. The modified version of Steel and Williams' argument also has an invalid form. Both of the previous two arguments are examples of affirming the consequent. (*Important*: Steel and Williams did not make this bad argument.)

Tri-Conditional

A **tri-conditional argument** has this form:

(1) If S1, then S2.
(2) If S2, then S3.
Therefore,
(3) If S1, then S3.

This form is valid. Both premises are conditionals, and so is the conclusion. The consequent in one premise is the antecedent in the other. The antecedent of the conditional in the conclusion is the antecedent of one of the premises, and its consequent is the consequent of the other premise.

A recent article in *Prevention* magazine argued that older people should go back to school. Experts cited there made the following argument:

(1) If people go back to school, then they'll get more exercise and stimulation.
(2) If they get more exercise and stimulation, then they experience improvements in overall health.
Therefore,
(3) If people go back to school, they'll experience improvements in overall health.

If you make

S1 = People go back to school.
S2 = People get more exercise and stimulation.
S3 = People experience improvements in overall health.

you'll see that this argument is an example of the tri-conditional form. (This is a simplified version of an argument presented by Borysenko 2006, 117–119.)

Technical Terms: Hypothetical Syllogism, Pure Hypothetical Syllogism, Pure Conditional

Other names for the tri-conditional argument form include "the hypothetical syllogism," "the pure hypothetical syllogism," and the "pure conditional argument."

Habits of a Critical Thinker

Carefulness, Attentiveness

A critical thinker is a careful, attentive thinker. The eight propositional argument forms look a lot like each other. The patterns of affirming and denying disjuncts, antecedents, and consequents can start to spin in your head. You have to be careful and attentive to get the form right. Carefully reviewing the differences between the eight forms is another part of the art of argument. One small difference, like where a "not" is located, can make all the difference in how you'll standardize an argument and whether it's valid or invalid. Don't try to take things too quickly. When you think you know an argument's form, go back to the passage and check to be sure.

If you look at the Guide for Finding, Standardizing, and Evaluating Propositional Arguments at the end of this chapter, you'll see another reason why critical thinkers have to be careful and attentive. It has fifteen steps! And you have to do them in the right order.

EXERCISE 5.4

A. Indicate whether the following passages contain an argument(s). If one or more arguments are present, indicate its form: denying a disjunct, affirming an inclusive disjunct, affirming an exclusive disjunct, affirming the antecedent, denying the antecedent, denying the consequent, affirming the consequent, tri-conditional, or some other form. Indicate whether the argument is valid. If a disjunction is present, indicate whether or not it's a false dichotomy.

1. If Tyler gets an A on the final, he'll pass the course, and I'm sure he'll get an A on the final. So Tyler will pass the course.

2. If Bobby doesn't come to class, Laura will be upset. But Bobby will come to class, so Kartik won't be upset.

3. If Anthony takes the job as a financial consultant, he'll have to move to New Jersey. He'll never move to New Jersey, so he'll never take the job.

*4. If hell freezes over, then the Atlanta Falcons will win the Super Bowl and if they win the Super Bowl, then I'm a monkey. That means that if hell freezes over, then I'm a monkey.

5. If Bobby doesn't come to class, Laura will be upset. But Bobby will come to class, so Laura won't be upset.

6. That dome must be made of gold or bronze and gold is way too expensive to be used to cover such a large surface so it must be made of bronze.

7. If Keela gets a set of Volrath pans for Christmas she'll be thrilled. And I bet she'd cook us up some really good stuff to eat. We should get her those pans.

*8. If 'twas brillig, and the slithy toves did gyre and gimble in the wabe, then Jay has slain the Jabberwock. 'Twas brillig, and the slithy toves did gyre and gimble in the wabe. Come to my arms, my beamish boy! O frabjous day! Callooh! Callay! Jay slew the Jabberwock! (This example is drawn with modifications from Carroll 2004, 220.)

9. "Federal prosecutors will probably call a former doctor for Barry Bonds as a witness if Bonds's perjury and obstruction of justice case goes to trial, according to court documents made public Thursday." (Schmidt 2007, C13)

10. "1. We are sometimes mistaken in our perceptual beliefs.

    2. If we are sometimes mistaken in our perceptual beliefs, then it is always logically possible that our perceptual beliefs are false.

    3. If it is always logically possible that our perceptual beliefs are false, then we never know that any of our perceptual beliefs are true.

    Therefore

    4. We never know that any of our perceptual beliefs are true." (Cornman 1992, 48)

11. "Opponents of channelizing natural streams emphasize that the practice is antithetical to the production of fish and wetland wildlife and, furthermore, the stream suffers from extensive aesthetic degradation." (Keller 2005, 225)

*12. "If Bonds and Clemens had not been linked to performance-enhancing drugs, they would sail through the voting process [for election to the Baseball Hall of Fame] and maybe challenge Tom Seaver's record of being named on 98.84 percent of the ballots. But because they have been accused of using illegal drugs to enhance their performances, the path to Cooperstown, N.Y., will be littered with endless debates." (Curry 2007, C12)

13. U.S. citizens will not need passports to enter the United States by land from Canada until mid-2009, if a bill passed by Congress is signed by President George W. Bush. A provision of the bill postpones plans by the Department of Homeland Security to require passports. Senator Patrick J. Leahy said that he expected Mr. Bush to sign the bill. Citizens living in border states have objected to the requirement.

14. "Walk down the hall in any building on your campus where professors have their offices. Do you see any bearded, disheveled men wearing rumpled pants and smoking pipes, hunched over their computers and mumbling to themselves? How about disheveled women wearing rumpled shirts, smoking pipes, hunched over their computers and mumbling to themselves? Researchers hard at work? No. Stereotypes of what [professors] look like and do? Yes. What you are more likely to see in the halls of your classroom building are men and women hard at work. They are committed to finding the answer to just another piece of the great puzzle that helps us understand [things] a little bit better than the previous generation." (Salkind 2006, 1, material omitted)

15. "I venture to affirm, that the rule here holds without any exception, and that every simple idea has a simple impression, which resembles it, and every simple impression a correspondent idea. That idea of red, which we form in the dark, and that impression which strikes our eyes in sun-shine, differ only in degree, not in nature. That the case is the same with all our simple impressions and ideas, it is impossible to prove by a particular enumeration of them. Every one may satisfy himself in this point by running over as many as he pleases. But if any one should deny this universal resemblance, I know no way of convincing him, but by desiring him to shew a simple impression, that has not a correspondent idea, or a simple idea, that has not a correspondent impression. If he does not answer this challenge, as it is certain he cannot, we may from his silence and our own observation establish our conclusion." (Hume 1896, 3)

B. Look for examples of affirming the antecedent, denying the antecedent, denying the consequent, affirming the consequent, or the tri-conditional in Exercise 5.3 above.

Chapter Summary

Propositional statements can be simple or compound. Simple statements are those that don't contain another statement. Compound statements contain at least one other statement. The four compound statements studied in this chapter are negations, disjunctions, conjunctions, and conditionals.

Disjunctions are two or more statements that can be joined by "or." Disjunctions are inclusive or exclusive. In exclusive disjunctions only one of the disjuncts can be true. In inclusive disjunctions more than one of the disjuncts can be true.

Conjunctions are two or more statements that can be joined by "and." Conjunctions claim that all of the conjuncts are true. If a conjunction has nineteen conjuncts and eighteen of them are true but one of them is false, then the conjunction is false.

Conditionals are compound statements that can be connected with "if . . . then." There are lots of different ways to express conditionals. The "if" part of a conditional is the antecedent, and the "then" part is the consequent. A conditional is true when its consequent is true or its antecedent is false.

There are eight common propositional argument forms. A proper deductive argument form is a called a "valid" form, and an improper deductive argument form is called an "invalid" form. Denying a disjunct, affirming an exclusive disjunct, affirming an antecedent, denying a consequent, and tri-conditionals are valid forms. Affirming an inclusive disjunct, denying an antecedent, and affirming a consequent are invalid forms.

GUIDE

Finding, Standardizing, and Evaluating Propositional Arguments

This Guide is an amplification of the "Guide for Finding, Standardizing, and Evaluating Arguments" from Chapter Two. The numbered sentences are copies from the Guide in Chapter Two. The paragraphs with "Prop" (for "Propositional") in front of them are additional materials that apply only to propositional arguments.

Finding Arguments

1. Look for an attempt to convince.

   Prop. Look for an attempt to convince that relies on the logical relationships *between* statements.

2. Find the conclusion.

3. Find the premises.

4. Review the following to make sure that you've correctly identified the conclusion and the premises: imperfect indicator words, sentence order, premises and/or conclusion not in declarative form, and unstated premises and/or conclusion.

5. Review the following to make sure that you haven't incorrectly identified something as a premise or a conclusion when in fact it isn't part of an argument: assertions, questions, instructions, descriptions, and explanations.

Standardizing Arguments

6. Rewrite the premises and the conclusion as declarative sentences. Make sure that each premise and the conclusion is a grammatically correct declarative sentence. Rewrite the premises and conclusion as necessary to make them clearer, but don't change the meaning of the passage. Remove pronouns from the sentences and replace them with the nouns or noun phrases to which they refer. Remove emotionally charged language.

7. Review any phrases you've omitted to be sure that they aren't premises or a conclusion.

8. Number the premises and the conclusion. Put [ ] around the number of an unstated premise or conclusion. Place the premises before their conclusion and insert "Therefore," between the premises and the conclusion. Use blank lines to indicate subarguments.

9. Compare your standardization to the original passage to make sure that you haven't omitted any arguments found in the passage and to be sure that you've correctly identified the premises and the conclusion.

Evaluating Arguments: The True Premises Test

10. Check to see whether the premises are accurate descriptions of the world.

11. Consider whether the premises are appropriate for the argument's audience.

12. Review the assumed premises to be sure that the assumptions are reasonable. Make sure that all assumed premises are uncontroversially true empirical statements, uncontroversially true definitional statements, or appropriate statements by experts. Make sure the definitions are good ones.

    Prop. If the argument contains a disjunction, check for a False Dichotomy.

Evaluating Arguments: The Proper Form Test

13. Determine whether the argument is a deductive argument or inductive argument.

14. Determine whether the premises are relevant to the conclusion. Look at each premise individually to see whether the truth of the premise provides some evidence for the truth of the conclusion. Look at the premises as a group to see whether the truth of all of them provides some evidence for the truth of the conclusion.

    Prop. Determine the form of the propositional argument. Compare it to the eight propositional argument forms discussed in this section. See the next page.

Evaluating Arguments: Checking for Fallacies

15. Compare the argument to the list of fallacies on page 410 to see whether the argument commits any of the fallacies.

Propositional Argument Forms

Denying a Disjunct

1. (1) S1 or S2 (or both).
(2) Not S1.
Therefore,
(3) S2.

2. (1) S1 or S2 (or both).
(2) Not S2.
Therefore,
(3) S1.

3. (1) S1 or S2 (but not both).
(2) Not S1.
Therefore,
(3) S2.

4. (1) S1 or S2 (but not both).
(2) Not S2.
Therefore,
(3) S1.

Fallacy: Affirming an Inclusive Disjunct

1. (1) S1 or S2 (or both).   **2.** (1) S1 or S2 (or both).
   (2) S1.   (2) S2.
   Therefore,   Therefore,
   (3) Not S2.   (3) Not S1.

Affirming an Exclusive Disjunct

1. (1) S1 or S2 (but not both).   **2.** (1) S1 or S2 (but not both).
   (2) S1.   (2) S2.
   Therefore,   Therefore,
   (3) Not S2.   (3) Not S1.

Affirming the Antecedent   **Fallacy: Denying the Antecedent**

  (1) If S1, then S2.   (1) If S1, then S2.
  (2) S1.   (2) Not S1.
  Therefore,   Therefore,
  (3) S2.   (3) Not S2.

Denying the Consequent   **Fallacy: Affirming the Consequent**

  (1) If S1, then S2.   (1) If S1, then S2.
  (2) Not S2.   (2) S2.
  Therefore,   Therefore,
  (3) Not S1.   (3) S1.

Tri-Conditional

  (1) If S1, then S2.
  (2) If S2, then S3.
  Therefore,
  (3) If S1, then S3.

6

Categorical Arguments

It is believed that the aorta is capable of undergoing passive stretching, because elastic arteries are the large arteries capable of undergoing passive stretching, and the aorta is an elastic artery.

—Paraphrased from Fritz (1999, 472)

Learning Outcomes

After studying the material in this chapter, you should be able to:

1. Recognize the four standard categorical statement forms: universal affirmative, universal negative, particular affirmative, and particular negative.

2. Put ordinary sentences into the standard categorical statement forms.

3. Illustrate the four standard categorical statement forms using Venn diagrams.

4. Recognize, standardize, and evaluate categorical arguments with one premise.

5. Recognize, standardize, and evaluate categorical arguments with two premises.

$\mathbf{T}$he argument on the previous page is a deductive argument, but it isn't an example of one of the eight propositional deductive forms discussed in Chapter Five. It's a categorical deductive argument. This chapter will look at some categorical argument forms. It will help you determine the form of the argument above and whether it passes the proper form test.

Identifying Categorical Statements

Categorical arguments focus on statements about categories of things. A category is a group, a collection of things with a shared characteristic. **Categorical statements** say that things of one category either are or aren't in some other category. Here's a categorical statement:

Some apples are red.

It says that some of the members of the category of apples are also in the category of red things.

There are lots of ways to make categorical statements. But they can all be put into four standard categorical statement forms. Because categorical statements assert that things in one *group* either are or aren't in some other *group*, we'll use the variables G1 and G2.

Key Concept
Categorical statements say that things of one category either are or aren't in some other category.

Connections

Chapter Two introduces the use of variables.

The Four Standard Categorical Statement Forms

Form	Name	Abbreviation	Example
All G1 are G2.	Universal Affirmative	UA	All apples are red.
All G1 are not G2.	Universal Negative	UN	All apples are not red.
Some G1 are G2.	Particular Affirmative	PA	Some apples are red.
Some G1 are not G2.	Particular Negative	PN	Some apples are not red.

Key Concept
The four standard categorical statement forms.

The four categorical statement forms have four parts. (1) They begin either with the word "all" or with the word "some." (2) Then they refer to one group, G1. (3) Then they have either "are" or "are not." (4) Finally, they refer to the second group, G2.

Part 1	Part 2	Part 3	Part 4
All/Some	G1	are/are not	G2

Part 1 is the **quantity** of the statement. If the quantity of a statement is "all," the statement is a **universal** statement. If the quantity of a statement is "some," the statement is a **particular** statement. Part 2 is the **subject** of the statement. Part 3 is the **quality** of the statement. If the quality of a statement is "are," the statement is an **affirmative**. If the quality of a statement is "are not," then the statement is a **negative**. Part 4 is the **predicate** of the statement. If the two groups are "college students" and "brilliant people," then the four forms are below. You can make these four forms for any two groups.

Key Concept
The four parts of categorical statements.

		Quantity	Subject	Quality	Predicate
Universal Affirmative	UA	All	college students	are	brilliant people.
Universal Negative	UN	All	college students	are not	brilliant people.
Particular Affirmative	PA	Some	college students	are	brilliant people.
Particular Negative	PN	Some	college students	are not	brilliant people.

Technical Terms: A, E, I, O

Some textbooks use the letters A, E, I, O instead of the abbreviations used in this book.

A = UA   E = UN   I = PA   O = PN

Why do you need categorical logic? Because some arguments have a proper form, but they don't seem to have a proper form if you treat them as propositional arguments. Look at this argument:

(a) (1) All apples are fruits.
     (2) Some apples are red.
     Therefore,
     (3) Some fruits are red.

Argument (a) has a proper form. But if you treat it as a propositional argument, it would look like this:

     S1 = All apples are fruits.
     S2 = Some apples are red.
     S3 = Some fruits are red.

(a1)(1) S1
    (2) S2
    Therefore,
    (3) S3

The propositional argument (a1) has an improper form. Propositional logic is the logic of relationships *between* statements but categorical logic is the logic of relationships *within* statements. The logic of argument (a) isn't captured by (a1).

You can correctly capture the form of (a) like this:

> G1 = apples
> G2 = fruits
> G3 = red things

(a2) (1) All G1 are G2.
     (2) Some G1 are G3.
     Therefore,
     (3) Some G2 are G3.

(a2) has a proper form. This is why you need categorical logic.

Remember from Chapters Two and Five that proper deductive argument forms are called "valid" arguments, and deductive arguments that fail the proper form test are called "invalid."

> **valid argument** = a deductive argument that passes the proper form test
> **invalid argument** = a deductive argument that fails the proper form test

Technical Terms: Aristotelian Logic, Classical Logic, Class Logic, Predicate Logic, First-Order Logic

Some texts call categorical logic "Aristotelian deductive logic." Other texts call it "classical logic" or "class logic." If you take an advanced logic class you'll learn that categorical logic and propositional logic can be combined into a more complex system that is called "predicate logic" or "first-order logic."

EXERCISE 6.1

A. For each of the following: (a) identify which of the four types of categorical statements it is (UA, UN, PA, PN), (b) if necessary, put it in one of the four standard categorical forms, and (c) identify its quantity, quality, subject, and predicate.

1. All people under 65 years of age are people who need health insurance.
2. All people 65 years old and older are people covered by Medicare.
3. All able-bodied people younger than 65 years old are not people covered by Medicare.
*4. Some people who work are not people covered by health insurance.
5. Some airline pilots are people in favor of extra screening of passengers who carry liquids on board the airplane.
6. All people who fly are people who are willing to undergo extra screening to increase airport security.
7. Some airport personnel are temporary employees without benefits.
*8. All broadcast media are recently developed technologies whose long-term effects are good and ill.
9. All of James' friends are people he has met at school.
10. Some of Theresa's friends are people she works with at the credit union.
11. Some of the people who work at the credit union are people who go to school with James.
*12. Not all Americans have health insurance.

13. "Those who are without insurance don't benefit much from advances in cancer care that are predicated on early discovery and treatment." (*Boston Globe* 2007)

14. "Many healthcare advocates would prefer one in which the state provides insurance for everybody." (*Boston Globe* 2007)

15. "People on Medicaid, the federal/state system for poor Americans, do not have as high survival rates as those with employer-sponsored insurance." (*Boston Globe* 2007)

Universal Affirmative: All G1 Are G2

People don't talk using the four categorical statement forms. They are technical terms defined by logicians. Don't try to figure them out as if they were something your friends would say. Think of them as words in a foreign language. Let's look at each one in more detail.

Key Concept
The form of a universal affirmative (UA) statement.

A **universal affirmative (UA) statement** is a statement that can be put into this form:

All G1 are G2.

Speaking roughly, the UA statement

All college students are brilliant.

says that every member of the category of college students is also a member of the category of brilliant people. Here are some other ways to make a UA statement.

Every college student is brilliant.
Each college student is brilliant.
Any college student is brilliant.
A college student is a brilliant person.
Only brilliant people can be college students.
College students are brilliant.

People often leave off the "all" and use words other than "are" and "is" to make a UA statement. Here are more examples:

Original	In Standard Categorical Form
Dogs have tails.	All dogs are things with tails.
Computers often break down.	All computers are things that break down often.
Toyotas get good mileage.	All Toyotas are cars that get good mileage.
Official baseballs weigh 5 to 5.25 ounces.	All official baseballs are things that weigh between 5 and 5.25 ounces.
Recessions lead to unemployment.	All recessions are things that lead to unemployment.

Categorical Statements: Important Details

Detail 1: Venn Diagrams

The philosopher John Venn invented diagrams to make the meaning of the standard statement forms clearer. Venn diagrams begin with two overlapping circles, one for each of the categories in a categorical statement.

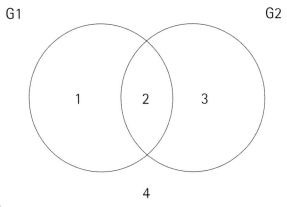

Venn Diagram 6.1

The circle on the left represents the G1 category. Things that are members of G1 are inside the G1 circle, and things that aren't members of G1 are outside the G1 circle. Things that are members of G2 are inside the G2 circle, and things that aren't G2 are outside the G2 circle. Area 1 represents those things that are G1 and are not G2. Area 2 represents those things that are both G1 and G2. Area 3 represents those things that are G2 and are not G1. Area 4 represents those things that are neither G1 nor G2.

If G1 = apples and G2 = red things, then a Venn diagram looks like this:

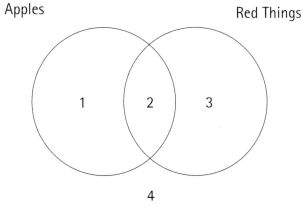

Venn Diagram 6.2

Area 1 represents things that are apples but aren't red. Golden Delicious apples are in Area 1. Area 2 represents things that are apples and are red. Red Delicious apples are in Area 2. Area 3 represents red things that aren't apples. Red sports cars and red hats are in Area 3. Area 4 represents things that aren't apples and aren't red. A white pickup truck, the Leaning Tower of Pisa, and you are in Area 4.

To represent the four categorical statements on a Venn diagram, you shade an area when it's empty, put an "X" in an area when it has something in it, and leave an area blank when a statement doesn't tell you whether the area is empty or it has something in it. Don't fall into the trap of thinking that a blank area is empty. A shaded area is empty. When an area is blank, that means that you don't know what's in that area because the statement doesn't say anything about it.

Let's look at this universal affirmative (UA):

(c) All apples are red.

This statement is false, but you can still represent it on a Venn diagram.

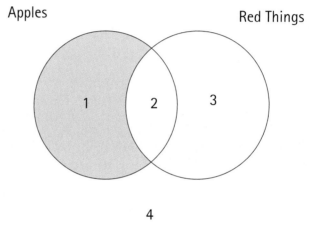

UA: All apples are red.

Venn Diagram 6.3

Area 1 is shaded because if "All apples are red," then there's nothing in Area 1. Area 1 represents those things that are apples and aren't red. But if all apples are red, then Area 1 is empty.

Detail 2: Empty Categories

When you look at "All apples are red" you might think that in addition to Area 1 being shaded out, there should be an "X" in Area 2 instead of it being blank. After all, you know that there are some red apples. Hold that thought and look at this UA statement:

(d) All werewolves are howlers.

You know that there aren't any werewolves. It's an empty category. You might think that the entire werewolf circle should be shaded. You might think that the Venn diagram of this statement should look like this:

UA: All werewolves are howlers.   WRONG

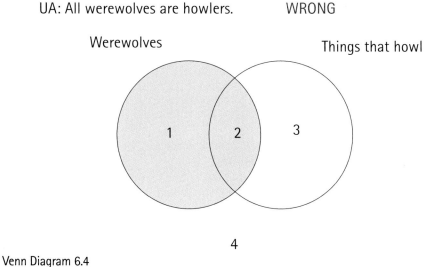

Venn Diagram 6.4

Now look at this UA statement.

(e) All *écureuils* are things with tails.

Are there any *écureuils*? You don't know. (*"écureuil"* is a word in French. If you speak French, pretend that you don't know what *"écureuil"* means.) But even though you don't know whether there are any *écureuils*, you still know that if statement (e) were true, nothing without a tail could be an *écureuil*. You know that there's nothing in Area 1 of this Venn:

UA: All *écureuils* are things with tails.

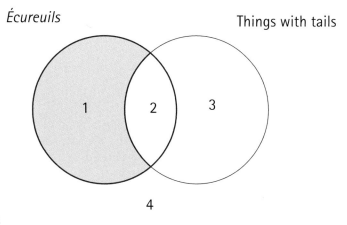

Venn Diagram 6.5

But because you don't know whether there are any *écureuils*, you don't know whether there's anything in Area 2. You have to leave it blank.

"All apples are red," "All werewolves are howlers," and "All *écureuils* are things with tails" show that sometimes the subject category has members,

Key Concept
The precise meaning of a UA statement is: If there's anything in the subject category, then it's also in the predicate category.

sometimes it doesn't, and sometimes you don't know whether it has members. But you always know that, if there's anything in the subject category, then it's also in the predicate category. This is the precise meaning of a UA statement. What is common to Venn Diagrams 6.3, 6.4, and 6.5 is that Area 1 is shaded. The Venn diagram of a UA statement represents the meaning that is common to

cases where the subject category has members
(All apples are red),
cases where the subject category doesn't have any members
(All werewolves are howlers), and
cases where you don't know whether the subject category has any members
(All *écureuils* are things with tails).

Later in this chapter, it will be important that the UA statement is defined with a conditional, an if … then statement.

Connections

Chapter Five discusses conditionals.

Technical Terms: The Assumption of Existence, Traditional/Aristotelian Interpretation, Modern/Boolean Interpretation

When they talk about categorical statements in which the subject category is empty, logicians distinguish between a modern (or Boolean) interpretation and a traditional (or Aristotelian) interpretation. The traditional interpretation (offered by the philosopher Aristotle) leaves open the possibility that at least one member exists for every subject category. The modern interpretation (offered by the mathematician George Boole) doesn't make this assumption of existence for members of UA and UN statements.

On the traditional interpretation, the UA statement "All werewolves are howlers" is false (because there aren't any werewolves), but on the modern interpretation it's true (because the UA statement is taken to mean "*if* there were any werewolves, they would be howlers"). In this chapter, we'll use the modern interpretation. But the traditional interpretation is also useful. Some versions of this book include a chapter that uses the traditional interpretation.

Detail 3: Category Variables

To make things easier, instead of using the variables G1 and G2, let's use meaningful capital letters in *italics* to stand for categories. These capital letters are called "category variables." You should use letters that help you remember the categories, like "*C*" to stand for "college students" and "*B*" to stand for "brilliant people." In that case, you can write the UA sentences about college students like this:

C = college students
B = brilliant people

All *C* are *B*.

Key Concept
When you take a statement in standard categorical form and replace the groups with variables, you have **formalized** the statement.

The letters you choose don't matter. When you take a statement in standard categorical form and replace the groups with variables, you have **formalized** the statement (because what you have done illustrates the statement's form).

Whenever you formalize a statement, you must indicate what the variables mean. Students sometimes forget and put something like this on a test:

Wrong: All *C* are *B*.

Also, variables have to stand for a group of things. They can't stand for an adjective or an adverb.

Wrong: *C* = college students

B = brilliant

All *C* are *B*.

B has been assigned to an adjective. "Brilliant" doesn't clearly refer to a category. Brilliant what? Brilliant stars? Brilliant colors? Brilliant arguments? The statement

UA   All college students are brilliant.

is referring to brilliant people, not brilliant stars, colors, or arguments.

Detail 4: Complex Categories

Statements about complex categories can be put in categorical form. Look at this sentence:

(a) Every major field has at least one guide to the resources that experienced researchers commonly use. (Booth 2003, 81)

By changing the verb, and recognizing that "every" means "all," you can standardize this statement into UA form and then formalize it.

(b) All major fields are fields that have at least one guide to the resources that experienced researchers commonly use.

M = Major fields

G = Fields that have at least one guide to the resources that experienced researchers commonly use

All *M* are *G*.

Statement (b) captures, in a more precise way, the meaning of (a).

Technical Term: Universal Assertion

"Universal assertion" is another name for UA statements.

Critical Thinkers

John Venn

John Venn (1834–1923) was a British logician and philosopher who taught moral sciences at Cambridge University in England. He's famous for developing the Venn diagrams used today in logic, computer science, and statistics. You can read the *Cambridge Philosophical Society Proceedings* article where Venn first introduced the diagrams in 1880, "On the Employment of Geometrical Diagrams for the Sensible Representation of Logical Propositions," at http://books.google.com/books?id=Gpl1AAAAI AAJ&tpg=PA47&dq=john+venn&as_brr=1#PPA47,M1.

Universal Negative: All G1 Are Not G2

A **universal negative (UN) statement** is a statement that can be put into this form:

> All G1 are not G2.

There are many different ways to make a UN statement.

> No college students are brilliant.
> Nobody who is a college student is brilliant.
> If anybody is a college student, that person isn't brilliant.
> There never was a college student who was brilliant, and there never will be.
> College students aren't brilliant.

Each of these statements would be correctly formalized as

> C = college students
> B = brilliant people
>
> All C are not B.

Here's another UN statement:

> None of us has been to Venus, but we believe that it's hot, dry, and mountainous. (Booth 2003, 10)

This statement doesn't use "are" or "are not," and it might look like it doesn't have a subject category. But "us" refers to people. You could standardize and formalize the statement like this:

> All people who believe that Venus is hot, dry, and mountainous are people who haven't been to Venus.
>
> B = People who believe that Venus is hot, dry, and mountainous
> V = People who have been to Venus
>
> All B are not V.

Make sure that your category variables stand for categories without negatives. "V" refers to "People who have been to Venus." It doesn't stand for "People who have *not* been to Venus."

> **Wrong:** B = People who believe that Venus is hot, dry, and mountainous
> V = People who have not been to Venus
>
> All B are not V.

This isn't correct because the "not" appears twice. The assignment of the category variable "V" and the UN statement both contain "not." When you formalize a passage, you shouldn't put a negative in the meaning of a category variable. The negative appears in the quality of the statement, not in the assignment of variables.

Remember that the precise definition of a UA statement is the conditional "if there's anything in the subject category, then it's also in the predicate category." The precise definition of a UN statement is also a conditional: if there's anything in the subject category, then it isn't in the predicate category. Think about werewolves again and look at the UN statement

> (a) All werewolves are not howlers.

You might think that this UN statement is false because there aren't any werewolves. But remember from Chapter Five that conditional statements are true when the antecedent is false or the consequent is true. This means that (a) is true because its antecedent is false. There aren't any werewolves.

Key Concept
The precise meaning of a UN statement is: If there's anything in the subject category, then it isn't in the predicate category.

Connections

Chapter Five discusses conditionals.

The UN statement "All apples are not red" is represented on a Venn diagram like this:

UN: All apples are not red.

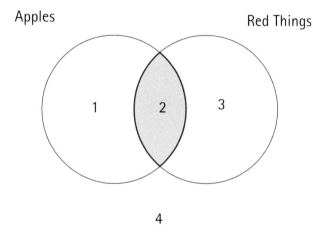

Key Concept
The representation of a UN statement with a Venn diagram.

Venn Diagram 6.6

Area 2 is shaded because if "All apples are not red," then there's nothing in Area 2. As with the UA statement, you might think that there should be an "X" in Area 1 because you know that there are some apples, and if none of them are red then that means that there are some that aren't red. But look at

All *écureuils* are not things with tails.

UN: All *écureuils* are not things with tails.

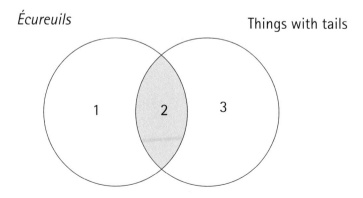

Venn Diagram 6.7

If there are *écureuils*, then there's something in Area 1. But if there aren't any *écureuils*, then there's nothing in Area 1. You don't know whether there are any *écureuils*, so you don't know whether there's anything in Area 1. That's why Area 1 is blank.

Technical Term: No G1 are G2

Some critical thinking books use

    (a) No G1 are G2.

in place of

    (b) All G1 are not G2.

Both (a) and (b) are ambiguous and you aren't likely to hear or come across either of them in normal conversation. As long as you understand what a UN statement means, it doesn't matter whether you use (a) or (b). We have to pick one for this book, and we have picked (b) to parallel the UA form.

Particular Affirmative: Some G1 Are G2

Key Concept
The form of a particular affirmative (PA) statement.

A **particular affirmative (PA) statement** is a statement that can be put into this form:

Some G1 are G2.

The precise meaning of a PA statement is

Key Concept
The precise meaning of a PA statement is: There's at least one member in the subject category that's also in the predicate category.

There's at least one member in the subject category that's also in the predicate category.

In deductive logic, the word "some" is a technical term. It means "at least one."

Some apples are red.

means that there's at least one apple that is red. On a Venn diagram it's represented like this:

PA: Some apples are red.

Key Concept
The representation of a PA statement with a Venn diagram.

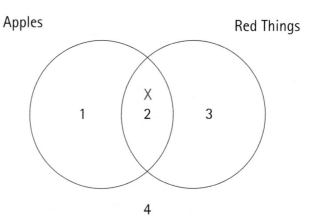

Venn Diagram 6.8

There's an "X" in Area 2 because "Some apples are red" tells you that there's at least one red apple. But it doesn't tell you anything else, so the other three areas are blank.

PA statements can be made with sentences like:

1. At least one college student is brilliant.
2. Some college students are brilliant.
3. A few college students are brilliant.
4. Most college students are brilliant.
5. Almost all college students are brilliant.
6. A great number of college students are brilliant.

Any of these statements can be formalized like this:

(a) C = college students
     B = brilliant people

     Some C are B.

When statements 2–6 are standardized with the PA form, part of the meaning is lost. If you asked people whether

Almost all college students are brilliant.

and

At least one college student is brilliant.

mean the same thing, most of them would say that they don't. But both of these statements are written as (a) because they both mean that there's at least one member in the first category that's also in the second category. Here's another way in which categorical statements, like all technical terms, don't match common usage.

Why have logicians made the decision to use "some" the way they do? "Some," "a few," "most," "almost all," and "a great number" are vague. Logicians want to make them precise and they want to be able to represent a wide variety of statements in PA form. What's common to all six of the statements above? All of them assert that at least one college student is brilliant. This precise meaning captures an important part of the meaning of statements 1–6 above.

Connections

Chapter Four discusses vague categories.

Particular Negative: Some G1 Are Not G2

A **particular negative (PN) statement** is a statement that can be put into this form:

Some G1 are not G2.

The precise meaning of a PN statement is

There's at least one member in the subject category that's not in the predicate category.

Key Concept
The form of a particular negative (PN) statement.

Key Concept
The precise meaning
of a PN statement is:
There's at least one
member in the subject
category that's not in
the predicate category.

"Some apples are not red" is a particular negative. On a Venn diagram it's represented like this:

PN: Some apples are not red.

Key Concept
The representation of
a PN statement with a
Venn diagram.

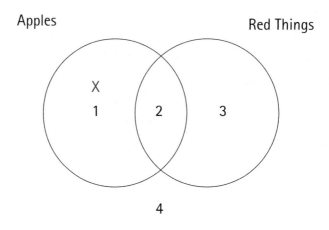

Venn Diagram 6.9

This statement tells you that there's at least one thing that is an apple but isn't red.

The PN statement

Some college students are not brilliant.

says that there's at least one college student who isn't brilliant. Claims such as

Most college students aren't brilliant.

Not all college students are brilliant.

can be formalized as a PN statement.

> C = college students
> B = brilliant people

Some C are not B.

As was the case with universal negatives, the formalization of a particular negative must use category variables that are assigned to affirmative categories. If you don't do this, you are likely to make the following mistake:

Wrong: Children don't always remain with their family.

> K = Children
> R = Things that *do not* always remain with their family.

Some K are not R.

It should be

> Children don't always remain with their family.

> K = Children
> R = Things that always remain with their family.

> Some K are not R.

Don't read anything extra into a PN statement. The statement

> (a) Some college students are not brilliant.

might be misinterpreted as meaning

> (b) Some college students are not brilliant and
>   some college students are brilliant.

But, speaking precisely, the PN statement

> C = college students   B = brilliant people

> (c) Some C are not B.

doesn't say that some college students *are* brilliant. The PN statement (c) says only that there's at least one college student who isn't brilliant. If someone says (a) and the context makes it clear that he means to say (b), you have to use two categorical statements to express the meaning of (a).

> C = college students
> B = brilliant people

> Some C are B.
> Some C are not B.

Technical Terms: Not all G1 are G2

Some categorical logic books write the PN form as "Not all G1 are G2." We write it as "Some G1 are not G2" to parallel the PA form.

Habits of a Critical Thinker

Making Precise Distinctions

It can be hard to distinguish UA, UN, PA, and PN statements. A good critical thinker can see when a distinction is needed and can make precise distinctions.

Suppose that someone says that God doesn't exist because there's evil in the world and a good God wouldn't allow evil. In response, someone says that evil isn't caused by God. It's caused by people. At this point a good critical thinker would see that there's

a distinction between different kinds of evils. Some seem to be caused by people (stealing), but some don't (earthquakes). As we have put it quickly here, this distinction isn't precise. Is the collapse of a building in an earthquake caused by the earthquake or the people who built the building? We don't have the space to go further into this complex topic. Our point is only that making good distinctions is important to thinking critically.

EXERCISE 6.2

A. Rewrite the following as one of the four standard categorical statements forms. In some cases, only the material in brackets needs to be put into one of the four forms.

1. Not all students in college are sophomores.
2. Any students who are sophomores aren't graduating.
3. If the moon were destroyed, the earth would have many tidal waves.
*4. If someone is eligible for Medicare, they don't need their own health insurance.
5. Every citizen has health insurance.
6. When it rains, it pours.
7. Polar bears live in northern climates.
*8. This has been a long day.
9. When it's raining, almost everyone carries an umbrella.
10. Because wood scratches, [metal is a better material for desks]. [Focus on the material in brackets.]
11. The costs of cell phone services have decreased and areas with coverage have increased so that [now there's no reason to ever use a pay phone]. [Focus on the material in brackets.]
*12. Some people mistakenly believe that there are no universal moral principles.
13. Only those who complete 120 credit hours graduate from college.
14. Not everyone believes that there are no universal moral principles.
15. At least one furlough day per month is required for all state employees.

B. Draw the correct Venn diagram for each of the exercises in 6.1 A and 6.2 A.

▌ Evaluating Categorical Arguments with One Premise

Key Concept
Categorical arguments are arguments that can be expressed with standard categorical statements.

Categorical arguments are arguments that can be expressed with standard categorical statements. There's an infinite number of categorical argument forms. This textbook will focus on some of the most common categorical argument forms. Let's start with categorical argument forms that have only one premise.

Technical Term: Immediate Inferences

Categorical arguments with one premise are also called "immediate inferences."

Contradiction

Key Concept
The two pairs of contradictories. Contradictory statements can't both be false and can't both be true.

There are two pairs of contradictories within the four standard categorical statement forms.

UA   All G1 are G2   << **Contradiction** >> PN   Some G1 are not G2

UN   All G1 are not G2   << **Contradiction** >> PA   Some G1 are G2

Contradictory statements can't both be false and can't both be true. One way to recognize categorical contradictories is that the pair of statements each have the opposite quantity and the opposite quality. If you assume that

(UA)   All apples are red.

is true, it follows that

(PN)   Some apples are not red.

is false. If you assume that (UA) "All apples are red" is false, then you can infer that (PN) "Some apples are not red." Similarly, if you assume that (PN) "Some apples are not red" is true, then you can infer that (UA) "All apples are red" is false. If you assume that (PN) "Some apples are not red" is false, then you can infer that (UA) "All apples are red" is true. This gives you four valid (= proper) argument forms based on the fact that UA and PN are contradictories.

1. (1) UA
    Therefore,
    (2) It is false that PN

2. (1) It is false that UA
    Therefore,
    (2) PN

3. (1) PN
    Therefore,
    (2) It is false that UA

4. (1) It is false that PN
    Therefore,
    (2) UA

UN and PA statements are also contradictories. Each one has the opposite quantity and the opposite quality. If you know that

(UN)   All apples are not red.

is true, then you know that

(PA)   Some apples are red.

is false. If you know that (UN) "All apples are not red" is false, then you know that (PA) "Some apples are red" is true. Similarly, if you know that (PA) "Some apples are red" is true, then you know that (UN) "All apples are not red" is false. And if you know that (PA) "Some apples are red" is false, then you know that (UN) "All apples are not red" is true. You've got four more valid argument forms.

5. (1) UN
    Therefore,
    (2) It is false that PA

6. (1) It is false that UN
    Therefore,
    (2) PA

7. (1) PA
    Therefore,
    (2) It is false that UN

8. (1) It is false that PA
    Therefore,
    (2) UN

Suppose you know that

> All bones are made of osseous tissue.

is true. You'd also be able to conclude that the statement

> Some bones are not made of osseous tissue.

is false. This is form 1 above. If scientists discovered in the future that there was a bone not made of osseous tissue, then you'd say

> All bones are made of osseous tissue.

is false. On that basis, you could validly conclude that

> Some bones are not made of osseous tissue.

is true.

If you know that any one of the four standard categorical statements is true, you will always be able to validly conclude that its contradictory is false and if you know that any one of the four statements is false, you can validly conclude that its contradictory is true. That's a quick way to double your knowledge!

Fallacy: Confusing a Contrary and a Contradictory

Look at the following argument:

UN (1) All the rooms in this house are not hot.
Therefore,
(2) It is false that some rooms in this house are cold.

Key Concept
The **Fallacy of Confusing the Contrary with the Contradictory** occurs when contraries are confused with contradictories.

This argument commits the **Fallacy of Confusing the Contrary with the Contradictory**. Hot and cold are contraries, not contradictories. If a room is hot, it can't be cold, and if it's cold, it can't be hot. But it could be neither. It could be room temperature.

Connections

The room temperature argument also commits the Fallacy of False Dichotomy. Chapter Five discusses this fallacy and contraries.

This table illustrates the difference between contraries and contradictories. Be careful not to confuse them.

Contraries	Neither	Contradictories
Hot–Cold	Room temperature	Hot–Not hot
Beautiful–Ugly	Unremarkable	Beautiful–Not beautiful
Enemy–Ally	Neutral	Enemy–Not an enemy
Democrat–Republican	Independent	Democrat–Not a Democrat
Rich–Poor	Middle-income	Rich–Not rich
In School–On vacation	Graduated	In School–Not in school

EXERCISE 6.3

A. Determine which of the following arguments have valid (= proper) form. For those that have a valid form, indicate which of the eight categorical argument forms it has.

1. (1) All Americans over 65 are protected by Medicare.
   Therefore,
   (2) It is false that some Americans over 65 aren't protected by Medicare.

2. (1) Some people on Social Security are young people who became disabled in a car accident.
   Therefore,
   (2) It is false that all people on Social Security aren't young.

3. (1) All students who are freshmen are students who live on campus.
   Therefore,
   (2) It is false that some students who are freshmen aren't students who live on campus.

*4. (1) It is false that all students who are freshmen are students who live on campus.
   Therefore,
   (2) Some students who are freshmen are students who don't live on campus.

5. (1) All students who attend college are people who have paid fees to use the library.
   Therefore,
   (2) It is false that some students who attend college aren't people who have paid fees to use the library.

6. (1) Some college students are football players.
   Therefore,
   (2) It is false that some college students aren't football players.

7. (1) Some college students aren't football players.
   Therefore,
   (2) Some college students are football players.

*8. (1) It is false that all college students aren't in the military.
   Therefore,
   (2) Some college students are in the military.

9. (1) Some food in the dining hall is organic.
   Therefore,
   (2) It is false that all food in the dining hall isn't organic.

10. (1) Some food that is good for you is organic.
    Therefore,
    (2) It is false that all food that is good for you isn't organic.

11. (1) It's not true that all salespeople are not capable of selling products they don't believe in.
    Therefore,
    (2) Some salespeople are capable of selling products they don't believe in.

*12. (1) Many people suffer from the common cold each year.
Therefore,
(2) If it false that no one suffers from the common cold each year.

13. (1) There's no vaccination for the common cold.
Therefore,
(2) Some vaccines are for the common cold.

14. (1) Antibiotics are prescribed for individuals with cold symptoms only if a doctor believes an individual has a bacterial infection.
Therefore,
(2) It is false that some antibiotics prescribed for cold symptoms aren't for people believed to have a bacterial infection.

15. (1) All pandas live in zoos throughout the world.
Therefore,
(2) Some pandas don't live in zoos throughout the world.

Conversion

Conversions are carried out by switching the subject and predicate of a statement. Here's how each of the four categorical statement forms can be converted.

	Original Statement	Converse	Valid
UA	All G1 are G2	All G2 are G1	No
UN	All G1 are not G2	All G2 are not G1	Yes
PA	Some G1 are G2	Some G2 are G1	Yes
PN	Some G1 are not G2	Some G2 are not G1	No

The conversions of UN and PA lead to valid (= proper) forms.

9. UN (1) All G1 are not G2.
Therefore,
(2) All G2 are not G1.

10. PA (1) Some G1 are G2.
Therefore,
(2) Some G2 are G1.

If you know that

All bookworms are not invertebrates.

then you can conclude by conversion that

All invertebrates are not bookworms.

And if you know that

> Some carpetbaggers are people who carry suitcases.

then you can conclude by conversion that

> Some people who carry suitcases are carpetbaggers.

The conversions of UA and PN lead to invalid (= improper) forms.

Invalid: UA   (1) All G1 are G2.
                   Therefore,
                   (2) All G2 are G1.

Invalid: PN   (1) Some G1 are not G2.
                   Therefore,
                   (2) Some G2 are not G1.

Even if you know that

> All stockbrokers are people who take risks.

you shouldn't conclude that

> All people who take risks are stockbrokers. After all, scuba divers, sky divers, and ordinary automobile drivers also take risks.

In a similar way, even though you know that

> Some dogs are not collies.

you can't conclude that

> Some collies are not dogs.

Distribution

One way to understand why conversion leads to a valid form for UN and PA statements but doesn't for UA and PN statements is to think about what logicians call "distribution." The subject and predicate categories of each of the four forms are either distributed or undistributed. Remember that a categorical statement says that members of the subject category are either in or not in the predicate category. Each categorical statement makes this claim about either all or some of the members in each category. A category is **distributed** when the statement says something about all members of that category.

Suppose that you brought pizza to class one day, and you brought in enough for everyone in your class to have a slice. You could say that you distributed pizza to all members of your class. But if you only brought one pizza, there probably wouldn't be enough to go around. You could say that you hadn't distributed pizza to all members of your class. Similarly, logicians say that if the statement says something about all members of the category, then that category is distributed. If the statement doesn't say something about all members, then that category isn't distributed.

Both universal statements (UA and UN) distribute their subject categories because they say "All" of the members of the subject are either in or not in the predicate category.

Key Concept
A category is **distributed** when the statement says something about all members of that category.

(UA)   All logicians are primates.

and

(UN)   All logicians are not amoebas.

tell you something about all logicians (either that they are all primates or that all of them are not amoebas).

Both particular statements (PA and PN) don't distribute their subject categories because they both say "Some" (not all) of the members in the subject are in or not in the predicate. Both

(PA)   Some apples are red.

and

(PN)   Some apples are not red.

don't tell you anything about all apples.

The predicates of affirmative statements (UA and PA) aren't distributed but the predicates of negative statements (UN and PN) are. The UA statement above ("All logicians are primates") doesn't tell you anything about all primates. Similarly, the PA statement above ("Some apples are red") doesn't tell you anything about all red things. The UN statement above ("All logicians are not amoebas") tells you something about all amoebas. It tells you that all amoebas are not logicians. The PN statement above ("Some apples are not red") tells you something about all red things, but what it tells you is a bit odd. It tells you that all red things are not one of the apples to which "some apples" refers. Here's a chart to help you remember distribution. The distributed categories are in red.

Key Concept
The distributed categories.

	Distributed Categories (in bold)
UA	All **G1** are G2
UN	All **G1** are not **G2**
PA	Some G1 are G2
PN	Some G1 are not **G2**

A rule for helping you to remember which categories are distributed is "subjects of universals and predicates of negatives."

If you know which categories are distributed, you can quickly figure out which ones will lead to a valid (= proper) form when converted. If the distribution stays the same in the conversion, reasoning from one statement to its converse is a valid form. If the distribution is changed in the conversion, then the conversion doesn't produce a valid form. You can see this most easily with UA. It distributes its subject category but doesn't distribute its predicate category. This is because a UA says *all* members of the subject are in the predicate category, but it *doesn't* say that all members in the predicate category are in the subject category. So when you convert a UA statement, you change which categories are distributed and change the meaning of the statement. This is why converting a UA produces an invalid form. (As you'll see later, distribution is also important when you evaluate categorical arguments with two premises.)

Complements

Before you can understand some more categorical argument forms with one premise, you have to understand the idea of a complement. The **complement** of a category is the category of all things that don't have that feature. The complement of the category of apples is non-apples. Non-apples include grapes, cars, computers, and pencils. The complement of the category of non-apples is apples. The complement often looks odd because the prefix "non" isn't used as frequently as "in," "un," "ir," or "a." Here are some examples of complements: visible and invisible, locked and unlocked, regular and irregular, theist and atheist.

Key Concept
The **complement** of a category is the category of all things that don't have that feature.

Contraposition

Contraposition is a two-step operation. You begin by switching the subject and predicate, just as you do for conversion. Then you complement both the subject and the predicate.

Key Concept
The two steps of contraposition and the contrapositives of the four categorical statement forms.

	Original Statement	Contrapositive	Valid
UA	All G1 are G2	All non-G2 are non-G1	Yes
UN	All G1 are not G2	All non-G2 are not non-G1	No
PA	Some G1 are G2	Some non-G2 are non-G1	No
PN	Some G1 are not G2	Some non-G2 are not non-G1	Yes

Reasoning from a UA statement to its contrapositive produces a valid (= proper) form.

11. (1) All G1 are G2.
    Therefore,
    (2) All non-G2 are non-G1.

The UA statement

All engineers are faced with decisions that require ethical reflection.

can be formalized like this:

E = Engineers
F = People faced with decisions that require ethical reflection

All E are F.

The contrapositive of this statement is

All non-F are non-E.

or

All those who are not faced with decisions that require ethical reflection are not engineers.

The contrapositive of a PN statement also produces a valid form.

12. (1) Some G1 are not G2
    Therefore,
    (2) Some non-G2 are not non-G1.

If you know that

Some birds are not eagles.

then you know that

Some non-eagles are not non-birds.

In more natural English, if you know that some birds aren't eagles, then you know that some things that aren't eagles are birds.

The reasoning from a UN or a PA statement to its contrapositive is invalid. You can tell this because the distribution of the categories is altered. From the UN statement

All cars are not birds.

you can't conclude that

All non-birds are not non-cars.

Some things that aren't birds are cars. And from the PA statement

Some dogs are non-collies.

you can't conclude that

Some collies are non-dogs.

It's true that some dogs are non-collies. Some are German Shepherds. But all collies are dogs.

Obversion

Like contraposition, **obversion** is a two-step operation: First, you change the quality of the statement. Then you complement the predicate. Changing the quality means that if the original statement is affirmative, you make it negative. If the original statement is negative, make it affirmative. Don't change the subject. Here's the obverse of the four standard categorical statement forms.

	Original Statement	Obverse	Valid
UA	All G1 are G2	All G1 are not non-G2	Yes
UN	All G1 are not G2	All G1 are non-G2	Yes
PA	Some G1 are G2	Some G1 are not non-G2	Yes
PN	Some G1 are not G2	Some G1 are non-G2	Yes

Obversion produces a valid form for all four statements.

13. UA (1) All G1 are G2.
     Therefore,
     (2) All G1 are not non-G2.

14. UN (1) All G1 are not G2.
     Therefore,
     (2) All G1 are non-G2.

15. PA (1) Some G1 are G2.
     Therefore,
     (2) Some G1 are not non-G2.

16. PN (1) Some G1 are not G2.
     Therefore,
     (2) Some G1 are non-G2.

The UN statement

All short bones are not irregular bones.

is a UN statement, and the predicate is a complement. Taking "irregular" as "non-regular," using S for the subject and R for the predicate, the statement would be formalized as

S = Short bones
R = Regular bones

All S are not non-R.

(Remember that category variables are assigned to affirmative categories.) The obverse of

All S are not non-R.

is

All S are R. (All short bones are regular bones.)

If you know the first statement is true, you can conclude that the obverse is true as well.

Here's an example of how you can use and misuse one-premise categorical arguments. Suppose that a study found that

All people who no longer smoke are people with increased lung cancer survival rates.

S = People who smoke
R = People with increased lung cancer survival rates

All non-S are R.

If you're a smoker, you might want to know what's true about smokers. To find out, you might be tempted to make this argument:

(a) (1) All non-S are R.
Therefore,
(2) All S are non-R.

(2) says that

(2) All smokers are people with non-increased lung cancer survival rates.

But argument (a) has an invalid form. It might be that some smokers have a genetic immunity to lung cancer. Argument (a) complemented the subject and predicate. But just complementing the subject and predicate isn't one of the valid forms for categorical one-premise arguments. It isn't an example of obversion because the quality isn't changed. It isn't an example of contraposition because the subject and predicate aren't switched.

But you can use contraposition to make this valid argument:

(b) (1) All non-S are R.
Therefore,
(2) All non-R are S.

This says that

(3) All people with non-increased lung cancer survival rates are smokers.

Arguments (a) and (b) have the same premise. But argument (b) is an example of valid form 11 above. If you're a smoker, this is a pretty good reason to quit!

GUIDE

Some Valid (= Proper) Categorical Argument Forms with One Premise

Contradiction

1. (1) UA.
Therefore,
(2) It is false that PN.

2. (1) It is false that UA.
Therefore,
(2) PN.

3. (1) PN.
Therefore,
(2) It is false that UA.

4. (1) It is false that PN.
Therefore,
(2) UA.

5. (1) UN.
Therefore,
(2) It is false that PA.

6. (1) It is false that UN.
Therefore,
(2) PA.

7. (1) PA.
Therefore,
(2) It is false that UN.

8. (1) It is false that PA.
Therefore,
(2) UN.

Conversion

9. UN (1) All G1 are not G2.
Therefore,
(2) All G2 are not G1.

10. PA (1) Some G1 are G2.
Therefore,
(2) Some G2 are G1.

Contraposition

11. (1) All G1 are G2.
Therefore,
(2) All non-G2 are non-G1.

12. (1) Some G1 are not G2.
Therefore,
(2) Some non-G2 are not non-G1.

Obversion

13. UA (1) All G1 are G2.
Therefore,
(2) All G1 are not non-G2.

14. UN (1) All G1 are not G2.
Therefore,
(2) All G1 are non-G2.

15. PA (1) Some G1 are G2.
Therefore,
(2) Some G1 are not non-G2.

16. PN (1) Some G1 are not G2.
Therefore,
(2) Some G1 are non-G2.

EXERCISE 6.4

A. For each of the following given statements, provide: (a) the contradictory, (b) the converse, (c) the complement of the predicate category, (d) the obverse, (e) the complement of the subject category, and (f) the contrapositive. You may first need to put the statement into standard categorical form.

1. Some pandas are animals that live in the wild.
2. Some vaccines are not for the common cold.
3. All cultural minorities are groups that need special rights.
*4. All bones are not made of cardiac tissue.
5. All learned behavior is the result of experience.

B. For each of the exercises in A, determine whether the reasoning from the original statement to the one you produced is an example of a valid form. If it is, indicate the number (1–16) of the form.

C. Determine whether the following arguments are valid (= pass the proper form test). If it is, indicate the number (1–16) of the form.

   1. (1) Some Democratic candidates for the U.S. presidency in 2008 were women.

   Therefore,

   (2) Some women were Democratic candidates for the U.S. presidency in 2008.

   2. (1) All African American candidates for the 2008 presidential race were Democrats.

   Therefore,

   (2) All non-Democrats were not non–African American candidates for the 2008 presidential race.

   3. (1) All candidates for the 2008 presidential race were U.S. citizens.

   Therefore,

   (2) All candidates for the 2008 presidential race were not non–U.S. citizens.

   *4. (1) All living beings on earth are carbon-based organisms.

   Therefore,

   (2) All carbon-based organisms are living beings on earth.

   5. (1) All social learning is assumed to underlie traditions.

   Therefore,

   (2) All animals that exhibit traditions will exhibit social learning.

   6. (1) In the wild, giant pandas are found in China, but a few pandas live in zoos throughout the world.

   Therefore,

   (2) Some pandas are not animals who live in the wild [wild = non-zoo].

   7. (1) All pandas eat bamboo.

   Therefore,

   (2) All bamboo eaters are pandas.

   *8. (1) All pandas eat bamboo.

   Therefore,

   (2) All bamboo eaters are not non-pandas.

   9. (1) All pandas are animals that belong to an endangered species.

   Therefore,

   (2) All pandas are not animals that belong to an unendangered species.

   10. (1) All defense of cultural practices is likely to have much greater impact on the lives of women and girls.

   Therefore,

   (2) All defense of cultural practices is likely to have a lesser impact on men and boys. (Simplified paraphrase from Okin 1996.)

11. (1) All cultural minorities are groups that need special rights.
    Therefore,
    (2) All nonminorities are not groups that need special rights.

*12. (1) All African Americans are people who are likely to fully comprehend the helplessness, loneliness, and anxieties of the unemployed.
    Therefore,
    (2) All people likely to fully comprehend the helplessness, loneliness, and anxieties of the unemployed are non–African Americans.

13. (1) It is contended that only inflation engenders concern and fear.
    Therefore,
    (2) All issues that are non-inflation [such as unemployment] are issues that do not engender concern and fear.
    (Simplified paraphrase from King 1976.)

14. (1) "Clearly, no one can predict the precise impact of global warming over the next century."
    Therefore,
    (2) All possible predictions about the impact of global warming will be imprecise at best.
    (Simplified paraphrase from Bennett 2007, 320–321.)

15. (1) All diseases that are classified as public health disorders are treated by public policy and not by individual medication.
    Therefore,
    (2) Some diseases not classified as public health disorders are not treated without public policy and only by individual medication.

Evaluating Categorical Arguments with Two Premises

Identifying Categorical Syllogisms

This section looks at categorical arguments with two premises. It focuses on categorical arguments with

1. precisely three categorical statements (two premises and a conclusion),
2. precisely three categories, and
3. each of the categories appearing in precisely two of the three statements.

Key Concept
The three features of **categorical syllogisms.**

Following tradition we'll call arguments that have these three features **categorical syllogisms.** Here's a categorical syllogism:

    (1) All fathers are not women.
    (2) Some stockbrokers are women.
    Therefore,
    (3) Some stockbrokers are not fathers.

The argument has precisely three statements (two premises and a conclusion). It has precisely three categories: fathers, women, and stockbrokers. Each of the three categories appears exactly twice. You can formalize the argument like this:

> F = Fathers
> W = Women
> S = Stockbrokers

> (1) All F are not W.
> (2) Some S are W.
> Therefore,
> (3) Some S are not F.

This argument passes the true premises test and is valid (= passes the proper form test).

You saw a categorical syllogism at the beginning of this chapter.

> It is believed that the aorta is capable of undergoing passive stretching, because elastic arteries are the large arteries capable of undergoing passive stretching, and the aorta is an elastic artery.

Here's a standardization:

> (1) Elastic arteries are the larger arteries capable of undergoing passive stretching.
> (2) The aorta is an elastic artery.
> Therefore,
> (3) The aorta is capable of undergoing passive stretching.

This argument isn't in the form of a categorical syllogism yet because its statements aren't in the four categorical statement forms.

The conclusion of the argument isn't a UN or PN because it's an affirmative statement. But is it a UA statement or a PA statement? The four categorical statement forms are precise, but the way people talk isn't so precise. Part of the art of argument is determining the best way to take ordinary speech and formalize it into categorical statements. You might think that (3) is a PA statement. After all, the aorta is only one artery and you've only got one aorta in your body. But, in spite of the word "the" at the beginning of the sentence, the author is making a claim about all aortas. The author is claiming that all aortas (yours, your friends', etc.) are capable of undergoing passive stretching. You can rewrite (3) as

> (3) All aortas are things capable of undergoing passive stretching.

Because this claim is about all aortas, it's a UA statement. You can formalize (3) like this:

> A = Aortas
> C = Things capable of undergoing passive stretching

> (3) All A are C.

Premise (2)

> (2) The aorta is an elastic artery.

also begins with "the." It might first appear to be about one particular aorta. But, on reflection, you see that the author is again making a claim about all aortas.

(2) All aortas are elastic arteries.

You can formalize (2) like this:

E = Elastic arteries

(2) All *A* are *E*.

Premise (1)

(1) Elastic arteries are the larger arteries capable of undergoing passive stretching.

is clearer than the others because the misleading word "the" isn't present. This is an affirmative claim about all elastic arteries. It says

(1) All elastic arteries are things capable of undergoing passive stretching.

or

(1) All *E* are *C*.

You can put all this together.

(1) All elastic arteries are capable of undergoing passive stretching.
(2) All aortas are elastic arteries.
Therefore,
(3) All aortas are capable of undergoing passive stretching.

A = Aortas
C = Things capable of undergoing passive stretching
E = Elastic arteries

(1) All *E* are *C*.
(2) All *A* are *E*.
Therefore,
(3) All *A* are *C*.

Critical Thinkers

Christine Ladd-Franklin

Christine Ladd-Franklin (1847–1930) taught at Columbia University and published more than 100 articles. Ladd-Franklin's most famous contribution is the invention of a technique for testing all syllogisms for validity with one formula (called the antilogism). Her method is still used today. You can read one of her articles, "On Some Characteristics of Symbolic Logic," at http://books.google.com/books?id=4NULAAAAIAAJ&jtp=543#v=onepage&q=&f=false.

EXERCISE 6.5

A. For each of the following, (a) determine whether it's a categorical syllogism. If it is, (b) put the argument into standard categorical form and (c) formalize it.

1. All dogs are collies and all collies are purple; therefore, all dogs are purple.

2. Some chickens are green because all chickens are ugly and some ugly things are green.

3. Some apples are fruits and some oranges are fruits, so it follows that some apples are oranges.

*4. All freshmen are students and no students are infants, so all infants are not students.

5. All seniors are graduating and all sophomores are not seniors, so some graduates are not sophomores.

6. Some politicians are honest so politicians must be unhappy because most honest people are unhappy.

7. Some New Yorkers belong to the Chinese Communist party because some people from China belong to the Chinese Communist party and some New Yorkers are from China.

*8. No Americans are wealthy, so Cindy is not wealthy because Cindy is an American.

9. All able-bodied people younger than 65 years of age are in need of their own health insurance because all able-bodied people younger than 65 are not eligible for Medicare whereas all people eligible for Medicare are not in need of health insurance.

10. Because animals cannot be moral agents, they cannot be said to have rights; therefore, if they are due moral consideration at all, it must be on some other basis. (Simplified paraphrase from Machan 1991.)

11. Residents of the congressional district of our state do not earn more than the minimum wage because residents of the congressional district of our state will not be affected by the upcoming tax hike and residents who do not earn more than the minimum wage will not be affected by the upcoming tax hike.

*12. All employees are stakeholders in the company so all CEOs should act in their favor because all CEOs are responsible to stakeholders of the company.

13. "All classrooms painted in non-white colors spark students' imaginations because classrooms painted white are boring and bored students do not engage their imaginations." (Sunstein 2007, 110)

14. "Most substances offer resistance to the flow of electricity, and this resistance changes with temperature. So most substances change with temperature." (Cutnell 2007, 363)

15. "All membership groups are constantly looking for new adherents to expand their resources and clout. Groups that rely on ideological appeals have a special problem because the competition in most policy areas is intense." (Janda 2008, 308)

B. Determine whether the following passages contain an argument. If it does contain an argument, determine whether the argument is a categorical syllogism. If the arguments is a categorical syllogism, put it into the form of a categorical syllogism and formalize it.

1. "People may say one thing in a focus group and do another thing in the voting booth." To get beyond this, some neuromarketers are tracking not only what people say on the survey, but also the time it takes them to respond, since their theory is that "faster responses indicate stronger feelings." (Alter 2007, W1 & W6, material omitted)

(The next three arguments are paraphrases from Vinicor 1994, 22, material omitted.)

2. Because diabetes can be ameliorated in large part by loss of weight and increase in exercise activity, and because weight control and exercise programs involve no medication and indeed can be advertised and administered publicly, it seems reasonable to conclude that diabetes is a public problem (not an individual's disease).

3. Reflecting on infectious conditions, it appears that disease burden, rapid change in disease incidence (suggesting preventability), and public concern about risk are three essential characteristics that define a public-health disorder. [Hint: Focus on the implied argument in the phrase "rapid change in disease incidence (suggesting preventability) defines a public-health disorder."]

*4. [M]ost would still consider diabetes primarily to be a clinical disease. In part, this perception is based on the fact that, in association with aging and a possible strong family history, diabetes and its complications may appear inevitable to many. [Hint: "Inevitable" means that it is not preventable.]

5 & 6. Find two categorical arguments in the following: Because it was assumed that scientific progress would displace people's need for religion, it was expected that religion would decline in the 20th century given the growth of scientific achievement. This did not happen. In fact, religion has been on the rise in the past few decades despite tremendous scientific achievements. (Paraphrased from Haviland 2007, 290.)

7. If the actual price is greater than the standard price per hour, the direct labor price variance is a positive number. If the direct labor price is positive, then there is indication of an unfavorable variance. Therefore, if the actual price is greater than the standard price per hour, then there is indication of an unfavorable variance. (Paraphrased from Ainesworth 2007, 258.)

*8. "'Terrorists are cold-blooded killers,' concluded President Bush after suicide bombers had just killed some 35 people in coordinated attacks on the Red Cross headquarters in Iraq, just as those years earlier were willing to kill innocent people in the World Trade Center." (Janda 2008, 191)

9 & 10. "[S]ociological theories claim to explain global inequality. The first, modernization theory, is a variant of functionalism. According to modernization theory, global inequality results from various dysfunctional characteristics of poor societies themselves. Specifically, modernization theorists say the citizens of poor societies lack sufficient capital to invest in Western-style agriculture and industry. They lack rational, Western-style business techniques of marketing, accounting, sales, and finance. As a result, their productivity and profitability remain low. They lack stable, Western-style governments that could provide a secure framework for investment. Finally, they lack a Western mentality: values that stress the need for savings, investment, innovation, education, high achievement, and self-control in having children. Societies characterized by these dysfunctions are poor." (Brym 2005, 241, material omitted)

*11 & 12. Several possibilities for standardizing categorical syllogisms are contained within the following:

> Proponents of dependency theory, a variant of conflict theory, have been quick to point out the chief flaw in modernization. For the last 500 years, the most powerful countries in the world deliberately impoverished the less powerful countries. Focusing

on internal characteristics blames the victim rather than the perpetrator of the crime. It follows that an adequate theory of global inequality should not focus on the internal characteristics of poor countries themselves. Instead, it ought to follow the principles of conflict theory and focus on patterns of domination and submission—specifically in this case on the relationship between rich and poor countries. That is just what dependency theory does.

According to dependency theorists, less global inequality existed in 1500 and even in 1750 than today. However, beginning around 1500, the armed forces of the world's most powerful countries subdued and then annexed or colonized most of the rest of the world. Around 1780 the industrial revolution began. It enabled the Western European countries, Russia, Japan, and the United States to amass enormous wealth, which they used to extend their global reach. They forced their colonies to become a source of raw materials, cheap labor, investment opportunities, and markets for the conquering nations. The colonizers thereby prevented industrialization and locked the colonies into poverty. (Brym 2005, 241, footnotes omitted)

13. The famous Athenian general and statesman, Pericles, supported going to war against Sparta and Sparta's allies. After several years of war, Sparta had invaded Athens twice and was winning. Athenians were growing demoralized. After the second invasion, Pericles gave a speech in which he is quoted as saying:

It does not matter whether a man prospers as an individual: if his city is destroyed, he is lost with it; but if he meets with misfortune, he is far safer in a fortunate city than he would be otherwise. Since, therefore, a city is able to sustain its private citizens in whatever befalls them, while no individual is strong enough to carry his city, are we not all obliged to defend it and not, as you are doing now, sacrifice our common safety? (Thucydides 1993, 52–53)

14. "Luther was anything but a fundamentalist. He did not attach equal importance to every [biblical] text. He boldly called Romans 'the most important document in the New Testament,' and he brushed aside the Epistle to St. James as 'an epistle of straw.'" [Note: Fundamentalists attach equal importance to every biblical text.] (Dickens 1968, 57, material omitted)

15. More than one possible categorical relationship is contained in the following:

Social responsibility arises from concern about the consequences of business's acts as they affect the interests of others. Business decisions do have social consequences. Business people cannot make decisions that are solely economic decisions, because they are interrelated with the whole social system. This situation requires that business persons' thinking be broadened beyond the company gate to the whole social system. Systems thinking is required. Social responsibility implies that a business decision maker in the process of serving his or her own business interests is obliged to take actions that also protect and enhance society's interests. (Shaw 2004, 213)

Evaluating Categorical Syllogisms: The Test Method

A set of four tests allows you to determine whether a categorical syllogism is valid. You can think of them as subtests. If a categorical syllogism fails one of these subtests, it's invalid (= fails the proper form test). If it passes all four subtests, it's valid (= passes the proper form test).

GUIDE

Validity of Categorical Syllogisms: The Test Method

1. The Equal Negatives Test: The number of negative statements in the conclusion must equal the number of negative statements in the premises.
2. The Quantity Test: If both premises are particulars, then the conclusion can't be a universal and if both premises are universal, then the conclusion can't be a particular.
3. The Distributed Conclusion Test: If a category is distributed in the conclusion, then it must also be distributed in a premise.
4. The Distributed Middle Category Test: The middle category must be distributed at least once.

Let's look at each of these tests.

The Equal Negatives Test

This test says that for a categorical syllogism to have a valid form, the number of UNs and PNs in the premises must be the same as the number of UNs and PNs in the conclusion.

In the aortas argument

A = Aortas
C = Things capable of undergoing passive stretching
E = Elastic arteries

(1) All E are C.
(2) All A are E.
Therefore,
(3) All A are C.

the number of negative statements in the premises of this argument is zero because both of the premises are in UA form. The number of negative statements in the conclusion is also zero because it's also a UA statement. The aortas argument passes the equal negatives test. In general, the following kinds of categorical syllogisms fail the equal negatives test:

arguments with two negative premises,
arguments with one or two negative premises and an affirmative conclusion, and
arguments with two affirmative premises and a negative conclusion.

Any time you see a passage standardized in any of these three ways, you'll know right away that it's invalid (= doesn't pass the proper form test).

The Quantity Test

This test says that if both premises are particulars, then the conclusion can't be a universal, and if both premises are universal, then the conclusion can't be a particular. In the aortas argument, both premises are universal but so is the conclusion. This argument passes the quantity test.

Most people quickly see that if the two premises of a syllogism are both particular statements (if they are both about only "some" of their subject category), then you can't validly draw any conclusion about "all" of anything. The argument

(1) Some apples are red.
(2) Some red things are cars.
Therefore,
(3) All apples are cars.

doesn't have a valid form.

It's harder to see that if both premises are universal, then the conclusion can't be a particular. If you look at an argument like this one:

(1) All apples are fruits.
(2) All fruits are things that are good to eat.
Therefore,
(3) Some apples are things that are good to eat.

you might think that a argument with two universal premises and a particular conclusion could have a valid form. But think again about werewolves and look at this argument:

(1) All werewolves are howlers.
(2) All howlers are things that make noise.
Therefore,
(3) Some werewolves are things that make noise.

Universal statements don't say that the subject category has any members. Remember that a UA statement is defined with a conditional. A UA statement says only that *if* the subject category has any members, *then* they will be included in the predicate category. This is why premise (1) of this argument is true even though there are no werewolves. And premise (2) is true. But remember that logicians defined "some" to mean "at least one member," so particular statements *do* say that the subject category has members. That's why the conclusion of this argument, statement (3), is false (because there are no werewolves). The argument about werewolves has true premises and a false conclusion. The truth of the premises doesn't guarantee that the conclusion is true. A categorical syllogism with two universal premises and a particular conclusion has an invalid form.

The Distributed Conclusion Test

You saw above that the notion of distribution helps you understand which conversions produce valid argument forms. It also helps you evaluate categorical syllogisms. You should go back and review the discussion of distribution and make sure you have it fresh in your mind.

The distributed conclusion test states that, if a category is distributed in the conclusion, then it must also be distributed in a premise. In the aortas argument, the conclusion is a UA statement, All *A* are *C*. Remembering the phrase "subjects of universals and predicates of negatives," you note that a UA statement distributes its subject but not its predicate. The conclusion distributes its subject, *A*. It doesn't distribute its predicate,

C. Test 2 concerns only what's distributed in the conclusion. Because *C* isn't distributed in the conclusion, you don't have to worry about whether *C* is distributed in the premises. But you need to make sure that *A* is distributed in a premise.

Category *A* isn't in premise (1) so it can't be distributed in premise (1). Premise (2) is a UA statement, and UA statements distribute their subjects. So *A* is distributed in premise (2), and the aortas argument passes the distributed conclusion test. The only category that is distributed in the conclusion is *A*, and this category is also distributed in a premise.

GUIDE

Doing the Distributed Conclusion Test

If the conclusion is a...	then check the distribution of...
1. UA	the subject of the conclusion.
2. UN	both categories.
3. PA	neither category.
4. PN	the predicate of the conclusion.

As you can see from the third row, if the conclusion is a PA statement, the argument automatically passes the distributed conclusion test.

The Distributed Middle Category Test

Key Concept
The **middle category** is the category that's not in the conclusion.

The distributed middle category test states that the middle category must be distributed at least one time. The **middle category** is the category that's not in the conclusion. In the aortas argument, the middle category is *E*. *E* is also the subject of premise (1) and the predicate of premise (2). Both premises are UA statements. UA statements distribute their subject, so *E* is distributed in premise (1). It isn't distributed in premise (2). Premise (2) is a UA statement, and a UA statement doesn't distribute its predicate. But the distributed middle category test only requires that the middle category be distributed once. The aortas argument passes the distributed middle category test. It passes all four tests so it's a valid argument.

By the way, because PA statements don't distribute either the subject or the predicate categories, any categorical syllogism with two PA premises automatically fails the middle category test.

EXERCISE 6.6

A. For each of the following categorical argument forms, determine which test, if any, it fails.

1. (1) All G1 are G2.
(2) All G3 are G2.
Therefore,
(3) All G1 are G3.

2. (1) All G1 are not G2.
(2) All G2 are not G3.
Therefore,
(3) Some G1 are not G3.

3. (1) All G1 are G2.
(2) Some G1 are not G3.

Therefore,
(3) Some G3 are not G2.

*4. (1) All G2 are G1.
(2) Some G2 are G3.
Therefore,
(3) All G3 are G1.

5. (1) Some G1 are G2.
(2) Some G2 are G3.
Therefore,
(3) Some G1 are not G3.

B. Use the Test Method to determine whether each argument in Exercise 6.5A and 6.5B has a valid form. If an argument fails one or more of the tests, indicate which test(s) it fails.

Evaluating Categorical Syllogisms: The Venn Method

You can use Venn diagrams to determine whether a categorical argument has a valid form. But the Venn diagrams discussed earlier in this chapter can't be used because they present only two categories, and categorical syllogisms have three categories. You need a Venn diagram with three circles to evaluate categorical syllogisms.

You begin by drawing the three circles. They must overlap because you need to be sure to represent every possible combination of the three categories.

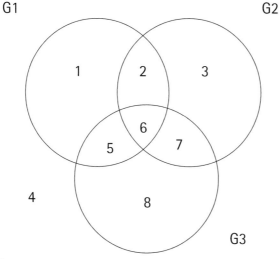

Venn Diagram 6.10

This Venn diagram has circles for G1 and G2 just as the other Venns did. But now there's a circle for a third category, G3. Let's say that G1 = Apples, G2 = Red things, and G3 = Things in Montana.

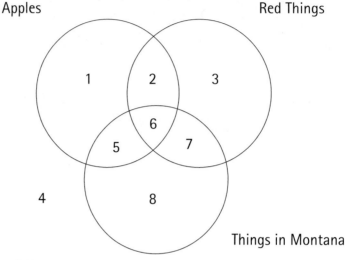

Venn Diagram 6.11

Because you have three overlapping circles instead of two, you have eight areas instead of four. Area 6 includes those red apples that are in Montana. Area 5 contains all apples that are not red but are in Montana. Area 8 includes things that are in Montana but are neither apples nor red (such as the town of Billings and Glacier National Park).

You can represent any of the four categorical statements on the Venn diagram with three circles. The UA statement "All things in Montana are red" can be represented like this:

UA: All things in Montana are red.

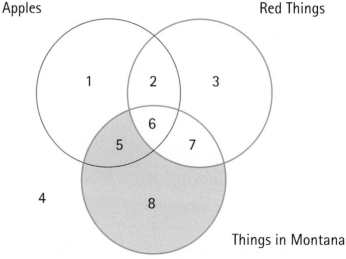

Venn Diagram 6.12

Areas 5 and 8 are shaded to indicate that they're empty. The statement "All things in Montana are red" doesn't tell you anything about Areas 1–4 and 6–7. They are all blank. As you look at Venn Diagram 6.12, tilt your head to the left and pretend that the Apples circle isn't there. You'll see that Areas 5 and 8 in Venn Diagram 6.12 are the same as Area 1 of Venn Diagram 6.3 on page 180.

A different UA statement has a different Venn diagram. Here is the Venn diagram of the UA statement "All red things are apples":

UA: All red things are apples.

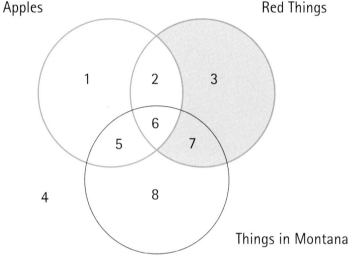

Venn Diagram 6.13

Here Areas 3 and 7 are filled in because this UA statement tells you that there's nothing in these areas.

The UN statement "All apples are not in Montana" can be represented like this:

UN: All apples are not in Montana.

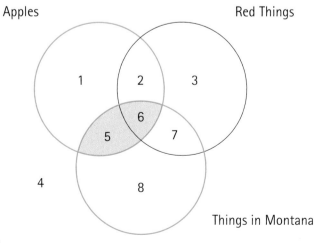

Venn Diagram 6.14

Areas 5 and 6 are shaded because this UN statement tells you that there are no apples in Montana.

The PN statement "Some apples are not red" can be represented like this:

PN: Some apples are not red.

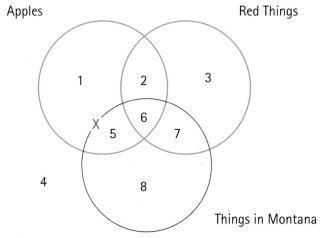

Venn Diagram 6.15

There's an "X" on the line between Areas 1 and 5 because this PN statement tells you that there's at least one thing in at least one of these two areas. It might be that the PN statement is true because there's only one Golden Delicious apple. The PN statement "Some apples are not red" doesn't tell you whether this Golden Delicious apple is in Montana (Area 5) or isn't in Montana (Area 1). So you put the "X" on the line between the two.

The PA statement "Some things in Montana are red" can be represented like this:

PA: Some things in Montana are red.

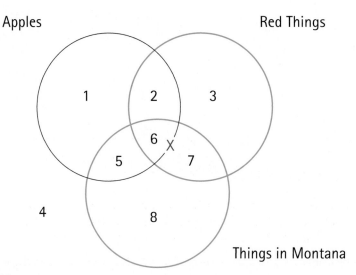

Venn Diagram 6.16

There's an "X" on the line between Areas 6 and 7 because this PA statement tells you that there must be at least one thing in at least one of these two areas but if this PA statement is true because there's only one red thing in Montana, this PA statement doesn't tell you whether it's an apple (Area 6) or not (Area 7).

A categorical syllogism has a valid form when the truth of the premises *guarantees* the truth of the conclusion. This means that a categorical syllogism has a valid form when the Venn diagram of both premises is sufficient (with no more diagramming) to be a Venn diagram of the conclusion. You first diagram each premise and then check to see whether you've diagrammed the conclusion.

GUIDE

Validity of Categorical Syllogisms: Venn Method

1. Draw three overlapping circles. Put the category that is the subject of the conclusion at the top left, the category that is the predicate of the conclusion at the top right, and the category that doesn't appear in the conclusion in the middle under the other two categories.

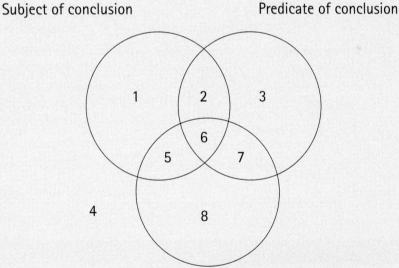

Venn Diagram 6.17

---

2. Diagram the premises. Diagram the universal premises, and then diagram the particular premises.
3. Compare the resulting diagram to the conclusion to see whether the diagram of the two premises has diagrammed the conclusion. If it has, the argument has a valid form. If it hasn't, the argument has an invalid form.

Look at this argument:

(1) All sea lions are mammals.
(2) All mammals are animals that nurse their young with milk.
Therefore,
(3) All sea lions are animals that nurse their young with milk.

You can formalize it like this:

 S = sea lions
M = mammals
 N = animals that nurse their young with milk

(1) All S are M.
(2) All M are N.
Therefore,
(3) All S are N.

Step 1. You set up the three-circle Venn diagram with the subject of the conclusion (S) on the top left, the predicate of the conclusion (N) on the top right, and the category that doesn't appear in the conclusion (M) in the middle below the other two.

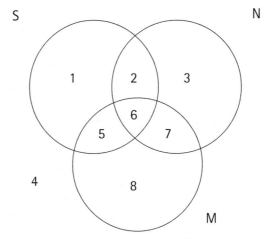

Venn Diagram 6.18

Step 2. In this case, both premises are universal so it doesn't matter which premise you diagram first. Diagram premise (1), All S are M, like this:

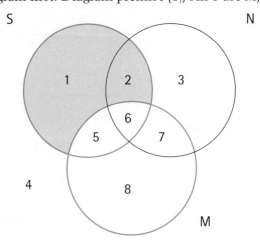

Venn Diagram 6.19

You shade Areas 1 and 2 because "All *S* are *M*" tells you that those two areas are empty.

You now add the shading for the second premise, "All *M* are *N*."

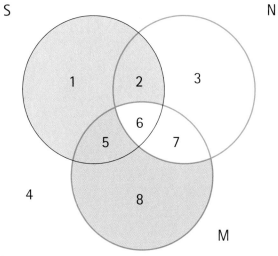

Venn Diagram 6.20

You add shading to Areas 5 and 8 because "All *M* are *N*" tells you that these areas are empty.

Step 3. Compare the resulting diagram to the conclusion to see whether the diagram of the two premises has diagrammed the conclusion. Look at Venn Diagram 6.20 and compare it to the conclusion of the argument, "All *S* are *N*." "All *S* are *N*" tells you that Areas 1 and 5 should be shaded. On Venn Diagram 6.20, both of these areas are shaded. The diagramming of the premises has diagrammed the conclusion. This argument has a valid form.

Let's look at a categorical syllogism with an invalid form.

(1) All sea lions are mammals.
(2) All wolves are mammals.
Therefore,
(3) All sea lions are wolves.

S = sea lions
M = mammals
W = wolves

(1) All *S* are *M*.
(2) All *W* are *M*.
Therefore,
(3) All *S* are *W*.

You set up the circles like this:

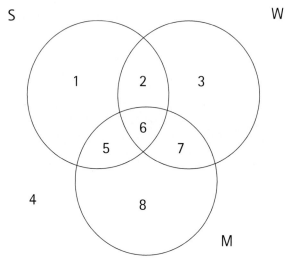

Venn Diagram 6.21

Then you diagram the first premise, "All *S* are *M*."

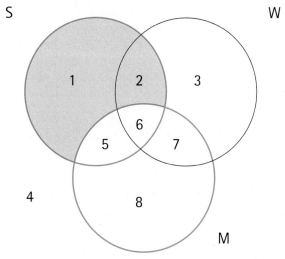

Venn Diagram 6.22

Then you diagram the second premise, "All *W* are *M*."

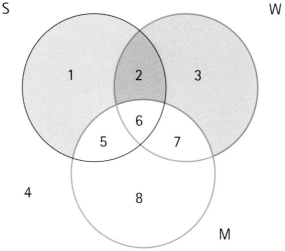

Venn Diagram 6.23

"All *W* are *M*" tells you to shade out Areas 2 and 3. You already shaded out Area 2 when you diagrammed premise (1). All you need to do is shade Area 3.

You now compare Venn Diagram 6.23 to the conclusion "All *S* are *W*." "All *S* are *W*" tells you that Areas 1 and 5 should already be shaded. But in Venn Diagram 6.23, Area 5 isn't shaded. The diagramming of the premises doesn't diagram the conclusion. This argument has an invalid form.

Let's look at some arguments with particular premises.

(1) All sea lions are mammals.
(2) Some sea lions are things that live in the Pacific Ocean.
Therefore,
(3) Some mammals are things that live in the Pacific Ocean.

  S = sea lions
M = mammals
  P = things that live in the Pacific Ocean

(1) All *S* are *M*.
(2) Some *S* are *P*.
Therefore,
(3) Some *M* are *P*.

You set up the circles with the categories in the right places.

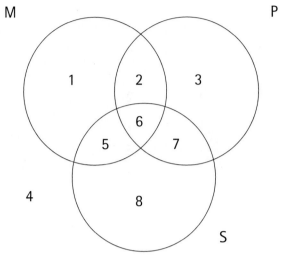

Venn Diagram 6.24

This argument has one universal premise and one particular premise. Remember to diagram the universal premise first. The universal premise is "All *S* are *M*."

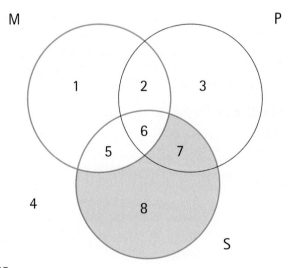

Venn Diagram 6.25

You shade out Areas 7 and 8 because "All *S* are *M*" tells you that these areas are empty.

You now add the diagram of the particular premise "Some *S* are *P*."

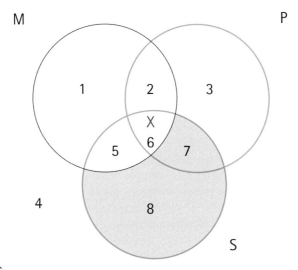

Venn Diagram 6.26

On its own, "Some *S* are *P*" would tell you that there should be an "X" on the line between Areas 6 and 7. "Some *S* are *P*" tells you that some sea lions live in the Pacific but it doesn't tell you whether they are mammals (Area 6) or not (Area 7). But premise (1) has told you that Area 7 is empty. You know that the sea lion that lives in the Pacific is a mammal. You put an "X" in Area 6. This shows why you should **diagram universal premises first**.

You now compare Venn Diagram 6.26 to the conclusion of the argument, "Some *M* are *P*." There's an "X" in Area 6. If there's an "X" in Area 6, then there's at least one thing that is a mammal that lives in the Pacific (and it happens to be a sea lion). The truth of the premises implies the truth of the conclusion, and the argument has a valid form.

Key Concept
You should diagram universal premises first.

Let's look at an invalid argument with one particular premise and one universal premise.

(1) All sea lions are mammals.
(2) Some things that live in the Pacific Ocean are mammals.
Therefore,
(3) Some things that live in the Pacific Ocean are sea lions.

S = sea lions
M = mammals
P = things that live in the Pacific Ocean

(1) All S are M.
(2) Some P are M.
Therefore,
(3) Some P are S.

After correctly placing the circles, you diagram the universal premise "All S are M."

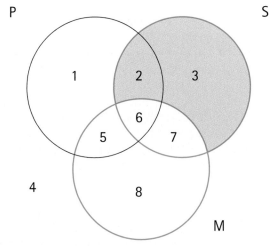

Venn Diagram 6.27

Then you add the diagram of the particular premise, "Some P are M."

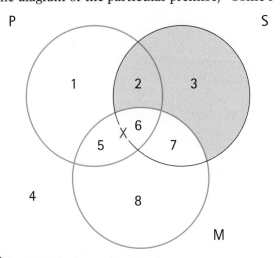

Venn Diagram 6.28

In this case, the universal premise hasn't excluded either Area 5 or Area 6. You put "X" on the line between these two areas.

You now compare Venn Diagram 6.28 to the conclusion "Some *P* are *S*." This conclusion says that there should be an "X" in Area 2 or an "X" in Area 6. In Venn Diagram 6.28, Area 2 is shaded, so there's no "X" there. And there isn't an "X" in Area 6 either. There's an "X" on the line between Areas 5 and 6. You know that something is in Area 5 or Area 6 but you don't know which. You don't know for sure that something is in Area 6. The diagram of the premises hasn't diagrammed the conclusion. This argument has an invalid form.

Finally, let's look at an argument with two particular premises.

(1) Some things that live in the Pacific Ocean are mammals.
(2) Some mammals are things that hibernate in the winter.
Therefore,
(3) Some things that live in the Pacific Ocean are things that hibernate in the winter.

H = things that hibernate in the winter
M = mammals
P = things that live in the Pacific Ocean

(1) Some *P* are *M*.
(2) Some *M* are *H*.
Therefore,
(3) Some *P* are *H*.

Because both premises are particular, you can diagram either one first. The first premise, "Some *P* are *M*," is diagrammed like this:

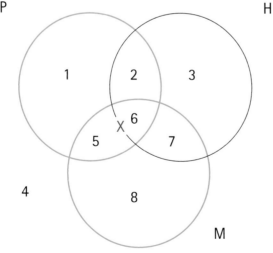

Venn Diagram 6.29

Then you add the diagram of the second premise, "Some *M* are *H*."

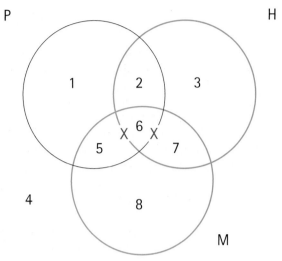

P   H

Venn Diagram 6.30

You now compare Venn Diagram 6.30 to the conclusion "Some *P* are *H*." You haven't diagrammed "Some *P* are *H*." The first premise tells you that there must be something in Area 5 or Area 6. The second premise tells you that there must be something in Area 6 or Area 7. The conclusion tells you that there should be an "X" in Area 2 or an "X" in Area 6. The premises don't put "X"s in Area 2 or on any of Area 2's lines. If the "X" on the line between Areas 5 and 6 turns out to be in Area 5 and the "X" on the line between Areas 6 and 7 turns out to be in Area 7, then there's no "X" in Area 6. The premises of the argument show that the conclusion *might* be true but they don't show that it *must* be true. This argument has an invalid form.

Habits of a Critical Thinker

Discipline

Many years ago, one of the authors of this book took the course you are now taking. He didn't think it was hard. He thought that he didn't need to practice much. He didn't have the discipline to practice using the four tests and doing Venn diagrams. When the final came along, it took him a long time to see if arguments had a valid form. He didn't have time to complete the final and he bombed the course. Over the summer, he spent an hour a day working on checking arguments for valid form. He took the course again and got a high A. The moral of the story is that a good critical thinker is disciplined. It takes work to think well. You need to practice and set up a schedule to keep yourself on track.

EXERCISE 6.7

A. Use the Venn Method to determine whether the arguments in Exercise 6.6A have a valid form.

B. Use the Venn Method to determine whether the arguments in Exercise 6.5A and 6.5B have a valid form.

Chapter Summary

Categorical arguments focus on statements that compare categories of things. Categorical statements assert that things of one category either are or aren't members of some other category. There are four standard categorical statement forms, each of which has four parts. The parts are: (a) the quantity (All or Some), (b) the subject category, (c) the quality (are or are not), and (d) the predicate category. These yield the four standard forms, universal affirmative (UA, All apples are red), universal negative (UN, All apples are not red), particular affirmative (PA, Some apples are red), and particular negative (PN, Some apples are not red).

A proper deductive argument form is called a "valid" form, and an improper deductive argument form is called an "invalid" form.

Some categorical arguments have only one premise.

UA and PN statements are contradictories. If one of them is true, then the other is false. UN and PA statements are also contradictories.

You convert a statement by switching the subject and predicate categories. When you convert a UN or PA statement, you produce an argument with a valid form. You contrapose a statement by converting the categories and then complementing both categories with a "non-." When you contrapose a UA or a PN statement,

you produce an argument with a valid form. You obvert a statement by changing the quality and complementing the predicate category. When you obvert any of the four categorical statement forms, you produce an argument with a valid form. Contradiction, conversion, contraposition, and obversion lead to sixteen valid argument forms.

Categorical syllogisms are arguments that have (a) precisely three statements (two premises and a conclusion), (b) precisely three categories, and (c) each of the categories appearing in precisely two of the three statements. The middle category of a syllogism is the category that doesn't appear in the conclusion.

Categorical syllogisms can be evaluated by two methods. The Test Method evaluates categorical syllogisms by seeing whether they pass four tests. Any categorical syllogism that fails one of the four tests has an invalid form. Any categorical syllogism that passes all four tests has a valid form. The Venn Method graphically depicts categorical statements and arguments. By mapping the premises onto the circles, one can see whether the conclusion appears. If it does, the argument has a valid form. If the conclusion isn't apparent, the argument has an invalid form.

GUIDE

Finding, Standardizing, and Evaluating Categorical Arguments

This Guide is an amplification of the "Guide for Finding, Standardizing, and Evaluating Arguments" that is in Chapter Two. The numbered sentences are merely copies from the Guide in Chapter Two. The paragraphs with "Cat" (for "Categorical") in front of them are additional materials that apply only to categorical moral arguments.

Finding Arguments

1. Look for an attempt to convince.

   Cat. Look for an attempt to convince that relies on the logical relationships *within* statements.

2. Find the conclusion.

3. Find the premises.

4. Review the following to make sure that you have correctly identified the conclusion and the premises: imperfect indicator words, sentence order, premises and/or conclusion not in declarative form, and unstated premises and/or conclusion.

5. Review the following to make sure that you haven't incorrectly identified something as a premise or a conclusion when in fact it's not part of an argument: assertions, questions, instructions, descriptions, and explanations.

Standardizing Arguments

6. Rewrite the premises and the conclusion as declarative sentences. Make sure that each premise and the conclusion is a grammatically correct declarative sentence. Rewrite the premises and conclusion as necessary to make them clearer but don't change the meaning of the passage. Remove pronouns from the sentences and replace them with the nouns or noun phrases to which they refer. Remove emotionally charged language.

   Cat. Put all the statements in the argument into one of the standard categorical statement forms (UA, UN, PA, or PN).

7. Review any phrases you've omitted to be sure that they aren't premises or a conclusion.

8. Number the premises and the conclusion. Put brackets [] around the number of any unstated premise and/or conclusion. Place the premises before their conclusion, and insert "Therefore" between the premises and the conclusion.

   Cat. Assign category variables and rewrite the argument using them.

9. Compare your standardization to the original passage to make sure that you haven't omitted any arguments found in the passage and to be sure that you have correctly identified the premises and the conclusion.

   Cat. Check to be sure that your formalization correctly captures the meaning of the argument as expressed in English.

Evaluating Arguments: The True Premises Test

10. Check to see whether the premises are accurate descriptions of the world.

11. Consider whether the premises are appropriate for the argument's audience.

12. Review the assumed premises to be sure that the assumptions are reasonable. Make sure that all assumed premises are uncontroversially true empirical statements, uncontroversially true definitional statements, or appropriate statements by experts. Make sure the definitions are good ones.

Evaluating Arguments: The Proper Form Test

13. Determine whether the argument is a deductive argument or inductive argument.

14. Determine whether the premises are relevant to the conclusion. Look at each premise individually to see whether the truth of the premise provides some evidence for the truth of the conclusion. Look at the premises as a group to see whether the truth of all of them provides some evidence for the truth of the conclusion.

Cat. Determine the form of the categorical argument. Determine whether it has one premise, two premises, or more than two premises.

Cat. If the argument has one premise, compare it to the sixteen forms of categorical arguments with one premise discussed in this chapter.

Cat. If the argument has two premises, verify that it meets the criteria for being a categorical syllogism. Use the test method or the Venn method to determine whether it passes the proper form test.

Evaluating Arguments: Checking for Fallacies

15. Compare the argument to the list of fallacies on page 410 to see whether the argument commits any of the fallacies.

7

Analogical Arguments

Look at the world. It is just one big machine subdivided into an infinite number of smaller machines. All these various machines are adjusted to each other with an accuracy that fills all with wonder. This fitting of means to ends throughout the natural world resembles the machines humans produce. Since the effects resemble each other we are led to infer, by all the rules of analogy, that the causes also resemble each other and that the author of nature is somewhat similar to us, although he has much greater powers proportionate to the greater work he has done. By this argument we can prove the existence of God and that his mind is similar to ours.

—David Hume, *Dialogues Concerning Natural Religion* (2007, 19, material omitted and simplified)

Learning Outcomes

After studying the material in this chapter, you should be able to:

1. Put analogical arguments into standard form.
2. Identify the analogues, the primary subject, the similarities, and the conclusory feature of analogical arguments.
3. Apply the true premises test to analogical arguments.
4. Apply the proper form test to analogical arguments.
5. Compose good analogical arguments.

Remember from Chapter Two that inductive arguments come in at least three kinds: analogical, statistical, and causal. This chapter discusses analogical arguments. Analogical arguments are based on comparisons. Hume's argument on the previous page is an analogical argument for the view that God exists. It compares the natural objects found in the world (eyes, legs, and the fingers on our hands) to the machines made by humans (cars, computers, and televisions). It argues that both natural objects and machines made by humans show the marks of design, the "fitting of means to ends." Because the machines made by humans have a designer, Hume suggests that natural objects also have a designer, God.

Analogical arguments are the basis of much of the reasoning in the law. They're also used whenever someone classifies something. Examples of this use of analogical arguments include chemistry's periodic table of elements and the classification of living things into species. Analogies are also fundamental to the proper form test.

Identifying Analogical Arguments

Analogical arguments are arguments based on comparison. Suppose that you're enrolled in Linguistics 101 and that you've never had a linguistics course before. The time for your first paper rolls around and you're not sure how to write it. What makes a good linguistics paper? Ideally, your linguistics professor would have given you lots of information, but let's suppose that your professor wasn't that organized.

You happen to have kept three handouts from three previous classes about how to write papers. One's from an English class, another is from a geology class, and the third is from an accounting class. The titles of these three handouts are: "How to Write a Good English Paper," "How to Write a Good Geology Paper," and "How to Write a Good Accounting Paper." Which of these three would be the most useful as a guide for writing your linguistics paper? As you think about this question, you're considering three different analogical arguments: one for the view that the English handout is the best guide, another for the view that the geology handout is the best guide, and another for the view that the accounting handout is the best guide. You're comparing linguistics to English, geology, and accounting and trying to decide which of these three subjects is most like linguistics.

It seems that the English guide would be the best one to use. Linguistics is more similar to English than it is to geology or accounting. English and linguistics are both the study of language, but geology and accounting aren't.

Key Concept

Analogical arguments are arguments based on comparison.

The Form of Analogies

Key Concept

The standard form of
analogical arguments.

Here's the standard form of analogical arguments:

(1) X1s have features F1, F2, F3, . . . , and
     feature Fn.
(2) X2s also have features F1, F2, F3, ...
Therefore,
(3) X2s probably have Fn.

"X"s are variables that refer to entities, and "F"s are variables that refer to features.

Connections

The use of variables is discussed in Chapter Two.

Analogical arguments aren't usually found in this form. The order of the premises is often different. People often leave premises unstated.

Here's Hume's argument about God in standard form:

(1) The objects made by humans have the fitting of means to ends and they have a designer.
(2) Natural objects have the fittings of means to ends.
Therefore,
(3) Natural objects have a designer, God.

X1 is the objects made by humans, X2 is natural objects, F1 is having the fitting of means to ends, and Fn is having a designer.

Key Concept

The four parts of an
analogical argument.

Analogical arguments have four parts. The **analogues**, X1s, are the things to which the entities in the conclusion are being compared. The **primary subjects**, X2s, are the things about which a conclusion is being drawn. The **similarities** (F1, F2, F3, . . .) are the features that the premises claim are shared by the analogue and the primary subject. The **conclusory feature**, Fn, is the feature in the argument's conclusion that's claimed to be a feature of the primary subject. The conclusory feature appears in a premise and then again in the conclusion. In standard form, the conclusory feature is on its own line in the first premise.

Giorgio Carnevale and Theodore Pietsch (2006) recently examined an unusual fossil that was found in Algeria (see Figure 1 below). It was the fossil of a fish. They wondered what kind of fish it was. On the basis of an analogical argument, they concluded that it was an extinct species of frogfish. Frogfish are small fish that live in shallow sea waters and spend most of their lives sitting immobile near the sea floor. They look like a rock or a piece of coral. They wiggle a fin that looks like a worm as a lure to draw other fish close. When another fish approaches to investigate the wiggling lure, the frogfish snaps it up. Some scientists believe that the snap of a frogfish is the fastest known movement in the animal kingdom. Scientists use the Latin name *Antennarius* to refer to frogfish. The fossil in Figure 1 is unusual because it shows one fish inside another. Figure 2 is a picture of a living frogfish.

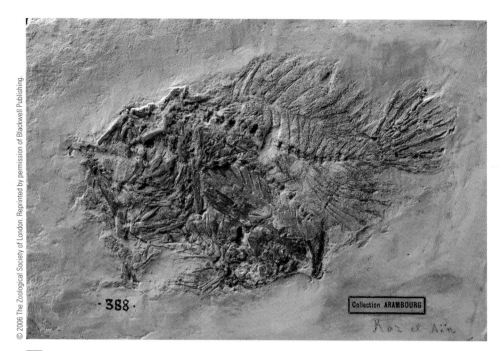

Figure 1 Fossilized frogfish.

Figure 2 Living frogfish.

Carnevale and Pietsch used an analogical argument to reach the conclusion that the fossil fish was a frogfish.

The classification of the specimen within the genus *Antennarius* is based on the occurrence of a combination of several diagnostic features shared by the living species of this genus, such as skin covered with close-set bifurcate dermal spinules, caudal fin rays bifurcate, epural present and meristic values. (2006, 452, material omitted)

In this argument, the similarities are

- having skin covered with close-set bifurcate dermal spinules
- having caudal fin rays bifurcate, and
- having epural present and meristic values

If you were evaluating Carnevale and Pietsch's analogy, you'd need to know a lot about these three features. But at this point it's enough to see that you can put their argument into the standard form of an analogy.

(1) Some existing fish have skin covered with close-set bifurcate dermal spinules, caudal fin rays bifurcate, and epural present and meristic values and
they're frogfish.
(2) The fossilized fish has skin covered with close-set bifurcate dermal spinules, caudal fin rays bifurcate, and epural present and meristic values.
Therefore,
(3) The fossil fish is probably a frogfish.

In this case, the analogue, X1, is existing fish that have the three similarities. The primary subject, X2, is the fossilized fish. The conclusory feature, Fn, is the feature of being a frogfish.

Technical Term: Analogy

In this book, "analogy" refers to an entire argument. But sometimes "analogy" is used to refer to the similarities. Carnevale and Pietsch might have written: "There are three analogies between the specimen and existing frogfish: skin covered with close-set bifurcate dermal spinules, caudal fin rays bifurcate, and epural present and meristic values." When you see the word "analogy" you need to read carefully to determine whether the word refers to the entire argument or only to the features common to the analogue and the primary subject.

The key to identifying an analogical argument is to look for an argument that relies on comparison. If you suspect that a passage contains an analogical argument, try to find the analogue, the primary subject, the similarities, and the conclusory feature. If one of these parts is missing, there probably isn't an analogical argument. (Don't forget that premises and conclusions can be unstated.) Sometimes you'll find an analogue, a primary subject, and some similarities but no conclusory feature. When that happens, you're probably looking at an illustrative analogy.

Giorgio Carnevale

Courtesy of Giorgio Carnevale

Giorgio Carnevale (1975–still finding fossils) is an Assistant Professor of Paleontology in the Department of Earth Sciences at the University of Perugia, Italy. Professor Carnevale's excellent use of analogical arguments has led to more than 50 articles that focus primarily on fossil fish.

Illustrative Analogies

Illustrative analogies are used to help people understand something instead of being used to make an argument. Here's an illustrative analogy from Hume, the philosopher who wrote the argumentative analogy at the beginning of this chapter. In 1740, he published *A Treatise of Human Nature*. This long book contains many complex arguments about difficult issues. It's divided into three parts. At the end of the first part Hume offers an illustrative analogy.

> Before I go into the immense depths of philosophy that lie before me, I want to stop here for a moment and think about the voyage I have made so far. It has undoubtedly required a great deal of skill and hard work. I am like a man who has grounded his ship on many sandbars and nearly wrecked it while passing a small island but who still has the nerve to put out to sea again in the same leaky weather-beaten boat and even hopes to go around the world in it. (Hume 1985, 311, material omitted and simplified)

Hume is drawing an analogy between working through the arguments in his book and traveling over the ocean in a ship. In the 1700s traveling on the ocean was dangerous. Many ocean voyages failed as ships got lost, sank in storms, or were overrun by diseases. Many long books fail because they don't establish their conclusions. Hume isn't attempting to make an argument. He's only attempting to illustrate the difficulties of evaluating arguments by comparing evaluating arguments to traveling on the ocean.

Metaphors are a kind of illustrative analogy. They're common in poetry. One reason people read poetry is to better understand themselves and the world. Poets often use analogies to point out overlooked or underappreciated features of things. Here's the poem "Marks" by Linda Pastan (1978):*

---

*Pastan, Linda. "Marks", from *The Five Stage of Grief* by Linda Pastan. Copyright © 1978 by Linda Pastan. Used by permission of W. W. Norton & Company, Inc.

My husband gives me an A
for last night's supper,
an incomplete for my ironing,
a B plus in bed.
My son says I am average,
an average mother, but if
I put my mind to it
I could improve.
My daughter believes
in Pass/Fail and tells me
I pass. Wait 'til they learn
I'm dropping out.

Pastan draws an analogy between the grades given to students by their teachers and the way that her family evaluates her. Pastan isn't making an argument. She's attempting to express the way that people can feel as if they're being graded. Illustrative analogies aren't argumentative analogies. They're a different and perfectly appropriate way to use analogies.

Connections

Chapter Four discusses metaphors.

EXERCISE 7.1

A. Which, if any, of the following are analogies?

1. A rose is a rose is a rose. not comparing anything
2. A rose by any other name would smell as sweet. not comparing
3. Life is like a bowl of cherries. yes   ilustative
*4. More primates live in North and South America compared to any other continent. Not
5. Fewer primates live in North America compared to any other continent. NO
6. Arguments are by nature divisive. NO
7. I like Atlanta, but my friend likes Boston. NO
*8. Why are astronomers like boxers? They both see stars. ilustative
9. Researchers at Very Cool University (VCU) have been studying the nervous system. They have focused on the nervous systems of crayfish and have learned how to cure disorders of the nervous system in crayfish. In both humans and crayfish, calcium plays a crucial role in the operation of nerves. Their discoveries about the role of calcium in nerve cells of crayfish may lead to important advances in treating such diseases as muscular dystrophy and Alzheimer's disease.
10. The Earth and the other planets such as Venus, Mars, Saturn, Jupiter, etc. have several things in common. They are approximately spherical, they revolve around the Sun and rotate around their own axis, they follow elliptical orbits, they are large, they have an irregular surface, and they have an atmosphere. The Earth contains several forms of life. It's probable that other planets contain several forms of life.

B. Which of the following passages contains analogies? If the passage contains an analogy, is it illustrative or argumentative?

1. The weather in Atlanta is hotter than the weather in Boston. I like the weather in Atlanta. My best friend likes the weather in Boston. *NO Comparison*

2. Monkeys and humans are medium-sized mammals and they live in groups. When monkeys are given substance X, they show reaction R. Consequently, if administered substance X, humans will show reaction R. *Yes analy argument*

3. In a *New Yorker* cartoon, two cats are chatting in front of a badly scratched lounge chair. One says to the other: "I have a couple of other projects I am excited about." (teNeues 2010) *NO*

*4. "[One way] of acquiring the notion of a being who directs the universe is by considering the end to which each thing appears to be directed. [W]hen I see a watch with a hand marking the hours, I conclude that an intelligent being has designed the springs of this mechanism, so that the hand would mark the hours. So, when I see the springs of the human body, I conclude that an intelligent being has designed these organs to be received and nourished within the womb for nine months; for eyes to be given for seeing; hands for grasping, and so on. (Voltaire 1989, 69, material omitted) *yes analy argument*

5. "A centipede was happy quite,

   Until a frog in fun *NO*

   Said, 'Pray, which leg comes after which?'

   This raised her mind to such a pitch,

   She lay distracted in the ditch

   Considering how to run."

   (Kronenberger 1935, 161)*

6. Richard Feynman, winner of the 1965 Nobel Prize in Physics, wrote as follows: "Nature uses only the longest threads to weave her patterns, so each small piece of her fabric reveals the organization of the entire tapestry." (Feynman 2006, 9A)

7. The planets are attracted to the sun in inverse proportion to the square of their distance from the sun, and they revolve around the sun in orbits, and electrons are attracted to the nucleus of an atom in inverse proportion to the square of their distance from the nucleus, so it seems likely that electrons revolve around the nucleus in orbits. *argumentive analy*

*8. "There is extensive evidence that permitting people to obtain clean needles will reduce the spread of HIV. An article in the *Journal of the American Medical Association* stated that needle exchange programs around the world, including Amsterdam, Sweden, Australia, Britain, and several cities in the United States, have led to reduced needle sharing among IDUs, as an increasing percentage of this population obtains clean needles from the program. That this should lead to a reduction in HIV infection is to be expected, and there is evidence pointing to that outcome." (Stoll 1998)

9. "Volcanic rocks dominate the surface of Mars. In the cold, dry conditions that prevail there today, these rocks can persist with little chemical alteration. But the recent discovery by Mars orbiters and landers of sulphate and clay deposits on the planet *argumentive analy*

---

*"A centipede was happy quite" An Anthology of Light Verse, Louis Kronenberger, ed. (New York: Random House, 1935).

indicates that Mars' ancient environment was different, and involved liquid water. Evidence that Mars was wetter before about 3.7 billion years ago comes from various geomorphic features. In particular, valleys with characteristic branching forms seem to have been eroded by water. The heavily degraded rims of ancient craters and crater infilling are similarly interpreted as fluvial features in some models." (Catling 2007, 31-32, material omitted)

10. "Capacity for the nobler feelings is in most natures a very tender plant, easily killed; not only by hostile influences, but by mere want of sustenance; and in the majority of young persons it speedily dies away if the occupations to which their position in life has devoted them, and the society into which it has thrown them, are not favorable to keeping that higher capacity in exercise." (Mill 1979, 10) *Illustrative*

C. Put all of the argumentative analogies identified in sections A and B above into standard form. Identify the primary subject, analogue, the similarities, and conclusory feature.

D. Background information: In 1976, Congress considered a Full Employment and Balanced Growth Act for establishing a national policy and procedure that would guarantee to all able adult Americans the availability of useful and rewarding employment. Many people testified before the committee when it met on May 14, 17, 18, and 19, 1976. One of those who testified was founder and co-chair of the Full Employment Action Council, Coretta Scott King, widow of Martin Luther King, Jr. Mrs. King's testimony offers many arguments in favor of full employment, including several analogies (as well as statistical and moral arguments). See how many analogies you can find in the following excerpt. Which are illustrative and which are argumentative? Put all of her argumentative analogies into standard form. Identify the primary subject, analogue, and conclusory feature.

It probably requires someone who is black to fully comprehend the helplessness, loneliness, and anxieties of the unemployed. It requires a black, because blacks are more than merely deprived. They are consciously and deliberately ignored as much as possible by the larger society.

"For so long, being black was to be invisible.

"With the same design great effort is made to hide the unemployed; to erase them from visibility and to blank out the constricted lives they live. The chilling resemblance of the dimly seen unemployed to the leper colonies of the Dark Ages is not too extreme an analogy.

"A very intense campaign has been under way to establish that no one really cares about unemployment. It is contended that only inflation engenders concern and fear. After all, it is said, 92.5 percent are employed and only 7.5 percent are unemployed.

"It does sound small when put in these bland, cold terms, and there are no cries of anguish to disturb the sleep of the vast majority. But now put it another way: 7,003,000 people—mostly adults—are without jobs. True, they eat—but not too much; they have some sort of shelter; some even have health care. But many, including children, are in chronic ill health, or are ill nourished, and living a life of punishment and systematic abuse as if they had done some evil to this Nation.

"Psychologically, they are mauled even more terribly. Because they are what the English call "redundant," they are struck with the sledgehammer of inferiority. To be deprived is bad, but to be deprived among the secure and privileged is far worse. At least 20 million Americans are afflicted with this tragic, crippling disease for which they bear no guilt and possess no means of cure. It is probably much more than 20 million counting family members and the huge uncounted numbers who have given up looking for employment because the scarring of constant rejection was too unbearable. Why are the unemployed hidden and their suffering silenced? For the same reason, the same slickly polished device was used for blacks. If they were unseen, if their hurts were unheard, people could be made to believe they were contented. Thus, people may not be made to act about the matter of correcting a crying injustice.

"The truth is millions of jobless living among us have lives of misery, and we have the ability to change it. The truth is, we should change the condition out of our moral concern. But if that be too feeble, there is another reason. The sordid existence they endure today may be ours tomorrow.

"We are then told we cannot change conditions—change must trickle down slowly as a benevolent monarch drops coppers into the uplifted palms of a beggar. This nauseating image of charity from the Middle Ages is still with us, institutionalized by the Ford administration's trickle-down theory. [Gerald Ford was president of the United States at the time of King's testimony.]

"We should believe them no more than we should have believed them 40 years ago in 1935 when they wailed that unemployment insurance and social security would bring an end to free enterprise and democracy.

"Let us put the issue sharply: We say the unemployed can be provided jobs at productive labor with decent wages. It has been done in other developed countries without curbing profits or liberties. Indeed, where some of the nations have encountered small increments of unemployment lately, it is due to the slowdown of our economy impinging on theirs.

"Let us keep squarely in mind that youth unemployment in the ghetto has reached some 40 percent—a horrifying figure. If we are to eradicate poverty, drug addiction, and crime, we have to offer work.

"A young person in the ghetto cannot find a job for $30 a day, but they can readily find criminal work for $100 a day and need no education nor skill. It is amazing the degree to which ethical barriers have held.

"Everyone today has a sense that the seams of society are under intense strain. In this circumstance, the powers that be are engaged in a substantial social gamble.

"Just as the stubborn and immoral pursuit of the Vietnam war nurtured and intensified the disaffection of tens of millions of Americans, and finally made Washington an oath rather than a seat of government, so will mulish adherence to retaining an army of unemployed lead to the growing contempt of Americans in their own Government.

"Have the powers that be learned nothing from trying to keep blacks in segregation and inferiority? Have they learned nothing from trying to stop trade union organizing in the 1930s? Have they learned nothing from trying to hide crimes of high government officials and agencies?

"They are all finally dealt with, and the more intense the effort to repress, the more turbulent the process of inevitable change. For black Americans in particular, the economic policies and actions of the past few years have been nothing less than a frontal assault on all the gains and victories of the 1960s. The legislation we black Americans struggled for, and at times died for, is now being literally undermined. To my mind current policies amount to nothing less than the repeal of the Civil Rights Acts of the 1960s, and the gutting of the promise of justice.

"What good is the legal right to sit in a restaurant if one cannot afford the price of the food? And what good is the promise of fair employment when there is no employment for black Americans?

"The deliberate creation of high unemployment has meant nothing less than the denial of the basic human right to live as full-fledged members of the American system." (King 1976, 636-638, material omitted)

Uses of Analogies

The rest of this chapter looks only at argumentative analogies and uses "analogy" to refer to argumentative analogies. Argumentative analogies are used in an amazing variety of ways. Let's look at some examples.

Sometimes analogies are used because people can't or shouldn't observe something. Leber congenital amaurosis (LCA) is a birth defect that affects both humans and purebred Briard dogs. Children or puppies with this disease either have no sight at birth or lose it within months. Guylene Le Meur and a group of researchers in Nantes, France, developed a treatment for this disease. The treatment involved injecting a genetically altered virus into LCA-affected eyes. Le Meur and her team hoped that the genetically altered virus would act to correct the birth defect. To test this treatment, they injected the genetically altered virus into the eyes of eight Briard dogs with LCA, seven puppies and one adult dog. The sight of the seven puppies was restored. The adult dog was unaffected. The Nantes scientists then concluded that:

> [A]nalysis of our results in dogs suggests that for successful gene therapy to occur in humans, patients should be treated at a relatively young age. (Le Meur 2007, 300)

In other words, they concluded this gene therapy might work on human infants. Here's their argument in standard form:

(1) Briard puppies with LCA have eight mutated genes that affect vision and
they were cured of their blindness by the genetically altered virus.
(2) Human infants with LCA also have eight mutated genes that affect vision.
Therefore,
(3) Human infants with LCA will probably be cured of their blindness by the genetically altered virus.

We've simplified this case by referring to only one of the many similarities noted by Le Meur and her team. Besides the eight mutated genes that affect vision, the other similarities noted were many complex properties of the eyes, genes, and nervous system that are common to both dogs with LCA and humans with LCA. In this case the scientists observed the effect of the genetically altered virus on the puppies because they know that it would be wrong to perform this experiment on human infants.

Sometimes the reason people can't observe something is that it's in the past or the future. Take a look at another analogy from the article about frogfish. Carnevale and Pietsch named their new species *Antennarius monodi*.

> The feeding behavior of *Antennarius monodi* seems to be consistent with that of [existing *Antennarius*]. A nearly complete [fish] can be easily observed in the abdominal region of the specimen. This fish evidently represents the last meal of [this] *Antennarius*. (Carnevale 2006, 453, material omitted. The abbreviation "*A.*" that stands for *Antennarius* is replaced with the full word.)

Carnevale and Pietsch conclude that the fish that became a fossil had eaten another fish right before it died. They're relying on an analogy between what people have observed happening when living frogfish eat other fish (that they go into the frogfish's abdominal region) and what would have happened in the past if the fossilized frogfish had eaten another fish.

Sometimes people draw analogies about one place from information about another place. Aletha Huston and a team of psychologists based at the University of Texas at Austin studied the effects of the New Hope Project. This project was conducted in Milwaukee. Working parents were given three benefits: an income supplement, assistance with childcare, and healthcare subsidies. The parents had to remain employed to keep these benefits. The study compared children in these families to another group of children in families whose parents didn't receive the three benefits. The group of families who didn't receive the benefits is the control families. Huston found that

> Children in New Hope families performed better than those in control families on academic achievement—particularly reading—as measured by three independent sources: standardized test scores, parent reports, and teacher reports. (Huston 2005, 915)

She concluded that

> The results of this evaluation suggest that the policies tested in New Hope may be beneficial to large parts of the population who have low incomes but are able to work. (Huston 2005, 916)

Huston is using an analogy between a project done in one place (Milwaukee) and projects that might be done in other places (other cities).

Sometimes people use analogies to argue that things should be treated in the same way. Analogies are central to the debate over abortion. Some people use analogies to argue that human fetuses should be treated more like adult humans and other people use analogies to argue that there is no moral requirement that human fetuses be treated like adult humans. The civil rights movement in the United States used many analogical arguments to defend the view that the law should treat blacks and whites in the same way.

Sometimes people use analogies to classify things. The Carnevale and Pietsch analogy about frogfish is an example. The periodic table of elements that you've seen in your chemistry classes is based on a large series of analogies. The classification of people into races, sexes, ethnic groups, income groups, age groups, and many other groups is based on analogies.

Key Concept
Analogies are used in many different ways.

Technical Terms: Temporal Analogies, Spatial Analogies, Equal Treatment Analogies, Classification Analogies

Scholars group analogies according to their usage. A temporal analogy is an analogy in which the conclusion is about an unobserved event in the past or the future. If the conclusion of a temporal analogy is about the future, the analogy is a forward-looking temporal analogy. If the conclusion of a temporal analogy is about the past, the analogy is a backward-looking temporal analogy. A spatial analogy is an analogy in which someone reasons from the claim that something happens in one place to the claim that the same thing will happen in another place. An equal treatment analogy is an analogy whose conclusion is that two things should be treated in the same way. A classification analogy is an analogy whose conclusion is that something should be classified in a particular way.

Logical Analogies

A **logical analogy** is an analogical argument that compares arguments. In this book, you've seen many logical analogies. The proper form test relies on logical analogies. In Chapter Two you saw that this argument:

(1) All roses are plants.
(2) All roses have thorns.
Therefore,
(3) All plants have thorns.

has the same logical form as this argument:

(1) All Germans are Americans.
(2) All Germans are people with large feet.
Therefore,
(3) All Americans are people with large feet.

When we (the authors of this book) compared these two arguments, we were drawing a logical analogy. We were pointing to a similarity between these two arguments. The similarity we were pointing to was that both arguments have this form:

(1) All G1 are G2.
(2) All G1 are G3.
Therefore,
(3) All G2 are G3.

(Remember that G1, G2, and G3 are variables that stand for groups.) Let's call the two arguments above the "roses argument" and the "Germans argument." Let's call the logical form above "Form M." We argued that the Germans argument failed the proper form test. We were making this argument:

(1) The roses argument has Form M and
     fails the proper form test.
(2) The Germans argument has Form M.
Therefore,
(3) The Germans argument fails the proper form test.

We also argued that *any* argument with Form M fails the proper form test. We were implicitly making a long series of analogical arguments that compared all arguments that have Form M. As you look at an argument to see whether it passes the proper form test, you're using logical analogies to determine whether the logical form of the argument in question has a proper form. You're implicitly making an argument like this:

(1) Argument X1 has Form F1 and
     it passes/fails the proper form test.
(2) Argument X2 also has Form F1.
Therefore,
(3) Argument X2 passes/fails the proper form test.

Refutation by Logical Analogy

Logical analogies can also be used to show that an argument has a flaw. Look at this argument:

It is not normal to be attracted to a member of the same sex. It violates the basic sexual structure which God created. It is a perversion. It is against nature. (Martin 1993)

Martin's unstated conclusion is that homosexuality is wrong. Suppose that Jay wanted to show that Martin's argument was a bad argument. He might attempt to draw a logical analogy between Martin's argument and this argument.

> It is not normal for humans to fly high in the sky. It violates the basic physical structure which God created. It is a perversion. It is against nature.

Jay is drawing an analogy between this argument:

> (1) It is not natural to be attracted to a member of the same sex.
> Therefore,
> (2) It is wrong to be attracted to a member of the same sex.

and this argument:

> (1) It is not natural to fly in an airplane.
> Therefore,
> (2) It is wrong to fly in an airplane.

He is making the following logical analogy:

> (1) The airplane argument has similarities, F1, F2, F3, . . . , and is a bad argument.
> (2) The homosexuality argument also has similarities, F1, F2, F3, ...
> Therefore,
> (3) The homosexuality argument is a bad argument.

Let's look at another example. Suppose that Luke offers the following argument:

> (1) If someone is President, then he or she lives in the White House.
> (2) Barack Obama lives in the White House.
> Therefore,
> (3) Barack Obama is President.

Danielle thinks that this argument isn't a good argument. She might attempt to show that it isn't a good argument by using a logical analogy. She might argue that Luke's argument is analogous to this one:

> (1) If someone is President, then he or she lives in the White House.
> (2) Michelle Obama lives in the White House.
> Therefore,
> (3) Michelle Obama is President.

Danielle is offering a refutation by logical analogy.

Connections

Danielle is correct. Luke's argument isn't good. It commits the fallacy of Affirming the Consequent. See Chapter Five.

Refutations by logical analogy are often persuasive. But they have a problem. Because people often use a refutation by logical analogy without explicitly noting the similarities they have in mind, refutations by logical analogy often don't tell you the exact problem with an argument. If someone doesn't point out the similarities between the two arguments they're discussing, the refutation doesn't tell you whether the argument fails the proper form test or the true premises test. It only tells you that there's a problem somewhere in the argument.

Habits of a Critical Thinker

Thinking Boldly

New ideas can make people uncomfortable. It may be that the discussions of God, abortion, and homosexuality in this chapter make you feel uncomfortable. They may raise issues and doubts. A good critical thinker is a bold thinker, one who isn't afraid to examine new ideas and question things that most people assume. David Hume, who wrote the quote at the beginning of this chapter, considered arguments for and against the existence of God. When Hume wrote (in the 1700s) it was bold to consider this issue. Hume was denied teaching positions because he was willing to consider the idea that God didn't exist. It's partly because of his bold mind that he's recognized as a great philosopher. Being bold enough to let your mind go where good arguments take you, even if it's to places that make you feel uncomfortable, may lead you to discoveries about the world and yourself.

EXERCISE 7.2

A. Constructing analogies.

1. Construct an analogy in favor of or against polygamy.

2. Construct an analogy in favor of or against capital punishment.

3. Construct a logical analogy between arguments A and B which concludes that argument B passes the proper form test.

   Argument A

   (1) If he's a senator, he's at least thirty.
   (2) He isn't thirty.
   Therefore,
   (3) He isn't a senator.

   Argument B

   (1) If he lives in New York, he lives in the United States.
   (2) He doesn't live in the United States.
   Therefore,
   (3) He doesn't live in New York.

*4. Use a logical analogy to refute the following argument.

   (1) If someone is French, she's European.
   (2) George Bush isn't French.
   Therefore,
   (3) George Bush isn't European.

5. Suppose a doctor argued that cloning is to be rejected because it would be equivalent to "playing God." Construct an analogy which shows that believing doctors shouldn't be playing God is inconsistent with other things most doctors believe.

6. Find a similarity (F1) and conclusory feature (Fn) that would make an analogy with "houses built in New Orleans" as the primary subject and "houses built on the Florida coast" as the analogue.

7. Construct an analogy given the following information: Stanley and Roger are both members of the family owning Hilton Hotels. You are told that Stanley is wealthy and unreliable.

*8. Using either "should be illegal" or "shouldn't be illegal" as the conclusory feature, construct an analogical argument for or against a woman's right to have an abortion.

9. Put the following analogy into standard form, from the child's point of view. When a child learns how to speak, she'll tend to apply the standard rules of verb formation

to irregular verbs as well. For example, the child will say "comed" rather than "came," "dived" rather than "dove," "ringed" rather than "rung," "runned" rather than "run," and so on, just as she'll say "loved," "helped," "cooked," "appeared," and so forth.

10. Construct an analogy that concludes that dinosaurs were probably killed by a giant meteorite. (You may need to do some research to do this exercise.)

For the next two exercises, consider the following background information: In the 1700s and 1800s, whale fishing, or whaling, was a major industry. Whales have huge amounts of fat called blubber. When heated, this blubber produces whale oil, and in the 1700s and 1800s whale oil lamps were a primary means of lighting homes. Before the invention of modern ships, whaling was very dangerous. Many men died hunting whales. Because of its economic importance and danger, whaling produced many folk songs. Here are the lyrics to part of one of them. It is called "The Greenland Whale Fishery":

Oh, Greenland is a dreadful place,
A land that's never green;
Where there's ice and snow, and the whale fishes blow
And the daylight's seldom ever seen, brave boys,
And the daylight's seldom ever seen.

(This song has been recorded many times. One accessible recording can be found on Almanac Singers 1996).
In the third line, the song refers to "whale fishes." In the 1800s whales were classified as a type of fish.

11. Construct an analogy for the view that whales should be classified as fish. Put your analogy into standard form.

12. Construct an analogy for the view that whales should be classified as mammals. Put your analogy into standard form.

*13. Put the argument in this passage into the standard form of an analogy. Fossils of an amphibian that lived more than 245 million years ago have been found in Antarctica, suggesting that the climate in Antarctica at that time was much warmer than it is today. The 60-centimeter piece of skull was found on Fremouw Peak in the Transantarctic Mountains, just six degrees from of the South Pole. Palaeontologists have identified it as a Parotosuchus, a two-meter-long salamander-like amphibian predator. The fossil shows that the weather in Antarctica in the late Early or Middle Triassic period was warm enough to let a cold-blooded creature live there. (Written by the authors of this book from information found in Sidor 2008)

14. Put the argument in this passage into the standard form of an analogy. "We come then to the question presented: Does segregation of children in public schools solely on the basis of race, even though the physical facilities and other 'tangible' factors may be equal, deprive the children of the minority group of equal educational opportunities? We believe that it does. We conclude that in the field of public education the doctrine of 'separate but equal' has no place. Separate educational facilities are inherently unequal. Therefore, we hold that the plaintiffs and others similarly situated for whom the actions have been brought are, by reason of the segregation complained of, deprived of the equal protection of the laws guaranteed by the Fourteenth Amendment." (*Brown v. Board of Education* 1954, 493, material omitted)

Evaluating Analogical Arguments

You evaluate analogies the same way you evaluate all other arguments, using the true premises test and the proper form test. But you need to know some important details about applying these tests to analogies.

The True Premises Test

When applying the true premises test to analogies, the most important detail is that analogies can use imaginary cases. Let's look at an example.

The philosopher Judith Jarvis Thomson has used an imaginary case in an analogical argument for the view that women are morally permitted to have an abortion. Many people think that a human fetus has a right to life. They also think that a woman has a right to choose what happens to her body, but they hold that, in the case of abortion, the fetus' right to life conflicts with the woman's right to choose what happens to her body. They think that, in that case, the fetus' right to life is stronger, more important, than the woman's right to choose. If the fetus' right to life conflicts with a woman's right to choose, the fetus' right ought to be respected and abortion is wrong. This argument can be standardized like this:

(A) (1) A human fetus has a right to life.
    (2) A woman has a right to choose what happens to her body.
    (3) The fetus' right to life is stronger than a woman's right to choose what happens to her body.
    (4) In the case of abortion, a woman's right to choose what happens to her body conflicts with the fetus' right to life.
    Therefore,
    (5) In the case of abortion, a woman ought to respect the fetus' right to life (and not have an abortion).

Thomson uses an analogy to argue that premise (3) is false.

> [L]et me ask you to imagine this. You wake up in the morning and find yourself back to back in bed with an unconscious violinist. A famous unconscious violinist. He has been found to have a fatal kidney ailment, and the Society of Music Lovers has canvassed all the available medical records and found that you alone have the right blood type to help. They have therefore kidnapped you, and last night the violinist's circulatory system was plugged into yours, so that your kidneys can be used to extract poisons from his blood as well as your own. The director of the hospital now tells you, "Look, we're sorry the Society of Music Lovers did this to you—we would never have permitted it if we had known. But still, they did it, and the violinist is now plugged into you. To unplug you would be to kill him. But never mind, it's only for nine months. By then he will have recovered from his ailment, and can safely be unplugged from you." Is it morally incumbent on you to accede to this situation? No doubt it would be very nice of you if you did, a great kindness. But do you have to accede to it? What if it were not nine months, but nine years? Or longer still? What if the director of the hospital says, "Tough luck, I agree, but you've now got to stay in bed, with the violinist plugged into you, for the rest of your life. Because remember this. All persons have a right to life, and violinists are persons. Granted you have a right to decide what happens in

and to your body, but a person's right to life outweighs your right to decide what happens in and to your body. So you cannot ever be unplugged from him." I imagine you would regard this as outrageous, which suggests that something really is wrong with [argument (A)]. (Thomson 1971, 48-49)

Thomson is drawing an analogy between the case of a person hooked to a famous violinist and the case of a woman who's pregnant. Let's call the famous violinist "Victor." Let's call the person hooked to the famous violinist "Hadia." Here's a standardization of Thomson's argument:

(B) (1) In the case of the famous violinist, Hadia's right to choose what happens to her body conflicts with Victor's right to life and it would not be wrong for Hadia to cause Victor to die (by unplugging herself).

(2) In the case of abortion, a woman's right to choose what happens to her body conflicts with the fetus' right to life.

Therefore,

(3) It is not wrong for a woman to cause the fetus to die (by having an abortion).

Therefore,

(4) The fetus' right to life is not stronger than a woman's right to choose. (Premise (3) of argument (A) is false.)

Thomson's analogy is one of the most famous philosophical arguments of the 20th century. But when it comes to the true premises test, the first premise of Thomson's argument is unusual. It's about an imaginary case. There never has been a person attached to a famous violinist. It seems that premise (1) of argument (B) is false. But it doesn't seem that the falsity of premise (1) is a problem with Thomson's argument. What's going on here?

People sometimes overlook that they have a good bit of knowledge about imaginary situations. No one reading this book has ever seen it snow at the mouth of the Amazon. The mouth of the Amazon is close to the equator, and temperatures there never come close to freezing. But let's imagine that it were to snow at the mouth of the Amazon. What color would this snow be? The answer is obvious. If it snowed at the mouth of the Amazon, the snow would be white. We all know that the snow would be white, even though none of us has ever seen it snow there.

Knowledge about imaginary cases isn't some sort of lesser knowledge. Our knowledge about imaginary cases can be very solid. Compare our knowledge about the color of snow falling at the mouth of the Amazon to our knowledge about the effects of cholesterol. (Cholesterol is a type of fat found throughout our bodies and particularly in our blood.) It turns out that cholesterol is a complex substance. Different kinds of cholesterol do different things, and cholesterol does different things in different parts of the body. Our views about the effects of cholesterol have changed dramatically over the past twenty years. On the other hand, our knowledge about the color of snow at the mouth of the Amazon hasn't changed at all over that time. (These facts about cholesterol are from Grundy 2002.)

Of course, some examples of knowledge about imaginary cases aren't as obvious as the Amazon snow knowledge. How would you react if you discovered that you had an identical twin? Imagine that you thought that you had no twin and then your twin walked up and said "Hi." Most of us don't have good knowledge about this imaginary case. We don't know how we'd feel. In some cases people have good knowledge about imaginary cases and in other cases they don't.

Technical Term: Counter factual

Imaginary situations are sometimes called "counter factual situations" or "counter factuals." When you imagine, you're imagining something that is counter to the facts. In other words, you're imagining a case that doesn't actually exist.

How do you apply the true premises test to analogies in which one of the premises relies on knowledge about imaginary cases? The audience of the analogy becomes crucial. For these analogies to have force, the people reading the analogy must have the same views about the imaginary case as the person making the analogy. Thomson's analogy includes the phrase "I imagine you would regard this as outrageous." Thomson is assuming that people who are reading about the imaginary case of the famous violinist will think that Hadia may unplug herself from Victor. Let's look more closely at premise (1) of Thomson's argument. It has two parts. The first part is

In the case of the famous violinist, Hadia's right to choose what happens to her body conflicts with Victor's right to life

The second part is

and it would not be wrong for Hadia to unplug herself from Victor.

It seems clear that people have good knowledge about the first part of Thomson's first premise. If Hadia existed and was plugged into Victor, her right to choose what happens to her body would conflict with Victor's right to life. The more controversial point is the second part of premise (1). Thomson claims that we all have this knowledge about this imaginary case. Someone who disagreed with Thomson's claim that it would not be wrong for Hadia to unplug herself from Victor would reject her claim of knowledge about this imaginary case and assert that her first premise doesn't pass the true premises test. Premises about an imaginary case pass the true premises test when the author and the audience have the same views about the imaginary case. If they don't, the premise fails the true premises test.

Key Concept
Premises about an imaginary case pass the true premises test when both author and audience have the same views about the imaginary case.

Critical Thinkers

Judith Jarvis Thomson

Courtesy of Judith Jarvis Thomson

Judith Jarvis Thomson (1929–still thinking up thought experiments) is a Professor of Philosophy at Massachusetts Institute of Technology. She's best known for her creative and incisive thought experiments, like the violinist case in this chapter. Professor Thomson has published widely in moral philosophy, philosophy of law, and metaphysics for more than 50 years. She was President of the American Philosophical Association in 1992–1993.

The Proper Form Test

Let's apply the proper form test to analogies. Look at this argument:

(1) Adult humans have the genetic code of the species *Homo sapiens* and a right to life.
(2) Human fetuses also have the genetic code of the species *Homo sapiens*. Therefore,
(3) Human fetuses have a right to life.

Suppose that Dusty made this argument, and Erica believes that Dusty's argument fails the proper form test. Erica can make two different kinds of points.

First, she can argue that just because a thing has the genetic code of the species *Homo sapiens*, that doesn't show that it has a right to life. Erica might point out that when Dusty cuts his fingernails he throws the part of his fingernails that he has removed into a trash can. But each of those cuttings from his fingernails has the genetic code of the species *Homo sapiens*. It seems that the cuttings from Dusty's fingernails don't have a right to life even though they all have the genetic code of the species *homo sapiens*. If she makes this type of argument, Erica is arguing that the similarity noted by Dusty isn't relevant. In this case, one of the issues that divides Dusty and Erica is whether having the genetic code of the species *Homo sapiens* is a *relevant similarity*.

Second, Erica might say that in the first trimester fetuses don't feel pain while adult humans do feel pain. Then she might argue that this is an important difference between human fetuses and adult humans. If she makes this type of argument, Erica is arguing that there's a *relevant dissimilarity* between Dusty's analogue and his primary subject.

The most important issue when it comes to determining whether an analogy passes or fails the proper form test is the *relevance* of similarities and dissimilarities. If someone can show either that the similarities cited in an analogy aren't relevant or that there are relevant dissimilarities between the analogue and the primary subject, then the analogy doesn't do well on the proper form test.

When it comes to relevance, you need to first look at the argument's conclusion. Think about two computers as they roll off the assembly line at a factory. You might be tempted to say that they're identical. Suppose that they're the same model, have the same amount of memory, have equally large hard drives, are the same color, etc. But even in such similar objects, there'll be some differences. The silicon in the chips in the two computers is made from different grains of sand. There'll be small differences in the electrical properties of the silicon in the two computers. No two silicon computer chips are exactly alike. Each is a tiny bit faster or slower than another.

But are any of these differences relevant? It depends. Suppose that you're trying to draw a conclusion about which of the two computers to buy. It may be that, from your perspective, there are no relevant differences between the two examples of the same model of computer. It may be that you look and look and can't find a reason to prefer one computer over the other. Both will do everything you want a computer to do (word processing, playing games, instant messaging, etc.) equally well. As you look at the two units of the same model of computer sitting next to each other in their identical boxes at the store, you'd probably be happy to choose between them by flipping a coin.

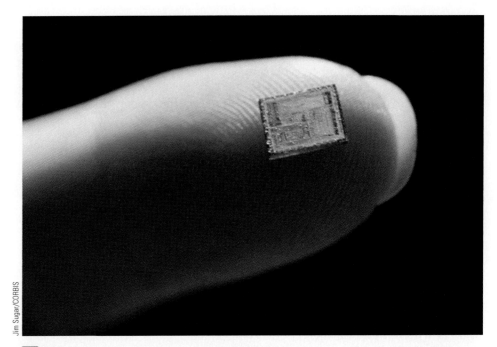

Jim Sugar/CORBIS

Figure 3 Modern silicon computer chips, quite small in size, hold about 2 billion tiny transistors.

On the other hand, suppose that you were a professor of engineering who studied the manufacturing techniques used in factories. You were seeking to draw a conclusion about the manufacturing processes in the factory where the computers were built. In that case, you might see relevant differences where a buyer would see none. Suppose that one computer took 5 fewer minutes to make than the other. A person buying a computer would probably see this as an irrelevant difference between the two computers. But the engineering professor would probably see this as a relevant difference. If the factory produces thousands of computers per year, producing each computer 5 minutes faster might substantially lower the costs of producing the computers. This case shows that when it comes to relevance, you should think about the argument's conclusion. If you were making an argument intended to convince someone to buy a particular model of computer, the differences between the individual computers of that model are probably irrelevant. If you were making an argument intended to show someone that one manufacturing process was superior to another, differences between individual computers of the same model may well be relevant.

When thinking about relevance you also need to consider background knowledge. Remember the frogfish analogy. Carnevale and Pietsch are presupposing that things such as "skin covered with close-set bifurcate dermal spinules, caudal fin rays bifurcate, [and] epural present and meristic values" are relevant features when it comes to the classification of a fish as a frogfish. They're also presupposing that having a backbone isn't relevant to the classification of a fish as a frogfish. They're presupposing that all their readers know that having a backbone can't be used to classify a fish as a frogfish because this feature is shared by many different kinds of fish and many things that aren't fish. Part of their readers' background knowledge about animals is that many of them (dogs, elephants, sharks, frogfish, etc.) have backbones. Having a backbone isn't a relevant feature when it comes to determining the species of a fossilized fish. They're also presupposing that their audience has background knowledge that all frogfish have "skin covered with close-set bifurcate dermal spinules, caudal fin rays bifurcate, [and] epural present and meristic values."

Chapter Two noted that the premises of an argument are relevant to the conclusion if the truth of the premises provides some evidence for the truth of the conclusion. This allows us to see the bottom line when it comes to the relevance of the features in an analogy. A feature is a **relevant similarity** when the fact that the analogue and the primary subject share that feature provides some evidence that the primary subject has the conclusory feature. A feature is a **relevant dissimilarity** when the fact that the analogue and the primary subject don't share that feature provides some evidence that the primary subject doesn't have the conclusory feature.

Chapter Two also noted that relevance is a matter of degree. The more evidence a relevant similarity provides, the stronger the analogy. The less evidence the similarity provides, the weaker the analogy. Relevant dissimilarities have the opposite effect on the strength of an analogy. The more evidence a relevant dissimilarity provides, the weaker the analogy. Avoid falling into the trap of attempting to classify all analogies as either good or bad. Analogies, like all inductive arguments, can be placed on a continuum of strength. Think of analogies not as good or bad but rather as better and worse.

Connections

See the discussion of relevance in Chapter Two.

Technical Terms: False Analogy, Faulty Analogy

Some books refer to a weak analogy as a "false analogy" or "faulty analogy." In some courses, "false analogy" or "faulty analogy" are applied to illustrative analogies as well as argumentative analogies.

> **Key Concept**
> A feature is a **relevant similarity** when the fact that the analogue and the primary subject share that feature provides some evidence that the primary subject has the conclusory feature. A feature is a **relevant dissimilarity** when the fact that the analogue and the primary subject don't share that feature provides some evidence that the primary subject doesn't have the conclusory feature.

Habits of a Critical Thinker

Perceptiveness

Some similarities are obvious, but many aren't. A good critical thinker is perceptive and sees similarities and dissimilarities that others overlook. One reason Judith Jarvis Thomson's case of the famous violinist is so well known is that Thomson is perceptive. She saw the similarities between abortion and the famous violinist case before anyone else did.

There are no recipes for how to be perceptive. The bottom line is that you have to think carefully about situations and try many different ideas. Perception has led to many breakthroughs in human thought. For example, in the late 1800s Marie Curie was perceptive enough to see that the mineral pitchblende, while rich in uranium, gave off more radioactivity than could be accounted for by its uranium. Then she was perceptive enough to conclude that pitchblende must contain another radioactive element. She and her husband, Pierre, discovered that pitchblende contains not one but two radioactive elements, which they named "polonium" and "radium." Her discoveries were the foundation for x-rays and radiation treatments for cancer. Curie was one of the world's most perceptive scientists who made lasting contributions to humanity, and she won two Nobel Prizes.

Analogies, Consistency, and False Beliefs

An analogy is a test of the *consistency* of a person's beliefs. Thomson is point-ing to what she sees as an inconsistency in the beliefs of someone who holds

> It is wrong for a pregnant woman to have an abortion.

and

> It is not wrong for Hadia to unplug herself from Victor.

Thomson is in effect saying to someone who holds these two views:

> Your views aren't consistent. When it comes to abortion, you think that a woman must remain attached to a fetus. But when it comes to the case of the famous violinist, you don't think that Hadia must remain attached to Victor.

Analogies are powerful arguments because they can reveal that someone's beliefs are inconsistent, and most people strongly desire to avoid inconsistent beliefs.

People try to avoid inconsistent beliefs because two inconsistent beliefs can't both be true. Let's suppose that Travis believes both (a) that his sister is in New York and (b) that she isn't in New York. His beliefs are contradictory. Even though you don't know where Travis's sister is, you know that one of his beliefs is false. His sister can't be in New York and not be in New York at the same time. Pointing out to people that they have inconsistent beliefs is important because people who have inconsistent beliefs have some false beliefs.

Connections

Chapter One discusses the consequences of false beliefs.

In the case of Thomson's argument, three options are available to people who wish to avoid the charge of having inconsistent beliefs. (1) They can agree with Thomson that the case of the famous violinist and the case of abortion are analogous and hold that both a woman's having an abortion and Had-ia's unplugging herself from Victor are permitted. (2) They can agree with Thomson that the case of the famous violinist and the case of abortion are analogous but hold that neither a woman's having an abortion nor Hadia's un-plugging herself from Victor is permitted. The third option is to hold that (3) the two cases are not sufficiently analogous either because there's a relevant dissimilarity or because the similarities between Victor and Hadia aren't rele-vant similarities.

In general, when presented with an analogy, you've got three possible ways to respond. (1) You can agree with the author of the analogy that the analogue and the primary subject are analogous and agree that both have the conclusory feature. (You can agree that X1s and X2s are analogous and that the similari-ties indicate that they both have Fn.) (2) You can agree with the author of the analogy that the analogue and the primary subject are analogous and claim that neither of them has the conclusory feature. (You can agree that X1s and X2s are analogous but hold that the similarities indicate that neither has Fn.) (3) You can claim that the analogue and the primary subject aren't sufficiently analogous either because there's a relevant dissimilarity between them or because the similarities between them are not relevant. (You can claim that X1s and X2s are not analogous.)

Let's end this chapter with a final look at the analogy about the impact of the New Hope project that was made by Huston. Remember that her conclusion was:

> The results of this evaluation suggest that the policies tested in New Hope may be beneficial to large parts of the population who have low incomes but are able to work.

Huston drew an analogy between a project done in one place (Milwaukee, Wisconsin) and projects that might be done in other places (that is, other cities). Huston hasn't overlooked the proper form test for an analogy. She's aware that there may be relevant dissimilarities between Milwaukee and other cities. Immediately after the sentence quoted above, she notes:

> There are limitations, of course. The program was initiated with broad community, business, and government support in Wisconsin, a state with a strong tradition of social programs and an aggressive system to move welfare recipients into employment. With low rates of unemployment in the late 1990s, jobs were relatively easy to find. Although programs offering some types of similar benefits in other northern states had positive effects on children's achievement, we cannot be sure how well the effects would replicate in different economic and policy climates or in different regions of the United States. The promising results of the demonstration in Wisconsin suggest that wider replication of the New Hope policy package would be worth testing and might lead to important developmental benefits for children in low-income families with working parents. (Huston 2005, 916, material omitted)

In this quote Huston uses the measured tone and draws the careful conclusions that are found in good critical thinkers' arguments. She points out some possible relevant dissimilarities between Milwaukee and other cities. Some other cities don't have "a strong tradition of social programs." Some other cities might not have low unemployment rates that make jobs "relatively easy to find." Huston has used her analogy well. She points out both the strengths and the weaknesses of her analogy and draws conclusions that are appropriately tempered by those strengths and weaknesses. Huston shows that a good critical thinker doesn't try to divide all analogies into two piles: the good analogies and the bad analogies. A good critical thinker sees that analogies can be better or worse. Few analogies are perfect and a less-than-perfect analogy can still lead you to important conclusions as long as you're careful not to reach too far.

EXERCISE 7.3

A. Which of the arguments you standardized in Exercises 7.1 and 7.2 pass the true premises test?

B. Which of the arguments you standardized in Exercises 7.1 and 7.2 pass the proper form test?

C. In the following passages, do the following:

  (a) Put the argument into standard form, and identify the analogues, the primary subject, the similarities, and the conclusory feature.

  (b) Apply the true premises test. Don't forget to check for imaginary cases.

  (c) Apply the proper form test, stating whether the purported similarities are relevant and whether there are any relevant dissimilarities.

  (d) If you don't think there are any relevant dissimilarities, bring up a dissimilarity you think isn't relevant and say why it's irrelevant.

  1. The Epicureans argue that death is annihilation—i.e., that there is no afterlife, and when you die, you simply cease to exist for eternity—and on this basis, they further argue that death should not be feared, since there is nothing bad about death for the person who dies. One of these arguments, the "symmetry argument," is given here: "Life is granted to no one for permanent ownership, to all on lease. Look back now and consider how the bygone ages of eternity that elapsed before our birth were nothing to us. Here, then, is a mirror in which nature shows us the time to come after our death. Do you see anything fearful in it? Do you perceive anything grim? Does it not appear more peaceful than the deepest sleep?" (Lucretius 2001, 94)

  2. Some people believe that it is morally wrong to raise and kill animals for the sake of eating their meat and to support this practice by purchasing meat. An argument against the view (that purchasing meat is wrong) is that these animals would not have existed in the first place if people did not purchase meat, and so we are doing them a favor by purchasing their meat. Henry Salt derides this as the "logic of the larder" when he points out that [the logic of the larder] must apply to mankind: "It has, in fact, been the plea of the slave-breeder; and it is logically just as good an excuse for slave-holding as for flesh-eating. It would justify parents in almost any treatment of their children, who owe them, for the great boon of life, a debt of gratitude which no subsequent services can repay. We could hardly deny the same merit to cannibals, if they were to breed their human victims for the table, as the early Peruvians are said to have done." (Salt 1914)

  3. In 2007, New York City was thinking about implementing a "congestion pricing" proposal, which would require drivers to pay $8 per day to use the streets of the southern half of Manhattan (excluding driving on marginal highways or during nights or weekends). Ken Livingston, Mayor of London, supported the proposal by pointing to London's use of a congestion pricing plan, because the situations of the two cities are similar. He writes, "London's business district was undergoing rapid growth, but it was at capacity in terms of traffic. [Lowering traffic speeds] led to business losses and a decrease in quality of life. Simultaneously, carbon emissions were mounting because of the inefficiency of engine use." Starting in 2003, all cars entering the London center city had to pay a charge of £5 (about $9) a day. Livingston claims, "This led to an immediate drop of 70,000 cars a day in the affected zone. Traffic congestion fell by almost 20 percent. Emissions of the greenhouse gas carbon dioxide were cut by more than 15 percent." Furthermore, feared negative side effects did not occur: increases in retail sales in the zone "significantly exceeded the national average," and the theatre district "has been enjoying record audiences." Livingston went on to cite statistics showing a shift away from car travel into public transportation and bicycling, and public support for the program shifting from about 50/50 before it began to 2-1 in favor. He adds, "This success had preconditions. In London, as will be the case in New York or any other city, an enhanced public transportation system was critical." He concludes, "Is London's success a guarantee that congestion charging will work in New York? Of course not. But it is an indicator that properly executed congestion pricing works, and works well." (Livingston 2007, material omitted)

*4. "Last July, Kelly White and her boyfriend became engaged. They had a cozy picnic of wine and cheese on a hill before he presented her with a watermelon-flavor Ring Pop and asked her to marry him. 'I'd rather not say if he got down on one knee or not,' she said. 'It's embarrassing.' But they won't end up at the altar anytime soon: they said they would not marry until gay and lesbian couples are also allowed to. 'I usually explain that I wouldn't go to a lunch counter that wouldn't allow people of color to eat there, so why would I support an institution that won't allow everyone to take part,' said Ms. White, 24, a law student at the University of California, Davis. 'Sometimes people don't buy that analogy.'" (Schaefer 2006, ST1)

5. "Existing frogfish are divided into six groups each of which has a Latin name: *Antennarius biocellatus*, *Antennarius nummifer*, *Antennarius ocellatus*, *Antennarius pauciradiatus*, *Antennarius pictus*, and *Antennarius striatus*. Each of these groups contains one or more species. For example, the frogfish whose Latin name is *Antennarius bermudensis* is in the *Antennarius nummifer* group. Carnevale and Pietsch present the following argument for the view that the fossil they are studying is a member of the group *Antennarius ocellatus*. They have named their new species of fish *Antennarius monodi*. "[I]t is possible to include *Antennarius monodi* with the *Antennarius ocellatus* group because of the presence of a distinct caudal peduncle, 13 dorsal-fin rays, eight bifurcate anal-fin rays, and 20 vertebrae." (Carnevale 2006, 453. Citations are omitted and punctuation altered to match conventions in this text.)

6. "The skeleton of a eutherian (placental) mammal has been discovered from the Lower Cretaceous Yixian Formation of northeastern China. The new eutherian has limb and foot features that are known only from scansorial (climbing) and arboreal (tree-living) extant mammals, in contrast to the terrestrial or cursorial (running) features of other Cretaceous eutherians." (Ji 2002, 816, material omitted) Ji and his collaborators concluded that the fossilized mammal was a climbing or tree-living eutherian mammal.

7. The Stoics Zeno and Chrysippus "affirmed that everything is fated. When a dog is tied to a cart, if it wants to follow it is pulled and follows, making its spontaneous act coincide with necessity, but if it does not want to follow it will be compelled in any case. So it is with men too: even if they do not want to, they will be compelled in any case to follow what is destined." (Hippolytus 1987, 386, material omitted)

*8. "We would be the Natives if attacked by aliens. The human race is to be considered as one civilization with multiple factions within it. Again the Native American analogy holds true since there were also many various Indian Nations. The Europeans, ETs this time, are coming we must assume. Will they be nice or nasty? Do we wish to become extinct as some Natives did? Do we wish to travel our own 'Trial of Tears'? Do we wish to be assimilated into a European society as happened to some of the Native Americans? Or will we fight back? Perhaps we should prepare for the worst and hope for the best. Now is the time for preparation, before it is too late!" (Taylor 2007, 14)

9. "No one is sent down to the black pit of Tartarus. Undoubtedly it is in our life that all those things exist which are fabled to be in the depths of hell. No unhappy Tantalus quakes at the huge rock hanging over him in mid-air, numbed by an empty terror. Rather, it is in life that an empty fear of the gods hounds mortals: each is afraid of the fall which his lot may bring him. Nor is it true that Tityos lies in hell with birds tunneling into him, or that they can really find an everlasting food supply to forage beneath his great chest. But we have our own Tityos here—the man who lies lovesick, torn apart by winged creatures and gnawed at by nervous agony, or rent by cares through some other passion. Sisyphus too exists before our eyes in real life. He is the man who thirsts to run for the rods and cruel axes of public office, and who always returns beaten and dejected. For to pursue the empty and unattainable goal of power, and in its pursuit to endure unremittingly hard toil, that is the struggle of pushing uphill a stone which, in spite of all, at the very peak rolls back and hurtles downward to the level ground below. Here on earth the life of the foolish becomes hell." (Lucretius 1987, 152–153, material omitted)

D. Apply the true premises and proper form tests to evaluate the analogies you constructed from the Coretta Scott King excerpt in Exercises 7.1 D above.

Chapter Summary

Analogical arguments are arguments based on comparison. But some analogies are not argumentative. They only illustrate a comparison. Argumentative analogies have four parts. The **analogues**, X1, are the things to which the entities in the conclusion are being compared. The **primary subjects**, X2, are the things about which a conclusion is being drawn. The **similarities** (F1, F2, F3, . . .) are the features that the premises claim are shared by the analogue and the primary subject. The **conclusory feature**, Fn, is the feature in the argument's conclusion that's claimed to be a feature of the primary subject. The standard form for analogy is

(1) X1 has features F1, F2, . . . and Fn.
(2) X2 has features F1, F2, ...
Therefore,
(3) X2 probably has feature Fn.

Analogies have many uses. Analogies can be used because people can't or shouldn't observe something. Sometimes the reason people can't observe something is that it's in the past or the future. People can draw analogies about one place from information about another place. People can use analogies to argue that things should be treated in the same way. People can use analogies to classify things.

Logical analogies are analogical arguments about arguments. A logical analogy is the basis of the proper form test. If two arguments have the same form, and one passes the proper form test, then by analogy, the argument being evaluated also passes the proper form test.

When doing the true premises test on an analogy, you need to be aware of imaginary cases. Good analogies can use imaginary cases. Premises about an imaginary case pass the true premises test when the author and the audience have the same views about the imaginary case.

When doing the proper form test on analogies, you need to consider relevant similarities and relevant dissimilarities. A feature is a relevant similarity when the fact that the analogue and the primary subject share that feature provides some evidence for the claim that the primary subject has the conclusory feature. A feature is a relevant dissimilarity when the fact that the analogue and the primary subject don't share that feature provides some evidence for the claim that the primary subject doesn't have the conclusory feature.

One reason analogies are important is that they can reveal whether a person's beliefs are consistent. If beliefs are inconsistent, at least one of them is false.

GUIDE

Finding, Standardizing, and Evaluating Analogical Arguments

This Guide is an amplification of the "Guide for Finding, Standardizing, and Evaluating Arguments" that is in Chapter Two. The numbered sentences are copies from the Guide in Chapter Two. The sentences with "Analogy" in front of them are additional materials that apply only to analogical arguments.

Finding Arguments

1. Look for an attempt to convince.
   Analogy. Look to see whether there is an attempt to convince that uses a comparison. Check to see whether the analogy is argumentative or illustrative.
2. Find the conclusion.
   Analogy. Find the primary subject and the conclusory feature.
3. Find the premises.
   Analogy. Find the analogue(s) and the similarities.
4. Review the following to make sure that you have correctly identified the conclusion and the premises: imperfect indicator words, sentence order, premises and/or conclusion not in declarative form, and unstated premises and/or conclusion.
5. Review the following to make sure that you have not incorrectly identified something as a premise or a conclusion when in fact it is not part of an argument: assertions, questions, instructions, descriptions, and explanations.

Standardizing Arguments

6. Rewrite the premises and the conclusion as declarative sentences. Make sure that each premise and the conclusion is a grammatically correct declarative sentence. Rewrite the premises and conclusion as necessary to make them clearer but do not change the meaning of the passage. Remove pronouns from the sentences and replace them with the nouns or noun phrases to which they refer. Remove emotionally charged language.
7. Review any phrases you have omitted to be sure that they are not premises or a conclusion.

8. Number the premises and the conclusion. Put brackets [] around the number of any unstated premise and/or conclusion. Place the premises before their conclusion and insert "Therefore," between the premises and the conclusion. Use blank lines to indicate subarguments.

Analogy. Put the standardization into the standard form of an analogical argument:

(1) X1s have features F1, F2, F3, . . . and
    feature Fn.
(2) X2s also have features F1, F2, F3, . . .
Therefore,
(3) X2s probably have Fn.

9. Compare your standardization to the original passage to make sure that you have not omitted any arguments found in the passage and to be sure that you have correctly identified the premises and the conclusion.

Evaluating Arguments: The True Premises Test

10. Check to see whether the premises are accurate descriptions of the world.
Analogy. Check for knowledge about imaginary cases. Evaluate it if it is present.
Analogy. Check to see whether the analogue and the primary subject have the features that the argument claims they do.
11. Consider whether the premises are appropriate for the argument's audience.
12. Review the assumed premises to be sure that the assumptions are reasonable. Make sure that all assumed premises are uncontroversially true empirical statements, uncontroversially true definitional statements, or appropriate statements by experts. Make sure the definitions are good ones.

Evaluating Arguments: The Proper Form Test

13. Determine whether the argument is a deductive argument or an inductive argument.
14. Determine whether the premises are relevant to the conclusion. Look at each premise individually to see whether the truth of the premise provides some evidence for the truth of the conclusion. Look at the premises as a group to see whether the truth of all of them provides some evidence for the truth of the conclusion.
Analogy. Consider whether the similarities are relevant. Check to see whether there are any relevant dissimilarities. Evaluate the importance of the similarities and the relevant dissimilarities.

Evaluating Arguments: Checking for Fallacies

15. Compare the argument to the list of fallacies on page 410 to see whether the argument commits any of the fallacies.

8

Statistical Arguments

In this study we used fecal steroid analysis to examine the effects of seasonal, reproductive, and social factors on female testosterone in a group of free-ranging hybrid baboons in the Awash National Park of Ethiopia. We collected behavioral and hormonal data from 25 adult females across an 11-month period. The results indicated that female dominance rank was positively related to testosterone measures.

—Jacinta C. Beehner, Jane E. Phillips-Conry, and Patricia L. Whitten, "Female Testosterone, Dominance Rank, and Aggression in an Ethiopian Population of Hybrid Baboons" (Beehner 2005, 101. Material has been omitted and the abbreviation "T" has been replaced with its referent, "testosterone.")

Learning Outcomes

After studying the material in this chapter, you should be able to:

1. Calculate the mean, weighted mean, mode, midrange, and median of a data set.

2. Identify statistical arguments.

3. Identify the sample, the N, the relevant properties, and the target of statistical arguments.

4. Identify representative and biased samples.

5. Correctly evaluate statistical arguments.

Statistical arguments are arguments that draw a conclusion about all members of a group by looking at part of the group. The quote on the previous page draws a conclusion about all female baboons by looking at some female baboons. Statistical arguments are used to determine everything from what shows remain on TV to which medications a doctor can prescribe. You use statistical arguments every time you start your car or walk to your favorite restaurant.

Descriptive Statistics

Descriptive statistics report and analyze data about things people have observed. **Argumentative statistics** draw generalizations about things that haven't been observed based on a sample of things that have been observed. You can't evaluate statistical arguments unless you know the basics of descriptive statistics. Mark Twain said that "there are three kinds of lies: lies, damn lies, and statistics" (1990, 185). Twain's remark is funny and accurate because many people know that others don't understand statistics and can be influenced by bad statistical arguments. For you to avoid falling into this trap, you need to understand descriptive statistics.

Technical Term: Inferential Statistics

Argumentative statistics are also called "inferential statistics."

Statistics are about data but what are data? They're not just numbers because numbers without a link to the world are meaningless. Suppose that someone tells you that they have "four." Four what? Numbers are only meaningful if you know what they're describing. The number "four," in the context of discussing the grade point average (GPA) of a student, becomes "4.0," an impressive number. Or is it? What if you found out that everyone at this student's college had a 4.0 GPA?

Let's look at a data set. Jacinta Beehner has studied the relationship between the amount of testosterone in female baboons and their dominance rank within their troop. Testosterone is a hormone usually associated with males, but in mammals both males and females have testosterone. To measure the level of testosterone in female baboons, Beehner collected their feces. To determine their rank with their troop, she observed the behavior of female baboons. Every baboon has a dominance rank. There is a dominant male and a dominant female, and all the other baboons in the troop rank below the dominant male and female but may be higher or lower than other baboons in the troop. The ranking can be measured by observing which baboons are aggressive, which ones retreat when confronted, and the grooming behavior of the baboons. If one baboon grooms another, then the baboon who does the grooming is ranked lower.

Key Concept
Descriptive statistics report and analyze data about things people have observed. **Argumentative statistics** draw generalizations about things that haven't been observed based on a sample of things that have been observed.

make sure I define

1. Baboon's Name	2. Mean Fecal Testosterone (nanograms/gram)	3. Relative Rank
Cecelia	1.48	0.00
Gari	1.50	0.32
Gigi	1.39	0.20
Goldilox	1.03	0.08
Handle	1.33	0.16
Jersey	1.52	0.72
Kitten	1.75	0.96
Koala	1.44	0.64
Lally	1.74	0.28
Loopy	1.61	0.80
Manx	1.30	0.24
Nicky	1.77	1.00
Pooh	1.61	0.92
Rita	1.72	0.56
Strep	1.44	0.12
Tibs	1.88	0.60
Tigger	1.64	0.36
Tripod	1.72	0.68
Wusha	1.51	0.52
(These numerical data were not in Beehner's (2005) article. They were reported in the form of a chart. The numerical data were graciously provided by Dr. Beehner. We've simplified it by changing one value.)		

Column 1 indicates the name of each baboon. Column 2 indicates the amount of testosterone found in the feces of that baboon. Column 3 indicates the rank of each baboon. Nicky has a rank of 1.00. She's the dominant female. All the other female baboons ranked below her. Cecelia had the lowest rank, 0.00. All the other female baboons ranked above her. Tibs's rank is 0.60. Sixty percent of the female baboons in this group ranked below her and 40% ranked above her. This chart can be used to illustrate a key point regarding descriptive statistics, that "average" has many meanings.

The Many Meanings of "Average"

Key Concept
An **average** is a way of describing the **center** of a set of data.

You probably know your GPA, but you might not have thought about the meaning of "average" in "grade point average." An **average** is a way of describing the **center** of a set of data. You can think of the center of a data set as its middle. The middle of something can be measured in different ways. Think about a car. You could measure its middle by measuring its length and dividing by two. Or you could find the place where half the car's weight is on either side. Like the middle of a car, the center of a data set can be measured in several ways, and all of them can be called the "average."

The Mean

Sometimes "average" means "mean." The **mean** of a set of numbers is calculated by adding the numbers together and dividing by the number of numbers in the set. A student could compute his GPA by the following method: add the grade points and divide by the number of courses taken.

Course	Letter Grade	Grade Points
1. Anthropology	A−	3.67
2. Biology	B	3.00
3. Business Statistics	F	0.00
4. Ceramics	B+	3.33
5. French	B	3.00
Total points		13.00

The total points (13.00) divided by number of courses (5) equals 2.60, the student's GPA. Strictly speaking, the GPA is the mean grade points earned. In the baboon data, the mean level of testosterone is 1.55 nanograms. (Check our math!)

Technical Term: Arithmetic Mean

The mean is also called the "arithmetic mean."

The Weighted Mean

At most colleges, the GPA isn't a mean. It's a weighted mean. A **weighted mean** is a mean in which some components have more of an effect than other components. Suppose that Biology is a four-hour course and Ceramics is a two-hour course. Biology will have a greater weight in the GPA than the three-hour courses, and Ceramics will have a lower weight.

Course	Letter Grade	Grade Points	Hours	Course Points
1. Anthropology	A−	3.67	3	11.01
2. Biology	B	3.00	4	12.00
3. Business Statistics	F	0.00	3	0.00
4. Ceramics	B+	3.33	2	6.66
5. French	B−	3.00	3	9.00
Total			15	38.67

Key Concept
The **mean** of a set of numbers is calculated by adding the numbers together and dividing by the number of numbers in the set.

Key Concept
A **weighted mean** is a mean in which some components have more of an effect than other components.

The Course Points equals the Grade Points times the number of Hours. The weighted mean is the total course points (38.67) divided by the total hours (15) and equals 2.58. The weighted mean is lower than the unweighted mean because the high grade in the two-hour Ceramics class has less effect on the weighted mean.

The Mode

> **Key Concept**
> The **mode** is the most frequently occurring value in a data set.

Sometimes the center of a data set is expressed by the most frequently occurring value in a data set, the **mode**. The mode of our student's grades is 3.0. The student got two Bs (two 3.0s) and only one of each of the other grades earned (A–, B+, and F). When a data set contains a tie for the most frequent value, it has multiple modes. In the baboon testosterone data, three values (1.44, 1.61, and 1.72) each appear twice. The other values each appear once. This data set has three modes, one at 1.44, one at 1.61, and one at 1.72.

Technical Term: Modal

The adjectival form of "mode" is "modal." Our student's modal grade was B or 3.00.

The Midrange

> **Key Concept**
> The **midrange** is the sum of the highest value and the lowest value, divided by two.

Sometimes "average" refers to the **midrange**. The midrange is the sum of the highest value and the lowest value, divided by two. The midrange of our student's grades is the sum of the highest grade (3.67) and the lowest grade (0.00), divided by two, 1.84. To get the midrange of the testosterone data, you add the highest value (1.88, Nicky) and the lowest value (1.03, Goldilox) and get 2.91. Then you divide by two and get the midrange, 1.455.

The Median

> **Key Concept**
> The **median** of a data set is a data point, D, such that at most half the set have values lower than D and at most half the set have values higher than D.

Sometimes "average" refers to the median. You can think of the median as the number you get when you arrange the numbers from highest to lowest and pick the middle number. Strictly speaking, a data set with an even number of data points doesn't have a median. If a data set has four points, then no data point has the same number of data points on either side of it. In this case, researchers often take the mean of the two middle values as the median. In other data sets, multiple points have the same value. In the grades above, the median is a B because the student has five grades (A-, B+, B, B, and F), and two grades are higher than the first B and two grades lower than or equal to this B. Speaking precisely, the **median** of a data set is a data point, D, such that at most half the set have values lower than D and at most half the set have values higher than D.

To see the median testosterone level of the baboons, arrange them from highest to lowest testosterone level.

1. Baboon's Name	2. Mean Fecal Testosterone (nanograms/gram)	3. Relative Rank
1. Tibs	1.88	0.60
2. Nicky	1.77	1.00
3. Kitten	1.75	0.96
4. Lally	1.74	0.28
5. Rita	1.72	0.56
6. Tripod	1.72	0.68
7. Tigger	1.64	0.36
8. Loopy	1.61	0.80
9. Pooh	1.61	0.92
10. Jersey	*1.52*	*0.72*
11. Wusha	1.51	0.52
12. Gari	1.50	0.32
13. Cecelia	1.48	0.00
14. Koala	1.44	0.64
15. Strep	1.44	0.12
16. Gigi	1.39	0.20
17. Handle	1.33	0.16
18. Manx	1.30	0.24
19. Goldilox	1.03	0.08

There are nineteen baboons, so the median testosterone is the data point with nine above it and nine below it. That's 1.52, and so Jersey is at the median.

Outliers and Resistance

Some data sets have outliers. **Outliers** are data points that are far away from the other points in the data set. In the baboon data, Goldilox is an outlier. Her testosterone level is far below the others'. Means and midranges are strongly affected by outliers, but medians aren't. In the grade example, the F has a much greater decreasing effect on the mean than the grade of B. If the highest value of a data set is an outlier, the midrange won't accurately reflect the data's center. When a measure of the center of a set of data is greatly influenced by outliers it has **low resistance**. Because medians aren't affected in the same

Key Concept
Outliers are data points that are far away from the other points in the data set. When a measure of the center of a set of data is greatly influenced by outliers it has **low resistance**.

way, they have higher resistance. The low resistance of means is especially obvious if the data set is small. If you have ninety hours and a 3.00 GPA and then you get an F in a three-hour class, your GPA will drop by 0.10 to 2.90. But if you have fifteen hours and a 3.00 GPA and then get an F, your GPA would drop by 0.50 to 2.50. You need to be careful about means when looking at small data sets.

Choose the measure of centrality that's relevant to your purposes. In 2005, U.S. mean household income was $63,344 but U.S. median household income was $46,326 (DeNavas-Walt 2006, 38). The mean is $17,018 (35%) higher than the median. In this case, median is a better measure of centrality than mean because of the mean's low resistance. The income of a very few very rich individuals pulls up the U.S. mean income. This makes the mean a bad indicator of the center of U.S. income.

Centrality isn't always relevant. Suppose that you're trying to decide whether to walk across a river and someone tells you that its mean depth is three feet. That information isn't very useful. What you want to know is how deep the river is at its deepest point. You don't care about centrality.

GUIDE

Mean	$(N1 + N2 + N3 + \ldots Nn) \div n$
Weighted Mean	$(N1 \times W1 + N2 \times W1 + N3 \times W3 + \ldots Nn \times Wn) \div n$
Mode	The most frequent value in the data set
Midrange	(Lowest value + highest value) $\div$ 2
Median	A data point, D, such that at most half the set have values lower than D and at most half the set have values higher than D.

Critical Thinkers

Jacinta Beehner

Courtesy of Jacinta Beehner

An Assistant Professor of Psychology and Anthropology at the University of Michigan, Jacinta Beehner researches the connections between social conditions and variations in individual living things. For much of her research, she gathers data on gelada baboons, who live in extremely large social groups (compared to most other primates). *Smithsonian* magazine published an article about her research (http://www.smithsonianmag.com/science-nature/Ethiopias-Exotic-Monkeys.html), and she has published more than twenty articles. You can see those at http://sitemaker.umich.edu/jacinta.beehner/published_research.

EXERCISE 8.1

A. For each of the following, determine whether or not an average number is reported. If an average is reported, identify which type of average it is (mean, median, etc.). Calculate as many of the following as you can given the data: (a) mean, (b) weighted mean, (c) mode, (d) midrange, and (e) median.

1. The average number of credit hours for the students in the following list is 16:

Aaron	12
Abigail	16
Brenda	15
Bret	18
Charles	19
Charlene	18
Deborah	15
Douglas	16
Edward	16
Edith	16

2. The average number of credit hours for the students in the list in Exercise 1 above is precisely 16.1.

*3. The average income for Wall Street's top ten income earners in 1996 was $258.7 million, based on the following table:

George Soros, Soros Funds	$800 million
Julian Robertson, Tiger Mgt.	$300
Henry Kravis, KKR	$265
George Roberts, KKR	$265
Stanley Druckmiller, Soros Funds	$200
Robert MacDonnell, KKR	$200
Sam Fix, Harbour Group	$190
Thomas Lee, Thomas H. Lee Co	$130
Nick Roditi, Soros Funds	$125
Jerome Kohlberg, KKR	$112

    (Philli ps 2002, 145)

*4. The average income for Wall Street's top ten income earners reported in Exercise 3 was $456 million.

5. "Prior to 1951, birth statistics came from a complete count of records received in the Public Health Service (now received in NCHS). From 1951 to 1971, they were based on a 50 percent sample of all registered births. Beginning in 1972, they have been based on a complete count for states participating in the Vital Statistics Cooperative Program (VSCP) and on a 50 percent sample of all other areas." (U.S. Census Bureau 2000, 63, material omitted)

    If you were to tally the number of births from 1951 through 1971 and divide by 21, what kind of average number of births would result?

6. "Three-fourths of college-educated men in these studies achieved some upward mobility, while only 12 percent of those who received no schooling did." (Schaefer 2006, 202)

7. "A 1994 almanac showed that Judaism had almost 18 million members, Christianity had roughly 1.8 billion members, Islam had almost 1 billion members, Hinduism had almost 733 million adherents, Buddhism about 315 million, and Confucianism about 6 million or more members." (Deiner 1977, 11) The average number of members among these six religious groups is 645 million.

   Refer to the following data for the next three passages.

Unemployment Rate and Educational Attainment			
Year	All	High–School Graduate	College Graduate
1992	6.7	7.7	2.9
1995	4.8	5.2	2.5
1998	4.0	4.8	1.8
1999	3.5	4.0	1.9

Data are based on civilian population 25 to 64 years of age. Total includes other categories, not shown separately (those with less than high-school diploma and those with some college but less than a bachelor's degree). (U.S. Census Bureau 2010, 424)

*8. Calculate the mean and median unemployment rates between 1992 and 1999 for those whose highest level of education is a high-school diploma.

9. Calculate the mean and median unemployment rate between 1992 and 1999 for those who have a college degree.

10. Calculate the mean average difference between the unemployment rates of those with a high-school diploma vs. those with a college degree for the years data are provided.

11. "The 'gender gap' in pay is a widely recognized fact. Even as recently as 2002, women who worked full time year round earned only 78 percent as much as men." (Giddens 2005, 287, material omitted)

*12. "[B]efore 1980, only 43 percent of women (or their partner) used a method of birth control at their first premarital intercourse. By 1999–2002, the proportion using a method at first premarital intercourse had risen to 79 percent." (Mosher 2004, 1)

13. "Whereas traditionally grain was grown for human consumption, an increasing percentage is being grown for animal consumption. Worldwatch Paper 103 reports that "roughly 38 percent of the world's grain—especially corn, barley, sorghum, and oats—is fed to livestock." (Durning 1991, 14)

14. "A survey of youth in more than fifteen countries finds that 75 percent of U.S. tweens want to be rich, a higher percentage than anywhere else in the world except India, where the results were identical. Sixty-one percent want to be famous." (Schaefer 2006, 54)

15. "For both whites and blacks, suicide was more common among men than women. The suicide rate for white men (25 suicides per 100,000 people) was about four times higher than the rate for white women (6). Among African Americans, the rate for men (12) was about six times that for women (2)." (Centers for Disease Control and Prevention 2009)

B. For each of the following sets of data, calculate as many of the following as you can given the data: (a) the mean, (b) the weighted mean, (c) the mode, (d) the midrange, and (e) the median.

1. Political and economic commentator Kevin Phillips (2002, 151) points out the declining employment in the top 500 U.S. industrial corporations over the last two decades of the 20th century. Based on the figures below, what is the average number of jobs across the time period from 1980 to 1993?

Year	Number of Jobs at the Top 500 Corporation
1980	15.9 million
1985	14.1 million
1990	12.4 million
1993	11.5 million

2. According to *Honest Work, A Business Ethics Reader* (Ciulla 2007, 166), the number of bankruptcies filed increased considerably from 1997 to 2002.

Year	Total	Non–Business	Business
2002	1,504,806	1,464,961	38,845
2001	1,307,857	1,271,865	35,992
2000	1,301,205	1,263,096	38,108
1999	1,419,199	1,378,071	41,128
1998	1,423,128	1,370,490	53,638
1997	1,247,065	1,193,057	54,008

3. Given the bankruptcy statistics in Exercise 2 above, are there any outliers?

*4. In Exercise 2 above, what was the lowest and what was the highest number of bankruptcies for business and for non-business filings?

5. Was there any year in which the number of bankruptcy filings decreased for businesses? For non-business filings?

*6. "Worldwatch Institute, an independent, nonprofit research organization, reported that the expanding global livestock industry has hidden costs. One of those costs is the amount of grain that cows, pigs, sheep, and poultry eat. Whereas traditionally grain was

Country/Region	Share of Grain Consumed by Livestock
United States	70
Eastern Europe	64
EC	57
Soviet Union	56
Brazil	55
Japan	48
Middle East	33
China	20
Southeast Asia	12
Sub-Saharan Africa	2
India	2

grown for human consumption, an increasing percentage is being grown for animal consumption. Worldwatch Paper 103 reports that roughly 38 percent of the world's grain—especially corn, barley, sorghum, and oats—is fed to livestock." (Durning 1991, 14–15)

*7. Which countries are outliers in Exercise 6 above?

8. Keep track of the number of servings of vegetables and fruits you eat for five days. Then calculate the "average" number of servings per day for each (vegetables, fruits) that you consume. Calculate the various types of "average" listed in the directions to this exercise.

9. Were there any outliers in your record, or was your consumption fairly uniform across all five days?

10. Were the numbers similar for vegetables and fruits, or was one much higher than the other?

11. Using an unofficial copy of your own transcript from college (or high school if this is your first year in college), calculate what your GPA would be for all types of "average" listed above in the directions to this exercise.

12. Were there any outlier semesters in your grades, or were your grades fairly uniform across the semesters?

*13. "In 1997, sales of VCRs numbered 16.7 million. In 2002, estimated sales of VCRs were 13.3 million." (Lial 2004, 219)

1995	World Total	Africa	Asia	Europe	Cen./S. America	N. America	Oceania
Population	5,686,775	719,497	3,437,791	728,034	476,641	296,644	28,168
Teachers	47,105	3,791	24,455	9,398	5,131	4,000	330
% of GNP	4.8	5.6	3.7	5.1	4.1	5.4	5.6

14. The population numbers are in thousands, so 5,686,775 = 5,686,775,000.

Standard Deviation

Key Concept

Standard deviation is a measure of the **spread** of data away from the mean.

Researchers are often interested in ways data deviate from the center. **Standard deviation** is a measure of the **spread** of data away from the mean. Roughly and non-mathematically speaking, the standard deviation is the amount that the numbers in a data set vary from the mean. This data set:

8, 8, 8

has a standard deviation of zero. The mean of the three points is 8, and all three points are at the mean. This data set:

0, 0, 1000, 1000

has a standard deviation of 577.35. The points are widely spread from the data set's mean (500). In the baboon data, the standard deviation of the testosterone level data is 0.20. The testosterone data has a narrow spread. This introductory text won't cover how to calculate a standard deviation.

(But if you have your data in Microsoft Excel, it can calculate standard deviation.)

Standard deviations can be used to indicate where a particular data point falls in the spread. This data set:

2, 2, 2, 2, 2, 2, 2, 2, 2, 2, 2, 2, 2, 2, 2, 2, 2, 2, 2, 2, 40

has twenty-one points. The mean is 3.81, and the standard deviation is 8.29. The data point 40 is an outlier. The data point 40 is 36.19 away from the mean (40 − 3.81 = 36.19). 36.19 divided by the data set's standard deviation is 4.37. Data point 40 is 4.37 standard deviations away from the mean. The data points of 2 are much closer to the mean. They are less than one standard deviation from the mean. Each data points of 2 is 1.81 away from the mean (3.81 − 2 = 1.81) and 1.81 is less than 8.29, the data set's standard deviation. Goldilox's testosterone level is about two and a half standard deviations away from the mean. The mean is 1.55, and Goldilox's level is 1.03. The difference is 0.52 (1.55 − 1.03). The standard deviation is 0.20. If you divide 0.52 by 0.20 you get 2.6.

Standard deviations are also clues to misleading means. If the standard deviation of a data set is large, then a mean may be hiding an odd distribution. Suppose that the standard deviation of a data set is 527 and its mean is 500. That's a clue that the mean is misleading. The standard deviation of this data set

0, 0, 0, 0, 0, 1000, 1000, 1000, 1000, 1000

is 527 and its mean is 500, but this mean is misleading because there are no data points near 500.

Distributions

To avoid making mistakes about measures of centrality and spread, look at the distribution of the data on a chart. This will often help you determine the best measure of centrality, whether an unusual distribution is producing the centrality, or whether centrality is relevant to your purposes. The **shape** of a data set can be thought of as the graphical illustration you see when you plot the data on a chart.

All measures of centrality can hide different distributions. A 3.0 GPA can be earned in many different ways. One student could have all Bs, whereas another might have half As and half Cs. One example of a distribution that's hidden by a measure of centrality is a bimodal distribution. Speaking roughly and non-mathematically, a **bimodal distribution** is one that, when graphed, has two peaks. Another often discussed type of distribution is a normal distribution. Again speaking roughly and non-mathematically, a **normal distribution** is one that, when graphed, has one peak and smooth equal sides on either side of the peak.

Suppose that the mean grade given in English 101 is 2.00 and that the mean grade given in Math 101 is also 2.00. You might think that the courses are roughly equally difficult. But then suppose you see the following charts of the distribution of grades. These two charts are examples of **bar charts**.

Key Concept
The **shape** of a data set can be thought of as the graphical illustration you see when you plot the data on a chart.

Key Concept
A **bimodal distribution** is one that, when graphed, has two peaks. A **normal distribution** is one that, when graphed, has one peak and smooth equal sides on either side of the peak.

Key Concept
Bar charts.

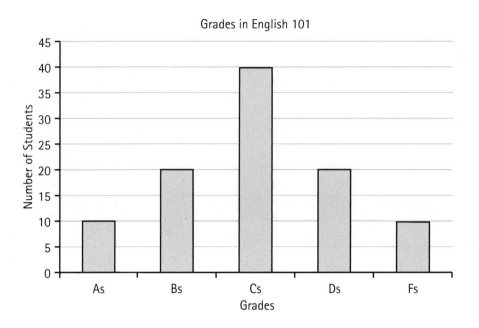

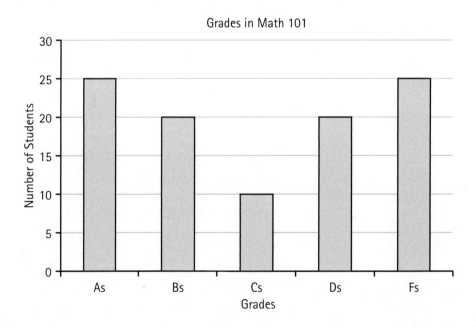

The bars indicate the number of students receiving each grade. There were 100 students in each class. In English 101, 10 students got an A. In Math 101, 25 students got an A. The grades in English 101 have a normal distribution. The grades in Math 101 have a bimodal distribution. Now you probably don't think that the courses are equally difficult. You probably think that the Math course is harder for some students and easier for others.

Technical Term: Gaussian Distribution

Normal distributions are also called "Gaussian distributions."

Plotting data on a chart can be done in several different ways. Besides the form of bar charts that you just saw, you can plot data in a **scatter chart**. Suppose that you think that Sallay, a college student, might be watching too much television. You decide to collect data to compare her GPA with the number of hours per week that she watched television that semester. Here are the data for Sallay's freshman and sophomore years.

Key Concept
Scatter charts.

Semester	Hours of TV Watched per Week	Semester GPA
Fall 1	3	3.8
Spring 1	10	3.3
Summer 1	13	2.7
Fall 2	18	2.5
Spring 2	27	2.2
Summer 2	30	2.0

Here's a scatter chart of this data.

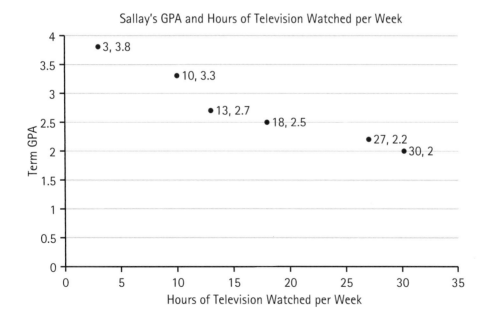

The numbers next to the point at the upper left are "3, 3.8" because they are the data collected for Fall 1. The data points fall roughly into a line. In the real world, data don't usually have such an obvious shape.

Here's a scatter plot of Beehner's data (Beehner 2005, 111):

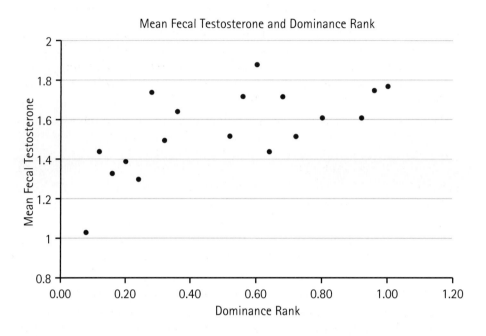

Key Concept
Line charts.

Another common type of chart is a line chart. Here's a **line chart** of the mean grades given by a particular instructor, Professor Manon, in one of her classes, Econ 101, over the course of the last six semesters:

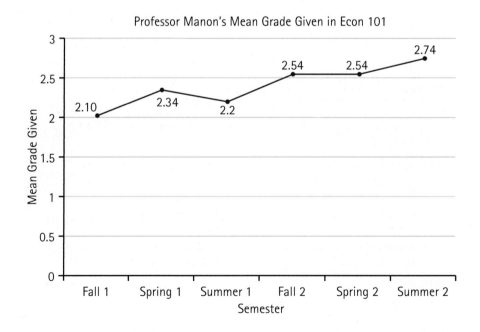

A line chart is similar to a bar chart. The only difference is that the tops of what would be the bars are connected by a line.

Technical Terms: Bar Graph and Scatter Plot

Bar charts are also called "bar graphs." Scatter charts are also called "scatter plots."

Different types of charts are used for different purposes. Line charts are often good ways to present change over time. The line chart that presents Professor Manon's grades is a good example. It indicates that over time her mean grade given has risen. Bar charts are often good ways to present quantities of things.

Here are some absolute rules about charts:

1. All charts should have a clearly labeled *x* axis (the horizontal axis) and a clearly labeled *y* axis (the vertical axis). In the chart of Professor Manon's grade, the *x* axis is clearly labeled "Semester" and the *y* axis is clearly labeled "Mean Grade Given." If we had put "Mean" on the *y* axis, that wouldn't have been clear and specific enough.

2. The units of measure on both axes should be clear. (Is a chart presenting the dollars of Cokes sold or the bottles of Cokes sold?)

3. The chart should have a clear title. The chart of Professor Manon's grades clearly indicates the course she is teaching and what the chart reports.

4. The source of the data presented should be correctly noted. (In this chapter there are some charts with no source because we invented the data.)

5. If different sets of data are put on one chart, the numbers, bars, or lines should be colored or shaded so that the different sets can be easily distinguished. If you put Professor Wilson's grades on the same chart with Professor Manon's, you should be sure that the different professors' grades can be easily distinguished.

A good chart is clear and useful. A bad chart is unclear and/or not useful. When you make a chart, look at it with the eyes of people who will see it. You need to be sure that it clearly and accurately presents the data to people who don't know the data as well as you do. Seeing charts from the point of view of other people is another part of the art of argument.

Technical Terms: Values on *x* and *y* Axes, Abscissa, Ordinate

When comparing two sets of data on one chart, you plot one set on the *x* axis of a chart and the other on its *y* axis. The *x* axis and the *y* axis have lots of different names. Here are some:

Names for the *x*-Axis Variable	Names for the *y*-Axis Variable
• explanatory variable	• response variable
• independent variable	• dependent variable
• criterion value	• predictor value
• domain	• range
• input value	• output value
• right-hand side	• left-hand side

The lines themselves also have names. The *x*-axis line is the abscissa, and the *y*-axis line is the ordinate.

Regressions

Regression lines are a way of describing the shape of a data set. The **regression line** of a data set is the line that best fits the data. Speaking roughly and

Key Concept
The **regression line** of a data set is the line that best fits the data.

non-mathematically, the regression line is the line that has the smallest total distance between the line and the data points. This introductory text won't indicate how to calculate a regression line. (But if you have your data in Microsoft Excel, it can draw the line for you.) You can use the scatter chart of Sallay's grades and add a regression line. You can do the same with the chart from Beehner's article.

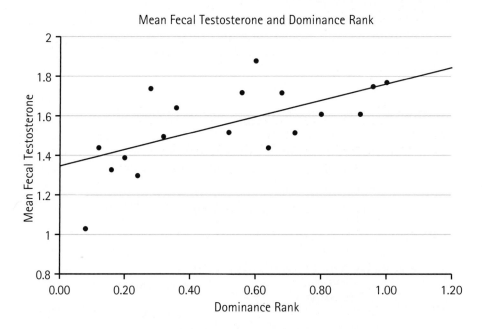

Regression lines are more than a way of describing the shape of a data set. Looking at the charts above, can you make a prediction concerning Sallay's semester GPA if she watched thirty-five hours of television per week in that semester? It looks like it would be about 1.50. On the basis of a pattern in the data you've observed, you've made an inference about something unobserved.

What would you predict about the testosterone level of a female baboon with a dominance rank of 0.50? This shows the value of regressions: you can use them to make predictions.

But you must predict with care. If you blindly followed the regression line on the chart of Sallay's GPA, you'd predict that if she watched enough television her GPA would become a negative number. But no student can have a GPA below zero. And many data sets don't have the shape of a line. One data set might have the shape of a wave, and you may only be seeing part of the wave. Learning how to use regression lines to draw conclusions is part of the art of evaluating statistical arguments, the topic of the last section of this chapter.

Technical Terms: Monotonic and Nonmonotonic

An increase or decrease is monotonic when it's uninterrupted. Look back at the chart of Professor's Manon's grades. Over time, they've increased. But the increase is nonmonotonic because from Spring 1 to Summer 1 her mean grade decreased (from 2.34 to 2.2) and because from Fall 2 to Spring 2, her mean grade didn't increase. It stayed steady at 2.54.

EXERCISE 8.2

A. For each of the data sets in Exercise 8.1 A 1, 3, 7, 8, 15, and 8.1 B 1, 2, 6, 8, 14, and 15, plot the data on a bar chart and line chart to see the shape of the data. Be sure to follow the five rules about charts discussed above.

B. For each of the data sets in Exercises 8.1 A 1, 3, 7, 8, 15, and 8.1 B 1, 2, 6, 8, 14, and 15, use Microsoft Excel to find the standard deviation and the regression line that fits the data. If you can find a regression line, use it to predict in each case what the next data point would be. In some cases, one problem includes more than one data set. In that case find the standard deviation for each data set in the problem.

▌ Identifying Statistical Arguments

Here are the standard forms of **statistical arguments**:

 General   (1) P% of the N observed things in G have F.
Therefore,
(2) P% of all the things in G have F.

Particular   (1) P% of the N observed things in G have F.
Therefore,
(2) P% of all the things in G have F.
(3) X is a thing in G.
Therefore,
(4) There is a P% chance that X has F.

 Key Concept
The standard forms of **statistical arguments.**

"P" and "N" are variables that refer to a number, "G" is a variable that refers to a group, and "F" is a variable that refers to a feature.

Connections

The use of variables is discussed in Chapter Two.

Here's an example of a statistical argument with the General form:

(1) During spring semester of 2006, 89% of 1,000 college students surveyed said that statistical arguments were their favorite type of argument.

Therefore,

(2) 89% of all college students would say that statistical arguments are their favorite type of argument.

This argument reasons from a premise about 1,000 college students whose views on statistical arguments have been observed (in a survey) to a conclusion about all college students. This is an example of the General form because the conclusion is about all college students.

Here's an example of a statistical argument with the Particular form:

(1) During spring semester of 2006, 89% of 1,000 college students surveyed said that statistical arguments were their favorite type of argument.

Therefore,

(2) 89% of all college students would say that statistical arguments are their favorite type of argument.

(3) Theo is a college student.
Therefore,

(4) There's an 89% chance that Theo would say that statistical arguments are his favorite type of argument.

This argument reasons from a premise about 1,000 college students to a conclusion about all college students and then to a second conclusion about one particular college student, Theo. This is an example of the Particular form because the second conclusion is about this particular college student.

The Particular form contains the General form. And the third premise of a Particular statistical argument is often easy to confirm or refute. The heart of a Particular statistical argument is a General statistical argument. This chapter focuses on the General form.

Parts of a Statistical Argument

Looking at the General standard form you can see that every statistical argument has five parts.

Key Concept
The five parts of a statistical argument.

1. The observed things in G are the **sample**.
2. The **N** is the number of things in the sample.
3. The features that these things have, the F, is the **relevant property**.
4. All the things in G are the **target**.
5. **P** is the percentage of the observed things that have F.

In our argument about college students,

1. Sample = the college students surveyed
2. N = 1,000
3. F = saying that statistical arguments were their favorite type of argument
4. Target = all college students
5. P = 89

Connections

Chapter Three noted that statements that report someone's observations are empirical statements. The premise of a statistical argument is the report of some observations. This means that statistical arguments are empirical arguments.

Technical Terms: Percentage of a Population, Sample Population, Target Population, Universe

Some researchers use the phrase "percentage of a population" or "sample population" to refer to the sample. Some researchers use the phrase "target population" to refer to the target. In some disciplines, the target is called the "universe" or the "universe of discourse."

Statistical arguments aren't usually found in standard form. The sample size may not be indicated. "P%" doesn't have to be expressed with a number. Statistical arguments often contain no numbers at all. Instead of referring to "100%," "85%," "50%," or "15%" of the sample, authors making a statistical argument can refer to "all," "most," "about half," or "some" of the sample.

You've probably gone to an ice cream shop and asked for a sample. The sample of ice cream you're given is a subset, a part, of all the ice cream of that flavor found in that store. When you decide on a flavor after sampling it, you're relying on a statistical argument. You're concluding that the unobserved (untasted) ice cream you're going to buy will have the same taste (the relevant property) as the ice cream you've observed (tasted).

Beehner's work on baboons includes a statistical argument.

We know that for the Awash females, testosterone is associated with rank and that rank is associated with aggression. Yet the stability of the female dominance

hierarchy makes it unlikely that testosterone mediates rank in this hybrid population. Pregnant females that were experiencing a surge in testosterone as the result of pregnancy did not rise in rank, and conversely, old females (with much lower testosterone levels than other females) did not fall in rank. Therefore, it seems that for baseline measures, our results are consistent with the hypothesis that rank determines testosterone levels, rather than the reverse. (Beehner 2005, 115–116)

Beehner uses information about her sample of female baboons to draw a conclusion about all female baboons. The conclusion that "our results are consistent with the hypothesis that rank determines testosterone levels, rather than the reverse" is about all female baboons (at least all those of the particular species Beehner studied). In this case,

1. Sample = the baboons observed
2. N = 19
3. F = having higher testosterone levels associated with higher rank
4. Target = all female baboons
5. P = not stated

Statistical Arguments and Analogical Arguments

What's the difference between a statistical argument and an analogical argument? In an analogical argument, you're comparing one group to another group and *the first group **is not** a subgroup of the second*. In a statistical argument, you're comparing one group (the sample) to another group (the target) and *the first group **is** a subgroup of the second*.

Let's return to the Briard dogs and humans with Leber congenital amaurosis (LCA) discussed in Chapter Seven. Remember that children and puppies

Habits of a Critical Thinker

Intellectual Humility

Critical thinkers are aware of their own intellectual limits. In letters to the editor, on cable news programs, and on talk radio, you hear lots of people who need more intellectual humility. They make their conclusions as definitive pronouncements and suggest that anyone who disagrees with them is an idiot. Here's a quote from Beehner that shows intellectual humility:

> The data presented here are suggestive rather than definitive, and there is certainly a need for more primate studies that examine individual hormone-behavior associations over time to bridge the gap between captive and freeranging studies. (Beehner 2005, 115)

Beehner doesn't say that her views are the complete truth that only idiots could deny. She says that her conclusions "are suggestive rather than definitive."

To be a critical thinker you must remember that everyone (including you) makes mistakes. If you lack intellectual humility, you're sure that you're right. And if you're sure that you're right, you aren't going to be open to suggestions for improvement or to good arguments that show that you're wrong.

with LCA either have no sight at birth or lose it very fast. Guylene Le Meur developed a treatment for this disease that involved injecting a genetically altered virus into LCA-affected eyes. She tested her technique on the eyes of eight dogs, seven puppies and an adult dog. The sight of the seven puppies was restored. The adult dog was unaffected. She concluded that this treatment might work on human infants. Is her argument an analogical argument between dogs and humans or a statistical argument with dogs as the sample and humans as the target?

Because dogs aren't a subset of humans, Le Meur is making an analogical argument. But she is also making a statistical argument. Her reasoning process has two steps. First, she uses a statistical argument to draw a conclusion about all Briard dogs. Because she can't study all the Briard dogs in the world, she studies a sample of them and then makes a statistical argument to draw a conclusion about all of them. Le Meur's sample was eight Briard dogs with LCA. She concluded that the therapy might restore the sight of all Briard dogs with LCA as long as the therapy was given while the dogs were puppies. The sample (the eight Briard dogs observed) is a subgroup of the target (all Briard dogs). Second, Le Meur makes an analogical argument to infer from the premise that the therapy restored sight to puppies with LCA (the analogues) to the conclusion that the therapy may restore the sight to human infants with LCA (the primary subjects). This is an analogical argument because dogs aren't a subgroup of humans.

Small changes can make what would be an analogical argument into a statistical argument. The argument about LCA contains an analogy because dogs aren't a subset of humans. But suppose that the scientists used the observations about Briard dogs to draw a conclusion about all mammals. In that case, the argument would be statistical because Briard dogs are a subset of mammals. (As you'll see in a moment, this would be a bad statistical argument because the sample would lack variety. Le Meur did not make this bad argument.)

Key Concept

In an analogical argument, you're comparing one group to another group and the first group is not a subgroup of the second. In a statistical argument, you're comparing one group (the sample) to another group (the target) and the first group is a subgroup of the second.

Technical Terms: Statistical Generalizations, Statistical Inferences, Inductive Generalizations Class, Set, Subclass, Subset, Individual, Member, Object Population Generalization, Environmental Generalization, Temporal Generalization

Statistical arguments are sometimes called "statistical generalizations," "statistical inferences," and/or "inductive generalizations." Some disciplines use "statistical generalization" to refer to the conclusion of a statistical argument. Others refer to the inference from the premise to the conclusion as "the generalization."

The groups in samples are often called "classes" or "sets," and subgroups are often called "subclasses," "subsets," or "strata." The things in samples are often called "individuals" (especially if the things are people), "members," or "objects."

Some researchers refer to "population generalizations," "environmental generalizations," and "temporal generalizations." While these terms are used in different ways, "population generalization" is usually another word for a statistical argument, whereas "environmental generalization" and "temporal generalization" are usually terms for analogical arguments.

EXERCISE 8.3

A. For each of the following, determine whether there's a statistical argument present. If there is, standardize it into either the General form or the Particular form. Identify the sample, the N, the relevant property or properties, the target, and the percentage. (In some cases, one or more of the five parts of a statistical argument in standard form may be missing.)

1. Five Green party members I have known are all French. Ralph Nader is a Green party member. Therefore, Ralph is probably French.

2. The tigers in the San Diego Zoo all have stripes. Thus, all tigers probably have stripes.

3. I ate at the new Char-Lee's restaurant yesterday and the food was pretty good, so I intend to eat there again today. It will probably be just as good today.

*4. So far this semester, my instructor has announced all quizzes ahead of time. She'll probably announce the next quiz ahead of time.

5. A survey of all the students taking Phil 1000 during Summer 2005 found that 60% of them earned either an A or a B in the course, thus the chances of other students getting an A or a B are better than 50-50.

6. Use Exercise 8.1 A 7.

7. Use Exercise 8.1 A 13.

*8. A line chart shows that the mean temperature increased steadily from 1955 to 2000 in the United States, Europe, and Antarctica. This shows that the global mean temperature probably also increased steadily during that time.

9. "One day while treating a patient, Freud encouraged her to relax on a couch. She rambled on about her physical problems and about issues that appeared to be unrelated to her physical complaints. Suddenly, she had a revelation that left her feeling better. Freud theorized that encouraging patients to say whatever comes to mind allowed them to recall forgotten memories that seemed to underlie their problems. This process, known today as free association, is one element of psychoanalysis, a therapy that Freud developed. From these experiences, Freud came to believe that the unconscious plays a crucial role in human behavior." (Pastorino 2006, 10)

10. "Contemporary American tweens and teens have emerged as the most brand-oriented, consumer-involved, and materialistic generations in history. And they top the list globally. A survey of youth in more than fifteen countries finds that 75 percent of U.S. tweens want to be rich, a higher percentage than anywhere else in the world except India, where the results were identical. Sixty-one percent want to be famous. More children here than anywhere else believe that their clothes and brands describe who they are and define their social status. American kids display more brand affinity than their counterparts anywhere else in the world; indeed experts describe them as increasingly 'bonded to brands.'" (Schaefer 2006, 54)

11. Use Exercise 8.1 A 15.

*12. Use Exercise 8.1 B 13.

13. "On August 1, 1981, Reagan signed the Economic Recovery Tax Act, which cut personal income taxes by 25 percent, lowered the maximum rate from 70 to 50 percent for 1982, cut the capital gains tax by one third, and offered a broad array of other tax concessions." (Bakeman 2007, 1007)

14. "A very intense campaign has been underway to establish that no one really cares about unemployment. It is contended that only inflation engenders concern and fear. After all, it is said, 92.5 percent are employed and only 7.5 percent are unemployed. It does sound small when put in these bland, cold terms, and there are no cries of anguish to disturb the sleep of the vast majority. But now put it another way: 7,003,000 people—mostly adults—are without jobs. True, they eat—but not too much; they have some sort of shelter; some even have health care. But many, including children, are in chronic ill health, or are ill nourished, and living a life of punishment and systematic abuse as if they had done some evil to this Nation." (King 1976, 636)

15. "We say the unemployed can be provided jobs at productive labor with decent wages. It has been done in other developed countries without curbing profits or liberties." (King 1976, 637)

Evaluating Statistical Arguments

You evaluate statistical arguments using the true premises test and the proper form test. But you need to know some details about how to apply the two tests to statistical arguments.

The True Premises Test

The application of the true premises test to statistical arguments is straightforward. Look back at the General form. Statistical arguments have only one premise, and this premise is a claim about something that someone observed. In applying the true premises test, you apply the test as it was outlined in Chapter Two with the revisions noted in Chapter Three. To jog your memory, Chapter Two said that a premise is true when it's a correct description of the world. But, as a report of someone's observation, the first premise of a statistical argument will often be an assumed premise, and you should use the guidelines for proper assumption from Chapter Three.

The Proper Form Test

A statistical argument with proper form can be put into the General form or the Particular form, but more than that is required for it to be a good argument. Think again about the ice cream shop. You ask for a sample of vanilla-chocolate-caramel swirl. You're relying on the following argument.

(1) 100% of 2 tablespoons in the tasted subset of the vanilla-chocolate-caramel swirl in the shop has taste T.
Therefore,
(2) 100% of all of the vanilla-chocolate-caramel swirl in the shop has taste T.

But suppose that, when you ask for a sample, the salesperson reaches in with the little sampling spoon and gives you a sample that contains only caramel—no chocolate and no vanilla. You'd object. "Hey, that's not a good sample! Give me a sample that includes vanilla, chocolate, and caramel!" If the sales person gave you a sample that contained some vanilla, some chocolate, and some caramel, that would be a good sample. A good sample is called "a representative sample."

To be more precise, a sample is perfectly **representative** when the proportions of every subgroup in the target are exactly matched by the proportions of the subgroups in the sample. A sample of vanilla-chocolate-caramel is perfectly representative if the proportions of vanilla, chocolate, and caramel in the sample are precisely the same as the proportions of vanilla, chocolate, and caramel in the tub of ice cream. Representativeness is a matter of degree. A sample is more or less representative. A statistical argument passes the proper form test when (a) it can be put into the General or Particular form and (b) the sample is sufficiently representative.

A sample that isn't representative is a biased sample. A sample is **biased** when the proportions of every subgroup in the target do *not* match the proportions of the subgroups in the sample. When the salesperson gives you a sample of vanilla-chocolate-caramel swirl that contains only caramel, that's a biased sample. Bias makes a statistical argument fail the proper form test.

Any interesting target contains things with many different properties. In many cases, it's almost impossible to get a sample that perfectly represents the proportions of *all* those properties. Think of the thousands of chemical properties of cancer cells. Getting a perfectly representative sample is also hard because you often don't know all the properties of the target and there's no practical way to find out. Think of all the things you don't know about all the different people in the world. To apply the proper form test, you need some guidelines to help you generate good (but not perfect) samples.

Guideline 1: Size

The larger the sample, the more likely that it is representative.

In general, the larger the sample, the greater the chance it's representative of the target, and therefore the stronger the argument. Beehner's argument would be stronger if she had observed more baboons.

When looking at sample size, you should look at the sample and the target. If the sample is a large proportion of the target, it's more likely to be a good sample. Suppose that one study has a target of all humans and another has a target of all 4th graders at a small elementary school. A sample of fifty is too small if the target is all humans, but if there are only 200 4th graders a sample of fifty is very large.

Guideline 2: Variety

The more varied the sample, the more likely that it is representative.

In general, the greater the variety in the sample, the greater the representativeness of the sample. Beehner's argument would be stronger if she had observed baboons in more parts of Africa. Suppose that a researcher was studying the nesting behavior of robins. Ideally, the researcher would observe some robins in every location where robins are found. If the researcher only observed robins in the state where the researcher lived, the sample would lack variety.

> **Key Concept**
> A sample is perfectly **representative** when the proportions of every subgroup in the target are exactly matched by the proportions of the subgroups in the sample.

> **Key Concept**
> A statistical argument passes the proper form test when (a) it can be put into the General or Particular form and (b) the sample is sufficiently representative.

> **Key Concept**
> A sample is **biased** when the proportions of every subgroup in the target do *not* match the proportions of the subgroups in the sample.

Jupiter Unlimited

The amount and kind of variety necessary to get a representative sample is determined by background knowledge. Suppose that someone objected to a statistical argument made by the robin researcher on the grounds that the sample didn't include robins living in cities whose names began with a vowel. This is a bad objection. There's no reason to think that the characteristics of the target (robins) vary according to the names of cities. On the other hand, because climate and other environmental conditions differ from state to state, you expect variation among robins living in different states.

Another way that background knowledge is relevant to sample variety is that you have information about the variety within different targets. A researcher studying the chemical properties of calcium doesn't have to worry about where the calcium came from. As long as it's pure calcium, background knowledge indicates that its chemical properties won't vary according to where it was found. Calcium is different from robins. If a researcher has good reason to think that there's little variation within a target, then he can use a smaller sample.

Adding to a sample makes it more representative only if the variety the things added is relevant to the conclusion. If you wondered whether the majority of the people living in the United States were college educated, and your first survey only included people from twenty-five states, adding data from the other twenty-five states would make your sample more varied and more representative. But if you added residents from Canada and Mexico, the variety of the sample would be increased but it wouldn't be relevant variety because your target is people in the United States.

Sampling Techniques

Because the representativeness of a sample is crucial, the methods used to select a sample are also crucial. There are several different kinds of samples, and part of the art of argument is determining which ones would be best for each different situation.

A **simple random sample** is one in which all the things in the target have an equal chance of being in the sample. In many cases, simple random samples are the best samples. But a simple random sample can be impractical. If a target is very large, it may be hard to randomly sample it. Another disadvantage of a simple random sample is that some random samples don't accurately reflect the actual distribution of things in the target. This problem often occurs if the sample is small. A lot of research in psychology and medicine uses nonrandom samples because of the great difficulty and expense of getting a large and varied simple random sample.

If the target contains different groups that will affect the research being conducted, a researcher might want to make sure that the sample includes things from each of the subgroups. Stratified random samples allow a researcher to select a sample that reflects the actual distribution in the target. In a **stratified random sample,** the target is first divided into subgroups and then a simple random sample is taken from each subgroup. These simple random samples are then combined to create the complete sample. A stratified random sample is often the best way to produce a sample that accurately reflects a varied target.

When researchers use a **systematic sample**, they select every Nth thing from a list of all things in the target. If you had a list of all college students in the country and chose every tenth student on the list until you had a sample of 1,000 students, you'd generate a systematic sample. A systematic sample may seem random, but in fact a researcher can greatly influence what things are in the sample, either by the ordering of the list or by the way in which the selection is made.

Voluntary response samples are composed of people who voluntarily choose to respond to a call for data. This sampling method is often used in surveys distributed by mail. Only those who actually fill out and return the survey are included in the data. The primary disadvantage of this form of sample is that some respondents might choose to respond solely because they have a vested interest in producing a particular result. In addition, these surveys often suffer from the **problem of nonresponse**. Some people in the sample don't supply data.

If someone chooses sample things for no reason at all but simply by whim, he has chosen a **haphazard sample**. Haphazard selection can result in biased samples in several ways. Someone might accidentally choose things that don't accurately represent the target as a whole. There could be unknown factors causing these things to be more likely to be selected. They may happen to be nearer the person making the selection, and this may turn out to be influential if things aren't similar in relevant properties to the target. Although both haphazard and random samples appear to be similar, they are different sampling techniques.

Key Concept
The many different kinds of samples.

Convenience samples consist of those things that are easiest for the researcher to reach. Convenience samples are geographically limited, and the samples they produce aren't likely to represent the entire target. But this method provides readily accessible data to the researcher. This advantage can be important. Given the cost and difficulty of getting a large random sample, it can be perfectly appropriate to use a convenience sample. A researcher might use a convenience sample in a pilot project to work out the problems in a study before conducting a simple random sample.

In a **purposive sample** the researcher selects from the target based on fixed proportions. The target is separated into subgroups, and a fixed proportion of the sample is taken from each subgroup to produce the final sample. If you want a ratio of 25% freshmen, 25% sophomores, 25% juniors, and 25% seniors to constitute a sample of 1,000 college students, you'd choose 250 freshman, 250 sophomores, 250 juniors, and 250 seniors. A purposive sample differs from a stratified random sample in that no randomized selection is used in a purposive sample.

The disadvantage of purposive sampling is that the proportions in the sample may not match the target. A college might have more than 25% freshmen and fewer than 25% seniors. The advantage of purposive sampling is that it avoids undercoverage. **Undercoverage** occurs when some groups in the target are underrepresented. If a researcher hadn't ensured that an equal number of students from each of the four classes were selected, the sample might include more students from one class than from the other three.

The problem of undercoverage is almost impossible to eliminate entirely. Suppose that you wanted to conduct a survey of American households by home telephone. This method of contacting people will rule out the possibility of including data from anyone who doesn't have a home phone. The widespread use of cell phones has led to a decrease in the number of people with a home phone. A researcher might contact a randomly selected group of home phone numbers and then add a purposive component to the sample by seeking out people who only have a cell phone.

If all things in a target are known and accessible, a census may be used. In a **census**, the researcher observes each and every thing in the target. A census isn't a sample because you have a sample when you observe less than everything belonging to the target. A census is obviously perfectly representative because you've observed all the things in the target.

> **Key Concept**
> **Undercoverage** occurs when some groups in the target are underrepresented.

> **Key Concept**
> In a **census**, the researcher observes each and every thing in the target.

Technical Terms: Cluster Sample, Quota Sample, Probability Sample, U.S. Population Census

Stratified random samples are sometimes called "cluster samples." Purposive samples are also called "quota samples."

"Probability sample" is used differently across different disciplines. Some use "probability sample" to refer only to simple random samples. Others use it to refer to any sample with a random component. And there are other uses as well. When you see the term "probability sample," remember to figure out what it means in that discipline.

The U.S. government sends out surveys every ten years to all households to determine the number of people residing in the country. The U.S. Census Bureau then sends people house-to-house to contact those who haven't responded. It also seeks out homeless people and people living in institutions. Because there's no way of determining the exact number of people residing in the country, the U.S. Census might be more accurately described as a voluntary response sample of the U.S. population. Data from the Census is used in many ways. For example, it determines the distribution of congressional seats and school districts.

EXERCISE 8.4

A. For each of the statistical arguments in Exercise 8.3 A, determine which sampling technique was used.

B. Evaluate each of the statistical arguments in Exercise 8.3 A. (Don't forget to do both the true premises test and the proper form test.)

C. Find three research studies using different sampling techniques, identify the technique used, and suggest one that would be make the argument stronger. Write a one-page essay to present and explain your results.

Statistical Fallacies

This chapter discusses three statistical fallacies: Hasty Generalization, Biased Sample, and Biased Questions.

Fallacy: Hasty Generalization

Key Concept
The Fallacy of Hasty Generalization occurs when a statistical argument uses a sample that's too small.

The Fallacy of Hasty Generalization occurs when a statistical argument uses a sample that's too small. According to Guideline 1, the larger the sample, the more likely that it's representative. In some cases, the sample of a statistical argument is so small that the argument should simply be ignored. If someone draws a conclusion about all children from a sample of two of them, that's an example of the Fallacy of Hasty Generalization. In this case, the statistical argument fails the proper form test.

Fallacy: Biased Sample

Key Concept
The **Biased Sample Fallacy** occurs when a sample has a serious lack of variety.

According to Guideline 2, the more varied the sample, the more likely that it's representative. The **Biased Sample Fallacy** occurs when a sample has a serious lack of variety. Suppose someone argued that 100% of the 2,000 dolphins he'd seen were grey; therefore, all dolphins are grey. The sample is large. But suppose that this person has only seen dolphins in the Gulf of Mexico. The sample lacks variety. In this case, the argument commits the Biased Sample Fallacy. Biased samples are harder to spot than small samples.

Think again about Le Meur's dogs with LCA. Le Meur tested her new treatment on the eyes of eight Briard dogs, seven puppies and an adult dog. The sight of the seven puppies was restored. The adult dog was unaffected. She concluded that this treatment might work on human infants. Remember that Le Meur is using both a statistical argument and an analogical argument. Let's focus on her statistical argument. Because Le Meur can't study all the Briard dogs in the world, she studied a sample of them. Her sample was eight dogs. She made a statistical argument to draw a conclusion about all Briard dogs. Here's her conclusion:

> In conclusion, we have demonstrated that targeted gene transfer can be used to correct the [sight of LCA] purebred Briard dogs. (Le Meur 2006, 9, material omitted)

She says that it "can" cure LCA. In other words, she concluded that the therapy *might* restore the sight of all Briard dogs with LCA (as long as the therapy was given while the dogs were puppies). Le Meur shows appropriate intellectual humility. She doesn't conclude that her new treatment *will* cure LCA in all Briard dogs.

But suppose that Peyton doesn't show proper intellectual humility. He reads Le Meur's article and concludes that

Le Meur's treatment will cure LCA in all dogs.

Peyton has committed the Fallacy of Hasty Generalization. A sample of eight dogs is much too small to conclude that the treatment *will* cure LCA in all Briard dogs. And he has committed the Biased Sample Fallacy. The sample has a serious lack of variety if the target is all dogs because Le Meur only tested one breed.

Fallacy: Biased Questions

The **Fallacy of Biased Questions** occurs when a survey asks for information with questions which are worded in a way that tends to encourage a particular response. The error could be intentional as in cases when a particular outcome is desired for political reasons. The error could be unintentional. Sometimes questions can be biased by the context (the time and place) in which they're asked. Asking people their views about gun control after they've seen a movie showing brutal murders is likely to bias the answers.

Suppose a university was thinking about a change in grading policy. They were thinking of changing from a letter-only grading system of A, B, C, D, or F to a plus/minus grading system of A+, A, A–, B+, B, etc. If students were asked whether they believed that a student earning an 89% on a test should get a higher grade than a student earning an 81% on the same test, most likely the majority of students would reply "Yes." On the other hand, if students were asked if they were in favor of an A– counting for less on their GPA than an A, it wouldn't be surprising if the majority replied "No." Both questions are about parts of the new policy, but the first question focuses the responders' attention on the possibility of an increase in GPA whereas the second focuses attention on the possibility of a decrease in GPA. Both questions would be instances of the Fallacy of Biased Questions.

Key Concept
The **Fallacy of Biased Questions** occurs when a survey asks for information with questions which are worded in a way that tends to encourage a particular response.

When you see data based on a survey, you need to remember to check for biased questions. Here's a list of questions you should ask about any data based on surveys:

1. What was the exact wording of the questions?
2. In what context were the questions asked?
3. Was there a problem of nonresponse?
4. What's the mean, the average, and the standard deviation?
5. Are there any outliers?

Habits of a Critical Thinker

Inquisitiveness

When you see a survey and ask these five questions you are showing an inquisitive attitude. Being inquisitive doesn't mean being confrontational or refusing to see what's good in an argument. It means asking probing questions. Inquisitive people don't believe something just because someone says it's true. They ask questions and evaluate arguments before deciding what to believe.

EXERCISE 8.5

A. In the following passages, determine whether any arguments are present. If an argument is present, determine whether any fallacy is committed. If a fallacy is committed, identify whether it's a statistical fallacy or another type of fallacy. Don't forget that statistical arguments can commit fallacies which aren't specific to statistical arguments as well as statistical fallacies.

1. I went to the Georgia Aquarium yesterday. All fish I saw there had no teeth. I bet that no fish have teeth.

2. In the fall of 2010 a survey was sent to all 10,000 students registered for classes at Very Cool University (VCU). Twenty percent of them returned the survey. In response to one question, 73% of the respondents indicated that they thought it should be illegal to make hiring decisions based on a person's sexual orientation. It seems that about three-fourths of all college students think that this kind of hiring practice should be illegal.

3. "Gallop surveyed people in October 2003 with the following question: 'When a patient is in a persistent vegetative state caused by irreversible brain damage, do you think his or her spouse should or should not be allowed by law to make the final decision to end the patient's life by some painless means?' Eighty percent of those surveyed said yes, the spouse should be allowed; 17% said no, and 3% said they had no opinion on the matter" (Janda 2008, 538–539). Suppose someone argued that he or she should be allowed to end a spouse's life because 80% of Americans believe it is the right of the spouse to do so. Would such an argument commit one or more fallacies, and if so, which one(s)?

*4. "[E]ducation plays a critical role in social mobility. The impact of formal schooling on adult status is even greater than that of family background (although as we have seen, family background influences the likelihood that one will receive higher education). Furthermore, education represents an important means of intergenerational mobility.

Three-fourths of college-educated men in these studies achieved some upward mobility, while only 12% of those who received no schooling did." (Schaefer 2006, 202)

 5. Use Exercise 8.1 A 13.

 6. Use Exercise 8.1 A 15.

 7. Use Exercise 8.1 B 13.

*8. Use Exercise 8.3 A 9.

 9. "On election day, [then Presidential candidate Ronald] Reagan swept to a decisive victory, with 489 electoral votes to 49 for [then President Jimmy] Carter, who carried only six states. The popular vote proved equally lopsided: 44 million (51 percent) to 35 million (41 percent), with 7 percent going to John Anderson, [who] ran on an independent ticket." (Bakeman 2007, 1007, material omitted)

10. "On August 1, 1981, Reagan signed the Economic Recovery Tax Act, which cut personal income taxes by 25 percent, lowered the maximum rate from 70 to 50 percent for 1982, cut the capital gains tax by one third, and offered a broad array of other tax concessions. The new legislation embodied an idea that went back to Alexander Hamilton, George Washington's Treasury secretary: more money in the hands of the affluent would benefit society at large, since the wealthy would engage in productive consumption and investment. The difference was that the Reagan tax cuts were accompanied by massive increases in defense spending, which generated ever-mounting federal deficits. The president, who in 1980 had pledged to balance the federal budget by 1983, had in fact run up debts larger than those of all his predecessors combined." (Bakeman 2007, 1007)

11. "This section presents vital statistics data on births, deaths, abortions, fetal deaths, fertility, life expectancy, marriages, and divorces. Vital statistics are compiled for the country as a whole by the National Center for Health Statistics and published in its annual report, Vital Statistics of the United States. Vital events occurring to U.S. residents outside the United States are not included in the data." (U.S. Census Bureau 2000, 63, material omitted) What effect on the enormous number of statistical arguments made on the basis of this data will there be, given the exclusion of residents outside the country? Suppose arguments using the data mentioned the qualification. Would there still be a fallacious effect on the argument? Why or why not?

*12. "We [Americans] read much more now that we did in the 1950s. In 1957, 17 percent of people surveyed in a Gallup poll said they were currently reading a book; in 1990, over twice as many did. In 1953, 40 percent of people polled by Gallup could name the author of Huckleberry Finn; in 1990, 51 percent could. In 1950, 8,600 new titles were published; in 1981, almost five times as many.

   "In fact, Americans are buying more books now than ever before—over 2 billion in 1992. Between the early '70s and the early '80s, the number of bookstores in this country nearly doubled—and that was before the Barnes & Noble superstore and Amazon.com. People aren't just buying books as status objects, either. A 1992 survey found that the average adult American reads 11.2 books per year, which means that the country as a whole reads about 2 billion—the number bought. There are more than 250,000 reading groups in the country at the moment, which means that something like 2 million people regularly read books and meet to discuss them." (MacFarquhar 2007, 64)

13. Aid from Coalition Support Funds to Pakistan

Year	Support in $Billions
2002	$1.25 billion
2003	$1.25 billion
2004	$700 million estimate
2005	$980 million estimate
2006	$780 million estimate
2007	$305 million estimate
2008	$300 million (pending approval)

Based on the data above, the *New York Times* concluded that aid to Pakistan has fallen. The support provided, known as Coalition Support Funds, is supposed to reimburse Pakistan for its military operations against terrorism, although there is some evidence that the money is used for nonmilitary governmental expenses. Congress has put a hold on some of the support until [then] Secretary of State Condoleezza Rice certifies that democratic rights have been restored (following Pakistani President Musharraf's declaration of a state of emergency on December 16, 2007). Is the conclusion about aid to Pakistan sufficiently supported by the data? (Information drawn from Rohde 2007, A1 & A6)

14. "The subprime mortgage crisis has been a financial catastrophe for much of Wall Street. At Goldman Sachs Group, Inc., thanks to a tiny group of traders, it has generated one of the biggest windfalls the securities industry has seen in years.

"The group's big bet that securities backed by risky home loans would fall in value generated nearly $4 billion of profits during the year ended November 30, [2007], according to people familiar with the firm's finances. Those gains erased $1.5 billion to $2 billion of mortgage-related losses elsewhere in the firm. On Tuesday, despite a terrible November and some of the worst market conditions in decades, analysts expect Goldman to report a record net annual income of more than $11 billion.

"Goldman has stood out on Wall Street for its penchant for rolling the dice with its own money. The upside of the approach was obvious in the third quarter: Despite credit-market turmoil, Goldman earned $2.9 billion, its second-best three-month period ever.

"Goldman's trading home run was blasted from an obscure corner of the firm's mortgage department—the structured-products trading group, which now numbers 16 traders.

"Goldman's success at wringing profits out of the subprime fiasco, however, raises questions about how the firm balances its responsibilities to its shareholders and to its clients. Goldman's mortgage department underwrote collateralized debt obligations, or CDOs, complex securities created from pools of subprime mortgages and other debt. When those securities plunged in value this year, Goldman's customers suffered major losses, as did units within Goldman itself. The question is now being raised: Why did Goldman continue to peddle CDOs to customers early this year while its own traders were betting that CDO values would fall? A spokesman for Goldman Sachs declined to comment on the issue." (Kelly 2007, A1 & A18, material omitted)

B. Standardize each of the arguments in A. Identify the sample, the N, the relevant property or properties, the target, and the percentage. (In some cases, one or more of the five parts of a statistical argument may be missing.)

C. Evaluate each argument in A by applying the true premises and proper form tests.

Chapter Summary

Statistical arguments are arguments that draw a conclusion about all members of a group by looking at part of that group. Descriptive statistics report and analyze data about observed things.

One way to describe data is by looking at its center. This is sometimes called the "average" of the data and can be calculated in several ways. Averages include the mean, the weighted mean, the mode, the midrange, or the median. You should use the type of average that's best for the issue being discussed. Data are also described by their spread, which is the amount the data points deviate from the center. Standard deviation is a primary measure of spread. A third way data are described is by looking at their shape on a chart. Statisticians use a method to find the line that best fits the data, the regression line. It's a useful tool for predicting trends or tendencies.

A proper statistical argument can be put into one of the following standard forms:

General   (1) P% of the N observed things in G have F.

Therefore,

(2) P% of all the things in G have F.

Particular   (1) P% of the N observed things in G have F.

Therefore,

(2) P% of all the things in G have F.

(3) X is a thing in G.

Therefore,

(4) There is a P% chance that X has F.

"P" and "N" are variables that refer to a number, "G" is a variable that refers to a group, and "F" is a variable that refers to a feature. Every statistical argument has five parts.

1. The observed things in G are the **sample**.
2. The **N** is the number of things in the sample.
3. The features that these things have, the F, is the **relevant property**.
4. All the things in G are the **target**.
5. **P** is the percentage of the observed things that have F.

Evaluating statistical arguments with the true premises test is straightforward. A premise is true if it's a correct description of the world. It can be assumed if the criteria for uncontroversial empirical statements are met.

Statistical arguments have proper form when they can be put into the General or the Particular form and the sample is representative of the target. Size and variety are two guidelines for evaluating representativeness. Larger samples with greater variety increase the chance that the sample is representative of the target.

Researchers use many sampling techniques to produce good samples. Types of samples include simple random samples, stratified random samples, systematic samples, voluntary response samples, haphazard samples, convenience samples, and purposive samples. Most of these types have both advantages and disadvantages.

As you evaluate statistical arguments, you should look for the Fallacy of Hasty Generalization (the sample is too small), the Biased Sample Fallacy (the sample isn't sufficiently varied), and the Biased Questions Fallacy.

GUIDE

Finding, Standardizing, and Evaluating Statistical Arguments

This Guide is an amplification of the "Guide for Finding, Standardizing, and Evaluating Arguments" that is in Chapter Two. The numbered sentences are copies from the Guide in Chapter Two. The paragraphs with "Statistical" in front of them are additional materials that apply only to statistical arguments.

Finding Arguments

1. Look for an attempt to convince.
   Statistical. Look to see if there's an attempt to convince that uses observations of a subset of a group to draw a conclusion about the entire group.

2. Find the conclusion.
   Statistical. Find the target and the relevant property.

3. Find the premises.
   Statistical. Find the sample.

4. Review the following to make sure that you've correctly identified the conclusion and the premises: imperfect indicator words, sentence order, premises and/or conclusion not in declarative form, and unstated premises and/or conclusion.

5. Review the following to make sure that you haven't incorrectly identified something as a premise or a conclusion when in fact it's not part of an argument: assertions, questions, instructions, descriptions, and explanations.

Standardizing Arguments

6. Rewrite the premises and the conclusion as declarative sentences. Make sure that each premise and the conclusion is a grammatically correct declarative sentence. Rewrite the premises and conclusion as necessary to make them clearer but don't change the meaning of the passage. Remove pronouns from the sentences and replace them with the nouns or noun phrases to which they refer. Remove emotionally charged language.

7. Review any phrases you've omitted to be sure that they aren't premises or a conclusion.

8. Number the premises and the conclusion. Put brackets [ ] around the number of an unstated premise or conclusion. Place the premises before their conclusion and insert "Therefore," between the premises and the conclusion. Use blank lines to indicate subarguments.
   Statistical. Put the standardization in the standard form of a statistical argument:

   General   (1) P% of the N observed things in G have F.

                   Therefore,

                   (2) P% of all the things in G have F.

   Particular   (1) P% of the N observed things in G have F.

                   Therefore,

                   (2) P% of all the things in G have F.
                   (3) X is a thing in G.

                   Therefore,

                   (4) There is a P% chance that X has F.

9. Compare your standardization to the original passage to make sure that you haven't omitted any arguments found in the passage and to be sure that you've correctly identified the premises and the conclusion.

Evaluating Arguments: The True Premises Test

10. Check to see whether the premises are accurate descriptions of the world.
Statistical. Check to see whether the sample has the relevant property that the argument claims it has.

11. Consider whether the premises are appropriate for the argument's audience.

12. Review the assumed premises to be sure that the assumptions are reasonable. Make sure that all assumed premises are uncontroversially true empirical statements, uncontroversially true definitional statements, or appropriate statements by experts. Make sure the definitions are good ones.

Evaluating Arguments: The Proper Form Test

13. Determine whether the argument is a deductive argument or inductive argument.

14. Determine whether the premises are relevant to the conclusion. Look at each premise individually to see whether the truth of the premise provides some evidence for the truth of the conclusion. Look at the premises as a group to see whether the truth of all of them provides some evidence for the truth of the conclusion.
Statistical. Evaluate the representativeness of the sample. Determine the sampling technique. Consider whether the sample is sufficiently large and sufficiently varied.

Evaluating Arguments: Checking for Fallacies

15. Compare the argument to the list of fallacies on page 410 to see whether the argument commits any of the fallacies.

9 Causal Arguments

NEW ORLEANS—Within a space of 15 hours on Aug. 29, three massive, concrete floodwalls in separate parts of the city suddenly fractured and burst under the weight of surging waters from Hurricane Katrina. The breaches unleashed a wall of water that swept entire buildings from their foundations and transformed what might have been a routine hurricane into the costliest storm in U.S. history. Today all three breaches are looking less like acts of God and more like failures of engineering that could have been anticipated and very likely prevented.

—Joby Warrick and Michael Grunwald, "Investigators Link Levee Failures to Design Flaws." (Warrick 2005, A01, material omittted)

Learning Outcomes

After studying the material in this chapter, you should be able to:

1. Identify causal arguments and determine whether their conclusions are making claims about necessary, sufficient, contributory, primary, remote, and/or proximate causes.

2. Evaluate causal arguments, using Mill's Methods, checking for reverse or third-party causation, and considering coincidental correlation.

3. Identify and avoid the Hasty Cause, Causal Slippery Slope, and *Post Hoc* Fallacies.

4. Recognize and correctly use causal arguments by elimination.

5. Recognize and correctly use the scientific method.

$\mathbf{E}$veryone wonders about causes. The passage on the previous page makes a claim about the cause of flooding in New Orleans. If you say that your home is chilly because your furnace pilot has gone out, you've made a causal argument. On a history exam you may have to write about events and conditions that led to World War I. In that case, you've been assigned to review a set of causal arguments. Causal arguments are common in science. The cause of global warming is currently a matter of great debate. Business courses rely on causal arguments when they consider causes of recessions.

The Many Meanings of "Cause"

A **cause** is an event or state of affairs that produces another event or state of affairs, the **effect**. This general definition is accurate, but it isn't specific enough. For one thing, what's the difference between events and states of affairs? In addition, there are at least seven different kinds of causes.

An **event** is something that happens at a particular time. A baseball shattering a pane of glass is an event. A **state of affairs** is a situation that persists for a period of time. States of affairs are also called "conditions." During the 1930s, in the United States, farming practices and a drought created an environmental state of affairs, the Dust Bowl, that caused crop failure and poverty.

The line between an event and a state of affairs is vague. Suppose that a bridge isn't built right and is slowly sinking into the sand of a river. Imagine that it takes a month for the bridge to finish sinking, and one day the bridge collapses and sinks. Is the sinking an event or a state of affairs? There's no clear answer because "event" and "state of affairs" are somewhat vague. In this book, we'll use the shorter word "event" to refer to states of affairs and events.

> **Key Concept**
> A **cause** is an event or state of affairs that produces another event or state of affairs, the **effect**.

> **Key Concept**
> An **event** is something that happens at a particular time. A **state of affairs** is a situation that persists for a period of time.

Connections

We've just made "event" into a technical term. Chapter Four discusses technical terms. Chapter Four also discusses vagueness.

Think about the flooding that occurred in New Orleans after Hurricane Katrina. At the beginning of this chapter you saw part of an article from the *Washington Post* that reports on a debate about the cause of this flooding. The article contains several examples of causal claims. We've numbered the paragraphs so that we can refer to them more easily.

1. NEW ORLEANS – Within a space of 15 hours on Aug. 29, three massive, concrete floodwalls in separate parts of the city suddenly fractured and burst under the weight of surging waters from Hurricane Katrina. The breaches unleashed a wall of water that swept entire buildings from their foundations and transformed what might have been a routine hurricane into the costliest storm in U.S. history.

2. Today all three breaches are looking less like acts of God and more like failures of engineering that could have been anticipated and very likely prevented.

3. [U.S. Army Corp of Engineers] spokesman Jason Fanselau said the agency's own data point to a massive surge that exceeded the height of the Industrial Canal floodwall by more than a few feet.

4. "Katrina flat-out overwhelmed the system," he said. "There was a huge wall of water that obliterated entire sections of the floodwall."

5. [However,] in the case of the 17th Street and London Avenue canals, independent investigators believe the floodwalls themselves were the problem. The reason was the naturally soft soil made up of river silts and swampy peat that has been the bane of builders here for two centuries.

6. Investigators now believe the walls collapsed when the soils beneath them became saturated and began to shift under the weight of relatively modest surges from the lake. And newly released documents show that the Corps was aware years ago that a particularly unstable layer of soil lay beneath both floodwalls.

7. "These levees did not overtop, yet they failed anyway," said Peter Nicholson, an engineering professor at the University of Hawaii at Manoa. "It's important that we find out now exactly what went wrong, because the Corps is already starting to rebuild."

8. Reports of problems with the soft underlayer began to surface even before the floodwalls were finished. In 1994, the now-defunct Pittman Construction Co., a New Orleans firm involved in levee construction, claimed in court documents that floodwall sections were failing to line up properly because of unstable soils. An administrative law judge dismissed the complaint on technical grounds in 1998, without specifically addressing the allegations about weak soils.

9. Corps officials are not yet convinced. "It is important not to jump to conclusions," said John Grieshaber, chief of the engineering division in the Corps' New Orleans district office. "It's hard to look at the aftereffects and say with a high level of certainty, 'This is what happened.'"

10. The Corps' actions since the storm, however, suggest that at least some officials are worried about weaknesses in the floodwalls' design. A proposal for rebuilding the floodwalls has set far tougher standards than existed 15 years ago. And the steel pilings, which formerly reached a depth of 20 feet, must now be driven through the peat layer to 40 feet, twice as deep as before. (Warrick 2005, A01, material omitted)

Cause as Necessary Condition

Many people think that Hurricane Katrina was the cause of the flooding in New Orleans. Look at the claim made in paragraph 4.

4. "Katrina flat-out overwhelmed the system," [Corps spokesman Jason Fanselau] said. "There was a huge wall of water that obliterated entire sections of the floodwall."

Why do people think that Katrina was the cause of the flooding? A first attempt to answer this question might be:

If Hurricane Katrina hadn't hit New Orleans, the flooding wouldn't have occurred.

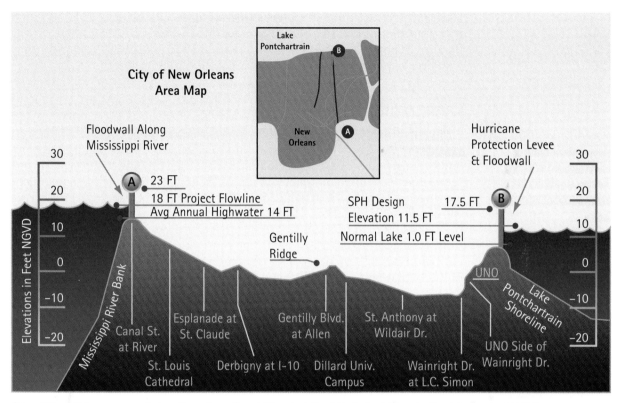

City of New Orleans ground elevations from Canal Street at the Mississippi River to the lakefront at U.N.O.

Most people think that this claim is true. After all, for many years, there wasn't any flooding. Then Katrina arrived and the flooding started. The claim in paragraph 4 is an assertion of a causal necessary condition. A **causal necessary condition** is an event that's required for the production of another event. Someone who says that Katrina is the cause of the flooding may be asserting that the arrival of Katrina was a necessary condition for the flooding. Many other necessary conditions also contributed to the flooding. New Orleans must have been built where it is (if it had been built farther inland, it wouldn't have flooded). The atmosphere of the Earth must contain water vapor (if the atmosphere of the Earth didn't contain water vapor, there would be no hurricanes).

Other people cited in this article claim that other conditions are necessary for the flooding. Look at the claims made in paragraphs 5 and 6.

5. [However,] in the case of the 17th Street and London Avenue canals, independent investigators believe the floodwalls themselves were the problem. The reason was the naturally soft soil made up of river silts and swampy peat that has been the bane of builders here for two centuries.
6. Investigators now believe the walls collapsed when the soils beneath them became saturated and began to shift under the weight of relatively modest surges from the lake.

Key Concept

A **causal necessary condition** is an event that's required for the production of another event.

Figure New Orleans Levee System, MIT Department of Architecture, 2006, http://stuff.mit.edu/afs/athena/course/4/4.196/OldFiles/www/New_Orleans_Levee_System.gif; http://soundwaves.usgs.gov/2006/01/NewOrleansMapLG.jpg; http://www.neworleansleveesystem.com/images/bigleveemap.gif; http://img.dailymail.co.uk/i/pix/2008/05_03/bradpittlevee_468x326.jpg

Here the *Washington Post* reports that some people believe that the incorrect placement of the levees on soft soil was a necessary condition for the flooding. They assert that if the levees hadn't been built on these soils, they wouldn't have failed and the flooding wouldn't have occurred.

Cause as Sufficient Condition

A **causal sufficient condition** is an event that, all by itself, will always produce another event. Causal sufficient conditions are hard to find. All by itself, no one event would have been sufficient to cause the flooding in New Orleans. Katrina isn't a sufficient condition for the flooding. The flooding didn't occur everywhere Katrina hit. In addition to the hurricane, certain local conditions were required in order for flooding to occur.

Examples of sufficient causal conditions usually seem artificial. Driving from Quebec to Atlanta is a sufficient cause of traveling from Canada to the United States It isn't necessary. You could fly from Ontario to Chicago. It's unlikely that you'd ever make causal claims like these.

Cause as Necessary and Sufficient Condition

A **causal necessary and sufficient condition** is an event that's required for the production of another event and will produce that event all by itself. Causal necessary and sufficient conditions are even harder to find than causal sufficient conditions. But here's one. The Earth can be divided into two hemispheres, the northern hemisphere and the southern hemisphere. The border between the two is the equator. Crossing the equator is a causal necessary and sufficient condition for moving from one of these two hemispheres to the other.

Contributory Cause

Suppose that you're filling a tank with water. To fill it, you're using twenty small containers. You pour the water from these containers into the tank. Pouring the water from all the containers into the tank causes the tank to fill up and overflow. None of these containers holds enough water in it to fill up the tank. None of them by itself is a sufficient cause of the overflow of the tank. None of them by itself is a necessary cause of the overflow. If you picked any one of the small containers and didn't pour it into the tank, the tank would still overflow. Of the twenty containers, any of them could be the one that makes the tank overflow. You can't point to any container as the one that causes the tank to overflow. You can't say that container #20 is required for the tank to overflow any more than you could say that container #1 is required for it to overflow. Yet each of the containers contributes to making the tank overflow. Each is a contributory cause.

One event is a **contributory cause** of other another event when the first event has an effect on the second but is neither a necessary cause nor a sufficient cause.

Contributory causes are common. The cause of an event is often a set of other events none of which is sufficient and none of which is necessary.

Suppose that you're wondering why your friend Oksana did better in an Educational Psychology class than your friend Christopher. It's likely that no one thing was a necessary cause of Oksana's better performance. It may be that she did a large set of different things that helped her do better and that failure to do any one of them wouldn't have made her do worse than he did. In that case, each of the different things is a contributory cause.

Primary Cause

In many cases, people will speak of something as *the* cause of an event even though they know that this cause was only a necessary cause or only a contributory cause. While the cause of the flooding in New Orleans is a matter of debate, no one asserts that the presence of water vapor in the Earth's atmosphere is *the* cause of the flooding. Everyone would admit that it was a causal necessary condition but no one would refer to it as *the* cause. The water vapor in the atmosphere isn't a relevant cause because water vapor is always present in the atmosphere and, even if you could remove the vapor, you wouldn't do that. (It would lead to the extinction of life on earth!)

When someone picks out a particular necessary, sufficient, or contributory cause for special attention, they're identifying a **primary cause**. The *Washington Post* article above indicates that some people think that Hurricane Katrina was the primary cause of the flooding but other people think that a flaw in the levees was the primary cause.

The primary cause of an event is partially a matter of the observers' interests and background. Imagine that aliens were observing Earth from another planet. Their planet's atmosphere doesn't contain water vapor. They had never seen a hurricane. They then observe with amazement the enormous storms on Earth. Their scientists study the matter. They might well conclude that the cause of hurricanes was the water vapor in the Earth's atmosphere.

Picking out a primary cause is often essential for drawing conclusions about what you should do to remove or produce causes for various effects. But you must be careful not to think that a primary cause is a sole cause. As you compose causal arguments, be careful not to assert that one type of event is the only cause of another type of event. As you evaluate causal arguments, look for claims that one event is the only cause of another event, when the author means to say that the first event is either a necessary or contributory cause.

Remote and Proximate Causes

Think about the series of events that came before the flooding. The breach of the levees occurred right before the flooding. Hurricane Katrina hit several hours before the flooding occurred. The supports for the 17th Street Canal Levee were put in years before the flooding occurred. Let's assume for the sake of argument that each of these three events (the breach of the levees, the arrival of the hurricane, and the improper placement of the levees) is a necessary cause of the flooding. In cases like this, scholars often speak of remote and proximate cause. The most proximate cause of the flooding was the failure of the levee. But you can then ask: What caused the levee to fail? The

Key Concept
When someone picks out a particular necessary, sufficient, or contributory cause for special attention, they're identifying a **primary cause.**

waters of Hurricane Katrina were a necessary cause. The levees had existed for years and survived many storms of lesser intensity. The hurricane was a more remote cause of the flooding than the failure of the levee. The design failures in the levees were a more remote cause of the flooding than the arrival of the hurricane.

Causes are more or less proximate or remote depending on how close they are in time to the effect. A **proximate cause** is a cause that is close in time to its effect. A **remote cause** is a cause that's far in time from its effect. As the levee case illustrates, causes aren't either proximate or remote. They're more or less proximate, more or less remote. Proximity of causation has nothing do to with whether a cause is a necessary cause, a sufficient cause, or a contributory cause. Any of these three kinds of causes can be more or less proximate.

Key Concept

A **proximate cause** is a cause that is close in time to its effect. A **remote cause** is a cause that's far in time from its effect.

EXERCISE 9.1

 *Contribute Cause x 2*

A. In the following passages, identify which of the many meanings of "cause" is being used: cause as necessary condition, cause as sufficient condition, cause as necessary and sufficient condition, primary cause, remote cause, proximate cause. Remember that a causal claim can fall into more than one category.

1. Jack: "Let's go to the movies at Cineplex after class. We have to get out of this building anyway."
   What type of cause is Jack implying by saying they "have to" leave the building?

2. Jill: "OK. If we can take the new Parkway, we can get there in half an hour."
   What type of cause is Jill claiming that taking the new Parkway is?

3. Jack: "Well, I'd rather take the old roads through town to get there, and they'll get us there just as quickly."
   Jill: "Maybe we can try out the new Parkway another time."
   What type of cause is Jack's claiming that taking the old roads is?

*4. Jack: "I hope that means you agree because I don't think the new Parkway will get us there, anyway. It hasn't been completely finished yet, and the construction that's open now stops short of where the theater is located."
   What type of cause is Jack denying that the new Parkway is?

5. Jill: "Oh, I didn't realize that. That's enough by itself to convince me to go on the old roads through town."
   What type of cause is Jill saying that Jack's last claim provides?

6. Jack: "So what you mean is that you weren't convinced by my claim that the old roads would get us there in half an hour?"
   Jill: Well, that helped but it wasn't enough by itself.
   What type of cause is Jill saying that the timing of the old roads route played in her decision?

7. Jack: "The main reason I wanted to go to the movies in the first place was that someone told me to go see *Into the Wild*, and I noticed today that it's playing at the Cineplex."

   What type of causal relation is implied by Jack's reference to an earlier recommendation to see the movie *Into the Wild*?

*8. What type of causal relation is Jack claiming about the fact that it's playing now at the Cineplex?

9. Jill: "I also heard that was a good movie. In addition, I know someone who said she knew Chris McCandless, the guy in the movie, when he was in college. She said he was an interesting writer, even then. I bet that is at least in part why he decided to go into the wild, because he wanted to write to his friends while he was there."
   What type of causal relation is Jill speculating about between McCandless' practice of writing and his going "into the wild"?

10. Jack: "Wait a minute. I don't think that I can go to the movies. I have a high fever and feel very weak. I bet that I have the flu."
    Which type of causal relation is implied between the symptoms of high fever and weakness and having the flu?

11. "Although many physical abilities decline over the adult years, it is not clear that these declines are inevitable. Life style factors such as a poor diet, smoking, drinking alcohol, and lack of exercise contribute to the decline in physical functioning for some people. Moreover, culture markedly influences the way we think about aging and our expectations of our physical abilities in middle and later adulthood. In Western cultures such as the United States, becoming old is associated with being frail, useless, and ill, so that many people attempt to push back the aging process." (Postortino 2006, 443, material omitted)

*12. "The growth and intensification of serfdom was a major tendency in Russian history. [A]t the end of the nineteenth century thirty-four million people out of a population of thirty-six million were reckoned as serfs." (Chamberlain 1965, 5, material omitted)
    What type of causal relation is Chamberlain claiming about the number of serfs?

13. "After regaining independence in 1952, Japan continued to profit from access to foreign raw materials, technology, and markets, including those of the United States. Because of popular sentiment, constitutional constraints, and the country's reliance on the American 'nuclear umbrella,' Japan was freed from the burden of supporting a large and costly military establishment, releasing funds and energies for economic development. At the same time, business benefited from a probusiness political system." (Schirokauer 2006, 634, material omitted) [Hint: There are three different types of causes in this passage.]

14. "The occurrence of hypertension in African-Americans is the highest in the world and plays a significant role in cardiovascular complications." (Campbell 2007, 90)

15. "The interaction between nicotine and alcohol, two of the most abused and co-abused drugs, can impact a person's ability to learn and could have implications for treating addiction, according to researchers at Temple University." (*Medical News Today* 2007)

Identifying Causal Arguments

A **causal argument** is an argument whose conclusion asserts that one event(s) caused another event(s). A large number of words indicate the presence of a causal argument.

Causal Argument Indicator Words			
because	produced	brought about	was responsible for
led to	created	affected	was the result of
influenced	effect	determined by	resulted from

There's no way to list all of the different ways people make causal claims. And some causal arguments have no indicator words. The statement, "She plugged in her microscope, and the lights in the lab went out," implies a cause and an effect. To be more explicit, you might say "Plugging in the microscope caused the lab lights to go out.

A **particular causal argument** is a causal argument whose conclusion asserts that one particular event causes another particular event. "Plugging in the microscope caused the lab lights to go out" is a particular causal claim. A **general causal argument** is a causal argument whose conclusion asserts that one *kind* of event causes another kind of event. "Overloading a circuit causes lights to go out" is a general causal claim. Particular causal arguments rely on general causal arguments because asserting that one particular event causes another particular event assumes that, if the same causal conditions occurred together at other times, the same effect would be produced. General causal arguments are fundamental. For this reason, this chapter will focus on general causal arguments.

The Form of a Causal Argument

Let's use the variable "E" to refer to types of events (or states of affairs). "E1" refers to one type of event, "E2" refers to another type of event, etc. Here's the standard form of a causal argument:

On Final

(1) E1 is correlated with E2.
(2) E2 is not the cause of E1.
(3) There is no E3 that is the cause of E1 and E2.
(4) E1 and E2 are not coincidentally correlated.
Therefore,
(5) E1 is a cause of E2.

Connections

Chapter Two discusses the use of variables.

Causal arguments aren't usually found in standard form. The order of the premises is often different. But, as you've seen before, the order in which premises are stated makes no difference to the evaluation of an argument. More difficult is the fact that the people who make causal arguments often leave one or more premises unstated.

Connections

Chapter One discusses unstated premises.

Premise (1). The first premise of a causal argument in the standard form says that two events are correlated. Speaking roughly and imprecisely, two events are correlated when they happen together. The position of a light switch (E1) is correlated with the light in the room (E2). When the switch is up, the light is on. When the switch is down, the light is off. E1 and E2 are correlated.

Premise (2). The second premise says that the first event wasn't caused by the second. You know that the light doesn't cause the switch to move. E2 doesn't cause E1.

Premise (3). The third premise says that there isn't any third thing that caused both E1 and E2. When you go into a room and find the light on, you generally assume that someone flipped the switch and that is what caused the light to be on. But some third event, E3, might have caused both the switch to go up and the light to come on. Perhaps a malfunction at an electrical substation caused a powerful surge of electricity that flipped the switch, fused it, and caused the light to come on. You'd discover this when you attempted to turn the light off and the switch didn't work. (This actually happened to the bathroom light in the house of one of the authors of this book.) But in the case of a normal light switch, there's no malfunction that causes both the switch to go up and the light to come on.

Premise (4). The fourth premise asserts that the correlation between the two events isn't a coincidence. You've experienced coincidences. Perhaps for two weeks, every time you don't brush your teeth at night, you stub your toe when getting out of bed. Many different events are happening all over the world all the time. Some of them are bound to correlate every now and then just by chance. But the correlation between the light and the switch isn't like that. E1 and E2 aren't coincidentally correlated.

You can put the argument into the standard form like this:

(1) The switch being in the up position is <u>correlated</u> with the light being on.

(2) The light being on is not the cause of the switch being in the up position.

(3) There is no third event that is the cause of both the switch being in the up position and the light being on.

(4) The switch being in the up position and the light being on are not coincidentally correlated.

Therefore,

(5) The switch being in the up position is a cause of the light being on.

EXERCISE 9.2

A. In the following passages,

(a) determine which ones contain causal arguments (some contain more than one),

(b) for each causal argument, determine which of the four premises are missing from the argument as explicitly stated in the passage, and

(c) if a causal argument is present, put it into standard form.

1. This patient has a high fever and feels very weak. The flu gives people a high fever and makes them weak. So, this patient might have the flu.

2. Why do I insist that you should do what I say? Just because I say so, that's why.

3. I had trouble sleeping last night. I bet I know why. I had a Coke Zero after dinner and whenever I have a Coke Zero or any other soda that has caffeine, I have trouble sleeping.

*4. Stefan: "Why didn't you reply to my text?" Willa: "Because I didn't get it. You know that your texts never go out when you send them from your Mom's."

5. Whenever it rains, I get a headache.

6. "Since communication can take place directly through the body, the body can be used to transmit information." (Norris 2001, 116, material omitted)

7. "The growth and intensification of serfdom was a major tendency in Russian history. [A]t the end of the nineteenth century thirty-four million people out of a population of thirty-six million were reckoned as serfs." (Chamberlain 1965, 5, material omitted)

*8. "Manipulation [of cash-settled contracts] has numerous deleterious effects, including dead-weight losses attributable to temporal and spatial distortions in consumption, production, storage, and transportation; reductions in hedging effectiveness; increases in future price volatility; reductions in the informativeness of future prices; and a decline in market liquidity." (Pirrong 2001, 222)

9. "[Alcohol] is a frequently abused, addictive drug that impairs cognitive function. It may disrupt cognitive processes by altering attention, short-term memory, and/or long-term memory. Interestingly, some research suggests that [alcohol] may enhance cognitive processes at lower doses. [Alcohol] enhanced short-term and long-term memory for contextual and cued conditioning at a low dose (0.25 g/kg) and impaired short-term and long-term memory for contextual and cued conditioning at a high dose (1.0 g/kg)." (Gulick 2007, 1528, material omitted)

10. "One of the most remarkable revelations in the wake of the September 11 attack on the United States was that six months after the tragedy the U.S. government's Immigration and Naturalization Service (INS) mailed a notice to a Venice, Florida, flight school informing it that Mohammed Atta and Marwan Al-Shehhi had been approved for student visas. Atta and Al-Shehhi were two of the hijackers who flew planes into the World Trade Center. Before the attack, the Federal Aviation Administration (FAA) had received numerous warnings and had actually issued four information circulars to commercial airlines, asking them to 'use caution.' But these bulletins sent to the airlines do not require any responses, and the airlines did nothing." (Janda 2007, 393)

11. "In the 1960s, psychologist Albert Bandura conducted several experiments on social learning that are now considered to be classic psychological experiments and contributed to his developing social learning theory. Collectively these experiments are referred to as the Bobo doll experiments because the experimental procedure utilized a blow-up plastic 'Bobo' doll, a popular child's toy.

"In the Bobo doll experiments, children watched films in which a woman beat up the Bobo doll. After viewing the films, Bandura and his colleagues placed the children in a room alone with the Bobo doll and observed the children's behavior without their knowledge. If the children imitated the characteristic behaviors of the model, then Bandura knew that learning had occurred.

[There were three movies, and the children were shown one of the three; in one film the person beating up the doll was punished; in another film the person was rewarded, and in a third there appeared to be no consequence (positive or negative) for the person beating up the doll.]

"As you might expect, the children who had seen the model rewarded for beating up Bobo were most likely to beat up on him themselves. However, an unexpected finding of the study was that the children who had seen the no consequences film were equally likely to beat up on Bobo! This means that seeing someone merely getting away with aggressive behavior is just as likely to lead to modeling as seeing aggression rewarded. The only thing that deterred the children's aggression toward Bobo was having seen the punishment film [in which the person beating up Bobo was punished]." (Pastorino 2006, 240, material omitted)

*12. "Clearly, global warming would mean a higher global average surface temperature for Earth. Beyond that simple statement, however, the issue of consequences becomes much more complicated and the uncertainties involved in prediction even greater.

"Changing weather patterns would ensure that different regions of Earth experienced different degrees of warming. Some regions would even become colder. Other regions might experience more rainfall or might become deserts. The greater overall warmth of the atmosphere would tend to mean more evaporation from the oceans, leading to more numerous and more intense storms.

"Another potential threat comes from rising sea level. Sea level has already risen some 20 centimeters in the past hundred years, and could rise another meter as the oceans warm. Secondary effects, such as those arising from changes to ocean currents or ecological changes, pose an even more intractable problem. For example, it is difficult to know how forests and other ecosystems will respond to climate changes induced by global warming. As a result, we cannot easily predict the impact of such climate changes on food production, fresh water availability, or other issues critical to the well-being of human populations.

"Given the current uncertainties, no one can predict the precise impact of global warming over the next century. However, the lesson is clear: Dramatic and deadly change can occur unexpectedly, and we do not know how our tampering might affect the finely balanced mechanisms that control Earth's climate." (Bennett 2007, 320–321, material omitted)

B. Refer to the following passage for these exercises.

"After regaining independence in 1952, Japan continued to profit from access to foreign raw materials, technology, and markets, including those of the United States. Because of popular sentiment, constitutional constraints, and the country's reliance on the American 'nuclear umbrella,' Japan was freed from the burden of supporting a large and costly military establishment, releasing funds and energies for economic development. At the same time, business benefited from a probusiness political system." (Schirokauer 2005, 634, material omitted)

1. Which event(s) is/are claimed to be correlated or causally related to the economic growth of Japan?

2. Identify the first premise of the causal argument found in the second sentence above, following the phrase "nuclear umbrella."

*3. Identify the second premise of the causal argument using the second sentence above, following the phrase "nuclear umbrella."

4. Is there a third premise for a causal argument provided or implied in the passage above?

5. If there is no third premise offered, are there rather one or more third party causes that are mentioned in the passage?

6. Is there any evidence provided in the passage above that would address the fourth premise of a causal argument?

Evaluating Causal Arguments

Now that you've examined the standard form of causal arguments, you're ready to look at how the true premises test and the proper form test apply to causal arguments. A causal argument passes the proper form test when it can be put into standard form. It passes the true premises test when each premise is true. Each of the premises in a causal argument in standard form is more complex than it looks at first. Let's look more closely at each one.

Premise (1): Correlation

The first premise of a causal argument in the proper form is

(1) E1 is correlated with E2.

Speaking roughly and imprecisely, two events are correlated when they happen together. In most parts of the United States, the months of September, October, and November are correlated with falling temperatures and falling leaves. The sound of your alarm clock is correlated with your getting out of bed. (This example illustrates that some correlations aren't perfect.) Correlations are things that people observe. The first premise of a causal argument in the proper form is an empirical premise, and causal arguments are empirical arguments.

Connections

Chapter Four notes that "empirical" means "based on observation."

Binary and Scalar Features

Key Concept

Binary features are features of events that the event either has or doesn't have. **Scalar features** are features of events that the event has to a greater or lesser degree.

Two different kinds of correlations correspond to two different kinds of features events can have. **Binary features** are features of events that the event either has or doesn't have. **Scalar features** are features of events that the event has to a greater or lesser degree. Both the position of the switch (up or down) and the state of the light (on or off) are binary features. If the light was on a sliding dimmer switch, the light and the switch would have scalar features. The light can be more or less bright and the switch can be slid higher or lower. Other binary features include a levee being breached or not being breached and a door being locked or unlocked. Other scalar features include a person's height and the amount of money a company makes in a year. (The root of "scalar" is the same as the root of the word "scale." Your bathroom scale is used to measure your weight, and your weight is a scalar feature.)

Technical Terms: Binary Variables, Dummy Variables, Indicator Variables, Scalar Variables, Continuous Variables, Linear Variables

In the mathematical representation of correlations, binary features are often represented by assigning the number 0 to one side of the feature and 1 to the other side. You might assign 0 to represent a state in which a light is off and a 1 to represent the state in which it's on. Scalar features are often represented by assigning a number from 0 to 1. The various levels of light output that a light on a dimmer switch can produce might be represented with numbers such as 0.01, 0.12, 0.57, etc. (For an example of this, see Chapter Eight's data on the rank of female baboons.) When working with binary and scalar features, researchers often talk of assigning variables to various features. Researchers might assign the variable "L" to the output of a light. They then might say, "L is a binary variable" or "L is a scalar variable." Binary variables are also called "dummy variables" and "indicator variables." Scalar variables are also called "continuous variables" and "linear variables."

Binary Correlation

Two types of events, E1and E2, have **positive binary correlation** when

> E1 is present when E2 is present and
> E1 is absent when E2 is absent.

A regular light switch is an example of positive binary correlation. When the switch is up (present) the light is on (present). When the switch is down (absent) the light is off (absent). If you assume that soils are either soft or not soft (as the article above about Hurricane Katrina seems to do), then the levee case is also a case of positive binary correlation. When the soil was soft (present) the levees failed (present), and when the soil wasn't soft (absent) the levees didn't fail (absent).

> Two types of events, E1and E2, have **negative binary correlation** when

> E1 is present when E2 is absent and
> E1 is absent when E2 is present.

You can transform any case of positive binary correlation into a case of negative binary correlation by changing what you call "present" and "absent." The levee case can be redescribed as a case of negative binary correlation by referring to firm soil instead of soft. When the soil was firm (present) the levees didn't fail (absent), and when the soil wasn't firm (absent) the levees failed (present).

Scalar Correlation

Scalar features can be entirely present or entirely absent (as when a light on a dimmer switch is turned all the way up or all the way down). But they can also be on a scale between present and absent. Two types of events, E1 and E2, have **positive scalar correlation** when

> E1 rises as E2 rises and
> E1 falls as E2 falls.

The case of a light on a dimmer switch is a case of positive scalar correlation. Other examples of positive scalar correlation include the relationship between how much a person eats and this individual's weight and the relationship between a person's income and the income tax this person pays.

Key Concept
Two types of events, E1and E2, have **positive binary correlation** when E1 is present when E2 is present and E1 is absent when E2 is absent. Two types of events, E1and E2, have **negative binary correlation** when E1 is present when E2 is absent and E1 is absent when E2 is present.

Key Concept
Two types of events, E1 and E2, have **positive scalar correlation** when E1 rises as E2 rises and E1 falls as E2 falls. Two types of events, E1 and E2, have **negative scalar correlation** when E1 rises as E2 falls and E1 falls as E2 rises.

Two types of events, E1 and E2, have **negative scalar correlation** when

E1 rises as E2 falls and
E1 falls as E2 rises.

Just as any example of negative binary correlation can be redescribed as a case of positive binary correlation, any example of negative scalar correlation can be redescribed as a case of positive scalar correlation. If you reversed the dimmer switch so that the light got dimmer as the switch went up, it would become a case of negative scalar correlation.

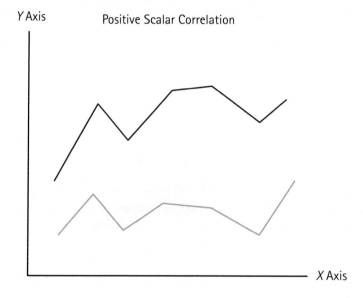

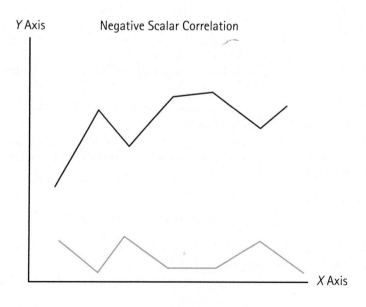

Technical Term: Concomitant Variation

Cases of scalar correlation are also called cases of "concomitant variation."

Not all events are correlated. There's **no correlation** between two events when there's neither binary nor scalar correlation. Grades and shoe size aren't correlated. The rate of inflation in the United States and the number of countries in the world aren't correlated.

The words "correlated" and "correlation" aren't that common. More common correlation indicator words are "associated," "linked," and "related." Various words regarding time and placement of objects can also be used to indicate correlation. Someone might say that E2 "occurred whenever E1 occurred," "always occurred after E1," "usually followed E1," or similar phrases about time. In the example of Hurricane Katrina, the correlation is between the parts of the levees that failed and the soils beneath those levees. As you read through the article above, you'll see that the word "correlation" is never used.

EXERCISE 9.3

A. Which of the following features are scalar and which are binary?

1. The degrees marked on a temperature scale.
2. The GPAs of students who have several immediate family members who have been to college as compared to the GPAs of students who have no immediate family members who have been to college.
3. Whether a given leopard does or doesn't have spots.
*4. Whether a given event occurred in the most recent Ice Age or not.
5. The amount of nitrogen in the air in a given area.
6. The human population density in various countries.
7. The human population density in the world.
*8. The annual percent of growth in the human population of the world.
9. The age of the ocean floor.
10. The number of places on Earth called "hot spots," whose volcanic centers result from hot materials produced deep in the mantle of the Earth's crust.
11. The amount of support given to Pakistan by the U.S. Congress to reimburse Pakistan's military actions against terrorism.
*12. "Friendship has one quality that renders it indissoluble and doubles its delight, a quality that love itself does not possess: certainty [of being understood]." (Balzac 2001, 224)
13. The financial disaster of the sub-prime mortgage crisis.
14. The Wall Street firms that have gone bankrupt due to the sub-prime mortgage crisis.
15. The "bailing out" of seven affiliated investment entities by Citigroup, Inc.

B. Provide two of your own examples of each of the following: binary correlation, scalar correlation, and no correlation.

Establishing Correlations: Mill's Methods

The philosopher John Stuart Mill pointed to four methods that are useful in establishing the existence of a correlation.

The Method of Agreement

The Method of Agreement helps you find binary correlations. Remember that two types of events, E1 and E10, have positive binary correlation when:

(a) E1 is present when E10 is present and
(b) E1 is absent when E10 is absent.

Suppose that you're wondering whether E10 is always present when E1 is present. You're trying to see whether (a) is true. You look at two different situations, call them "Case 1" and "Case 2," and see whether E1 is present in both. You collect some data and find that

(A) In Case 1, **E1** E2 E3 E4 are present and **E10** E11 E12 E13 are present.
In Case 2, **E1** E5 E6 E7 are present and **E10** E14 E15 E16 are present.

Only E1 and E10 are present in both cases. This gives you a reason to think that statement (a) is true, that E1 is present when E10 is present. If you only look at two cases, however, you don't have much evidence that E1 and E10 are correlated. If you look at more and more cases and find that E1 is present when E10 is present, you have more and more evidence that E1 is present when E10 is present.

You and four friends go out to dinner, and later that evening you all throw up. You wonder about the cause of the vomiting. All five of you ordered completely different things to eat and drink except that you all had a green salad. You'd suspect that the salad was the cause of the illness. Given the information you have so far, you shouldn't conclude that the salad was the cause. You and your friends have many other things in common besides eating the salad. You all used the restaurant's silverware. Perhaps it was all contaminated.

The information you have doesn't yet establish the presence of a correlation between the salad and being sick. The information allows you to conclude that:

(a) Salad is present when the stomach illness is present.

But you only have half of what it takes to establish a correlation. You haven't yet established that:

(b) Salad is absent when the stomach illness is absent.

The next method, the Method of Difference, is designed to help you establish that (b) is true.

The Method of Difference

You're wondering whether E1 and E10 are correlated. You look at two different situations, collect some data, and find:

(B) In Case 1, **E1** E2 E3 E4 are present and **E10** E11 E12 E13 are present.
In Case 3,   E2 E3 E4 are present and   E11 E12 E13 are present.

Only E1 and E10 are absent in Case 2. This gives you a reason to think that E1 is absent when E10 is absent. Here's part (b) of what you need to establish in order to show that E1 and E10 are correlated. As before, you'd need more cases to have good reason to think that E1 is absent when E10 is absent.

Suppose that, after you and your friends have recovered from your stomach illness, you go out to dinner again. But this time you all order the exact same things. But after dinner is over, you decide to have dessert. None of your friends has dessert. Later that night, you throw up but none of your friends gets sick. In this case, you'd suspect that the dessert was the cause of your illness. The Method of Difference provides evidence for part (b) of what it takes to establish a correlation. As before, given the evidence you have, you shouldn't do more than suspect the dessert. There were many other differences between you and your friends. You ate with different pieces of silverware than they did. Perhaps there was something on your fork that wasn't on their forks.

The Joint Method of Agreement and Difference

As its name indicates, the Joint Method of Agreement and Difference occurs when someone uses the Method of Agreement and the Method of Difference at the same time. Using the same format, the Joint Method of Agreement and Difference would look like this:

Key Concept
The Joint Method of Agreement and Difference.

(C) In Case 1, **E1** E2 E3 E4 are present and **E10** E11 E12 E13 are present.
In Case 2, **E1** E5 E6 E7 are present and **E10** E14 E15 E16 are present.
In Case 3, E2 E3 E4 are present and E11 E12 E13 are present.

This information provides evidence that E1 is correlated with E10. Comparing Cases 1 and 2 provides evidence that

E1 is present when E10 is present.

Comparing Cases 1 and 3 provides evidence that

E1 is absent when E10 is absent.

Let's suppose that you recover from your last stomach illness. You and your four friends again go out to dinner. This time you and one of your friends throw up but your other three friends don't get sick. You and the friend who got sick had only one item of food in common. You both had chicken parmesan. This would be the Agreement half of the Joint Method. Suppose that none of your other three friends had the chicken parmesan. This would be the Difference half of the Joint Method. You'd have evidence both for the view that the chicken parmesan was present when the illness was present and evidence for the view that the chicken parmesan was absent when the illness was absent.

The Method of Scalar Variation

Because the first three of Mill's Methods focus entirely on the presence and absence of various events, they can't be used to establish the existence of scalar correlation. Mill was aware of this problem. The Method of Scalar Variation tells you to look for scalar correlations. It tells you to look for cases in which

Key Concept
The Method of Scalar Variation.

E1 rises as E2 rises and
E1 falls as E2 falls.

You're taking an economics class and are assigned to investigate the causes of cycles of boom and bust in the housing industry. Your professor says that the number of new homes built per year goes up at some times and down at other times. One way to begin the search for the cause of this pattern would be to look for other economic events that follow the same pattern. You should look for both positive and negative scalar correlations. You should look for economic events that are more frequent or have higher levels when the number of new homes built rises. You should also look for economic events that are less frequent or have lower levels when the number of new homes falls. As you conduct your research, you'll be using Mill's Method of Scalar Variation.

The investigation of causal relationships can't be done correctly without Mill's Methods. But the Methods have limits. Look back at (A), (B), and (C) above. These lists of events might or might not be correlated with E10. Suppose that the real cause of E10 was omitted from our list. In that case, you wouldn't find the correlation between the cause and E10 because you never looked for it! Mill's Methods are a way to check to see whether something you think might be correlated with an event is in fact correlated. But they don't help generate a list of types of events to check.

When you draw up lists of types of events that you'll check using Mill's Methods, you're relying on your background knowledge. When you're thinking about the cause of the stomach illness, you don't look for correlations between the styles of clothes and illness. Relying on your background knowledge about the ways that illnesses spread, you look for the various different ways that you've previously seen illnesses transferred from one person to another.

Correlation Is Not Causation

If there were only two things you could remember about correlation and causation, they should be:

Key Concept
If there is no correlation, there can't be causation. Establishing correlation doesn't show causation.

1. *If there is no correlation, there can't be causation.*

   Corr~~ela~~tion ⟶ *Therefore* ⟶ *Caus~~ati~~on*

2. *Establishing correlation doesn't show of causation.*

   Correlation ⟶ *The~~refo~~re* ⟶ *Causation*

Critical Thinkers

John Stuart Mill

In addition to developing the Methods discussed in this chapter, John Stuart Mill (1806–1873) is famous for his work in political and ethical theory. Mill learned Greek at the age of three, began his studies of Latin and algebra when he was eight, and started working on logic when he was twelve (by reading Aristotle's work on logic in Greek). Among other political causes, he was a strong advocate for women's rights. You can read more about Mill's life, his intense depression as a young man, his belief in the importance of education, and his interest in scientific method in *The Autobiography of John Stuart Mill*. Most of his work is available free online, including *On Liberty*, *The Subjection of Women*, and *Utilitarianism*.

London Stereoscopic Company/ Hulton Archive /Getty Images

If two events aren't correlated, then neither event is the cause of the other. The color of a car isn't correlated with the emissions of a car. This tells you that the color of the car doesn't cause any increase or decrease in emissions.

That two events are correlated doesn't mean that one caused the other. The fact that the light switch in the up position is correlated with the light being on doesn't show that the light causes the switch to move up. If E1 is correlated with E2, there are four possible explanations for this correlation:

1. It could be that E1 causes E2.
2. It could be that E2 causes E1.
3. It could be that E3 causes E1 and E2.
4. It could be that the correlation between E1 and E2 is a coincidence.

Look back at the proper form of a causal argument. Premises (2), (3), and (4) require you to rule out possibilities 2, 3, and 4. If you can show that E1 and E2 are correlated, *and* you can show that E2 isn't the cause of E1, *and* you can show that there's no E3 that causes both E1 and E2, *and* you can show that E1 and E2 aren't coincidentally correlated, then *and only then* do you have the evidence you need to conclude that E1 is a cause of E2. When it comes to causal argument, ruling out possibilities 2, 3, and 4 is an important part of the art of argument.

Fallacy: Hasty Cause

The **Hasty Cause Fallacy** occurs when someone offers an argument with the following improper form:

(1) E1 is correlated with E2.
Therefore,
(5) E1 is a cause of E2.

The conclusion is numbered (5) to highlight that this argument form jumps from the first premise of the proper form of a causal argument to the conclusion without thinking about possibilities 2, 3, and 4. Someone who commits the Hasty Cause Fallacy moves too hastily from the claim that E1 is correlated with E2 to the claim that E1 is the cause of E2.

Technical Terms: False Cause, Objectionable Cause

The Hasty Cause Fallacy is also called "The Fallacy of False Cause" and "The Fallacy of Objectionable Cause."

One of the authors of this book has a computer monitor with a light in the bottom right-hand corner. The color of this light is correlated with whether the monitor is on. When the monitor is off, the light is yellow. When the monitor is on, the light is blue. If someone were to argue that this correlation shows that the light turning blue causes the monitor to come on, then that would be an example of the Hasty Cause Fallacy.

Key Concept
The form of a **Hasty Cause Fallacy**.

Fallacy: Causal Slippery Slope

If a person makes a series of causal claims, one or more of which commit the Fallacy of Hasty Cause, that person has committed the **Causal Slippery Slope Fallacy**. In 1925, John Scopes, a high school biology teacher, was put on trial for violating a Tennessee law that banned teaching the theory of evolution in public schools. Scopes' lawyer, a man named Clarence Darrow, made the following argument:

> If today you can take a thing like evolution and make it a crime to teach it in the public school, tomorrow you can make it a crime to teach it in the private schools, and the next year you can make it a crime to teach it in the church. At the next session you may ban books and the newspapers. Soon you may set Catholic against Protestant and Protestant against Protestant, and try to foist your own religion upon the minds of men. After [a] while, your honor, it is the setting of man against man and creed against creed until with flying banners and beating drums we are marching backward to the glorious ages of the sixteenth century when bigots lighted fagots to burn the men who dared to bring any intelligence and enlightenment and culture to the human mind. (Darrow 1925, 87, material omitted)

Here Darrow argues, without providing any causal evidence, that if the United States bans the teaching of evolution in school, we'll return to a time like that of the European wars of religion. He has committed Causal Slippery Slope Fallacy.

EXERCISE 9.4

A. In the following passages, indicate whether one of Mill's Methods is present and, if a Method(s) is present, which Method(s) it is.

1. Jack always ate beans and never ate steak and never got ill. Jake always ate steak and never ate beans and became ill. Jack said that the steak was the cause of Jake's illness.

2. Suppose Jack had argued instead that Jake became ill because he (Jake) never ate beans.

3. Suppose Jill, a friend of Jack and Jake, said that Jake became ill because he ate steak AND didn't eat beans.

*4. Suppose that Jill ate beans, but never as many as Jack, and now and again ate steak, but never as much as Jake. What would you conclude if Jill never became ill?

The next three exercises are excerpted from the Centers for Disease Control and Prevention (2009).

5. "[The Food and Drug Administration] FDA has evidence to support classifying the recall of product distributed from the PCA [Peanut Corporation of America] Plainview, Texas facility from January 1, 2007 forward as a Class 1 recall. This determination was based upon inspectional findings, epidemiological data, internal test results from PCA that are positive for *Salmonella*, test results from consumer samples that match the outbreak strain of *Salmonella typhimurium*, and FDA positive samples of finished product (post-processed peanut meal collected at the PCA Texas facility) that match the outbreak strain. The Texas Department of State Health Services (DSHS) also collected a sample of peanut meal from the same lot collected by FDA at the PCA Texas facility and has detected the outbreak strain of *Salmonella typhimurium*."

6. "This is an ingredient-driven outbreak; that is, potentially contaminated ingredients affected many different products that were distributed through various channels and consumed in various settings. The recalled products made by PCA, such as peanut butter and peanut paste, are common ingredients in cookies, crackers, cereal, candy, ice cream, pet treats, and other foods. Consumers are advised to discard and not eat products that have been recalled. To help consumers identify affected products, FDA has initiated a searchable database of recalled products that is updated daily or as additional recalls are identified. To date, more than 2,100 products in seventeen categories have been voluntarily recalled by more than 200 companies, and the list continues to grow."

7. "In January, the recall list was expanded to include some pet-food products that contain peanut paste made by PCA. Salmonella can affect animals, and humans who handle contaminated pet-food products also are at risk. It is important for people to wash their hands—and to make sure children wash their hands—with hot water and soap before and, especially, after handling pet-food products and utensils."

For the next three exercises, take into account the following background information: Diseases and illnesses are normally treated clinically by medical personnel focusing on each and every individual who suffers from the condition. But some diseases and illnesses are treated as a public health issue. The main examples are infectious epidemics, where treatment is not focused solely on affected individuals but rather on practices that will help the entire community, affected and unaffected individuals alike. The polio vaccine of the 1950s is an example: preventative practices were instituted and administered throughout the country. Drs. Bowman and Vinicor, of the Centers for Disease Control and Prevention (CDC), believe that we should also treat diabetes as a public health problem. Read the following excerpts from their work (Bowman 2005) and identify any use or potential use of Mill's Methods.

*8. "Type 2 diabetes makes a compelling case study for public health action. The disease respects no boundaries. It is increasingly common—occurring in both developed and developing countries, in men and women, at earlier ages than in past decades, and in persons of every race and ethnic group."

9. "Family history and genetic factors appear to further increase the risk for type 2 diabetes in Hispanic/Latino Americans. In the United States, the prevalence of diabetes was estimated to be 18.2 million people (6.3% of the population) in 2002, with dramatic increases predicted in the future."

10. "The determinants of type 2 diabetes are largely understood. Two of the most important risk factors, obesity and physical inactivity, are modifiable. The natural history involves progression from prediabetes, a condition in which blood glucose metabolism is abnormal (although not yet in the diabetes range), to the development of type 2 diabetes. The rate of progression from prediabetes to type 2 diabetes is between 3% and 10% per year. However, progression from prediabetes to diabetes can be prevented or delayed with sustained weight loss and increased physical activity. The magnitude of the change needed for primary prevention of type 2 diabetes is relatively modest: a 7% to 10% weight loss and sustained moderate physical activity, at least 30 minutes per day."

B. Review the passages in A above. This time, look for examples of the Hasty Cause Fallacy and the Causal Slippery Slope Fallacy.

C. This passage contains a causal conclusion. Put the argument in this passage into proper form.

Background information: Jens Herberholz and a group of researchers at Georgia State University studied the response of young crayfish to being attacked by dragonflies. Here is part of their summary of their research.

"The neural systems that control escape behavior have been studied intensively in several animals, including mollusks, fish, and crayfish. Surprisingly little is known, however, about the activation and the utilization of escape circuits during prey–predator interactions. To complement the physiological and anatomical studies with a necessary behavioral equivalent, we investigated encounters between juvenile crayfish and large dragonfly nymphs in freely behaving animals using a combination of high-speed video-recordings and measurements of electric field potentials. During attacks, dragonfly nymphs rapidly extended their labium, equipped with short, sharp palps, to capture small crayfish. Crayfish responded to the tactile stimulus by activating neural escape circuits to generate tail-flips directed away from the predator. Tail-flips were the sole defense mechanism in response to an attack, and every single strike was answered by tail-flip escape behavior." (Herberholz 2004, 1855)

Premise (2): Causation and Time

Passing first grade is correlated with knowing how to do simple addition. At the end of first grade, most children know how to add. This doesn't tell you whether knowing how to add causes someone to go to first grade (perhaps because children have been required to learn to add before they enter first grade) or, alternatively, whether going to first grade causes children to know how to add. But let's then add another piece of information. Most children don't know how to add *before* they go to first grade. You've now got some evidence that entering first grade is a (contributory) cause of knowing how to add.

The second premise of a causal argument in the proper form is

(2) E2 is not the cause of E1.

Key Concept

Reverse causation occurs when people think that E1 caused E2 but in fact E2 caused E1.

When people think that E1 caused E2 but in fact E2 caused E1, you have a case of **reverse causation**. The direction of causation is the opposite of what people think it is.

Premise (2) is usually based on the fact that the cause never comes after the effect. This claim asserts that either (a) the cause occurs at the same time as the effect or (b) the cause occurs before the effect. As an example of (a), let's assume that you're now sitting in a chair. What's causing your body to remain two feet above the floor? The molecular structure of the chair and the fact that the chair is under your body are the causes of your body remaining about two feet above the floor. In this case, the cause occurs at the same time as the effect.

That causes never occur after effects gives you a tool to rule out the possibility that E2 causes E1. You can use an argument with the following proper form.

(T) (1) E2 came after E1.
    (2) If E2 came after E1, then E2 is not the cause of E1.
Therefore,
    (3) E2 is not the cause of E1.

The conclusion of argument (T) is the second premise of a causal argument in the proper form. Argument (T) is a subargument for that premise and is an example of affirming the antecedent.

Connections

Chapter Five notes that any argument that affirms the antecedent has a proper form.

Fallacy: Post Hoc

The **Post Hoc** Fallacy occurs when someone misunderstands the relationship between causation and time. It has the following form:

(1) E1 occurs before E2.
Therefore,
(2) E1 is a cause of E2.

If you know that the first premise of this argument is true, you've got good reason to think that E2 *isn't* the cause of E1. But the fact that E1 occurs before E2 doesn't allow you to conclude that E1 *is* the cause of E2. It only provides some reason to think that E1 and E2 are correlated. And, as you saw above, you can't move directly from the claim that two events are correlated to the claim that one caused the other.

Here's an example of the *Post Hoc* Fallacy:

The only policy that effectively reduces public shootings is right-to-carry laws. Allowing citizens to carry concealed handguns reduces violent crime. In the 31 states that have passed right-to-carry laws since the mid-1980s, the number of multiple-victim public shootings and other violent crimes has dropped dramatically. Murders fell by 7.65%, rapes by 5.2%, aggravated assaults by 7%, and robberies by 3%. (*The Phyllis Schlafly Report* 2000)

The authors of this passage move from the claim that

the number of public shootings has fallen *after* people were allowed to carry concealed handguns

to the claim that

allowing people to carry concealed handguns *causes* a reduction in public shootings.

At most, the evidence indicates that these two types of events are correlated. The authors make no attempt to review and rule out other possible causes. It might be that an increase in prison sentences for shootings caused their number to fall. It might be that a drop in the number of young adults (who commit more crimes than other age groups) led to a drop in all crimes. Unless these possibilities (and others) are examined, you shouldn't conclude that allowing people to carry concealed handguns caused the reduction in

Key Concept
The form of the *Post Hoc* Fallacy.

Habits of a Critical Thinker

Avoiding Superstition

The *Post Hoc* Fallacy is at the root of many superstitions. Suppose that a baseball player has fried chicken for lunch two days in a row and he hits a home run on both those days. This is a coincidence. The player may develop the superstitious belief that if he eats fried chicken for lunch, he'll hit more home runs. Superstitious beliefs occur when someone believes that events that are causally unrelated have some causal effects on each other. Superstitious beliefs are tempting.

A playful superstition does no damage. Perhaps you always sing a silly song before you start a long car trip and joke to others that it keeps you from being in an accident. There's no harm in that. But if you really believed that singing the song prevented accidents, this would be dangerous. It might lead you to drive recklessly. A good critical thinker doesn't take superstitions seriously.

shootings. (Another problem with this argument is that it provides no evidence for the view that right-to-carry laws are the *only* policies that effectively reduce public shootings. But this second problem with the argument isn't an example of the *Post Hoc* Fallacy.)

Technical Terms: *Post Hoc, Ergo Propter Hoc*

The name of the *Post Hoc* Fallacy comes from the Latin phrase "*post hoc, ergo propter hoc.*" This translates as "after this, therefore because of this." This book usually avoids Latin, but we don't do that in this case because the name "*Post Hoc* Fallacy" has become common.

Premise (3): Third–Party Causation

In most homes, the furnace coming on is correlated with the lights coming on. The furnace tends to come on in the evening and so do the lights. Later at night, many people's furnaces drop to a lower temperature and their lights go out. Then in the morning, the furnace comes on again and so do the lights. After people leave for work, their furnaces again drop to a lower temperature and their lights go out. Do furnaces cause lights to go on? Do lights coming on cause furnaces to come on? Neither of these is the case. Some third thing besides lights and furnaces causes the correlation between furnaces and lights. In this case, the third thing is people. People turn on lights when it gets dark. They turn on furnaces when it gets cold and they aren't asleep. When it gets dark, it gets colder. People tend to turn on lights at the same time they turn up their furnace and then tend to turn off lights at the same time as they turn down their furnace. You have a case of third-party causation. **Third-party causation** occurs when one kind of event is the cause of two other kinds of events.

> **Key Concept**
>
> **Third-party causation** occurs when one kind of event is the cause of two other kinds of events.

The third premise of the form of a causal argument in the proper form asserts that there's no third-party causation.

(3) There is no E3 that is the cause of E1 and E2.

Third-party causation can be hard to discover. Smoking and car accidents are correlated. Smokers have more car accidents than nonsmokers. Does smoking cause car accidents? When people light a cigarette, they aren't watching the road. They might be more likely to have an accident. When a person is

Critical Thinkers

Ida B. Wells

Library of Congress

Ida B. Wells (1862–1931) was a journalist, editor, political activist, and leader of the civil rights movement. Wells published *Southern Horrors: Lynch Law in All Its Phases* in 1892 and *A Red Record: Tabulated Statistics and Alleged Causes of Lynchings in the United States* in 1895. She presented brilliantly documented research in order to disprove a popular view that lynching was caused by accusations of rape. Wells showed that the correlation between lynchings and accusations of rape were not as high as was believed and that the majority of lynching cases did not involve rape accusations. Wells argued that there was a third-party cause—fear of African-American economic progress—which was the primary cause of both lynchings and accusations of rape. You can read about her amazing life and work in the biography by Paula Giddings, *Ida: A Sword among Lions: Ida B. Wells and the Campaign against Lynching.*

holding a cigarette, they might not be able to control a car well if an emergency maneuver is required. On the other hand, this may be a case of third-party causation. Smoking is risky, and people have different personalities. Some people avoid taking risks, but other people enjoy taking risks. Some people seek out risky activities such as hang gliding, climbing cliffs, and deep sea diving. It may be that the correlation between smoking and car accidents is the result of a third-party cause: people who are less concerned about risk are smokers, and they engage in risky actions when driving. This might be why people who smoke have more car accidents. Moreover, these two causal explanations could both be true. It could be that distraction and attitudes toward risk are both contributory causes of car accidents. (For more on this issue, see Jonahl 1997.)

Don't confuse third-party causation with chains of causation. You might have one of those programmable thermostats in your home. You can set it so that the temperature varies at different times of the day. Suppose that in the summer you mistakenly set the thermostat to go from 72 degrees to 68 degrees at 4 a.m. This may well set off a chain of causation. The thermostat causes the AC to come on, the AC causes the temperature to drop, and this causes you to wake up and pull a blanket over yourself. This is a chain of causation because E1 causes E2 and then E2 causes E3. In a case of third-party causation, E3 causes both E1 and E2 but E1 doesn't cause E2.

Chain Causation   E1   → causes →   E2   → causes →   E3

Third–Party Causation   E1   → causes →   E2 & E3

Causal Arguments by Elimination

Third-party causation is another case in which background knowledge is crucial. The only way to determine whether third-party causation exists is to come up with a list of possible third-party causes and check to see whether each of them is actually a cause. You use your background knowledge to develop a list of third-party causes and use a set of causal arguments by elimination to attempt to show that they aren't third party causes.

Showing that one type of event *is not* the cause of another type of event is easier than showing that one type of event *is* the cause of another type of event. There are two ways to show that there's no causal link between two types of events: elimination by correlation and elimination by time.

Elimination by correlation begins with the premise that there's no correlation between two types of events and concludes that there's no causal link between them. As you saw above, if two types of events aren't correlated, neither event causes the other.

Elimination by time begins with the premise that one type of event, E2, occurs after another type of event, E1, and concludes that E2 isn't a cause of E1. As noted above, causation doesn't work backwards in time. If E3 occurs after E1 and E2, E3 isn't a third-party cause of E1 and E2.

Premise (4): Coincidental Correlation

The National Football League (NFL) is divided into two conferences: the National Football Conference (NFC) and the American Football Conference (AFC). Some have noted that if a team from the AFC wins the Super Bowl, the stock market has tended to fall and if a team from the NFC wins the Super Bowl, the stock market has tended to rise. This legend has proved accurate 30 of 37 times, an accuracy rate of more than 80%. Is there a causal link between the Super Bowl and the stock market? Our background knowledge doesn't provide any reason to think that a winning performance by an NFC team causes the stock market to rise. This correlation is just a coincidence. (For more on this correlation, see Hendrick 1999.)

Coincidences occur because billions of events are occurring in the world. By chance, some of these events will be correlated. If enough monkeys took the SAT, one of them would get a perfect score. This wouldn't mean that this monkey is any smarter than any other monkey. The fourth premise of a causal argument in the standard form

(4) E1 and E2 are not coincidentally correlated.

asserts that a correlation isn't a coincidence. One can provide a subargument for this premise in two ways.

First, for a causal claim to be justified, it must cohere with our background knowledge. You can tell that a particular team winning the Super Bowl–stock market correlation is coincidental because your background knowledge about football and the stock market indicates that there's no plausible causal link between these two events. Again you see that background knowledge is crucial.

Second, a coincidental correlation is unlikely to persist over time. If you wanted to see whether the monkey who got a perfect score on the SAT was actually smarter than other monkeys or whether its performance was only a coincidence, you could have the monkey take the SAT three, four, or more times. The monkey probably won't do as well the next time it took the test. But suppose this monkey consistently scored over 1400. Imagine that the monkey scored over 1400 on twenty consecutive tests. In that case, you'd have good reason to think that this particular monkey was actually smarter than other monkeys, that this correlation wasn't coincidental.

Key Concept

Elimination by correlation begins with the premise that there's no correlation between two types of events and concludes that there's no causal link between them. **Elimination by time** begins with the premise that one type of event, E2, occurs after another type of event, E1, and concludes that E2 isn't a cause of E1.

Technical Term: Accidental Correlation

Another term for coincidental correlation is "accidental correlation."

Habits of a Critical Thinker

Resisting Oversimplification

It's tempting to look for simple causal stories. But the author H. L. Mencken noted that "for every complex question, there is a simple answer—and it's wrong." Critical thinkers don't look for simple answers. They look for good answers. When it comes to causes, the good answer is usually a complex answer. A good answer to a question such as "What was the cause of the Great Depression?" will distinguish necessary from contributing causes, see that there may be many contributing causes, point to cases of third-party causation, etc. A good critical thinker is suspicious when someone says: "It's really very simple...."

EXERCISE 9.5

A. For each of the following passages,

  (a) identify whether there are one or more causal arguments present or implied,
  (b) if there are, standardize each one,
  (c) if premises are missing, insert them,
  (d) construct a sub-argument for each premise,
  (e) explain how one could use one or more of Mill's Methods to establish the premises.

1. Stop it, please! Your constant bragging gives me a headache. I'm not kidding, can't we just have a normal conversation with some give-and-take?

2. The vast majority of people who get small-cell lung cancer are or were cigarette smokers.

3. Amir loves seafood, but when Amir ate crab at the Red Lobster restaurant last night, he became violently ill. Amir's mother said he also became ill when he ate crayfish at the Mardi Gras some years ago. So, Amir now believes he is allergic to shellfish because he eats fish dinners at fast food restaurants all the time and never gets sick.

*4. According to my biology lab instructor, if you pour an acid on litmus paper, it will turn the litmus paper red.

5. "It is a nobrainer to say that the credit crunch is making liquidity scarce. It is less clear why central banks are powerless to do anything to stop it contracting, and why this shrinkage will sabotage economic growth as economies fall prey to the credit drought in places as far-flung as the Baltic states to China, as well in the OECD countries. But to back up for a minute, what is liquidity? Two years ago, when confronted with financial-sector balance sheets and asset prices that were growing at a multiple of GDP and money supply that wasn't, we at Independent Strategy found our answer. At the time, there was precious little correlation between money and financial-asset prices. That seemed strange. Unless return on assets, measured by corporate return on capital, was rising exponentially, there was no justification for asset prices to be doing so.

  "Further research indicated that what was driving asset prices was the supply of copious and cheap credit with which to buy them. This type of asset money or credit was not counted in the traditional definition of liquidity, which is simply broad money, made up of central-bank money and bank lending.

"The reason for the exponential growth in credit, but not in broad money, was simply that banks didn't keep their loans on their books any more—and only loans on bank balance sheets get counted as money. No longer could central banks determine how much debt was created. Now that the loans didn't stay on banks' balance sheets, lending capacity became almost infinite—for a while. The credit tide is now ebbing. Since August, the credit system has been frozen solid. Debt issuance for all sectors of the economy has plummeted. Banks don't trust each other's balance sheets. For these reasons the Federal Reserve this week announced joint actions with central banks around the world to ease liquidity conditions.

"The Fed's [actions] will help fulfill the responsibility of the central bank to ensure proper functioning of financial markets by providing temporary liquidity. But they are not an additional easing of monetary policy or bailout of banks' bad assets.

"Therein lies the problem: [The Federal Reserve's actions] address a liquidity shortage but can't address the solvency problem inherent in the balance sheets themselves. The junk assets that the banks moved off balance sheets will have to be financed by the banks, and a lot of them will have to be moved back onto the balance sheets. As this happens, bank lending capacity gets used up reducing lending capacity. All this means lower liquidity expansion, particularly of asset money, and lower economic growth.

"In a globalized system, no one is immune. The big shock of 2008 will be that the China bubble pops. After all, where would China be without excessive global liquidity flowing into its domestic markets? We are about to find out." (Roche 2007, A21, material omitted)

6. See Exercise 9.2 A 8.

7. This is a conversation between the famous detective Sherlock Holmes and his friend Dr. Watson:

"You have an extraordinary genius for minutiae," I [Watson] remarked.

"I appreciate their importance. Here is my monograph upon the tracing of footsteps, with some remarks upon the uses of plaster of Paris as a preserver of impresses. Here, too, is a curious little work upon the influence of a trade upon the form of the hand, with lithotypes of the hands of slaters, sailors, cork cutters, compositors, weavers, and diamond-polishers. That is a matter of great practical interest to the scientific detective,—especially in cases of unclaimed bodies, or in discovering the antecedents of criminals. But I weary you with my hobby."

"Not at all," I answered, earnestly. "It is of the greatest interest to me, especially since I have had the opportunity of observing your practical application of it. But you spoke just now of observation and deduction. Surely the one to some extent implies the other."

"Why, hardly," [Holmes] answered, leaning back luxuriously in his armchair, and sending up thick blue wreaths from his pipe. "For example, observation shows me that you have been to the Wigmore Street Post-Office this morning, but deduction lets me know that when there you dispatched a telegram."

"Right!" said I. "Right on both points! But I confess that I don't see how you arrived at it. It was a sudden impulse upon my part, and I have mentioned it to no one."

"It is simplicity itself," he remarked, chuckling at my surprise,—"so absurdly simple that an explanation is superfluous; and yet it may serve to define the limits of observation and of deduction. Observation tells me that you have a little reddish mould adhering to your instep. Just opposite the Seymour Street Office they have taken up the pavement and thrown up some earth which lies in such a way that it is difficult to avoid treading in it in entering. The earth is of this peculiar reddish tint which is found, as far as I know, nowhere else in the neighborhood. So much is observation. The rest is deduction."

"How, then, did you deduce the telegram?"

"Why, of course I knew that you had not written a letter, since I sat opposite to you all morning. I see also in your open desk there that you have a sheet of stamps and a thick bundle of post-cards. What could you go into the post-office for, then, but to send a wire? Eliminate all other factors, and the one which remains must be the truth." (Doyle 1994, 4–5)

*8. "Emotion must be included in a discussion of body intelligence because it is one of the means by which our bodies communicate knowledge to conscious awareness." (Norris 2001, 113)

9. "Malinowski's famous study of Melanesian sexual beliefs and practices provides evidence that sexual jealousy really does have a genetic rather than a purely cultural explanation. The tribe that he studied did not believe in physiological paternity; they thought the only function of sexual intercourse was to enlarge the vagina so that spirits could implant the fetus in the womb. Nevertheless, men were as jealous as in societies in which the male role in procreation is understood. (Posner 1992, 97–98, material omitted)

10. "Since communication can take place directly through the body, the body can be intentionally used to transmit information." (Norris 2001, 116)

11. In the following argument, Counselor Smart claims that the defendant, Shifty McRogue, is guilty of robbing a local bank. Several witnesses confirmed that the defendant has been in desperate need of money ever since he lost his job at the cracker factory. And McRogue has the profile of a criminal, anyway, since we know he has established a prior criminal record: he served thirty days in jail just last year for driving under the influence. Moreover, I have an expert witness, Dr. Quack, the famous phrenologist, who will testify that McRogue has a predisposition to rob banks. In fact, if found guilty, this would be the defendant's third conviction; under the state's "three strikes" legislation, he would automatically serve the maximum sentence for his crime. Ever since his release from jail, McRogue has been seen regularly in the company of Max Cheatem, an ex-convict who himself served time for armed robbery. Two weeks ago, Max Cheatem lent McRogue his blue two-door Ford—a car of the same make, model, and color as the getaway vehicle used in the robbery. And finally, the bank was held up by an assailant carrying a .22 pistol; three days before the robbery, the defendant purchased a .22 pistol. Therefore, McRogue is guilty of robbing the bank.

*12. See Exercise 9.2 A 10.

13. See Exercise 9.2 A 11.

14. See Exercise 9.2 A 12.

15. For the following passage, look for any causal claims made or implied from the point of view of the House Committee and from the point of view of the Hollywood Ten.

> "Since 1938 the [U.S. Congressional] House [of Representatives] Un-American Activities Committee (HUAC) had kept up a barrage of accusations about supposed subversives in the federal government.
>
> "In 1947 the HUAC subpoenaed nineteen prominent Hollywood writers, producers, and actors, intending to prove that the Communist party members dominated the Screen Actors Guild, that they injected subversive propaganda into motion pictures, and that President [Franklin] Roosevelt had brought improper pressure to bear upon the industry to produce pro-Soviet films during the war [World War II]. Ten of the witnesses, the so-called Hollywood Ten, jointly decided to use the First Amendment as a defense, and each of them refused to answer the question as a matter of principle, claiming that party membership was their business, especially since membership in the Communist party at that time was not illegal in the United States. They were all judged to be in contempt and were sentenced to up to a year in prison. But greater punishment awaited them. The movie industry blacklisted the Hollywood Ten, denying them further work." (Tindall 2007, 893)

B. Evaluate the arguments you standardized in A above by applying the true premises test and the proper form test. When applying the proper form test, determine whether any of the arguments commit fallacies of Hasty Cause, *Post Hoc*, Causal Slippery Slope, or any other non-causal fallacy.

C. For each of the following, determine whether the argument notes these possibilities:

(a) E2 could be the cause of E1,
(b) there might be an E3 that caused both E1 and E2, and
(c) the correlation is coincidental.

1. In an article noting that hypertension is higher among African-Americans than anyone else in the world, reporter Denise Campbell cites Elijah Saunders, M.D., Professor of Medicine and head of the Hypertension Section of Cardiology at the University of Maryland's School of Medicine in Baltimore. Dr. Saunders points out that "in today's competitive environment, a number of socioeconomic factors such as career pressure, unemployment or underemployment, substandard living conditions, racism, and other stress-related conditions also affect blood pressure. How stress contributes to hypertension and heart disease is not known, but the association is quite clear. Stress stimulators often trigger the development of calcification, which causes injury to the cells. The accumulated calcium becomes a marker for atherosclerosis, a thickening and hardening of artery walls that eventually blocks the arteries." (Campbell 2007, 90)

2. "For many years the American bald eagle was rarely seen. Consequently, the bird was placed on the Endangered Species List. In 1999 it was removed from the Endangered Species List and has been seen in greater numbers in more places. Both its removal from the Endangered Species List and the increased sightings are signs that bald eagles are no longer endangered." (Rieke 2006, 343)

3. "People like their names so much that they unconsciously opt for things that begin with their initials. Tom is more likely to buy a Toyota, move to Totowa, and marry Tessa than is Joe, who is more likely to buy a Jeep, move to Jonestown, and marry Jill— and Susie sells seashells by the seashore. Even weirder, they gravitate toward things that begin with their initials even when those things are undesirable, like bad grades or a baseball strikeout.

"In what they call 'moniker maladies,' a pair of researchers find that although no baseball player wants to strike out, players whose names begin with K (shorthand for strikeout) fan more often than other players. Most students want As, but those whose names begin with C or D have lower grade point averages than students whose names begin with A and B.

"The eerie coincidences also held for law schools. Scrutinizing data on 170 law schools and 392,458 lawyers, the researchers found that the higher the school's ranking (by *U.S. News & World Report*), the higher the proportion of lawyers with the initials A or B. Adlai and Bill are more likely to go to Stanford than Chester and Dwight. (In the study, people with conflicting initials—Douglas Avery—were eliminated from the analysis.) Clearly, the effect is not all-powerful. This SB [Sharon Begley, author of this passage] married an EG, lives in P, and named her children D and S. [Researcher Leif Nelson says he is] pretty sure they eliminated all other explanations for the weird link between initials and performance." (Begley 2007, material omitted)

*4. "A trademark must be sufficiently distinct to enable consumers to identify the manufacturer of the goods easily and to distinguish between those goods and competing goods.

"Fanciful, arbitrary, or suggestive trademarks are generally considered to be the most distinctive, (strongest) trademarks. This is because these types of marks are normally taken from outside the context of the particular product and thus provide the best means of distinguishing one product from another.

"Fanciful trademarks include invented words, such as 'Xerox' for one manufacturer's copiers and 'Kodak' for another company's photographic products. Arbitrary trademarks include actual words used with products that have no literal connection to the words, such as 'English Leather' used as a name for an aftershave lotion (and not for leather processed in England). Suggestive trademarks are those that suggest something about a product without describing the product directly. For example, the trademark 'Dairy Queen' suggests an association between the products and milk, but it does not directly describe ice cream." (Cross 2007, 333)

5. "Some animals have evolved very differently, exhibiting bright warning coloration. These animals are usually distasteful, and many are poisonous—such as the yellow jacket with its bright yellow and black stripes. Poisoning a predator is small consolation for an organism that has already been eaten; thus, the bright colors declare, 'Eat me at your own risk!' One unpleasant experience is enough to teach predators to avoid such conspicuous prey." (Audesirk 2005, 544)

6. "While measuring and analyzing the first process of digestion (salivation), [Russian physiologist Ivan] Pavlov noticed that his dogs would start to salivate before he gave them meat powder. The salivation had initially occurred only after the dogs were given the meat powder. To further study this curious response, Pavlov performed experiments to train the dogs to salivate to other non-food stimuli. Pavlov's experiments were important as examples of how behavior is the product of stimuli and responses." (Pastorino 2006, 11, material omitted)

7. "Since 1938 the [U.S. Congressional] House [of Representatives] Un-American Activities Committee (HUAC) had kept up a barrage of accusations about supposed subversives in the federal government.

"In 1947 the HUAC subpoenaed nineteen prominent Hollywood writers, producers, and actors, intending to prove that the Communist party members dominated the Screen Actors Guild, that they injected subversive propaganda into motion pictures, and that President [Franklin] Roosevelt had brought improper pressure to bear upon the industry to produce pro-Soviet films during the war [World War II]. Ten of the witnesses, the so-called Hollywood Ten, jointly decided to use the First Amendment as a defense, and each of them refused to answer the question as a matter of principle, claiming that party membership was their business, especially since membership in the Communist party at that time was not illegal in the United States. They were all judged to be in contempt and were sentenced to up to a year in prison. But greater punishment awaited them. The movie industry blacklisted the Hollywood Ten, denying them further work." (Tindall 2007, 893)

Focus on the argument implied by the House Committee's correlation between actors' affiliations and President Roosevelt's policies.

*8. Focus on the argument implied in #7 above by the action of the Hollywood Ten's refusal to admit or deny their membership in the Communist party.

9. Focus on the argument implied in #7 above from the point of view of the movie industry's decision to blacklist the Hollywood Ten.

10. See Exercise 9.1 A 11.

The Scientific Method

The scientific method is a series of steps to follow to develop and confirm a causal theory. To illustrate the method, think about an example that has probably happened to you: your computer freezes up. Let's apply the scientific method to examine this problem.

Step 1: Identify the Question to Be Answered

The scientific method begins with a question to be answered. Identifying a specific causal question to study is important: in most cases, what motivates a person is a particular problem and the question must match that problem. Think about the case of your malfunctioning computer. Perhaps you're interested in finding a necessary cause of the malfunction so that you can take steps to remove it. Or you may not care about the primary cause of the malfunction. You may only be interested in finding a sufficient cause of getting the malfunctioning to stop. One question seeks an answer to the primary cause of the malfunction; the other question seeks a cause of a solution to the malfunction. When a computer has a problem, people often reboot it. This often fixes the problem. If rebooting fixes a problem with a computer and the problem doesn't reoccur, most people don't care about the cause of the problem. They've found an action that caused the malfunction to stop. That's all they care about.

Suppose that you call a friend who is a computer geek and ask her to help you fix your malfunctioning computer. She comes over and spends three hours working on your computer. You have a paper due the next day, and you're impatiently waiting for the computer to work. Your friend loves working on computers. You just want to finish your paper. Suppose that after three

Key Concept
The steps in the scientific method.

326 Chapter 9 Causal Arguments

hours working you ask: "Do you think you can get it working soon?" She responds: "Oh, I can get it working in ten minutes. All I have to do is reinstall your word processing software. That will definitely fix the problem. But I want to figure out what caused the problem. Isn't it interesting to figure out the exact cause of a computer's problem?" You and she are seeking to answer different causal questions. You want to know: What's the quickest way to cause this problem to go away? She wants to know: What's the primary cause of the problem? This shows that it's crucial to identify the correct causal question.

Step 2: Formulate a Tentative Theory

When your computer malfunctions, you must start somewhere. You'll come up with a tentative theory. A tentative theory is a theory that's proposed for testing. You might think about the theory that your flash memory drive has gone bad or the theory that a reinstallation of the word processor will fix the problem. The first is a tentative theory about the cause of the problem. The second is a tentative theory about how to quickly fix the problem. Your first tentative theory is unlikely to be true. But you have to start by focusing on one theory or another.

The development of a tentative theory is another example of the importance of background knowledge. When your computer malfunctions, you have many options. You could cover it with a nice warm blanket, but you probably won't do this. You have background knowledge about the nature of electrical machines that indicates that covering them with nice warm blankets isn't likely to help. As our background knowledge increases, our tentative theories will get better. Your computer-geek friend has more background knowledge about computers than you do. Her tentative theories about your computer problem are more likely to be correct than yours. Your tentative theories are more likely to be correct than one offered by a person transported from the 1500s and placed in front of your computer.

Step 3: Check for Correlations

Once you have formulated a tentative theory, you must look for evidence of its truth or falsity. This requires checking for correlations. You determine what sort of correlations would exist if the theory were true. Scientists sometimes call this "deducing the consequences of a theory." But this phrase is misleading because the reasoning that tells you what sort of correlations would exist if the tentative theory were true is an example of inductive reasoning. Because of the possibility of third-party causes and coincidental correlation, the statement of an empirical theory about a correlation or a cause never deductively implies any future consequences. It would be more accurate if scientists said they were "inferring the consequences of a theory."

Once you infer that if some particular theory is true, then some correlations should exist, you're in a position to see whether those correlations do in fact exist. At this point you'll use Mill's Methods. To test the nice warm blanket theory, you can use the computer when it has a nice warm blanket on it and then use it when it doesn't have a nice warm blanket. You're checking to see whether the problem is present when the blanket is absent and whether the problem is absent when the blanket is present. If the problem is present when the blanket is absent, that would be a confirmation of the tentative theory. If the problem is absent when the blanket is present, that would be another confirmation of the theory. Information confirms a theory when a correlation that was inferred from the tentative theory has been shown to exist. But suppose, as is more likely, that the presence or absence of the nice warm blanket isn't correlated with the malfunction. In that case, each case of non-correlation between the blanket and the malfunction is a disconfirmation of the nice warm blanket theory. Evidence **confirms** a theory when that evidence indicates that a correlation inferred from the theory is present. Evidence **disconfirms** a theory when that evidence indicates that a correlation inferred from the theory isn't present.

To test the theory that you have a bad flash memory drive, you check for correlations between the presence of the flash memory drive and the computer freezing up. If the problem was present when the flash memory drive was present and absent when the flash memory drive was absent, that would be an example of Mill's Methods providing you with evidence that the problem with your computer was correlated with the presence of the original flash memory drive. But you'd need to be careful to avoid committing the Fallacy of Hasty Cause. You shouldn't draw the conclusion that the flash memory drive is the cause of the problem before checking for the other possibilities noted above. You need to follow Steps 4 and 5.

Step 4: If Necessary, Formulate a New Theory

If you've worked with malfunctioning computers, you know that your first tentative theory is usually wrong. When you use Mill's Methods to check for the correlations that would be present if that tentative theory were true, you find that they don't exist. The problem might occur when you used any of three flash memory drives. This disconfirms the bad flash memory drive theory, and you'll need to formulate a new theory. While you were testing for the correlations you inferred from your theory that you had a bad flash memory, you might have noticed something that gave you an idea for a new theory. You might have noticed another correlation—that the problem only occurs when you're using files that had been e-mailed to you by one of your friends. You might then formulate the theory that the files your friend sent you were corrupted.

Habits of a Critical Thinker

Avoid Confirmation Bias

Humans have a psychological flaw. Once you hold a view, you tend to see confirming evidence and overlook or discount disconfirming evidence. Suppose you think that unemployment is usually caused by laziness. You would be psychologically primed to see evidence that confirms this theory and psychologically resist the relevance of disconfirming evidence.

All humans are subject to confirmation bias. What can you do about it? Well, forewarned is forearmed. If you know about confirmation bias, you can try to resist it by actively looking for disconfirming evidence. Those who don't know about confirmation bias are more likely to fall into its trap.

The Scientific Method   **329**

At this point you reach the first loop in the scientific method. This new theory is now your current tentative theory, and it must be tested just as your first tentative theory was. You return to Step 3. You'll repeat this process until you come up with a theory whose inferred correlations turn out to be true.

Step 5: Check for Reverse Causation, Third-Party Causation, and Coincidental Correlation

Step 5 might be called "Avoiding the Hasty Cause Fallacy." As noted above, the Hasty Cause Fallacy occurs when someone makes an argument with the following form:

(1) E1 is correlated with E2.
Therefore,
(5) E1 is a cause of E2.

To avoid the Fallacy of Hasty Cause, you must check for reverse causation, third-party causation, and coincidental causation. If you find one of these problems, you must return to Step 4 and formulate a new theory. Here's the second loop in the scientific method.

Suppose that the correlations predicted by your theory that your friend's files are corrupted are present. You infer that if the problem is your friend's files, then other files sent by your friend should also cause the malfunction. You check and they do. It would then be time for you to check for reverse causation, third-party causation, and coincidental causation.

Step 6: Develop New Questions

You might think that if a theory made it past Step 5, you'd be done. In many cases, you would be. If you just want your computer malfunctions fixed you may not want to know more. But you may want to know more. The theory that your friend's files are corrupted raises new questions. Why were they corrupted? How can you keep your files from being corrupted again? You come to the third and final loop in the scientific method. When these new questions are raised, you'll return to Step 1 and begin the process again. The more you want to know, the more questions you'll raise, and the more work you'll have to do to really understand the problem.

An Example of the Scientific Method

Let's end this chapter by illustrating how the scientific method might be used in the case of Hurricane Katrina. (You should go back and look at the article excerpt on pp. 295-296.)

Step 1. Identify the Question to Be Answered. Precise identification of the question is crucial. The question isn't: Was Katrina a necessary cause of the flooding that occurred when the 17th Street Canal Levee failed? This isn't the question to be asked because everyone agrees that Katrina was a necessary cause. Rather, the researchers are seeking to determine whether there was another necessary cause, a design flaw in the levee. They're seeking to answer the following question: What was the proximate and primary cause of the failure of the 17th Street Canal Levee?

Step 2. Formulate a Tentative Theory. One tentative theory is that the levee failed because water rose higher than the top of the levee. The water then ran down the backs of the levees, washed away their supports, and they failed. Let's call this the high water theory. Fanselau proposes this theory in paragraph 4.

4. "Katrina flat-out overwhelmed the system," he said. "There was a huge wall of water that obliterated entire sections of the floodwall."

Step 3. Check for Correlations. Given this tentative theory, the next step is to infer some correlations from it and see whether those correlations exist. If the high water theory is true, the levees should have failed where they were overtopped and not failed where they weren't overtopped. In paragraph 7, Nicholson claims that this correlation doesn't exist. He claims that the high water theory is disconfirmed.

7. "These levees did not overtop, yet they failed anyway."

Let's assume that Nicholson is correct. In that case, you need to move to Step 4.

Step 4. Formulate a New Theory. Paragraphs 5 and 6 propose a new theory.

5. [However,] in the case of the 17th Street and London Avenue canals, independent investigators believe the floodwalls themselves were the problem. The reason was the naturally soft soil made up of river silts and swampy peat that has been the bane of builders here for two centuries.
6. Investigators now believe the walls collapsed when the soils beneath them became saturated and began to shift under the weight of relatively modest surges from the lake. And newly released documents show that the Corps was aware years ago that a particularly unstable layer of soil lay beneath both floodwalls.

On this theory, the levees were built on soft soils and weren't adequately anchored to firm soils underneath. You now have a new tentative theory, the soft soil theory, and you must return to Step 3.

Step 5. Check for Correlations (Again). You now infer some correlations from the soft soil theory. If this theory is true, the levees should have failed when built on soft soil and held when built on firm soil. Paragraph 8 says that this correlation exists.

8. Reports of problems with the soft underlayer began to surface even before the floodwalls were finished. In 1994, the now-defunct Pittman Construction Co., a New Orleans firm involved in levee construction, claimed in court documents that floodwall sections were failing to line up properly because of unstable soils.

The information in paragraph 8 confirms the soft soil theory. Let's assume that all the correlations confirm this theory. The article doesn't mention any disconfirming cases. (Disconfirming cases would be of one of two kinds: cases in which levees built on firm soil failed and cases in which levees built on soft soil didn't fail.) In that case, you move to Step 5.

Step 6. Check for Reverse Causation, Third-Party Causation, and Coincidental Correlation. Reverse causation can be easily ruled out. The levees were built and soft soil was present long before Katrina arrived. You can rule out the possibility that the flooding caused the soft soil. But third-party causation and coincidental correlation are much harder to rule out. The article you're reading was written only eight weeks after the hurricane. At that time, researchers were only beginning to study the levees. Grieshaber's comment in paragraph 9 is accurate.

>   9. Corps officials are not yet convinced. "It is important not to jump to conclusions," said John Grieshaber, chief of the engineering division in the Corps' New Orleans district office. "It's hard to look at the aftereffects and say with a high level of certainty, 'This is what happened.'"

It's unlikely that enough research could be done in the eight weeks after a hurricane to rule out third-party causation and coincidental correlation. But let's pretend that over the next year or two the soft soil theory was confirmed over and over again. When (and only when) that happened, it would be time to move to Step 6.

Step 7. Develop New Questions. The article above indicates that some people have already started thinking about Step 6. They've already started thinking about the new questions that would arise if the soft soil theory is well confirmed. One obvious question is: How can the levees be built to counter the effects of soft soil? Here's a possible answer from paragraph 10.

>   10. A proposal for rebuilding the floodwalls has set far tougher standards than existed 15 years ago. And the steel pilings, which formerly reached a depth of 20 feet, must now be driven through the peat layer to 40 feet, twice as deep as before.

If the scientific method is followed properly and the researchers are good critical thinkers, what's learned from Hurricane Katrina will reduce the amount of damage and death caused by future hurricanes.

EXERCISE 9.6

A. For each of the passages included or referred to below, answer the questions and follow these instructions.

(a) Does it explicitly or implicitly put forth a causal hypothesis?

(b) If so, determine which, if any, of the steps in the scientific method appear to have been considered in formulating the hypothesis.

>   1. The thunder must have caused the rain and lightning, because I definitely heard it first. In fact, I heard the thunder several minutes, it seemed to me, before I felt any rain or saw any lightning, and obviously, the cause comes before the effect.

>   2. There were a couple of break-ins last spring, at the new university dormitory. So this fall, the university decided to hire campus police to walk around the grounds of the dormitory in the evenings. So far, no more break-ins have occurred.

>   3. There was an end-of-term office party one semester at the university. Pizza, snacks, and drinks were served, and everyone appeared to be enjoying themselves. Later that afternoon, however, several members of the staff became violently ill. Luckily they hadn't left work so they knew about each other's illness, and they weren't too sick to speculate. After consultation, they realized that they had all eaten the pepperoni pizza. They made a pact that next term they would eat the mushroom pizza instead.

*4. During an illness, a friend brought Jeri a lovely plant. She kept it in the living room of her apartment and it flourished for several months. However, at some point, it appeared to be lighter than usual, and the leaves looked bedraggled. Jeri's cousin has a green thumb, so Jeri asked her what could be the problem. Jeri's cousin Zhouzhou said it needed transplanting because it had used up all its dirt. She took the plant to her home and moved it into a larger pot with new potting soil. There followed a few days in which the plant looked very bad, and during which time Jeri became depressed, thinking her plant was dying, and that it was a sign that she herself wasn't going to get well. But then, one day, Zhouzhou brought the plant back to Jeri's apartment, and it began to flourish again. Was it that the plant missed its home where the temperatures had been higher or was it simply that it takes a few days to get used to the new potting soil and shock of transplanting?

5. Professor McX was writing out exercises one day when all of a sudden she felt a tightening in her chest. Was it a heart attack coming? Indigestion? While pondering these two possible explanations, the Professor noticed that the people cleaning the building had just spilled some liquid on the rug outside her office. By this time, Professor McX had several other symptoms, including a headache, stomachache, and throat closing. It isn't a heart attack, she thought, as she began to pack up her belongings to get out of the range of the now obviously toxic fumes from the liquid spilled. Upon leaving she noticed that the equipment said "pest control" on it, so she presumed that the spilled material was pesticide, perhaps not 'spilled' at all, but rather purposely applied. The symptoms were severe enough to last the night, causing difficulty sleeping, but they began to wane by the next morning. Professor McX decided not to venture into the hall that day and worked elsewhere on her exercises.

6. (The following is part of a song heard during the childhood of one of the authors of this book.)
There was an old lady who swallowed a fly.
I dunno why she swallowed that fly,
Perhaps she'll die.
There was an old lady who swallowed a cow.
I don't know how she swallowed a cow!
She swallowed the cow to catch the goat...
She swallowed the goat to catch the dog...
She swallowed the dog to catch the cat...
She swallowed the cat to catch the bird...
She swallowed the bird to catch the spider
That wriggled and jiggled and wiggled inside her.
She swallowed the spider to catch the fly.
But I dunno why she swallowed that fly
Perhaps she'll die.
There was an old lady who swallowed a horse—
She's dead, of course.

7. Kamuela's dorm room shares a shower with another room. When he went to shower this morning, he couldn't turn the hot water completely off. The faucet handle appeared to be stripped, as it just turned around and around to no effect. Kamuela called the apartment staff and when the maintenance engineer came, Kamuela was surprised that she fixed the

handle almost instantaneously. Kamuela's theory was that the threads on the faucet were stripped so that the knob couldn't get a grip. If right, that theory would mean having to replace the faucet itself, certainly a job which would take more than an instant. It would probably entail the maintenance engineer going to purchase a new part before installing it. Clearly this didn't happen, so Kamuela inferred he was wrong in his hypothesis.

After the maintenance engineer left, Kamuela went back into his bathroom and looked at the hot water faucet. It worked great, but how had it been fixed so quickly? Upon further closer examination, he noticed that there was a tiny screw in the faucet handle. Aha! So the engineer had merely tightened up that screw which allowed the handle to grip the faucet and turn off the water. A loose screw had been the cause!

*8. Jahai was puzzled. He went to cook dinner for a couple of his friends two weeks ago, and after he'd been working for a few minutes there was some water on the tile floor. At first, he just figured he'd spilled something. But then the next night when he began fixing dinner, he saw that the same thing happened, and he'd just started chopping an onion. There was simply no way he could have spilled something. There's a hot water tank in Jahai's apartment, just next to the stove and across from the sink. Jahai called the apartment manager and said, "I think there's a leak in my hot water tank. I have water that seems to be coming up through the kitchen tile." The apartment manager sent over the maintenance engineer, who took the cover off and inspected the hot water heater. The maintenance engineer found nothing, no obvious leak, so she simply removed a few tiles, remarked that she'd replace them soon, and proceeded to vacuum up the water. Jahai was somewhat dissatisfied, as he was pretty sure there had to be a leak in the hot water heater. Where else could it come from? His apartment was on the second floor, so it wasn't coming in the front door from outside. Oddly enough, for the next week, or more, everything appeared to be ok. No water leaking out while he cooked each night. So even though Jahai was unconvinced that his theory was wrong, he had to admit that vacuuming up the water and repositioning a few tiles appeared to have been sufficient to solve the problem.

However, two nights ago, the water on the floor was back! What could have happened? Jahai intended to call the maintenance engineer again, but was too busy studying yesterday and didn't have time. Today there was a huge rainstorm. Jahai had time to call today, but chose not to do so because he was afraid that if he called today the apartment staff would assume that the recent downpour had caused the situation. He knew this couldn't be the case because it happened the night before the rain, but he felt sure that most people would assume the closely connected events would have to be causally related, so he decided to wait until a few days after the rain has stopped.

9. Look again the conversation between Sherlock Holmes and his friend Dr. Watson found in Exercise 9.5 A 7 above. Show how Holmes uses the scientific method to prove where Watson has been and why he has been there.

10. When sleeping, "the images evoked by the cortical activation often incorporate memories of episodes that have occurred recently or of things that a person has been thinking about lately. Presumably, the circuits responsible for these memories are more excitable because they have recently been active. Hobson and Pace-Schott (2002) suggest that both slow-wave sleep and REM sleep work together. Memories that are consolidated during slow-wave sleep are reactivated during REM sleep and consolidated with other memories. The activation of this brain mechanism produces fragmentary images; our brains try to tie these images together and make sense of them by creating

or synthesizing a more or less plausible story. This theory is known as the activation-synthesis theory, because it proposes that activation of the cortex by the pons causes the brain to create a subjective interpretation of what this activity means. When we communicate these interpretations to ourselves, we call them dreams." (Carlson 2006, 288)

*11. Background information: Diseases and illnesses are normally treated clinically by medical personnel focusing on each and every individual who suffers from the condition. Some diseases and illnesses, however, are treated as a public health issue. The main examples are infectious epidemics, where treatment is not focused solely on affected individuals, but rather on practices that will help the entire community, affected and unaffected individuals alike. The polio vaccine of the 1950s is an example: preventative practices were instituted and administered throughout the country. This type of response seems obvious in cases of infectious diseases. But Dr. Frank Vinicor, of the Centers for Disease Control and Prevention, hypothesizes that we should also treat diabetes as a public health problem, even though diabetes is currently treated simply as a clinical disease. See if you can standardize the steps of the scientific method from Vinicor's argument as found in the following passage:

"In the U.S., certain health conditions are readily accepted as 'public-health disorders,' and others continue to be primarily viewed as 'clinical diseases.' Reflecting on infectious conditions, it appears that disease burden, rapid change in disease incidence (suggesting preventability), and public concern about risk are three essential characteristics that define a public-health disorder. By any one of several criteria, diabetes is associated with a very high burden to individuals with the disease, as well as to society in general. Further, there is convincing and increasing evidence that primary, secondary, and tertiary prevention strategies are effective in reducing the disease burden associated with diabetes. Yet most would still consider diabetes primarily to be a clinical disease. In part, this perception is based on the fact that, in association with aging and a possible strong family history, diabetes and its complications may appear inevitable to many. Further, much of the burden associated with diabetes is insidious, coming on gradually only after a considerable number of years. Thus, the burden associated with diabetes has not dramatically increased in the past few months or years; it has been here for some time and is increasing steadily. Finally, our understanding of public concern is only now being systematically investigated. To effectively establish these public-health perspectives, public concern must be incorporated into efforts to define the burden of diabetes and our extant ability to prevent and thereby reduce this burden." (Vinicor 1994, 22)

*12. Ten years after writing the article that argued diabetes should be treated as a public health issue, Drs. Barbara Bowman and Frank Vinicor wrote an editorial that clearly shows the progress made, both in the classification of diabetes as a public health issue and in the greater articulation given to explain that classification. That is, scientists Bowman and Vinicor offer an improved version of Vinicor's original argument, which is, in effect, providing steps four, five, and six of the scientific method. See if you can standardize the steps from the passage below:

"Type 2 diabetes makes a compelling case study for public health action. The disease respects no boundaries. It is increasingly common—occurring in both developed and developing countries, in men and women, at earlier ages than in past decades, and in persons of every race and ethnic group, with a high prevalence in Hispanic/Latino

Americans and in other minority groups, including non-Hispanic blacks, American Indians, Alaska Natives, Asian Americans, and Native Hawaiian and other Pacific Islanders. As noted by Martorell and Saldaña, family history and genetic factors appear to further increase the risk for type 2 diabetes in Hispanic/Latino Americans. In the United States, the prevalence of diabetes was estimated to be 18.2 million people (6.3% of the population) in 2002, with dramatic increases predicted in the future. The determinants of type 2 diabetes are largely understood. Two of the most important risk factors, obesity and physical inactivity, are modifiable. The natural history involves progression from prediabetes, a condition in which blood glucose metabolism is abnormal (although not yet in the diabetes range), to the development of type 2 diabetes. The rate of progression from prediabetes to type 2 diabetes is between 3% and 10% per year. However, progression from prediabetes to diabetes can be prevented or delayed with sustained weight loss and increased physical activity. The magnitude of the change needed for primary prevention of type 2 diabetes is relatively modest: a 7% to 10% weight loss and sustained moderate physical activity, at least 30 minutes per day. Today, the number of adults with prediabetes in the United States is estimated to be at least 41 million. Type 2 diabetes leads to devastating health and economic consequences for individuals, their families, and society. The most serious complications include blindness, kidney disease, lower-limb amputations, and acceleration of coronary heart disease and stroke. After type 2 diabetes is diagnosed, treatment requires an increasingly intensive and complex regimen to control glucose, blood pressure, and lipids, in addition to ongoing preventive care for the eyes, kidneys, and feet. Health care and complications attributed to diabetes are costly: in 2002, the total cost of diabetes was estimated to be $132 billion, $92 billion of which was spent on direct medical costs and $40 billion of which was spent on indirect costs, including disability, work loss, and premature mortality. Clearly, ongoing access to high-quality health care is a paramount concern for preventing complications and death from diabetes. Such care is expensive, and much of the cost of drugs and supplies is not reimbursed, even for those with insurance coverage. While it is improving, the quality of clinical care for people with diabetes still falls short of established guidelines. Because of continued increases in the prevalence of obesity, the outlook for the future is ominous—the health system will likely be overwhelmed by type 2 diabetes. As detailed by Cohen et al in the series of articles from the Border Health Strategic Initiative, the solution to type 2 diabetes control must begin in the community. Extensive dialogue is a first step in engaging communities and identifying the priorities for community action. The papers by Cohen and associates demonstrate how communities and researchers can—and must—collaborate to assess targets for intervention and develop sustainable solutions to control type 2 diabetes. Insights gained from these interventions also can guide the development of effective community-based approaches for primary prevention of type 2 diabetes. Improving the public's health will require rapid translation and dissemination of effective, community-based strategies for diabetes prevention and control and the commitment to sustain and reinforce these interventions. As shown by this promising initiative, collaboration across and within national and state borders and communities will be essential and must involve the entire community: where people live, work, play, and go to school. Improved clinical care alone will not be sufficient. One strategy now being implemented uses the essential public health services as strategic levers to strengthen the public health response to diabetes. Development, implementation, and evaluation of such strategies are needed urgently." (Bowman 2005)

13 & 14. "Two main sociological theories claim to explain global inequality. The first, modernization theory, is a variant of functionalism. According to modernization theory, global inequality results from various dysfunctional characteristics of poor societies themselves. Specifically, modernization theorists say the citizens of poor societies lack sufficient capital to invest in Western-style agriculture and industry. They lack rational, Western-style business techniques of marketing, accounting, sales, and finance. As a result, their productivity and profitability remain low. They lack stable, Western-style governments that could provide a secure framework for investment. Finally, they lack a Western mentality: values that stress the need for savings, investment, innovation, education, high achievement, and self-control in having children. Societies characterized by these dysfunctions are poor.

"Proponents of dependency theory, a variant of conflict theory, have been quick to point out the chief flaw in modernization. For the last 500 years, the most powerful countries in the world deliberately impoverished the less powerful countries. Focusing on internal characteristics blames the victim rather than the perpetrator of the crime. It follows that an adequate theory of global inequality should not focus on the internal characteristics of poor countries themselves. Instead, it ought to follow the principles of conflict theory and focus on patterns of domination and submission—specifically in this case on the relationship between rich and poor countries. That is just what dependency theory does.

"According to dependency theorists, less global inequality existed in 1500 and even in 1750 than today. However, beginning around 1500, the armed forces of the world's most powerful countries subdued and then annexed or colonized most of the rest of the world. Around 1780 the industrial revolution began. It enabled the Western European countries, Russia, Japan, and the United States to amass enormous wealth, which they used to extend their global reach. They forced their colonies to become a source of raw materials, cheap labor, investment opportunities, and markets for the conquering nations. The colonizers thereby prevented industrialization and locked the colonies into poverty." (Brym 2005, 241, material omitted)

15. In 1995, the Centers for Disease Control and Prevention (CDC) created the Well Integrated Screening and Evaluation for Women Across the Nation (WISEWOMAN) program, authorized by Congress in the Breast and Cervical Cancer Mortality Prevention Act of 1990 (Public Law 101-354). WISEWOMAN, as an early detection program, screens for risk factors associated with cardiovascular disease and lifestyle intervention services for women aged 40 to 64 years. In the following passage, CDC public health scientists Melanie Besculides, Heather Zaveri, Rosanne Farris, and Julie Will theorize how to decide which practices are best suited to WISEWOMAN's goal. The scientists call their theory a "mixed-methods" approach, aimed at minimizing the limitations of particular causal arguments (that are informative for only one event) while maximizing the benefit of using different types of particular and general causal arguments, with a goal of discovering what will maximize prevention of certain types of cancer. Based on the excerpt below of their abstract and introduction, see if you can standardize their approach and hypothesis according to the steps of the scientific method.

Introduction: Recommendations on best practices typically are drawn from unique settings; these practices are challenging to implement in programs already in operation.

We describe an evaluation that identifies best practices in implementing lifestyle interventions in the Centers for Disease Control and Prevention's WISEWOMAN program and discuss our lessons learned in using the approach.

Methods: We used a mixed-methods evaluation that integrated quantitative and qualitative inquiry. Five state or tribal WISEWOMAN projects were included in the study. The projects were selected on the basis of availability of quantitative program performance data, which were used to identify two high-performing and one low-performing site within each project. We collected qualitative data through interviews, observation, and focus groups so we could understand the practices and strategies used to select and implement the interventions. Data were analyzed in a multi-step process that included summarization, identification of themes and practices of interest, and application of an algorithm.

Results: Pilot testing data collection methods allowed for critical revisions. Conducting preliminary interviews allowed for more in-depth interviews while on site. Observing the lifestyle intervention being administered was key to understanding the program. Conducting focus groups with participants helped to validate information from other sources and offered a more complete picture of the program.

Conclusion: Using a mixed-methods evaluation minimized the weaknesses inherent in each method and improved the completeness and quality of data collected. A mixed-methods evaluation permits triangulation of data and is a promising strategy for identifying best practices.

Introduction to Report: There is no doubt that public health programs should follow best practices. In the programmatic setting, best practices are the processes that lead to the implementation of the most appropriate intervention for a given location and population. Identifying and applying best practices is complex—largely because recommendations on what works are based typically on experimental or other one-of-a-kind settings. As a result, the practices recommended are not likely to be relevant to most other settings. An alternative is to identify best practices by collecting data from existing programs and to use two or more complementary methods, or a mixed-methods approach, to data collection. A mixed-methods approach can be a combination of one or more qualitative methods or a mix of qualitative and quantitative methods. A mixed-methods approach strengthens evaluation research, because no single method is without weakness or bias. Quantitative data, for example, may be objective, but they often lack the depth needed to elucidate how and why a program works. Qualitative data can enhance understanding of program implementation and operation but are considered less objective. By combining the two, research can be both objective and rich. There are several qualitative methods, each with strengths and weaknesses. For instance, although interviews with program staff can provide a detailed picture of program operations, they cannot objectively provide the range of participants' perspectives. Focus group participants can provide information on program experiences and effects, but this information is not generalizable because focus group members typically do not represent all program participants. Although the cardiovascular screening is undoubtedly important, the lifestyle intervention offered through WISEWOMAN is a key service intended to modify the behaviors associated with increased risk for cardiovascular and other chronic diseases. In fact, the intervention is predicated on the notion that obesity, poor diet, physical inactivity, and tobacco use can be modified to reduce high blood pressure and elevated serum cholesterol levels at relatively low cost and with minimal risk to participants. Theoretically, a reduction in risk factors leads to a decreased incidence of cardiovascular events such as myocardial infarction. The literature on lifestyle interventions suggests that a combination of diet and physical activity is most effective in reducing the risk factors for cardiovascular disease in women. The CDC not only requires all WISEWOMAN programs to offer a lifestyle intervention but also encourages them to use the national guidelines for heart-healthy eating, physical activity, and tobacco cessation in developing their interventions. Beyond this, the CDC does not prescribe the lifestyle intervention, preferring instead to have projects develop or select a culturally appropriate intervention shown by scientific evidence to be effective either in lowering blood pressure or cholesterol levels or in improving diet and physical activity. Lifestyle interventions therefore vary among states and tribes. Although state or tribal programs often dictate which intervention should be used at their local sites, they sometimes allow flexibility in how sites implement the intervention. To distill a set of best practices from these highly variable interventions, Mathematica Policy Research, Inc (MPR) reviewed the literature on lifestyle interventions and collected qualitative data from sites through interviews, observation, and focus groups. The best practices identified will be disseminated to existing and new WISEWOMAN practitioners through a user-friendly toolkit. (Besculides 2006, material omitted)

Chapter Summary

Causal arguments are arguments whose conclusion states that some event or state of affairs caused some other event or state of affairs. The standard form of a causal argument has four premises, each of which usually requires a subargument.

(1) E1 is correlated with E2.
(2) E2 is not the cause of E1.
(3) There is no E3 that is the cause of E1 and E2.
(4) E1 and E2 are not coincidentally related.
Therefore,
(5) E1 is a cause of E2.

Causal arguments can be made for several different types of causes. Necessary causes are required for the effect to occur. Sufficient causes are enough, all by themselves, to bring about the effect. Contributory causes are causes which have an effect on the event but are themselves neither necessary nor sufficient. Causes can be either proximate (meaning they happen close in time to the event) or remote (meaning they occur farther back in time from the event). A primary cause is the necessary, sufficient, or contributory cause that's the most important cause for an audience.

The first premise of a standardized causal argument asserts the existence of a correlation. Correlations can be either binary or scalar. There's a positive binary correlation when E1 and E2 are present simultaneously and absent simultaneously. There's a negative binary correlation when E1 is present in E2's absence, and E2 is present in E1's absence. There's a positive scalar correlation if E1 and E2 increase and/or decrease together. There's a negative scalar correlation if E1 increases as E2 decreases or E2 increases as E1 decreases. Correlations can be established by Mill's Methods. Some causal arguments jump from premise (1), establishing correlation between E1 and E2, to the conclusion that E1 causes E2. Because it omits premises (2), (3), and (4), such an argument fails the proper form test and commits Hasty Cause Fallacy.

The second premise of a standardized causal argument rules out reverse causation. The most common evidence for premise two is that E1 didn't happen later in time than E2. No cause can happen later in time than its effect. Causal arguments that commit the *Post Hoc* Fallacy assert that because E1 occurred before E2, E1 caused E2.

The third premise rules out third-party causation. Establishing premise (3) requires evidence that there's no other event (E3) that's the cause of the two events in question (E1 and E2). It isn't possible to rule out all third-party causes.

But ruling out several events as possible causes will greatly strengthen the argument. The two methods for doing this are to show that there's no correlation and to show that E3 happened later in time.

The fourth premise rules out the possibility that the correlation between E1 and E2 is only a coincidence. The causal link between E1 and E2 must be plausible given background knowledge. If there's a plausible causal link, the correlation must be present a sufficient number of times to rule out coincidence.

The scientific method is a series of steps used by scientists to establish causal theories. After identifying the precise question of interest, a tentative theory is proposed and the consequences of this theory are inferred. At this point, Mill's Methods are used to see if the correlations inferred from the theory exist. If they don't, a new tentative theory is formulated. If they do, you must rule out reverse causation, third-party causation, and coincidental correlation. The final step is to think about questions for further research.

GUIDE

Finding, Standardizing, and Evaluating Causal Arguments

This Guide is an amplification of the "Guide for Finding, Standardizing, and Evaluating Arguments" that is in Chapter Two. The numbered sentences are copies from the Guide in Chapter Two. The paragraphs with "Causal" in front of them are additional materials that apply only to causal arguments.

Finding Arguments

1. Look for an attempt to convince.
   Causal. Look to see if there's an attempt to convince someone that some event or state of affairs is caused by some other event or state of affairs.
2. Find the conclusion.
   Causal. Determine which kind of causal claim the conclusion is making: particular/general cause, necessary cause, sufficient cause, contributory cause, primary cause, remote/proximate cause.

3. Find the premises.
4. Review the following to make sure that you've correctly identified the conclusion and the premises: imperfect indicator words, sentence order, premises and/or conclusion not in declarative form, and unstated premises and/or conclusion.
   Causal. Identify the causes and the effects.
5. Review the following to make sure that you haven't incorrectly identified something as a premise or a conclusion when in fact it isn't part of an argument: assertions, questions, instructions, descriptions, and explanations.

Standardizing Arguments

6. Rewrite the premises and the conclusion as declarative sentences. Make sure that each premise and the conclusion is a grammatically correct declarative sentence. Rewrite the premises and conclusion as necessary to make them clearer but don't change the meaning of the passage. Remove pronouns from the sentences and replace them with the nouns or noun phrases to which they refer. Remove emotionally charged language.
7. Review any phrases you've omitted to be sure that they aren't premises or a conclusion.
8. Number the premises and the conclusion. Put brackets [ ] around the number of an unstated premise or conclusion. Place the premises before their conclusion and insert "Therefore," between the premises and the conclusion. Use blank lines to indicate sub-arguments.
   Causal. Put the standardization in the standard form of a causal argument:
   (1) E1 is correlated with E2.
   (2) E2 is not the cause of E1.
   (3) There is no E3 that is the cause of E1 and E2.
   (4) E1 and E2 are not coincidentally correlated.
   Therefore,
   (5) E1 is a cause of E2.
9. Compare your standardization to the original passage to make sure that you haven't omitted any arguments found in the passage and to be sure that you've correctly identified the premises and the conclusion.

Evaluating Arguments: The True Premises Test

10. Check to see whether the premises are accurate descriptions of the world.
    Causal. Premise (1). Use Mill's Methods to determine whether the events are correlated.
    Causal. Premise (2). Use information about time to check for reverse causation.
    Causal. Premise (3). Check for third-party causation.
    Causal. Premise (4). Check for coincidental correlation.
11. Consider whether the premises are appropriate for the argument's audience.
12. Review the assumed premises to be sure that the assumptions are reasonable. Make sure that all assumed premises are uncontroversially true empirical statements, uncontroversially true definitional statements, or appropriate statements by experts. Make sure the definitions are good ones.

Evaluating Arguments: The Proper Form Test

13. Determine whether the argument is a deductive argument or an inductive argument.

14. Determine whether the premises are relevant to the conclusion. Look at each premise individually to see whether the truth of the premise provides some evidence for the truth of the conclusion. Look at the premises as a group to see whether the truth of all of them provides some evidence for the truth of the conclusion.

Evaluating Arguments: Checking for Fallacies

15. Compare the argument to the list of fallacies on page 410 to see whether the argument commits any of the fallacies.
Causal. Check for the Hasty Cause Fallacy and the *Post Hoc* Fallacy.

10 Moral Arguments

The day may come when the rest of the animal creation may acquire those rights which never could have been [withheld] from them but by the hand of tyranny. The French have already discovered that the blackness of the skin is no reason why a human being should be abandoned without redress to the caprice of a tormentor. It may one day come to be recognized that the number of the legs, the [amount of hair on] the skin, or the [shape of the pelvic bone], are reasons equally insufficient for abandoning a sensitive being to the same fate. What else is it that should trace the insuperable line? Is it the faculty of reason, or perhaps the faculty of discourse? But a full-grown horse or dog is beyond comparison more rational, than an infant of a day, or a week, or even a month, old. But suppose they were otherwise, what would it avail? The question is not, can they reason? nor, can they talk? but, can they suffer?

—Jeremy Bentham, *Introduction to the Principles of Morals and Legislation* (1907, 311, first published in 1781, material omitted and capitalization modernized)

Learning Outcomes

After studying the material in this chapter, you should be able to:

1. Identify moral arguments.
2. Identify consequentialist moral arguments.
3. Identify deontic moral arguments.
4. Identify aretaic moral arguments.
5. Correctly evaluate moral arguments.

The quote on the previous page makes a moral argument that animals should have more legal rights than they currently have. You've probably heard moral arguments about abortion, the invasion of Afghanistan, and taxes. In these cases, the fact that moral arguments are being used is obvious. But moral arguments are often unstated presuppositions. In fact, they are presuppositions of everything you do.

Identifying Moral Arguments

A **moral argument** is an argument whose conclusion asserts that something is morally good or morally bad. Moral arguments don't usually contain the words "good" or "bad." An argument with a conclusion that a person is corrupt is a moral argument because it points to one way that a person can be morally bad. An argument with a conclusion that an action is generous is a moral argument because it points to one way that an action can be good. The many different ways a thing can be good or bad are revealed by the variety of moral words. Here's a list of more than one hundred words of moral praise.

Key Concept
A **moral argument** is an argument whose conclusion asserts that something is morally good or morally bad.

Moral Argument Indicator Words

accepting	contented	fair	humble
altruistic	cooperative	faithful	idealistic
appreciative	courageous	farsighted	imaginative
assertive	courteous	flexible	impartial
autonomous	creative	focused	independent
aware	critical	forgiving	industrious
balanced	cunning	free	innocent
beautiful	curious	friendly	inventive
beneficent	defiant	frugal	joyful
benevolent	dependable	funny	just
brave	detached	generous	kind
caring	determined	gentle	loving
cautious	devoted	good	loyal
charitable	diligent	graceful	merciful
chaste	discerning	grateful	moderate
clean	disciplined	happy	modest
committed	discrete	helpful	moral
compassionate	empathic	honest	nonviolent
confident	enduring	hopeful	nurturing
considerate	enthusiastic	hospitable	obedient

(Continued)

open	reliable	sharing	tolerant
optimistic	respectful	simple	tough
orderly	responsible	sincere	tranquil
patient	restrained	sober	trusting
peaceful	reverent	spiritual	trustworthy
perfect	righteous	spontaneous	truthful
perseverant	self-aware	strong	understanding
pious	self-disciplined	sympathetic	unselfish
prudent	has self-esteem	tactful	well-mannered
pure	self-reliant	temperate	wise
purposeful	sensitive	thankful	witty

Key Concept
Virtues are morally good features of people, and **vices** are morally bad features of people.

Even this list is incomplete. It only includes words that are used to indicate that people are morally good. There are just as many ways to say that someone is morally bad. **Virtues** are morally good features of people, and **vices** are morally bad features of people. In addition to being good or bad, features of people can be morally indifferent. Having a birthmark on the left arm is a morally indifferent feature.

Moral words are also used to say that actions and things are good or bad. Actions that are morally bad are sometimes called "forbidden." Actions that are morally indifferent are sometimes called "permitted." Actions that are morally good are sometimes called "obligatory." "Wrong" is sometimes used to refer to forbidden actions. Hurting people simply for your own amusement is wrong, forbidden. Having chocolate ice cream is permitted. If you have children, raising them well is obligatory.

"Rights" is another moral argument indicator word. To say that someone has a right is either to say that someone is morally obligated to do something for that person ("I have a right that you give me my car keys") or is morally obligated to let that person do something ("I have a right that you let me sit at this lunch counter").

Values: Often Overlooked Presuppositions

As the philosopher Aristotle noted (2009, 5), everything you do relies on moral claims. The fact that you are doing something usually means that you *value* what you're doing. When a baseball player practices hitting a baseball, he indicates that he thinks it's good to hit a baseball well. Scholars rely on moral claims. Remember the argument made by Aletha Huston regarding the effects of the New Hope Project. The New Hope Project gave working parents an income supplement, assistance with child care, and healthcare subsidies. Huston's study compared children in these families to another group of children in families (the control families) whose parents didn't receive these benefits. Huston found that:

> Children in New Hope families performed better than those in control families on academic achievement—particularly reading—as measured by

three independent sources: standardized test scores, parent reports, and teacher reports. (Huston 2005, 915)

She concluded that

The results of this evaluation suggest that the policies tested in New Hope may be beneficial to large parts of the population who have low incomes but are able to work. (Huston 2005, 916)

Huston is relying on the moral claim that academic achievement, particularly reading, is a good thing. The second quote contains the moral argument indicator word "beneficial." The fact that you are in college suggests that you are also relying on the moral claim that academic achievement is valuable.

Huston and the baseball player don't explicitly make the moral claims on which their activities rely. They haven't done anything wrong. It would be annoying if people always said that they value what they are doing. On the other hand, you should be aware of the values presupposed by an activity because those values may be controversial. Here's an old joke: an economist is a person who knows the price of everything and the value of nothing. This joke is unfair to economists (who probably value their children and families as much as anyone else). But it points out that economics assumes that the study of prices is important. Someone who makes this joke is hinting that he thinks that the study of prices isn't as valuable as economists think it is. He hints that we should spend less time studying prices and more time studying other things, perhaps how to paint an amazing painting, how to speak a second language, or how to cure a terrible disease.

EXERCISE 10.1

A. Review the following passages. Determine whether or not they contain a moral argument. Determine whether the passage contains a moral presupposition and, if so, what it is.

1. "Call me Ishmael. Some years ago—never mind how long precisely—having little or no money in my purse, and nothing particular to interest me on shore, I thought I would sail about a little and see the watery part of the world." (Herman Melville, *Moby-Dick*. See the epigraph of Chapter One.)

2. "[The Catholic Church] holds that it is not admissible to ordain women to the priesthood, for very fundamental reasons. These reasons include: the example recorded in the Sacred Scriptures of Christ choosing his Apostles only from among men; the constant practice of the Church, which has imitated Christ in choosing only men; and her living teaching authority which has consistently held that the exclusion of women from the priesthood is in accordance with God's plan for his Church." (Pope Paul VI, "Response to the Letter of His Grace the Most Reverend Dr. F. D. Coggan, Archbishop of Canterbury, concerning the Ordination of Women to the Priesthood." See the epigraph of Chapter Two.)

3. "It is a truth universally acknowledged, that a single man in possession of a good fortune, must be in want of a wife." (Jane Austen, *Pride and Prejudice*. See the epigraph of Chapter Four.)

*4. "'My dear Mr. Bennet,' said his lady to him one day, 'have you heard that Netherfield Park is let at last?'
Mr. Bennet replied that he had not.
'But it is,' returned she; 'for Mrs. Long has just been here, and she told me all about it.'
Mr. Bennet made no answer.
'Do you not want to know who has taken it?' cried his wife impatiently.
'You want to tell me, and I have no objection to hearing it.'
This was invitation enough."
[Hint: This conversation illustrates that Mr. and Mrs. Bennet have different moral presuppositions. What are they?] (Jane Austen, *Pride and Prejudice*. See the epigraph of Chapter Four.)

5. "Nanuwak had a difficult time processing the salmon with the ground-slate knife. Not long into the fish cutting, the blade showed several chips at the cutting surface. At the start she found that the stone knife cut the flesh more easily than the salmon's skin. Eventually she was sawing at the flesh and using 'lots of muscle' to cut it." (Lisa Frink, Brian Hoffman, and Robert Shaw, "Ulu Knife Use in Western Alaska: A Comparative Ethnoarchaeological Study." See the epigraph of Chapter Three.)

6. "I reasoned thus with myself: I am wiser than this man, for neither of us appears to know anything great and good; but he fancies he knows something, although he knows nothing; whereas I, as I do not know anything, so I do not fancy I do. In this trifling particular, then, I appear to be wiser than he, because I do not fancy I know what I do not know." (Socrates, as reported in Plato 1897, 19)

7. "It is believed that the aorta is capable of undergoing passive stretching, since elastic arteries are the large arteries capable of undergoing passive stretching, and the aorta is an elastic artery." (Sandy Fritz, Kathleen Maison Paholsky, and M. James Grosenbach, *Mosby's Basic Science for Soft Tissue and Movement Therapies*. See the epigraph of Chapter Six.)

*8. "Look at the world. It is just one big machine subdivided into an infinite number of smaller machines. All these various machines are adjusted to each other with an accuracy that fills all with wonder. This fitting of means to ends through all of the natural world resembles the machines humans produce. Since the effects resemble each other we are led to infer, by all the rules of analogy, that the causes also resemble each other and that the author of nature is somewhat similar to us, although he has much greater powers proportionate to the greater work he has done. By this argument we can prove the existence of God and that his mind is similar to ours." (David Hume, *Dialogues Concerning Natural Religion*, material omitted and simplified. See the epigraph of Chapter Seven.)

9. "Studies on the relationship between female testosterone measures and behavior, particularly in free-ranging primate populations, remain scant. In this study we used fecal steroid analysis to examine the effects of seasonal, reproductive, and social factors

on female testosterone in a group of free-ranging hybrid baboons in the Awash National Park of Ethiopia. We collected behavioral and hormonal data from 25 adult females across an 11-month period. The results indicated that female dominance rank was positively related to testosterone measures." (Jacinta C. Beehner, Jane E. Phillips-Conroy, and Patricia L. Whitten, "Female Testosterone, Dominance Rank, and Aggression in an Ethiopian Population of Hybrid Baboons." See the epigraph of Chapter Eight.)

10. "NEW ORLEANS — Within a space of 15 hours on Aug. 29, three massive, concrete floodwalls in separate parts of the city suddenly fractured and burst under the weight of surging waters from Hurricane Katrina. The breaches unleashed a wall of water that swept entire buildings from their foundations and transformed what might have been a routine hurricane into the costliest storm in U.S. history.

"Today all three breaches are looking less like acts of God and more like failures of engineering that could have been anticipated and very likely prevented." (Joby Warrick and Michael Grunwald, "Investigators Link Levee Failures to Design." See the epigraph of Chapter Nine.)

11. "As Benazir Bhutto's body was laid to rest, violence and looting broke out across Pakistan, challenging President Pervez Musharraf's control over the nation." (Wonacott 2007, A1)

*12. "What happens where there are [only] two, three, or several firms? How do competitive forces play out when each firm faces only a limited number of rivals? Will prices be cut to (marginal) costs, or will firms compete instead with advertising and other promotional devices?" (Pepall 2005, 4)

13. "It is very important that you take or use this exactly as directed. Do not skip doses or discontinue unless directed by your doctor." (A warning label on some prescription drugs.)

14. "The bell that measures time is ringing. Time here is measured by bells." (Atwood 1986, 8, material omitted)

15. "Anyone who works for an employer receives a paycheck that itemizes not only the money received but also the money deducted for various taxes. One of the big items for most people is FICA, which stands for Federal Insurance Contributions Act. This is the money taken out of your paycheck for the Social Security and Medicare systems, which provide income and medical care for retired and disabled Americans.

"At the time of writing, most Americans paid 7.65 percent of their earnings in FICA. But this is literally only the half of it: employers are required to pay an equal amount.

"In fact, most economists believe that the real effect of the FICA is to reduce wages by the full amount of the combined employee and employer payments.

"The reason economists think that workers, not employers, really pay the FICA is that the supply of labor is much less responsive to the wage rate than is the demand for labor. [S]ince workers are relatively unresponsive to decreases in the wage rate, employers can easily pass the burden of the [FICA] tax on to them through lower wages." (Krugman 2006, 103–104, material omitted)

The Nature of Moral Arguments

Before looking at the evaluation of moral arguments, you need to know two things about them. The first is about the link between morality and truth.

Moral Arguments and Truth

Remember that an argument is an attempt to provide reasons for thinking that some belief is *true*. Every argument is composed of two or more statements. A statement is a sentence that makes a claim that is either true or false.

Connections

Chapter One discusses these definitions of "argument" and "statement."

Most people think that moral judgments are statements. In other words, most people think that moral judgments make claims that can be true or false. Most people think that

(a) Slavery is wrong.

is true and that

(b) You are permitted to run over people whenever you drive your car.

is false. But some people think that there aren't any moral statements because they think that judgments about morality don't make claims that are true or false. If moral judgments aren't true or false, they can't be statements, and if there can't be any moral statements, there can't be any moral arguments. People who think this are noncognitivists. **Noncognitivists** believe that there are no moral statements that are true or false, and therefore there can't be any moral arguments.

Noncognitivists believe that (a) and (b) above aren't statements because neither of them can be true and neither of them can be false.

Noncognitivists don't deny that people talk and write about right and wrong. They deny that what people say and write about right and wrong is true or false. Noncognitivists don't deny that there's moral disagreement. They think that this disagreement is similar to expressing emotions. One form of noncognitivism holds that sentences like (a) and (b) are ways of expressing emotions. On this view, (a) might better be written as

(a1) Slavery. Boo! Hiss!

and (b) might better be written as

(b1) Driving over people with your car. Yeah! Love it!

Neither (a1) nor (b1) is true or false. When someone at a football game yells "Go Bears!" and someone else yells "Go Packers!" they are disagreeing. But the fans aren't making claims that can be true or false. They're just expressing their feelings. On this version of noncognitivism, moral disagreement is a kind of shouting match with each side expressing its emotions. Just as it would make no sense to argue that "Go Bears!" is true, noncognitivists think that it makes no sense to argue about right and wrong. **Cognitivists** believe that there are moral statements that are true or false, and therefore there can be moral arguments.

Key Concept
Noncognitivists believe that there are no moral statements that are true or false, and therefore there can't be any moral arguments.

Key Concept
Cognitivists believe that there are moral statements that are true or false, and therefore there can be moral arguments.

Critical Thinkers

David Brink

Courtesy of David Brink

David Brink (1958–still making moral arguments) is Professor of Philosophy at the University of California, San Diego. He's also an editor of the journal *Legal Theory*. Professor Brink has written several books and many articles on ethics and philosophy of law, but he's most important to you because the moral arguments he made in his book *Moral Realism and the Foundations of Ethics* (New York: Cambridge University Press, 1989) were so good that they are one of the main reasons the authors of this textbook are cognitivists.

Some people think that abortion is immoral, and some people think that it isn't. But the arguments you see in the newspaper about abortion assume that

Abortion is wrong.

is either true or it's false. If the people who were discussing abortion were noncognitivists, the debate would be much less heated. If people felt that they were expressing their emotions about the issue but that there was no correct answer, they'd probably be less concerned about the outcome of the abortion debate.

This introductory textbook won't discuss the arguments for or against noncognitivism. If you're interested in this issue (and we think this issue is fascinating), you should talk to a professor in the philosophy department of your college. He'll be able to direct you to a course where this issue is discussed. Outside of a philosophy class, most people assume that cognitivism is true. This book will also make that assumption.

Moral Arguments, Emotion, and Self-Interest

The second thing you need to know about moral arguments is that they are often bound up with emotion and self-interest. Its emotional force makes language useful and beautiful. You need to be able to tell your family that you love them and to express your anger. But when it comes to choosing what beliefs to hold, emotion is often a distraction. You can be fooled by bad arguments dressed up in emotional language. Standardization removes much of the emotional force and allows you to see whether an argument is providing good reasons or only beautiful words.

Key Concept
Moral arguments are often bound up with emotion and self-interest.

Connections

Chapters One, Three, and Four discuss the fact that standardization removes much of the emotional force of language.

This warning about the danger of emotions is especially relevant when it comes to moral arguments. Most people want to be good people. When you're discussing moral arguments, you're frequently arguing that someone did something wrong or is bad person. The person is likely to react emotionally. When this happens, your critical thinking skills are extremely useful. Try to get beyond emotional reactions to correctly evaluate the arguments presented.

Self-interest and self-deception can also blind people to good arguments. You've seen cases in which you're sure that someone believes something based on bad arguments because those arguments support beliefs that are in that person's self-interest. Because you've seen this in so many other people, you'd be guilty of a poor analogical argument if you thought that you were immune to the effects of self-interest. Because you care about seeing yourself as a good person, you've got self-interested motives to hold on to your moral views. Learning to recognize the presence and influence of emotions and self-interests on composing and evaluating claims is another part of the art of argument.

EXERCISE 10.2

A. In the following passages:
  (a) indicate whether they'd be written by a cognitivist, by a noncognitivist, or by both,
  (b) indicate whether the passage indicates that the writer is too emotional (for someone concerned to think critically).

  1. Take the example of "You shouldn't kill people." All that's going on when someone says this is that they are commanding someone else not to kill people.

  2. We must do this because Durga commands it. (Note: Durga is a Hindu goddess.)

  3. The killing of innocent children is a grave moral wrong.

  *4. Moral obligations are important! You can't just ignore them!

  5. Moral judgments are just piles of junk. I mean, look at how they are used!

  6. Why is religion such a divisive issue?

  7. Is it right or wrong for women to drive? It depends. In societies where most people think that it's okay for women to drive, it's right. In societies where most people think it's wrong for them to drive, it's wrong.

  *8. What? You think that in some places it's okay for women not to be allowed to drive? That's nuts. Only an idiot would deny that women have a universal human right to drive.

  9. It's very important to pay your taxes. If you don't, people will suffer.

  *10. When someone says that taxation is unfair, all they mean is that they don't like taxation.

Evaluating Moral Arguments

For now, let's focus on moral arguments about actions. They have a wide variety of forms, but underlying all of them is one basic form. If the conclusion of a moral argument is about actions, it can be put into this basic form:

Action (1) Action A has feature F.
(2) It is morally good/bad to do actions that have feature F. Therefore,
(3) H should/should not do A.

The variable "A" refers to an action, the variable "H" refers to a human being, and the variable "F" refers to a feature.

Key Concept
The basic form of a moral argument with a conclusion about an action.

Connections

Chapter Two discusses the use of variables.

Premise (1) of the **Action** form asserts that an action has a particular feature, F. Premise (2) asserts that it's morally good or bad for an action to have this feature. The phrase "can be put" in the sentence before the **Action** form is crucial. All moral arguments that draw a conclusion about actions *can be put* into this form even though few of them are actually found in this form in ordinary conversation.

The second premise is often unstated. Here's an example from Chapter One:

As part of their study, Dr. Frederick's research group is considering giving the drug miconazole to a group of children. However, they should not do this because miconazole always has three serious side effects that harm children. It causes vomiting, bloody stools, and severe abdominal cramping.

If you look at the explicit statement of the argument, it appears that it should be standardized like this:

(1) Giving miconazole to children causes vomiting, bloody stools, and severe abdominal cramping.
Therefore,
(3) Dr. Frederick's research group should not give miconazole to children.

But the argument is missing a step. Here's the missing premise:

[2] It is morally bad to do actions that harm children by causing vomiting, bloody stools, and severe abdominal cramping.

Most likely, the author of this argument can rely on the assumption that people shouldn't do things that harm children by causing vomiting, bloody stools, and severe abdominal cramping.

Connections

Chapter One discusses unstated premises.

EXERCISE 10.3

A. Determine which of the following passages contain a moral argument. If the conclusion is about an action, put the argument into the **Action** form. Insert any necessary unstated premises or conclusions.

1. Hang up and drive! (Seen on a bumper sticker.)

2. If you let the ads tell you how to vote, you deserve what you get. (Seen on a bumper sticker.)

3. Because the acid in your beakers is very strong, you must be careful not to spill it.

*4. Because the liquid in your beaker is sulfuric acid, many minerals would dissolve if you dropped them into your beaker.

5. What a jerk! He dinged my car and didn't even stop!

6. Galileo demonstrated that some extra-terrestrial objects do not orbit the Earth by showing that Jupiter has moons.

7. Cut it out! You can't practice the drums at 2 a.m. You'll wake the entire neighborhood!

*8. I don't think that I'd trust her. She told me that she'd help me study but then never came to the study session.

9. I saw you! That was so nice. You didn't have to stop and push that guy in the wheelchair.

10. Murder is the taking of an innocent human life, and that's something we should never do.

11. Laws against homosexual conduct deprive people of control of fundamental decisions in their lives. Fundamental decisions such as these shouldn't be made by the government.

*12. "[A] housing shortage [caused by price controls] is not merely annoying: like any shortage induced by price controls, it can be seriously harmful because it leads to *inefficiency*." (Krugman 2006, 86)

13. "In 1992, the price of Renault Company's Clio RT Hatchback in Britain was $7,519. This was more than 30 percent higher than the $5,750 charged for the car in Belgium. The two cars were identical in most respects, but they differed in one dimension. The one marketed in Britain had its steering wheel on the right-hand side, the proper placement for a country in which cars are driven on the left-hand side of the street." (Pepall 2005, 100, material omitted)

14. "House Speaker Glenn Richardson's much-publicized plan to eliminate most school property taxes could mean higher federal income taxes for some homeowners and higher costs of living for senior citizens, tax experts say.

    "Richardson would do away with most school taxes, the biggest part of a homeowner's annual property tax bill, and replace the lost revenue with a sales tax on more goods and services—everything from groceries and haircuts to auto and appliance repairs.

    "Tax experts point out that Richardson also would be eliminating an important income-tax deduction.

    "'For a homeowner, I would no longer be paying property taxes, but I would no longer be getting a deduction on those taxes,' said Roger Lusby, an Atlanta CPA and partner in Frazier & Deeter.

    "In addition, senior Georgians, who in many counties pay little or no school property taxes because of special exemptions, could end up paying higher taxes overall because they would be paying sales taxes on more goods and services, noted Lt. Gov. Casey Cagle, a critic of the Richardson plan." (Salzer 2007, A1)

15. "[A]ctions are right in proportion as they tend to promote happiness, wrong as they tend to produce the reverse of happiness." (Mill 1906, 9)

Consequentialist Moral Arguments

When is premise (2) of the **Action** form true? In other words, what features of actions make them morally good/bad?

Many people think that the effects of actions make them good or bad. Look again at the premises of the argument about miconazole. Premise (1) is a causal claim. It claims that miconazole *causes* vomiting, bloody stools, and severe abdominal cramping. Premise [2] says that people shouldn't do things that cause a certain effect. In a **consequentialist moral argument** someone argues that some action causes a particular effect (its consequences), that causing this particular effect is wrong, and therefore people should not do the action in question. Here's the **consequentialist** version of the **Action** form:

(1) Action A will produce C.
(2) It is morally good/bad to produce C.
Therefore,
(3) H should/should not do A.

"C" is a variable that refers to consequences. If someone were to ask you why it was wrong to give miconazole to children, a natural response would be to point to the consequences of the drug. According to consequentialist moral arguments, actions that have bad consequences are bad actions and actions that have good consequences are good actions.

Key Concept
The form of a **consequentialist moral argument**.

Technical Term: Consequentialism

In philosophy classes, the word "consequentialism" usually refers to the view that whether an action is right or wrong depends *only* on the consequences of the action. But outside of philosophy classes, consequentialist arguments are often combined with the other kinds of moral arguments.

Many different moral arguments have a consequentialist form. Each of these different versions of consequentialism can be seen as filling in "C" of the basic consequentialist argument form in different ways. The different versions of consequentialism can be classified by how they answer three questions:

1. What sorts of consequences are morally important?
2. Who is morally important?
3. What's the correct amount of the morally important consequences?

Let's look at each of these questions.

What Sorts of Consequences Are Morally Important?

Look at the second premise of the basic consequentialist argument form.

(2) It is morally good/bad to produce C.

You need to fill in C so that premise (2) is true. Actions have all sorts of different kinds of consequences. Which of these consequences are morally important and which are morally irrelevant? Here's a (silly) example of a consequentialist version of the **Action** form:

(1) Action A will produce as much Dr. Pepper as possible.
(2) It is morally good to produce as much Dr. Pepper as possible.
Therefore,
(3) H should do A.

The range of consequences valued by humans is enormous. Think of all the things that people like to do: skiing, hang gliding, sitting quietly, shopping, working in the yard, hanging out with friends, being alone, etc. And different people value different things. It seems hard to figure out what sorts of consequences are morally important. There seem to be too many options and too many different points of view.

To attempt to solve this problem, philosophers distinguish between instrumental and inherent value. Think about flu shots. They're unpleasant. If flu shots are unpleasant, why do you get a flu shot? The obvious answer is that you get one because you don't want to get the flu. Flu shots are something you get because they produce something else that you value. Flu shots are only valuable as means, as an instrument, to getting something else. Flu shots have only instrumental value.

Now think about pleasure. Why do you value pleasure? The question sounds funny. You just seem to value pleasure, period. Most people don't value pleasure as a means to getting something else. Something is **valued instrumentally** when it's valued as a means to getting something else. Something is **valued inherently** when it's valued for its own sake. Most people think that flu shots are instrumentally valuable and that pleasure is inherently valuable.

With notions of instrumental and inherent value, the question "What sorts of consequences are morally important?" can be reformulated as "What sorts of consequences are inherently morally important?" The instrumental/inherent distinction shows that there may be less disagreement about valued consequences. Someone who liked skiing and hated shopping might agree with someone who liked shopping and hated skiing that both of these activities are valued instrumentally and that they are both valued because they produce pleasure. It may be that both the skier and the shopper agree that pleasure has inherent value. At least three different sorts of consequences have been proposed as the kinds of consequences that are inherently morally important.

Pleasure and the Avoidance of Pain. Many people think that one inherently morally important consequence is the production of pleasure and the avoidance of pain. Why do most people like to eat chocolate? At least in part because it's pleasurable. Why do most people prefer that others not kick them? At least in part because it hurts. Lots of different things are pleasurable. The list includes eating, sleeping, reading good books, playing sports, and working in the garden. Lots of different things are painful. The list includes being sick, losing a loved one, being injured, and sitting through a boring lecture.

The Satisfaction of Desires. People sometimes confuse pleasure and the avoidance of pain with the satisfaction of desires. But they aren't the same thing. People sometimes don't feel pleasure when they get what they want. But the satisfaction they get is still valuable to them. In many cases, someone works hard for something but when he finally gets what he has been working for, he has a feeling of satisfaction or perhaps even disappointment. One of the authors of this book worked hard to write a previous book. He pulled all-nighters and gave up movies, dinners, and sporting events. It took him six years and the book finally got published. But he didn't feel any pleasure. He felt a grim but deep satisfaction. Many people think that the satisfaction of desires is inherently morally valuable, even when it doesn't produce pleasure.

People often work hard to satisfy their own desires or the desires of others. You might work hard to help a friend satisfy his desire for a new lawn. You undoubtedly have some desires of your own that you work to satisfy.

Some people think that the inherent value of pleasure is overrated. They think that the notion that pleasure has inherent moral value rests on an over-simplified picture of human psychology. Think about how you feel when you complete a major project and how you feel when you have something good to eat. Many people think that those feelings aren't similar enough to classify them both as pleasure. In addition, they think that, even if pleasure has some inherent value, desire satisfaction does as well, and desire satisfaction has more inherent value than pleasure.

The Development of Talents. Many people think that the development of talents and abilities is an inherently important consequence. Artists work to make themselves better artists. Football players work to make themselves better football players. Accountants work to make themselves better accountants. Many people strive to be a better mother, a better father, or a better friend. Some people think that the development of talents has only instrumental value (as a means to pleasure and/or a desire satisfaction), but others think that it has inherent value.

What sorts of consequences are inherently morally important? It seems that pleasure, desire satisfaction, and talent development are three plausible candidates. It will be useful to have one word to refer to pleasure, desire satisfaction, talent development, or whatever else has inherent moral value. Philosophers have tended to use the word "happiness" for this word. Let's do that too. In light of this, the consequentialist version of the **Action** form can be reformulated like this:

(1) Action A will produce happiness.
(2) It is morally good/bad to produce happiness.
Therefore,
(3) H should/should not do A.

Technical Term: Hedonism

Hedonism is the view that the *only* consequence that is inherently morally important is pleasure and the avoidance of pain. Look again at the quote from Bentham that begins this chapter. Bentham is a hedonist. He thinks that the only inherently morally important consequence is pleasure and the avoidance of pain. This explains why he thinks that the "question is not, can they reason? nor, can they talk? but, can they *suffer*?"

EXERCISE 10.4

A. Write a short essay in which you defend your view about what has inherent value. Your instructor will tell you how long your essay should be.

Who Is Morally Important?

The formulation of the basic consequentialist argument form isn't sufficiently precise because actions have different consequences for different people. If Sara sends a love letter to Edward, this might make Edward happy and make Justin unhappy. Here's a (silly) example of a consequentialist version of the **Action** form:

(1) Action A will produce happiness, but only for people more than six feet tall.
(2) It is morally good to produce happiness, but only for people more than six feet tall.
Therefore,
(3) H should do A.

Key Concept
Universalism holds
that everyone is equally
morally important.

Universalists hold that the answer to the question "Who is morally important?" is "Everyone." **Universalism** holds that everyone is equally morally important. Look at this famous sentence from the U.S. Declaration of Independence:

> We hold these truths to be self-evident, that all men are created equal, that they are endowed by their Creator with certain unalienable Rights, that among these are Life, Liberty, and the pursuit of Happiness.

The claim that "all men are created equal" is usually understood to mean that all men and all women are created equal. If this phrase says that all men and women have equal physical or mental abilities, then it's false. When it comes to basketball, LeBron James is a much better player than either of the authors of this textbook. But the Declaration is claiming that all men and women are equally morally important. Universalistic consequentialists think that the second premise of the basic consequentialist argument form is

(2) It is morally good to produce happiness for everyone in the world (and everyone's happiness is of equal importance).

According to this version of the consequentialist argument, you act rightly when your actions produce the most happiness for everyone in the world. You should consider your own happiness as well as everyone else's. And you should consider everyone's happiness equally. You shouldn't give any greater weight to your own happiness.

As the quote that begins this chapter illustrates, some philosophers think that "everyone" should include every being that can feel pleasure or pain, every being that can "suffer." Hedonists are particularly drawn to this view. If someone thinks that pleasure and pain have inherent value, it's plausible to hold that they have inherent value whether they occur in humans or non-humans. Some see this as a strength of hedonism, but others see it as a weakness.

Egoism

Most people think that universalistic consequentialism is a proper argument form. Most people think that another version of consequentialism, egoism, is an improper argument form. **Egoism** is the view that an action by any person is right when it produces the most pleasure for that person. The egoistic consequentialist version of the **Action** form is

(1) Action A will produce happiness for H.
(2) It is inherently morally good to produce happiness for H (and nothing else is inherently morally good).
Therefore,
(3) H should do A.

Key Concept
Egoism is the view that an action by any person is right when it produces the most pleasure for that person.

According to this argument, you should produce as much of your own happiness as you can, and everyone else should make himself as happy as possible. Someone who is an egoistic consequentialist won't sacrifice his own happiness for others. People who are egoists are selfish, and being selfish is usually regarded as a moral flaw. Most people think that the second premise in the argument above is false.

Technical Term: Restricted Egoism

Some business management theories discuss a technical version of egoism. In restricted egoism, the "ego" doesn't refer to a person. It refers to the corporation or to the corporation's owners collectively (its stockholders). The restriction on this form of egoism is that the corporations' actions must not violate any law or ethical custom in the country in which it does business.

What's the Correct Amount of the Morally Important Consequences?

How much happiness should a person seek to produce? One answer that springs to mind is: as much as possible. Consequentialists who think that you should produce as much happiness as possible are maximizing consequentialists. Nonmaximizing consequentialists can hold many different views. A nonmaximizing consequentialist might hold that an action is good if it contributes to everyone's having an equal amount of happiness. According to this view, you should perform actions that contribute to distributing happiness equally, even if that would decrease the total happiness in the world. Other versions of nonmaximizing consequentialism hold that happiness should be distributed according to merit or according to need.

Maximizing consequentialism is a common version of consequentialism. To get a more precise understanding of maximization, let's pretend that happiness can be measured with numbers. (This can't really be done. You can tell roughly how happy and unhappy people are, but you can't measure happiness with numbers. The numbers only provide a clearer understanding of what "maximizing" means.) On the chart below, positive numbers indicate happiness, negative numbers indicate unhappiness, and zero indicates indifference. Suppose that six actions are possible in a certain situation and that four (and only four) people (including yourself) are affected by your actions.

Actions	People				Total
	H1 (You)	H2	H3	H4	
A1	-2	-2	-3	-6	-13
A2	12	10	10	-40	-8
A3	2	2	2	2	8
A4	10	-10	4	4	8
A5	5	5	5	5	20
A6	5	20	-10	10	25

On this chart, each of the six actions you can do is represented by a row (A1–A6). Each of four people affected by your choice of action is represented by a column (H1–H4). From your personal perspective, Action 2 is the best. It produces the most happiness for you (12). The action that maximizes happiness is Action 6. It produces a total of 25 units of happiness, more than the total of any other action. If the only options open to you decrease happiness, how do you maximize happiness? Suppose that you had to choose between Action 1 and Action 2. In that case, you maximize by choosing the action that produces the least unhappiness, Action 2. If the only actions open to you produce the same amount of happiness, how do you maximize happiness? Suppose that you had to choose between Action 3 and Action 4. In this case, maximizing consequentialism says that you may pick either action. Between Action 3 and Action 4, you might pick Action 4 because it produces more happiness for you.

<aside>
Key Concept
The **universalistic maximizing consequentialist** version of the **Action** form.
</aside>

Here's the **universalistic maximizing consequentialist** version of the **Action** form:

(1) Action A will maximize happiness for everyone in the world.
(2) It is morally good to maximize happiness for everyone in the world. Therefore,
(3) H should do A.

Many people think that this is a proper argument form.

EXERCISE 10.5

A. Consequentialist views vary in three different ways. These correspond to the three questions noted on p. 353. Looking at those questions and the material above, develop five different consequentialist moral theories. Be sure to specify how each of your five theories answers each of the three questions.

B. Write an essay in which you argue that one of your five consequentialist moral theories is better than the other four. Your instructor will tell you how long your essay should be.

Critical Thinkers

Jeremy Bentham

UCL Art Collections, University College London, UK/ The Bridgeman Art Library

Jeremy Bentham (1748–1832), a British economist and social reformer, is best known as the first advocate of utilitarianism. Utilitarianism is a consequentialist theory, or more specifically, it's hedonist, universalistic, maximizing consequentialism. Bentham believed education should be available to all regardless of wealth, race, political beliefs, or religious affiliation. In his day, this was a radical view. Bentham was a prolific writer on many subjects including individual freedom, equal rights, separation of church and state, the abolition of slavery, and the end of the death penalty.

Deontic Moral Arguments

Most people think that, in addition to consequentialist forms, there are proper deontic argument forms. **Deontic** moral arguments include a premise that says that an action has a certain intrinsic feature. ("Deontic" is pronounced "dee-on-tick.")

What are intrinsic features? Think about mowing your lawn. Like every action, this one has consequences. Your grass is shorter. You've burned some calories. Here are some intrinsic features of mowing the lawn. It's an action of mowing. If your lawn mower is red, it's an action that's done with a red object. If you live in Missouri, it's an action done in Missouri. The **intrinsic features** of an action are all its features except its consequences.

Suppose Jacob tells Elisa that he'll meet her for lunch, but he isn't going to meet her. He just wants to get rid of her. One consequence of his lie is likely to be that Elisa goes to the restaurant where Jacob promised they'd have lunch. When Jacob doesn't show up, Elisa is likely to be hurt. But not all lies have bad consequences. Perhaps Elisa's car breaks down and she never makes it to the restaurant. In that case, Jacob's lie had no bad consequences. But whether Elisa is hurt or not, a lie is a lie. All lies have the intrinsic feature of being lies. Many people think that Jacob's lie was wrong even if it had no bad consequences. They endorse an argument with this form:

(1) H1's telling H2 that he would meet her for lunch (Action A) had the feature of being a lie (F).
(2) It is morally bad to do actions that have the feature of being a lie (F). Therefore,
(3) H1 should not have told H2 that he would meet her for lunch.

In general, deontic versions of the **Action** form look like this:

(1) Action A has intrinsic feature F.
(2) It is morally good/bad to do actions with intrinsic feature F. Therefore,
(3) H should/should not do A.

> **Key Concept**
> Deontic moral arguments include a premise that says that an action has an intrinsic feature.

> **Key Concept**
> The **intrinsic features** of an action are all its features except its consequences.

> **Key Concept**
> The form of a deontic moral argument.

Deontic moral arguments are common. The Ten Commandments from the Bible are making a set of deontic claims (Exodus 20:2–17). Three of the Commandments are

You shall not murder.
You shall not commit adultery.
You shall not steal.

These Commandments don't assert that you should refrain from doing these things because these actions have bad consequences.

Which intrinsic features, if inserted into premise (2) of the basic deontic moral argument, will make the argument a good one? No book could look at all the possibilities. It seems that actions that have features such as being a lie, being a theft of someone else's property, being an example of cheating, and being unfair (to name only a few) are morally wrong. Look back at the list of virtues at the beginning of this chapter. For many of them, you can think of a corresponding intrinsic feature that many people would think makes an act right. To solve this problem, philosophers have attempted to determine whether deontic arguments can be boiled down to one underlying intrinsic feature that accounts for all the others. Let's call such an underlying intrinsic feature a "fundamental intrinsic feature," and let's look at two possible fundamental intrinsic features: universalizability and cooperation.

Universalizability

The philosopher Immanuel Kant proposed a test to determine whether there was a good deontic argument against doing an action.

Do I want everyone at all times to do actions that have the same intrinsic features as the action I'm thinking of doing?

You've probably heard people using Kant's test. Suppose that someone wants to do something and another person thinks it's wrong. When this happens, people sometimes ask: "What if everybody did that?" On Kant's view, to determine whether an action is immoral, you should ask yourself if you'd want everyone to do what you're thinking of doing. An action that passes Kant's test is a **universalizable** action. Kant suggests the following deontic version of the **Action** form:

Key Concept
An action that passes Kant's test is a **universalizable** action.

Key Concept
The Kantian version of the **Action** form.

(1) Action A is not universalizable.
(2) It is morally bad to do actions that are not universalizable.
Therefore,
(3) H should not do A.

Whether an action is universalizable is an intrinsic feature of an action. On Kant's view, universalizability is the fundamental intrinsic feature. (The Golden Rule, do unto others as you would have them do unto you, is a version of Kant's test.)

Could Jacob really believe that he'd want everyone to lie? When you lie, you say something false and hope that someone else will still believe what you say. Why do people usually believe what other people say? Because people usually tell the truth. If everyone started lying, lying wouldn't work.

Immanuel Kant (1724–1804), the 18th-century German philosopher work continues to influence philosophy today. One of his most prominent works is the *Critique of Practical Reason*, a discussion of the foundations of morality that remains a classic statement of deontic moral views.

Lying only works when it's the exception to the rule. (Remember the story of the boy who cried "Wolf!")

Here's the question that Kant thinks Jacob should ask himself as he's thinking about whether to lie to Elisa:

Do I want everyone at all times to tell lies?

Kant thinks that the answer must be "No" because it's impossible for everyone to lie at all times. If everyone were speaking falsehoods all the time, no one would be fooled and the practice of lying wouldn't exist. This means that lying is not universalizable, and so it's wrong.

Technical Term: The Categorical Imperative

Kant called his test "the Categorical Imperative." He offered three versions of it. Here's the one used as the basis for the discussion above.

I ought never to act except in such a way that I could also will that my maxim should become a universal law. (Kant 1997, 15)

Cooperation

A second thing many people view as a fundamental intrinsic feature is cooperation. The value of cooperation is often illustrated with an example about prisoners, the prisoner's dilemma:

> Christina and Bernard rob a bank together. They are both arrested and placed in separate cells. Both of them were arrested in possession of an illegal gun. The prosecutor has plenty of evidence to convict each of them on the illegal gun charge, which carries a sentence of one year. However, the prosecutor doesn't have enough evidence to convict them of bank robbery. The prosecutor goes into each of their cells and offers them the same deal. "If you testify against the other and the other person remains silent, I'll drop the gun charge and let you go free and the other person will go to jail for ten years for bank robbery. If you remain silent and the other person testifies, I'll drop the gun charge and let the other person go free and you'll go to jail for ten years. If you both remain silent, you'll both go to jail for a year. If you both testify, you'll both go to jail for five years.

You can put this situation on a chart

	Column 1 Bernard Does Not Testify	Column 2 Bernard Testifies
Christina Does Not Testify	*Outcome A* Christina serves a year. Bernard serves a year.	*Outcome B* Christina serves ten years. Bernard goes free.
Christina Testifies	*Outcome C* Christina goes free. Bernard serves ten years.	*Outcome D* Christina serves five years. Bernard serves five years.

Let's look at the situation from Christina's perspective. Assume that she's an egoist. What will she do? She doesn't know what Bernard will do. But she knows that Bernard will either keep silent or testify. Let's look at each of these two possibilities.

Suppose that Bernard doesn't testify. That's Column 1 on the chart. In that case, Christina chooses between Outcomes A and C. She'll serve a year if she doesn't testify (Outcome A). She'll go free if she testifies (Outcome C). If Bernard doesn't testify, Christina the egoist will testify because going free is better than spending a year in jail.

Suppose that Bernard testifies. That's Column 2 on the chart. In that case, Christina chooses between outcomes B and D. She'll serve ten years if she doesn't testify (Outcome B). She'll serve five years if she testifies (Outcome D). If Bernard testifies, Christina the egoist will testify because serving five years is better than serving ten years.

No matter which option Bernard picks, Christina will testify. Bernard is in the exact same position that Christina is in. He doesn't know whether she'll testify or not. If she doesn't testify, he'll go free if he testifies or serve a year if he doesn't testify. If she does testify, he'll serve ten years if he doesn't testify and five years if he does testify. No matter what Christina decides, if Bernard is an egoist, he'll testify.

Both Christina and Bernard will go through this reasoning process. They'll both decide to testify. They'll both spend five years in prison. They'll end up with Outcome D. But they'd both be better off with Outcome A than they are with Outcome D. If they cooperated with each other and both refused to testify, they'd both only spend a year in prison instead of five.

Prisoner's dilemmas may seem like odd cases. But prisoner's dilemmas are common. In fact, it seems that society is one large prisoner's dilemma. Think about driving laws.

	Other Person Drives Cooperatively	**Other Person Drives Uncooperatively**
You Drive Cooperatively	*Outcome A* You get where you're going in 20 minutes. Other person gets where she's going in 20 minutes.	*Outcome B* You get where you're going in 45 minutes. Other person gets where she's going in 15 minutes.
You Drive Uncooperatively	*Outcome C* You get where you're going in 15 minutes. Other person gets where she's going in 45 minutes.	*Outcome D* You get where you're going in 30 minutes. Other person gets where she's going in 30 minutes.

You drive cooperatively when you follow the traffic rules. You drive uncooperatively if you don't. If everyone but you follows the rules and there are no cops (Outcome C), you'll be able to drive in all sorts of crazy ways and thus cut down on your driving times. But other people are also thinking: "If everyone but me follows the rules, I'll be able to drive in all sorts of crazy ways and get to where I'm going faster." If everyone were to think this way and drive uncooperatively (Outcome D), everyone would get to their destinations more slowly than if everyone were to drive cooperatively (Outcome A).

You've seen someone driving uncooperatively, driving too fast and changing lanes abruptly without signaling. A person who drives like this is assuming that others will drive cooperatively, that others will stay calmly in their lanes as he swerves between them. If everyone started swerving as he's doing, he could no longer predict where they'd be and he could no longer use swerving to move ahead.

Society makes many rules that you have to follow. Stand in line, don't punch people who annoy you, and pay your taxes. If everyone *but you* was required to follow the rules, you'd be able to go to the front of lines, punch people who annoyed you, and avoid paying your taxes. But if everyone does this, we'd all be worse off. Chaos would rule. Many people think that cooperating is a fundamental intrinsic feature. They think that the following deontic version of the **Action** form is a proper form:

(1) Action A is uncooperative.
(2) It is morally bad to do actions that are not cooperative.
Therefore,
(3) H should not do A.

Key Concept

The cooperation version of the **Action** form.

EXERCISE 10.6

A. Determine which of the following passages contain a moral argument. If the conclusion is about an action, determine whether it's a consequentialist or deontic argument and put it into either the consequentialist or the deontic argument form. In some cases, no argument is present but the passage is a statement of a either a consequentialist or deontic moral view.

1. Watch it! If you touch that, you will burn yourself.

2. Step on a crack and you break your mother's back.

3. Don't lie to me!

*4. If you falsely claimed that the book they sent you was defective and asked for another, that would be theft. You should never steal.

5. Careful with that PDA! I bought it, so you should be careful not to break it!

6. You have committed a crime most foul. I sentence you to fifteen years in prison.

7. Evelyn's car is old and right now it's really dirty. But it never fails to get her where she wants to go.

*8. You shouldn't even think about climbing that boulder. If you fell, you'd really hurt yourself.

9. "As members of the academic community, students are expected to recognize and uphold standards of intellectual and academic integrity. The university assumes as a basic and minimum standard of conduct in academic matters that students be honest and that they submit for credit only the products of their own efforts. Both the ideals of scholarship and the need for fairness require that all dishonest work be rejected as a basis for academic credit." (Georgia State University 2007, 70)

10. "I begin with the assumption that suffering and death from lack of food, shelter, and medical care are bad. My next point is this: if it is in our power to prevent something bad from happening, without thereby sacrificing anything of comparable moral importance, we ought, morally, to do it. People do not feel in any way ashamed or guilty about spending money on new clothes or a new car instead of giving it to famine relief. (Indeed, the alternative does not occur to them.) This way of looking at the matter cannot be justified." (Singer 2007, 529–530, material omitted)

11. "Poland's new government is right to be taking a skeptical second look at the Bush administration's proposal to station 10 interceptor missiles there as part of a European-based missile-defense system. The pragmatic conservatives voted into power in October want to make sure that the project offers real security benefits to Poland that outweigh its potential diplomatic costs." (The *New York Times*, "The Poles Get Cold Feet" 2007, WK7)

*12. "New Year's Eve tends to be the day of the year with the most binge drinking (based on drunken driving fatalities), followed closely by Super Bowl Sunday. Likewise, colleges have come to expect that the most alcohol-filled day of their students' lives is their 21st birthday. So, some words of caution for those who continue to binge and even for those who have stopped: just as the news is not so great for former cigarette smokers, there is equally bad news for recovering binge-drinkers who have achieved a sobriety that has lasted years. The more we have binged—and the younger we have started to binge—the more we experience significant, though often subtle, effects on the brain and cognition." (Steinberg 2007, A31)

13. "After 32 years of ruling Indonesia with an iron fist and a grabbing hand, then-President Suharto [of Indonesia] was forced to step down in 1998. While gone from power, he clearly is not forgotten. A few months ago, an Indonesian court ordered *Time* magazine to pay the former dictator a judgment now valued at about $111 million in a libel case. The verdict, which *Time* is challenging, should not be allowed to stand. [The court's decision is a threat to a free press. We hope the panel that hears *Time*'s appeal will see Suharto's suit for what it really is—the last grasp for vindication by an autocrat with no legitimate case to argue." (The *New York Times*, "Time and the Dictator" 2007, A30, material omitted)

14. "In the course of robbing a Holiday Inn in Dallas, Texas in late 1985, Miller-El and his accomplices bound and gagged two hotel employees, whom Miller-El then shot, killing one and severely injuring the other. During jury selection in Miller-El's trial for capital murder, prosecutors used peremptory strikes against 10 qualified black venire members. Miller-El objected that the strikes were based on race and could not be presumed legitimate, given a history of excluding black members from criminal juries by the Dallas County District Attorney's Office. The trial court received evidence of the practice alleged but found no 'systematic exclusion of blacks as a matter of policy' by that office and therefore no entitlement to relief under *Swain v. Alabama*." (*Miller-el* 2005, 544, material omitted)

15. "The present case does not involve minors. It does not involve persons who might be injured or coerced or who are situated in relationships where consent might not easily be refused. It does not involve public conduct or prostitution. It does not involve whether the government must give formal recognition to any relationship that homosexual persons seek to enter. The case does involve two adults who, with full and mutual consent from each other, engaged in sexual practices common to a homosexual lifestyle. The petitioners are entitled to respect for their private lives. The State cannot demean their existence or control their destiny by making their private sexual conduct a crime. Their right to liberty under the Due Process Clause gives them the full right to engage in their conduct without intervention of the government." (*Lawrence v. Texas* 2003, 558)

Aretaic Moral Arguments

So far, we've focused on moral arguments about actions. But this chapter began with a long list of words that are used to indicate moral praise of people. In English, words used to indicate moral praise of people are virtues, and the opposite of a virtue is a vice. **Aretaic moral arguments** are moral arguments whose conclusion is a statement about the moral evaluation of a person, a statement indicating that someone has a virtue or vice. ("Aretaic" is pronounced "ar-eh-tay-ick.")

Key Concept

Aretaic moral arguments are moral arguments whose conclusion is a statement about the moral evaluation of a person, a statement indicating that someone has a virtue or vice.

Consequentialists and deontologists tend to think that conclusions about virtues are based on premises about the moral status of actions. The basic idea is that a good person is a person who does good actions with a good motive, and good motives are motives that produce good actions. On this view, the evaluation of actions is more fundamental than the evaluation of people. According to these consequentialists and deontologists, the form of an aretaic moral argument is

(1) H has motives that lead to good actions.
Therefore,
(2) H has good motives.
(3) H does good actions.
Therefore,
(4) H is a good person.

Key Concept
The consequentialist/ deontological form of an aretaic moral argument.

Some people, called "**virtue ethicists**," hold that the moral evaluation of people is more fundamental than the moral evaluation of actions. They argue that instead of reasoning from premises about the moral status of actions to a conclusion about the moral status of a person, you should reason from premises about the moral status of people to the moral status of actions. Here's the virtue ethics version of the **Action** form:

(V) (1) Action A is an action that would be done by a person with virtue V.
  (2) It is morally good to do actions that would be done by a person with virtue V.

Therefore,

(3) H should do A.

Key Concept
Virtue ethicists
hold that the moral evaluation of people is more fundamental than the moral evaluation of actions.

Key Concept
The virtue ethics version of the **Action** form.

How do you know when premise (1) of (V) is true? There have been many different proposed answers to this question. Let's look at one.

Following the philosopher Aristotle, some people argue that a virtuous person is a person who's flourishing. But what makes a person flourish? Aristotle thought that humans flourish when they reason well. On this view, a virtuous person is a person who does things by reasoning well. You can't reason well when you're tired or hungry. You can't reason well unless you have an education, some leisure time, and a wide variety of experiences, particularly experiences involving contact with other people. You reason better when your life contains things such as being loved, learning how to do things, and having time in nature. On this view, all these things would be important for the creation of virtuous people. Some people think that the list at the beginning of this chapter is a list of the attributes of people who reason well. If this view is correct, then (V), the virtue ethics version of the **Action** form, should be revised like this:

(1) Action A is an action that would be done by a person who reasons well.
(2) It is morally good to do actions that would be done by a person who reasons well.

Therefore,

(3) H should do A.

Key Concept
The Aristotelian version of the **Action** form.

Moral Conflict

Most people use all three kinds of moral arguments: consequentialist, deontic, and aretaic. Suppose that you're in a history class and that you're studying the Civil War. One day, you might read a newspaper editorial from the 1800s that makes a consequentialist argument for the view that slavery should be preserved. Another day you might read an aretaic argument by a historian who argues that General Ulysses Grant wasn't very intelligent. On yet another day, you might read a deontic argument in defense of the view that the North had a right to go to war against the South. These three conclusions are different but they don't conflict with each other.

But things don't always work out so nicely. Sometimes there seem to be good moral arguments on both sides of an issue. This happens with other types of arguments as well. You could have two causal arguments that appear to be equally good. It can be hard to tell which of two proposed analogical arguments with contradictory conclusions is better. But many people find it particularly troubling when two moral arguments have contradictory conclusions. If you're arguing about non-moral matters, you can sometimes set the issue aside for a while. But moral arguments are often about action, and you're often forced to act. Think about the moral arguments for and against affirmative action. One reason that these debates are so sharp is that the issue can't be set aside. When people apply for a job or admission to a university, the company or school has to make a choice between using and not using affirmative action.

Moral conflict occurs when there seem to be good arguments for the view that X is morally good *and* for the view that X is morally bad. Moral conflict takes different forms. In some cases, moral arguments of the same type conflict with each other. Two consequentialist arguments might conflict because people hold different views about what has inherent value or different views about the consequences of an action. Two deontic arguments might conflict because people hold different views about intrinsic features. Perhaps the most difficult sorts of moral conflict are cases in which different sorts of moral arguments conflict. Let's illustrate this with a famous example, the case of the southern sheriff.

In a southern town in the United States during the 1940s, a white woman claims that she was raped. The sheriff can't find any evidence that would allow him to determine whether her claim is correct or, if it's correct, who attacked the woman. The white people in the town are threatening to go on a rampage through the black part of town, destroying homes and killing many black people. From past experience, the sheriff knows that they'll carry out this threat and that the only way he can prevent this rampage is to arrest, convict, and hang a black man. He knows that the people in this town are so racist that they'll convict and hang any black man that he arrests. The unhappiness that the rampage will cause is greater than the unhappiness that would be caused by killing one black man. Many innocent black people will die if a rampage takes place but only one will die if the sheriff frames an innocent black man.

Key Concept

Moral conflict occurs when there seems to be good arguments for the view that X is morally good *and* for the view that X is morally bad.

The sheriff faces a conflict between consequentialist and deontic arguments. He must either frame an innocent black man or do nothing and allow many innocent black people to die. On the one hand, there seems to be a strong universalistic maximizing consequentialist argument for the view that he should frame an innocent black man. Because the racial atmosphere in this town is so poisonous, at least one black person will die. It seems plausible that it would be better for one black person to die than for many black people to die. On the other hand, convicting an innocent person seems to be the kind of intrinsic feature that makes for a proper deontic moral argument. An action that has the intrinsic feature of being an act of convicting an innocent person of a serious crime seems wrong.

Cases of moral conflict can be matters of life and death. On a personal level, they can be gut-wrenching. When faced with such cases, people can (and should) agonize over their decisions. The philosopher John Rawls has offered a description of how people should try to resolve cases of moral conflict. This view of moral conflict is called "**reflective equilibrium**."

Key Concept
The method of reflective equilibrium.

Reflective equilibrium begins with considered moral judgments. Your considered moral judgments are moral judgments that you make under circumstances that make for good critical thinking. They are moral judgments that you've made when you're well rested, not angry, and not distracted by emotions. They're also judgments that you've made after you have a good understanding of the matter at hand. You know the meaning of all the words used in the judgment, and you've checked for errors in language and definition. You've checked the empirical claims. You've made sure that no fallacies are present.

Some moral judgments are about particular cases, and others are about principles. When you read the southern sheriff case, you probably made a judgment about what you thought the sheriff should do. That judgment is an example of a moral judgment about a particular case. When you read about the universalistic maximizing consequentialist argument form, you probably made a judgment about this form of moral argument. You made a judgment about a moral principle. Some moral judgments are controversial and others are less controversial. Think about the moral principle that racism is wrong. Most people think that this principle isn't controversial (at least not today). Think about the moral judgment that it's wrong to segregate swimming pools based on race. This judgment about a particular case isn't controversial. But many moral judgments are controversial. Think about the judgment that it's wrong to give financial aid to college students on the basis of race. Many moral principles are also controversial. Some think that it's always important to tell the truth. Others think that it's important not to tell the truth in some cases.

The method of reflective equilibrium says that when faced with a case of moral conflict, you should first set it aside for a moment. The method suggests that you focus first not on the conflict but rather on your uncontroversial moral judgments, both about cases and about principles. You should see what they imply about the controversial case. Their implications about the controversial case may be plausible. If so, this may help you see the resolution of the moral conflict. But the implications of your uncontroversial moral judgments about controversial cases may be implausible. In that case you have a reason to look back at those uncontroversial moral judgments and see whether they are really uncontroversial. If they have implausible implications, one or more of them may be flawed. In this way, you work back and forth between uncontroversial judgments about cases and principles to views about controversial cases. Your goal in this process is to get all your judgments into equilibrium. When your views are in reflective equilibrium, none of your considered moral judgments conflict with any of your other considered moral judgments. No one is actually in reflective equilibrium. Everyone is always considering new cases and thinking about new views.

You see reflective equilibrium at work in many cases of moral conflict. When people argue about abortion, one side often tries to show the other that their views aren't in reflective equilibrium. Those who think that abortion is wrong often argue that the view that abortion is permitted isn't consistent (isn't in reflective equilibrium) with views about the importance of human life. Those who think that abortion is permitted often argue that the view that abortion is wrong isn't in reflective equilibrium with views about the importance of humans making their own decisions about their own lives. As this case illustrates, reflective equilibrium is a difficult process that isn't guaranteed to resolve the conflict. However, many people think that reflective equilibrium is a useful way to make progress.

A Final Thought

As you took the course that assigned this book, you may feel that it was just one hard grind. Work, work, and more work. There's a kernel of truth in that feeling. Becoming a good critical thinker isn't easy. This introduction to critical thinking only pours a foundation. The house remains to be built in future classes and in the rest of your life. The house won't get built unless you work to build it.

But our final thought isn't about work. It's about joy. If you see college as nothing more than a series of assignments to be completed in order to get a piece of paper, you'll find it very hard and not much fun. But we think that critical thinking is fun. An innovative argument is a pleasure to see. The interplay of the human mind with the world has important consequences for our lives, and there's joy in the marvel of the human ability to think, to do more than simply react to the sensations the world throws at us. Our final thought is this: your ability to think critically, to practice the art of argument, will make your life better in material ways, and (perhaps more importantly) your ability to think critically allows you to experience the joys of discovery and understanding.

Chapter Summary

A moral argument is an argument whose conclusion asserts that something is morally good or morally bad. Values are often presuppositions of arguments. You need to be careful to correctly recognize arguments that rely on moral claims but don't explicitly state them. Taking H to refer to human beings, A to actions, and F to features, the following is the standard moral argument form about actions:

Action (1) Action A has feature F.

(2) It is morally good/bad to do actions that have feature F.

Therefore,

(3) H should/should not do A.

Consequentialist moral arguments hold that an action is good or bad because of its consequences, its effects. Actions have many kinds of consequences, but they can be divided into instrumental (values that are means to another value) and inherent (values that are valued for themselves and not as a means to something else). Pleasure, the avoidance of pain, the satisfaction of desires, and the development of talents are the inherent values most often seen in consequentialist moral arguments. In philosophy classes, it's common to refer to these collectively as "happiness." Every consequentialist theory must make a claim about who's morally important. Egoism is a moral theory that says that a person should produce happiness only for himself. Most people think that the egoist version of the **Action** form isn't a proper form. The most common form of consequentialism is universalistic consequentialism, which asserts that everyone's happiness is equally important. Maximizing consequentialists argue that you should do those actions that produce the maximum amount of happiness.

Deontic moral arguments hold that actions are good or bad based on their intrinsic features (not their consequences). Two common views about which intrinsic features are fundamentally important are universalizability and cooperation.

Aretaic moral arguments draw a conclusion about the moral evaluation of a person.

Consequentialists and deontologists tend to think that the evaluation of actions is more fundamental than the evaluation of people, but virtue ethicists think that the moral evaluation of people is more fundamental than the moral evaluation of actions.

Moral conflict occurs when there seem to be good arguments for the view that H should do A and for the view that H shouldn't do A. Moral conflicts involve some of the thorniest problems in life. Reflective equilibrium is one method for beginning to handle them.

GUIDE

Finding, Standardizing, and Evaluating Moral Arguments

This Guide is an amplification of the "Guide for Finding, Standardizing, and Evaluating Arguments" that is in Chapter Two. The numbered sentences are only copies from the Guide in Chapter Two. The paragraphs with "Moral." in front of them are additional materials that apply only to moral arguments.

Finding Arguments

1. Look for an attempt to convince.
   Moral. Look to see whether there's an attempt to convince someone that some person or action is morally good or morally bad.
2. Find the conclusion.
   Moral. Determine which statement makes a moral claim about people or about actions.
3. Find the premises.
4. Review the following to make sure that you have correctly identified the conclusion and the premises: imperfect indicator words, sentence order, premises and/or conclusion not in declarative form, and unstated premises and/or conclusion.
5. Review the following to make sure that you haven't incorrectly identified something as a premise or a conclusion when in fact it isn't part of an argument: assertions, questions, instructions, descriptions, and explanations.

Standardizing Arguments

6. Rewrite the premises and the conclusion as declarative sentences. Make sure that each premise and the conclusion is a grammatically correct declarative sentence. Rewrite the premises and conclusion as necessary to make them clearer, but don't change the meaning of the passage. Remove pronouns from the sentences and replace them with the nouns or noun phrases to which they refer. Remove emotionally charged language.
7. Review any phrases you have omitted to be sure that they aren't premises or a conclusion.
8. Number the premises and the conclusion. Put brackets [ ] around the number of an unstated premise or conclusion. Place the premises before their conclusion and insert "Therefore," between the premises and the conclusion. Use blank lines to indicate sub-arguments.
   Moral. Determine whether the argument is a consequentialist, deontic, or aretaic moral argument.
9. Compare your standardization to the original passage to make sure that you haven't omitted any arguments found in the passage and to be sure that you have correctly identified the premises and the conclusion.

Evaluating Arguments: The True Premises Test

10. Check to see whether the premises are accurate descriptions of the world.
11. Consider whether the premises are appropriate for the argument's audience.
12. Review the assumed premises to be sure that the assumptions are reasonable. Make sure that all assumed premises are uncontroversially true empirical statements, uncontroversially true definitional statements, or appropriate statements by experts. Make sure the definitions are good ones.

Evaluating Arguments: The Proper Form Test

13. Determine whether the argument is a deductive argument or inductive argument.

14. Determine whether the premises are relevant to the conclusion. Look at each premise individually to see whether the truth of the premise provides some evidence for the truth of the conclusion. Look at the premises as a group to see whether the truth of all of them provides some evidence for the truth of the conclusion.

Evaluating Arguments: Checking for Fallacies

15. Compare the argument to the list of fallacies on page 410 to see whether the argument commits any of the fallacies.

Moral Argument Forms

Action (1) Action A has feature F.
(2) It is morally good/bad to do actions that have feature F.
Therefore,
(3) H should/should not do A.

The Consequentialist Version of Action

(1) Action A will produce C.
(2) It is morally good/bad to produce C.
Therefore,
(3) H should/should not do A.

The Universalistic Maximizing Consequentialist Version of Action

(1) Action A will maximize happiness for everyone in the world.
(2) It is morally good to maximize happiness for everyone in the world.
Therefore,
(3) H should do A.

The Deontic Version of Action

(1) Action A has intrinsic feature F.
(2) It is morally good/bad to do actions with intrinsic feature F.
Therefore,
(3) H should/should not do A.

The Virtue Ethics Version of Action

(1) Action A is an action that would be done by a person with virtue V.
(2) It is morally good to do actions that would be done by a person with virtue V.
Therefore,
(3) H should do A.

Answers to Selected Exercises

Chapter One

EXERCISE 1.1 A

4. Statement. This claim can be true or false. It's true.

8. Statement. This claim can be true or false. It's true.

12. Statement. It's true or false depending on the views of the person who says it. Compare it to "Broccoli, uck!" which isn't a statement.

EXERCISE 1.1 C

4. Two. You break it. You bought it.

8. Two. He'll have soup. He'll have salad.

12. Three. I know myself as a creation of God. Everyone else and everything else are also God's creation. I am obliged to remember that everyone else and everything else are also God's creation.

EXERCISE 1.1 D

4. It's a command, not a statement. So it can't be a premise as it stands.

8. This is not a statement, so it can't be a premise.

12. This is a statement, so it could be a premise.

EXERCISE 1.1 E

4. This could be a conclusion. It's a statement.

8. This can't be a conclusion because it isn't a statement. It's a question.

12. This can't be a conclusion because it isn't a statement. It's a command.

EXERCISE 1.2 B

4. There's an argument. The premises are (1) gas prices will rise and (2) the housing market will continue to slump. The conclusion is (3) the United States will surely fall into a recession next year.

8. There's an argument. The premise is (1) I've seen him at Starbucks most days at about this time. The conclusion is (2) he's at Starbucks.

12. There's no argument.

EXERCISE 1.2 C

1.1 D

4. It's a command, not a statement. So it can't be a premise as it stands. If transformed into a declarative sentence, it would be controversial and so is unlikely to be a premise.

8. This is not a statement, so it can't be a premise.

12. This is a statement, so it could be a premise. But it's controversial and so it's unlikely to be a premise.

1.1 E

4. This is likely to be a conclusion. It's a statement and is something about which people might disagree.

8. This can't be a conclusion because it isn't a statement. It's a question.

12. This can't be a conclusion because it isn't a statement. It's a command.

EXERCISE 1.3 A

4. This isn't an argument. There's only one statement, and arguments must have at least two.

8. This is a collection of assertions (statements), but it isn't an argument because none of these statements is an attempt to provide reasons for any other statement.

12. It's possible that this author might be addressing someone who made an argument that everyone has a right to free speech at all times. But within the limited context we have here, this isn't an argument. There are two statements, but the author does not intend either one to support the other.

EXERCISE 1.4 A

4. Unstated conclusion: The U.S. should adopt a single-payer health care system.

8. Unstated premise: The precipitate is either calcium or sodium.

12. Unstated premise: (1) Amphibians can only live in climates warmer than that currently found in Antarctica. The argument also relies on the assumption that if Antarctica were warmer, the rest of the world must have been warmer as well. But this isn't an unstated premise. It's an overlooked assumption.

EXERCISE 1.5 A

Argument 1:
   (1) There's a mean giant at the top of this beanstalk.
   Therefore,
   (2) We shouldn't climb this beanstalk.
Argument 2:
   (1) A book said that there was a mean giant at the top of a beanstalk.
   Therefore,
   (2) There might be a mean giant at the top of this beanstalk.

EXERCISE 1.5 B

4. Command.

8. This is such a bad argument that it's close to not being an argument at all. But one might say it's an argument:

(1) The works of every political thinker presuppose that people are evil.

Therefore,

(2) All genuine political theories presuppose that people are evil.

12. This is a collection of assertions (statements), but it isn't an argument because none of these statements is an attempt to provide reasons for any other statement.

EXERCISE 1.5 C

4. This passage contains one argument and two explanations. The argument looks like this:

(1) The dinosaur's right foot was deformed.

Therefore,

(2) This dinosaur could barely walk.

The first explanation is an explanation of why the right foot was deformed. The explanans is that the foot was broken and healed badly. The explanandum is that the right foot was deformed.

The second explanation is an explanation of why the dinosaur died. The explanans is that the dinosaur could barely walk, and the explanandum is that the dinosaur died. This explanation relies on background knowledge, such as the fact that dinosaurs that could not walk could not get food and that without food, a dinosaur would die.

The key point that shows the presence of an argument is that whether a dinosaur could walk is not something that can be observed. It's controversial. But the deformation of the foot due to a break is something that trained people can observe in fossils. Similarly, there's no disagreement about the fact that the dinosaur is dead, so what is offered is an explanation for this death, not an argument that the dinosaur is dead.

8. There's an explanation. The explanans is that the Cherokees believed they had a sacred duty to avenge the deaths of fallen comrades, and the explanandum is that war parties formed quickly following a death.

12. There's no *explicit* explanation here. It's just a series of assertions. But the author suggests that being Protestant (the explanans) explains being a scientist (the explanandum).

EXERCISE 1.6 A

The arguments are in standard form in the answers above.

EXERCISE 1.6 B

The arguments are in standard form in the answers above.

EXERCISE 1.6 C

4. This is a question, not an argument.

8. This isn't an argument. It's a series of descriptions and assertions. It could also be an explanation for Holle's conviction for murder. In that case, the explanandum is that Holle was convicted of murder. The explanans are: the felony murder law, that Holle lent his car to a friend, that this friend used the car to drive to commit a burglary, and that someone was murdered during the course of the burglary.

12. This is a collection of assertions (statements), but it isn't an argument because none of these statements is an attempt to provide reasons for any other statement.

EXERCISE 1.7 B

Because each of the arguments above has one premise and a conclusion, they all have the same diagram.

Chapter Two

EXERCISE 2.1 A

4. This argument passes the true premises test and fails the proper form test.

8. This argument passes both the true premises test and the proper form test.

12. In this argument, you don't know for sure whether it passes the true premises test because you don't know who "I" is. However, it's unlikely that it passes the true premises test. The argument passes the proper form test.

EXERCISE 2.2 A

4. Likely to know that it's true: people who were schoolteachers from 1997 through 2007.

Not likely to know: people over 80 years old.

8. Likely to know: students taking this class.

Not likely to know: someone who has never had a critical thinking class.

12. Only "they aren't making any more of it" is a statement. "Buy land" is a command.
Likely to know: anyone over 12 years old.
Not likely to know: people under 4 years old.

EXERCISE 2.4 A

4. Other form.

8. Other form.

12. Form C.

EXERCISE 2.5 A

4. This argument is a deductive argument. It passes the proper form test (is valid) because if the premises are true, they will guarantee the truth of the conclusion.

8. This argument is inductive. It's a bad argument because the author has only one observation.

12. This argument is a deductive argument. It passes the proper form test (is valid) because if the premises are true, then the conclusion must be true.

EXERCISE 2.5 B

4. (a) Deductive and passes the proper form test (is valid):
(1) If humans are social animals, then most people prefer to eat in the company of other people.
(2) Humans are social animals.
Therefore,
(3) Most people prefer to eat in the company of other people.
(b) Inductive and passes the proper form test (is strong):
(1) The Gallup survey interviewed 10,000 people who said they preferred to eat in the company of other people.
Therefore,
(2) Most people prefer to eat in the company of other people.

8. (a) Deductive and passes the proper form test (is valid):
(1) If I am a hamster, then my mother is a hamster.
(2) I am a hamster.
Therefore,
(3) My mother is a hamster.
(b) Inductive and passes the proper form test (is strong):
(1) The mothers of all my best friends and neighbors are hamsters.
Therefore,
(2) My mother is a hamster.

EXERCISE 2.5 C

4. (1) Francis had pepperoni and mushrooms on her pizza.
Therefore,
(2) Francis had pepperoni on her pizza.

8. (1) My son started talking when he was two years old.
Therefore,
(2) All children start speaking when they are two years old.

12. (1) The earth is either flat or spherical.
(2) If the earth is flat, it does not project a circular shadow on the moon during a lunar eclipse.
(3) If the earth is round, it projects a circular shadow on the moon during a lunar eclipse.
(4) The earth projects a circular shadow on the moon during a lunar eclipse.
Therefore,
(5) The earth is spherical.

EXERCISE 2.6 A

4. The first statement is relevant to the second.

8. The first statement is relevant to the second.

12. The first statement is relevant to the second.

EXERCISE 2.7 A

4. There's an argument:
   (1) If you walk on the lines in the sidewalk, you'll be eaten by bears.
   (2) Sometime in the next week, someone will walk on the lines in the sidewalk.
   Therefore,
   (3) Sometime in the next week, someone will be eaten by bears.
   The premises are relevant to the conclusion. They are dependent premises.

8. There's an argument:
   (1) Many people think that air pollution is a serious problem.
   (2) Vehicle emissions are a significant cause of air pollution.
   Therefore,
   (3) Most people support laws requiring a reduction in the emissions produced by cars.
   The premises are relevant to the conclusion. They are dependent premises.

12. There are two arguments:
   (1) Segregation in schools that is not a part of the law has detrimental effects on black children.
   (2) Segregation enforced by the law is taken to imply the inferiority of blacks.
   (3) A sense of inferiority reduces children's motivation to learn.
   Therefore,
   (4) The impact of segregation is greater when segregation is enforced by the law.
   Therefore,
   (5) Segregation enforced by the law has the tendency to retard development of black children and deprive them of benefits received in integrated schools.

   In the argument (1)–(4), the premises are relevant to the conclusion. The premises are dependent. In the argument (4)–(5), the premise is relevant to the conclusion and is independent.

EXERCISE 2.7 B

2.6 A

4. This contains an argument. The first statement is relevant to the second. Because there's only one premise, it's independent.

8. The context makes it difficult to determine if the author is attempting to convince, so it seems that this is just two assertions, without an argument.

12. The context makes it difficult to determine if the author is attempting to convince, so it seems that this is just two assertions, without an argument.

EXERCISE 2.9 A

4. Appeal to Novelty.

8. Appeal to Tradition.

12. Appeal to Tradition.

EXERCISE 2.9 B

4. A fallacious appeal to tradition.
(1) For centuries, people have believed that the earth is flat.
Therefore,
(2) The earth is flat.
A fallacious appeal to novelty.
(1) People only recently started to believe that the earth is flat.
Therefore,
(2) The earth is flat.

EXERCISE 2.10 A

4. *Ad Hominem*.

8. No fallacy.

12. No argument and therefore no fallacy.

Chapter Three

EXERCISE 3.1 A

4. Empirical.

8. Empirical.

12. Empirical.

EXERCISE 3.1 B

4. This cannot be assumed.

8. This can be assumed. It's an uncontroversially true empirical statement.

12. This can't be used as a premise in an argument. It's a question, not a statement.

EXERCISE 3.1 C

4. "The potatoes were salty" is a testimonial statement.

8. Not testimonial.

12. "There are invisible winged horses in the dining hall" is testimonial.

EXERCISE 3.2 A

4. Not a definition.

8. Not a definition.

12. Not a definition.

EXERCISE 3.2 B

4. Not a definition.

8. Not a definition.

12. This is a definition. It can be assumed to pass the true premises test as an uncontroversially true definitional statement.

EXERCISE 3.2 D

4. "A star is a heavenly body capable of core fusion" would make a good premise because it's an uncontroversially true definitional statement.

EXERCISE 3.2 F

4. This is a testimonial statement. Dunch is reporting what he read. The statement

> Lixin defends the view that American missionaries, rather than being tools of cultural or other imperialism, were actually engaged in 'cultural exchange,' making a significant contribution to China's modernization in the late Qing period.

can be assumed to pass the true premises test as a plausible statement made by a reliable expert on China (Dunch).

The statement

> American missionaries, rather than being tools of cultural or other imperialism, were actually engaged in 'cultural exchange,' making a significant contribution to China's modernization in the late Qing period.

can't be assumed to pass the true premises test. It's a controversial empirical statement.

EXERCISE 3.3 A

4. The claim that

> Roger Penrose (1989, 1994) has argued that creative mathematicians do not think in a mechanistic way, but that they often have a kind of insight into the Platonic realm.

is made by Brown. It can be assumed to pass the true premises test as a plausible statement made by a reliable individual (Brown).

The claim that

> Creative mathematicians do not think in a mechanistic way, but they have a kind of insight into the Platonic realm.

can't be assumed to pass the true premises test. It's a controversial empirical statement that can't be assumed based only on Penrose's testimony.

The sentences

> [Roger Penrose] has enjoyed some of the most profound mathematical experiences of recent times. If he has nothing more than a mere hunch that he is glimpsing into the Platonic realm, that in itself is something for us all to ponder.

are an argument. Its conclusion is that we should ponder the fact that Penrose says he is glimpsing the Platonic realm. It isn't making any claims by an expert. It's claiming that Penrose's expertise gives us reason to consider his thoughts about math.

8. This is an argument.
(1) Communication can take place directly through the body.
Therefore,
(2) The body can be intentionally used to transmit information.
Statement (1) isn't clear enough to be plausible.

12. The claim that

> Raymond asserted that the number of caravanserais serves as a definitive index of the amount of economic activity in a city and that the urban khan governs the level of wholesale trade in an exclusive fashion, thereby serving as an absolute indicator of the amount of large-scale commercial activity in a given city.

can be assumed to pass the true premises test. There's no reason to think that Um is lying about Raymond's view. However, the claims that

> The number of caravanserais serves as a definitive index of the amount of economic activity in a city.

and that

> The urban khan governs the level of wholesale trade in an exclusive fashion, thereby serving as an absolute indicator of the amount of large-scale commercial activity in a given city.

can't be assumed to pass the true premise test. They are controversial empirical statements.

EXERCISE 3.3 B

4. Because Kelly is a reliable *Wall Street Journal* reporter, the statement that someone *told* her that Mr. Blankfein's income will be $70 million can be assumed as an uncontroversial premise. However, the statement that Mr. Blankfein's income will be $70 million cannot be assumed, because Kelly says that her source for the claim is only one person who is not identified.

8. Berman is a professor of anthropology specializing in the southwestern U.S. The statement may be assumed as an uncontroversial definition by an expert.

12. These statements can't be assumed to pass the true premise test based merely on Henderson-King's expertise. You would need to see the data to evaluate this controversial empirical claim. In addition, this statement cannot be assumed to pass the true premises test because it's vague. It appears to be a causal claim, but "is associated with" is too vague to know what the author is specifically claiming.

EXERCISE 3.4 B

4. The scope of this conclusion isn't sufficiently clear. "Usually" means more than 50% of the time, but how much more isn't clear. The strength of the conclusion seems to be high. The author does not temper the conclusion in any way. It seems that the author is fairly certain of this conclusion.

8. The author implicitly asserts that these claims about flax seed have broad scope, that *all* flax seeds have the properties indicated. Since our background knowledge about seeds indicates that flax seeds probably don't vary that much, this scope is warranted. As for certainty, there are different claims made with different levels of strength.

Alpha linolenic acid is a type of plant-derived omega 3 fatty acid, similar to those found in fish such as salmon.

Stated with high strength.

Benefits of flax seed include lowering total cholesterol and LDL cholesterol (the bad cholesterol) levels.

Stated with high strength.

[F]lax seed may also help lower blood triglyceride and blood pressure.

With the word "may," this is stated with moderate strength.

It may also keep platelets from becoming sticky, therefore reducing the risk of a heart attack.

With the word "may," this is stated with moderate strength.

Aside from alpha linolenic acid, flax seed is rich in lignan.

Stated with high strength.

Lignan is a type of phytoestrogen (antioxidant) and also provides fiber.

Stated with high strength.

Researches reveal that lignan in flax seed shows a lot of promise in fighting disease—including a possible role in cancer prevention, especially breast cancer.

With the phrases "shows a lot of promise" and "a possible role," this is stated with moderate strength.

You should include a moderate amount of flax seed in your diet.

Stated with high strength.

The original passage expresses a command, but the context makes it clear the sentence is meant to be a statement of the conclusion. The strength of this conclusion is not warranted because it's stated with high strength, but many of the premises are stated with only moderate strength. It would be better to conclude with something like: "It may well be beneficial to include a moderate amount of flax seed in your diet."

12. This is a set of claims about one particular house. There's no group, so there's no scope. As for strength, the claim

It's possible that this upper door, rather than the front entrance to the house, acted as the true threshold to the domestic space.

with the phrase "it's possible" is stated with low strength. The rest of the statements are made with high strength.

EXERCISE 3.4 C

4. There are many correct answers. Here's one:
To show that it's certain that global warming is caused by humans, you would need a lot more evidence than you would need if you wanted to show that global warming might be caused by humans.

8. (a) This scope is warranted by the information in the passage. "Some" might mean "more than one," and the study reports that at least two children who had prenatal exposure to fish oil had better hand-eye coordination than those without prenatal exposure to fish oil.

(b) This scope isn't warranted by the information in the passage. In fact, the study reports that "the differences were not statistically significant" until they controlled for several variables.

(c) This scope isn't warranted by the information in the passage. In fact, the study reports that "the differences were not statistically significant" until they controlled for several variables.

(d) This is not correct. See the comments above. There's enough information in the passage to make some judgments about scope.

12. (a) All youth exposed to alcohol advertising drink more than all youth not exposed.

Practically speaking, it's impossible to show that (a) is true. You would have to examine every youth that had ever lived!

Chapter Four

EXERCISE 4.1 A

4. The extension is: every instance of writing. This includes a huge collection of books, papers, magazines, notes, lists, etc. The intension is: any collection of meaningful characters put on paper or an electronic storage medium.

8. The extension has only one thing in it: the theological view that all human beings will eventually be saved.
The intension is: the theological view that all human beings will eventually be saved

12. The extension is: all those instances of courage. This includes a large collection of courageous actions.
The intension is: the mental strength to venture, persevere, and withstand danger or fear.

EXERCISE 4.1 B

4. This passage contains a definition. The extension of "roof" is all roofs, the ones on houses, office buildings, factories, sheds, etc. The intension is: the cover on top of a building.

8. This passage contains a definition. The extension of this use of "professor" is all assistant, associate, and full professors at any institution of higher education. It doesn't include visiting professors, research professors, clinical professors, etc. The intension is: a faculty member of the highest academic rank at an institution of higher education who also has one of the three indicated titles.

12. This passage doesn't contain a definition.

EXERCISE 4.2 A

4. This passage doesn't contain a definition. (Some textbooks would call this an ostensive definition, but this book focuses on definitions that can be put in genus/species format.)

8. This passage doesn't contain a definition.

12. This passage contains a definition. The extension is every instance of matter. This would be a very long list. The intension is stated in the definition itself: "anything that occupies space, displays a property known as *mass*, and possesses inertia." It's in genus/species format. The genus is "thing," and the species is "occupies space, displays a property known as *mass*, and possesses inertia."

EXERCISE 4.3 A

4. This passage contains a definition. It's a technical definition. It's being used for convenience.

8. This passage contains three definitions. The definition of "e-mail spam" is a dictionary definition. The definitions of "UBE" and "ICE" are technical definitions used for convenience.

12. This passage contains a definition. It's a technical definition used for greater precision.

EXERCISE 4.4 A

4. This passage contains a definition. It isn't a good definition because it uses synonyms. The word "concept" is part of the term being defined and part of the definition. In addition, the word "grasp" is metaphorical.

8. This passage contains a definition, but it's probably a joke definition. This isn't a good definition because it's both too narrow and too broad. It's too narrow because many economists know the value of things like their family and friends, and no one knows the price of everything.

12. This passage contains the dictionary definition of "atmosphere." The definition is "a life-giving gaseous envelope," which is too narrow. Some atmospheres aren't life-giving. Some are poisonous.

EXERCISE 4.5 A

4. There's no ambiguity in this passage. The word "yellow" is vague, but since there's very little context here, it's hard to tell if it's inappropriately vague.

8. There's no ambiguity or inappropriate vagueness in this passage.

12. There's no ambiguity or inappropriate vagueness in this passage. It's only a joke.

EXERCISE 4.6 A

4. The term "differently abled" is a euphemism. There're no rhetorical devices.

8. There's no emotionally charged language and no rhetorical devices. "W.C." is an abbreviation for the euphemism "watcr closet," which is an old-fashioned word for a room in which there's a toilet.

12. There's no emotionally charged language although the alliterative use of 'dismal' and 'disturbing' heightens the humor.

Chapter Five

EXERCISE 5.1 A

4. Compound. Inclusive disjunction.

8. This passage contains two simple statements. Neither is a negation or a disjunction. (1) Rem stands for *roentgen equivalent for man*. (2) Rem is a measure of the effect of the radiation when a person absorbs 1 roentgen.

12. This is a compound statement, but it's neither a negation nor a disjunction. The two statements are "I'll wait" and "you make haste." See the answer to Exercise 5.2 number 12 below.

EXERCISE 5.2 A

4. Compound. Conditional.

8. Compound. Conjunction.

12. Compound. Conditional.

EXERCISE 5.2 C

4. This is an argument.
(1) Wood scratches.
Therefore,
(2) Metal is a better material for desks.
Both premise and conclusion are simple statements.

8. This is a compound statement. It's long string of conjunctions.

12. This is an argument.
(1) Policymakers are reliant on the public for reelection.
(2) Organized interests represent citizen interests.
Therefore,
(3) Policymakers that are accountable to the public should be more responsive to civil society organizations.
Both premises and the conclusion are simple statements.

EXERCISE 5.3 A

4. The passage contains an argument. It denies a disjunct. The disjunct does contain a false dichotomy because the person's keys could be somewhere else.

8. The passage contains an argument. It denies a disjunct. This disjunct doesn't contain a false dichotomy because the catalog says you must take one of the two.

12. The passage contains two arguments.
(a) Henry is arguing for choosing freedom over slavery.
(1) We'll be free or we'll be slaves.
[2] We shouldn't be slaves.
Therefore,
[3] We should be free.
Therefore,
(4) We should take up arms against the British.

The first argument in this standardization is a denial of a disjunct. It contains a false dichotomy.

(b) Henry is also arguing that there's no time for ceremony, that rapid action is required.

(1) The question before the house (the Virginia legislature) is a question of freedom or slavery.

(2) If a question is a question of freedom or slavery, it's vitally important (it's of awful moment).

Therefore,

(3) The question before the house is vitally important.

(4) If a question is vitally important, then we should vote quickly (there's no time for ceremony).

Therefore,

(5) We should vote quickly.

This standardization contains two cases of affirming the antecedent.

EXERCISE 5.4 A

4. The passage contains an argument. It's a tri-conditional.

8. The passage contains an argument. It affirms the antecedent.

12. The passage contains an argument. It denies the antecedent.

EXERCISE 5.4 B

In Exercise 5.3 A 4, 8, and 12, there are no examples of affirming the antecedent, denying the antecedent, denying the consequent, affirming the consequent, or the tri-conditional. See the answers to Exercise 5.3 A 4, 8, and 12 above.

Chapter Six

EXERCISE 6.1 A

4. PN. Quantity: particular. Quality: negative. Subject: people who work. Predicate: people covered by health insurance.

8. UA. Quantity: universal. Quality: affirmative. Subject: broadcast media. Predicate: recently developed technologies whose long-term effects are good and ill.

12. PN. Not all Americans have health insurance = Some Americans are not people who have health insurance. Quantity: particular. Quality: negative. Subject: Americans. Predicate: people who have health insurance.

EXERCISE 6.2 A

4. All people who are eligible for Medicare are not people who need their own health insurance.

8. All days that are today are days that have been long.

12. Some people are people who mistakenly believe that there are no universal moral principles.

EXERCISE 6.2 B   Venn for 6.1 A #4

Some people who work are not people covered by health insurance.

People who work   People covered by health insurance

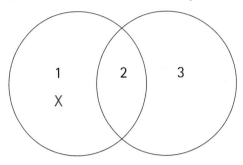

4

EXERCISE 6.2 B   Venn for 6.1 A #8

All broadcast media are recently developed technologies whose long-term effects are good and ill.

Broadcast media

Recently developed technologies whose long-term effects are good or ill.

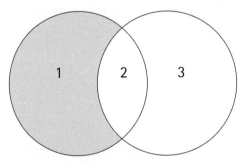

4

EXERCISE 6.2 B   Venn for 6.1 A #12

Some Americans are not people who have health insurance.

Americans   People who have health insurance

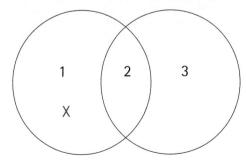

4

EXERCISE 6.2 B   Venn for 6.1 B #4

All people who are eligible for Medicare are not people who need their own health insurance.

People who are eligible
for Medicare

People who need
health insurance

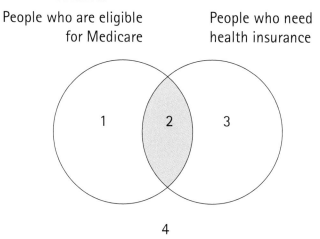

4

EXERCISE 6.2 B   Venn for 6.1 B #8

All days that are today are days that have been long.

Days that are today   Days that have been long

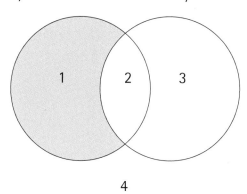

4

EXERCISE 6.2 B   Venn for 6.1 B #12

Some people are people who mistakenly believe that there are no universal moral principles.

People

People who mistakenly believe that there
are no universal moral principles

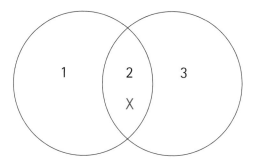

4

EXERCISE 6.3 A

4. Valid. Form 2.

8. Valid. Form 6.

12. Valid. Form 7.

EXERCISE 6.4 A

4. (a) Contradictory of statement 4: Some bones are body parts made of cardiac tissue.
(b) Converse of statement 4: All body parts made of cardiac tissue are not bones.
(c) Complement of the predicate category of statement 4: Non-body-parts-made-of-cardiac-tissue.
(d) Obverse of statement 4: All bones are non-body-parts-made-of-cardiac-tissue.
(e) Complement of the subject category of statement 4: non-bones.
(f) Contrapositive of statement 4: All non-body-parts-made-of-cardiac-tissue are not non-bones.

EXERCISE 6.4 B

(a) Contradictory. Invalid.
(b) Converse: Valid. Form 9.
(c) Complement of the predicate category: No statement was produced.
(d) Obverse: Valid. Form 14.
(e) Complement of the subject category: No statement was produced.
(f) Contrapositive: Invalid.

EXERCISE 6.4 C

4. Invalid.

8. Invalid.

12. Invalid.

EXERCISE 6.5 A

4. It isn't a categorical syllogism. The category "freshman" is used only once. In a categorical syllogism, each category appears exactly twice.

8. It's a categorical syllogism.
(1) All Americans are not wealthy.
(2) All people who are Cindy are Americans.
Therefore,
(3) All people who are Cindy are not wealthy.
A = people who are American
W = people who are wealthy
C = people who are Cindy
(1) All A are not W.
(2) All C are A.
Therefore,
(3) All C are not W.

12. It's a categorical syllogism.
(1) All stakeholders are people within the realm of CEOs' responsibility.
(2) All employees are stakeholders.
Therefore,

(3) All employees are people within the realm of CEOs' responsibility.
E = employees
S = stakeholders
R = people within the CEO's realm of responsibility
(1) All S are R.
(2) All E are S.
Therefore,
(3) All E are R.

EXERCISE 6.5 B

4. The key to understanding this argument is to see that the use of the words "most" and many" are misleading. Typically, you would standardize an argument using "most" or "many" with particular statements, either PA or PN, using the word "some." However, the actual argument in this passage isn't about the many or most people mentioned. The passage is about the kind of disease that diabetes is. The passage gives an argument to account for why many or most people still consider diabetes to be a clinical disease. One way to standardize the argument is:
(1) All cases of diabetes are cases that appear to be inevitable.
(2) All cases that appear to be inevitable are clinical diseases.
Therefore,
(3) All cases of diabetes are clinical diseases.
D = cases of diabetes
I = cases of inevitable disease
C = clinical diseases
(1) All D are I.
(2) All I are C.
Therefore,
(3) All D are C.

8. (1) Some terrorists are people who are willing to kill innocent people.
(2) All people willing to kill innocent people are cold-blooded killers.
Therefore,
(3) All terrorists are cold-blooded killers.
T = terrorists (including suicide bombers)
W = people willing to kill innocent people
C = cold-blooded killers
(1) Some T are W.
(2) All W are C.
Therefore,
(3) All T are C.

11 & 12 Problems 9, 10, 11, and 12 come from the same passage. It's easier to understand 11 and 12 after reading 9 and 10. The entire passage is about two competing explanans for global inequality. The excerpt in Problems 9 and 10 offers the modernization theory. The excerpt in 11 and 12 offers an argument against the modernization theory and presents a counter explanation, the dependency theory.

11. Proponents of the dependency theory are concerned with the explanandum (the global inequality in the world), and their explanans focus on the way in which poor societies became poor. The dependency theorists claim that wealthy societies used their capital, investment, and Western style of government to exploit colonized societies that had much material wealth, such as raw materials, but no capital to invest. This exploitation dominated the colonized societies and eventually made them poor. Based on these explanans, the dependency theorists argue that modernization theory isn't an adequate theory.

(1) All modernization theories that focus on the internal characteristics of the poor societies are theories that blame the victim instead of the perpetrator.

(2) All theories that blame the victim instead of the perpetrator are not adequate theories.

Therefore,

(3) All modernization theories are not adequate theories.

M = modernization theories
B = theories that blame the victim instead of the perpetrator
A = adequate theories

(1) All M are B.
(2) All B are not A.
Therefore,
(3) All M are not A.

12. The dependency theory also argues that an adequate theory to explain global inequality must take into account patterns of domination. Dependency theorists claim that patterns of domination hold between rich and poor societies.

(1) All adequate theories are theories that focus on the characteristics of rich societies that have dominated poor societies since 1500.

(2) All theories that focus on characteristics of rich societies that have dominated poor societies since 1500 are dependency theories.

Therefore,

(3) All adequate theories are dependency theories.

A = adequate theories
F = theories that focus on the characteristics of rich societies that have dominated poor societies since 1500
D = dependency theories

(1) All A are F.
(2) All F are D.
Therefore,
(3) All A are D.

EXERCISE 6.6 A

4. The Equal Negatives Test: Passes. There are no negations in the conclusion and none in the premises.
The Quantity Test: Passes. One premise is a universal and one is a particular.
The Distributed Conclusion Test: Fails. G3 is distributed in the conclusion but not in either premises.
The Distributed Middle Category Test: Passes. G2 is distributed in premise (1)
The argument is invalid.

EXERCISE 6.6 B

6.5 A

4. It isn't a categorical syllogism.
8. Passes all four tests. The argument is valid.
12. Passes all four tests. The argument is valid.

6.5 B

4. Passes all four tests. The argument is valid.
8. Fails the distributed conclusion test because T is distributed in the conclusion but not in either premise. The argument is invalid.

11. The argument passes all four tests. It's valid.

12. The argument passes all four tests. It's valid.

EXERCISE 6.7 A   Venn for 6.6 A #4

4.

(1) All G2 are G1.
(2) Some G2 are G3.
Therefore,
(3) All G3 are G1

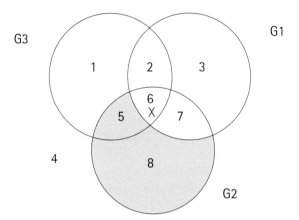

The argument is invalid. To correctly diagram the conclusion, All G3 are G1, Areas 1 and 5 would need to be shaded. But only Area 5 is shaded.

EXERCISE 6.7 B   Venn for 6.5 A #8

4. No Venn because this argument isn't a categorical syllogism.

8. (1) All A are not W.

(2) All C are A.
Therefore,
(3) All C are not W.

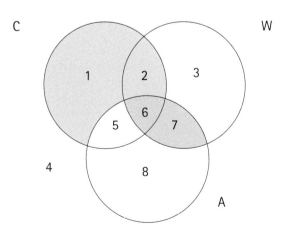

The argument is valid. To correctly diagram the conclusion, All C are not W, Areas 2 and 6 would need to be shaded. And they are shaded.

EXERCISE 6.7 B   Venn for 6.5 A #12

12. (1) All S are R.
    (2) All E are S.
    Therefore,
    (3) All E are R.

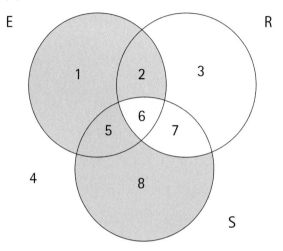

The argument is valid. To correctly diagram the conclusion, All E are R, Areas 1 and 5 would need to be shaded. And they are shaded.

EXERCISE 6.7 B   Venn for 6.5 B #4

4. (1) All D are I.
    (2) All I are C.
    Therefore,
    (3) All D are C.

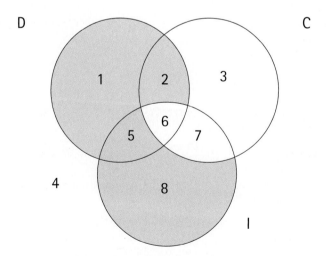

The argument is valid. To correctly diagram the conclusion, All D are C, Areas 1 and 5 would need to be shaded. And they are shaded.

EXERCISE 6.7 B   Venn for 6.5 B #8

8. (1) Some T are W.
  (2) All W are C.
  Therefore,
  (3) All T are C.

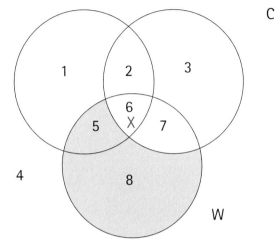

The argument is invalid. To correctly diagram the conclusion, All T are C, Areas 1 and 5 would need to be shaded. But Area 1 isn't shaded.

Chapter Seven

EXERCISE 7.1 A

 4. No analogy

 8. There's an analogy.

EXERCISE 7.1 B

 4. There's an analogy. It's argumentative.

 8. There's no analogy. But there's a statistical argument. See Chapter Eight.

EXERCISE 7.1 C

7.1 A

 4. There's no analogy.

 8. This analogy isn't argumentative, so it can't be put into standard form.

7.1 B

 4. (1) Watches have an end to which they appear to be directed, and they're designed.
  (2) Human bodies also have an end to which they appear to be directed.
  Therefore,
  (3) Human bodies probably are designed.

  Primary subject: human bodies

  Analogue: watches

  Similarities: having an end to which it appears to be directed

  Conclusory feature: being designed

 8. There's no analogy.

EXERCISE 7.2 A

4. (1) If someone is French, she's European.
   (2) George Bush isn't French.
   Therefore,
   (3) George Bush isn't European.
   There're many possible correct answers, including:
   (1) If someone is French, she's European.
   (2) Queen Elizabeth of England isn't French.
   Therefore,
   (3) Queen Elizabeth of England isn't European.
   This is a refutation by logical analogy because both premises are true, but the conclusion is false.

8. Against:
   (1) Adult human beings have the genetic code of the species *homo sapiens*, and
       killing adult human beings should be illegal.
   (2) Human fetuses also have the genetic code of the species *homo sapiens*.
   Therefore,
   (3) Killing human fetuses should be illegal.
   For:
   (1) A woman's decision to have a child is a fundamental part of a woman's freedom, and
       a woman's decision to have a child should be legal.
   (2) A woman's decision not to have a child is also a fundamental part of a woman's freedom.
   Therefore,
   (3) A woman's decision not to have a child, to have an abortion, should be legal.

13. (1) There're places where amphibians live today, and
       these places are much warmer than Antarctica is today.
    (2) Antarctica 245 million years ago is a place where amphibians lived.
    Therefore,
    (3) Antarctica 245 million years ago was much warmer than it's today.

EXERCISE 7.3 A and B

See the standardizations above.

7.1 B

4. This argument passes the true premises test. One reason it passes is that "appear to" in the premises means that (2) doesn't assert that human bodies are directed. It only asserts that they appear to be.

   Whether this argument passes the good form test is controversial. Some think that there're few relevant similarities and many relevant dissimilarities between watches and human bodies, but others disagree. This is a famous argument for the existence of God.

7.2 A

4. The premises pass the true premises test. As the refutation by logical analogy above indicates, this argument fails the proper form test.

13. The argument passes the proper form test fairly well, but you'd need more background information to be sure. If you could rule out the possibility that the Parotosuches fossil might have come from elsewhere, that would strengthen the argument. For example, the fossil might have floated there from further north. It would also be a stronger argument if the authors had listed the similarities between the Parotosuches and today's amphibians.

EXERCISE 7.3 C

4. (a). Standard form
  (1) The institution of lunch counters that don't serve people of color is immoral and
      it would be wrong to participate in that institution.
  (2) The institution of courthouses that won't marry gays and lesbians is also immoral.
  Therefore,
  (3) It would be wrong to participate in that institution.
  Primary subject: courthouses that won't marry gays and lesbians.
  Analogue: lunch counters that don't serve people of color.
  Similarities: being immoral.
  Conclusory feature: being wrong to participate in an institution.
(b). Premise (1) seems to clearly pass the true premises test, but premise (2) is controversial and needs the support of subargument.
(c) and (d). The main issue when it comes to similarities/dissimilarities is whether the fact that many courthouses won't marry gays and lesbians is immoral.

8. (a) Standard form
  (1) When Europeans arrived in the North American, the Native Americans were divided and unprepared, and they suffered greatly.
  (2) If aliens arrived on Earth now, we'd be divided and unprepared.
  Therefore,
  (3) If aliens arrived on Earth now, we'd probably suffer greatly.
  Primary subject: aliens arriving on Earth.
  Analogue: Europeans arriving in North American.
  Similarities: being divided and unprepared.
  Conclusory feature: suffering greatly.
(b) These premises pass the true premises test. They are uncontroversial empirical statements.
(c) and (d). The purported similarities are relevant, but the author overlooks a number of relevant dissimilarities. Even if we assumed that aliens arriving here would act like Europeans, our weapons technology might not be behind that of aliens to the extent that the Native Americans' weapons technology was behind that of Europeans. In addition, another important factor in the suffering of Native Americans was their inability to fight off European diseases. Things might have gone differently if the Native Americans were able to fight off the European diseases but the Europeans weren't able to fight off the diseases of the Native Americans. Similarly, it might be that aliens are unable to fight off human diseases.

There's no reason to suppose that aliens would be like Europeans since, after all, they are aliens. If the aliens arrived with an attitude of cooperation and desire for communication, the presence of the similarities would be irrelevant.

Chapter Eight

EXERCISE 8.1 A

3. This is the mean.

4. This is the midrange.

The mean is $258.7M. See number 3.

You can't calculate a weighted mean with the data provided.

There're two modes, one at $265M and another at $200M.

Because there're ten data points, there's, strictly speaking, no median, but the mean of the fifth and sixth points on the list is $200M.

8. Mean: 5.425%

Median: Because there're ten data points, there's, strictly speaking, no median, but the mean of the second and third place values (5.2% and 4.8%) is 5.0%.

12. From the data provided, it isn't possible to calculate (a) the mean, (b) the weighted mean, (c) mode, (d) the midrange, or (e) the median.

EXERCISE 8.1 B

4. Lowest non-business: 1,193,057

Highest non-business: 1,464,961

Lowest business: 35,992

Highest business: 54,008

6. Mean: 38.09

Weighted mean: From the data provided, it isn't possible to calculate the weighted mean.

Mode: 2

Midrange: 36

Median: 48

7. Sub-Saharan Africa and India. There's a different of 10 between these two and Southeast Asia (between 2 and 12). No other difference is that great.

13. From the data provided, it isn't possible to calculate (a) the mean, (b) the weighted mean, (c) mode, (d) the midrange, or (e) the median.

EXERCISE 8.2B

8.1 A

  8.

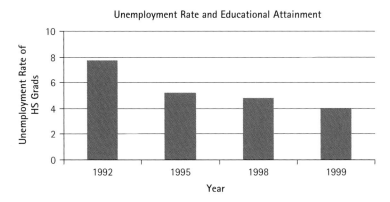

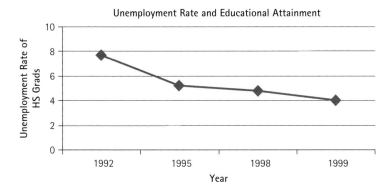

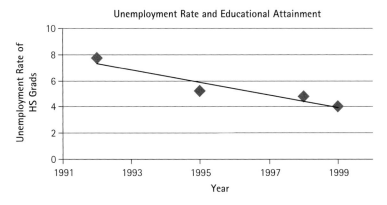

8.1 B

6.

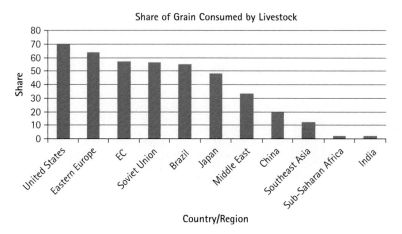

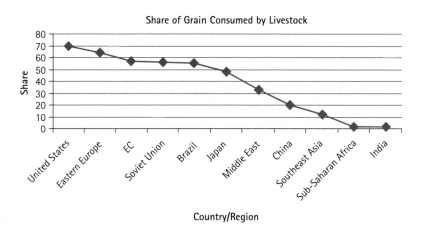

EXERCISE 8.3 A

4. There's a statistical argument. It has a particular conclusion.

Sample: the quizzes previously given.

N: the author doesn't state the N. It's the number of quizzes previously given.

Relevant property: being announced ahead of time.

Target: the next quiz.

Percentage: all, 100%.

(1) 100% of the N quizzes previously given in the class were announced ahead of time.

Therefore,

(2) 100% of the quizzes in the class will be announced ahead of time.

(3) The next quiz is a quiz in the class.

Therefore,

(4) The next quiz will probably be announced ahead of time.

8. This is a statistical argument with the General form.

Sample: mean temperatures from 1955 to 2000 in the United States, Europe, and Antarctica.

N: 3, the three areas where temperatures were observed.

Relevant property: increasing over time.

Target: Temperatures in other parts of the world.

Percentage: 100%.
(1) 100% of the 3 observed areas of the world (US, Europe, Antarctica) have had increasing mean temperatures.
Therefore,
(2) 100% of all areas of the world have had increasing mean temperatures.

12. There's no statistical argument.

EXERCISE 8.4 A

4. Convenience sample.

8. Convenience sample.

12. There's no statistical argument.

EXERCISE 8.4 B

4. True premises test: It's hard to do the true premises test because you don't know who is speaking. But if the person speaking is reliable, the statements made are plausible.

Proper form test: The sample size isn't stated. Is it early in the semester and the professor has given only two quizzes, or is it late in the semester and the professor has given fifteen quizzes? The more quizzes, the more likely that the sample is representative. The sample appears to have good variety because it includes all the quizzes that have been given.

8. True premises test: The source of the information isn't stated. Therefore, the premise can't be assumed to pass the true premise test.

Proper form test: As it stands, this argument is weak. The three areas weren't chosen at random, and our background information indicates that climate varies from one part of the world to another. This argument fails the proper form test.

12. There's no statistical argument.

EXERCISE 8.5 A

4. (1) 75% of college-educated men in these studies achieved some upward mobility.
Therefore,
(2) 75% of all college-educated men will achieve some upward mobility.
(3) College-educated men have features F1, F2, F3, etc. and 75% of college-educated men will achieve some upward mobility.
(4) College-educated women also have features F1, F2, F3, etc.
Therefore,
(4) 75% of all college-educated women will also achieve upward mobility.
Therefore,
(5) Education plays a critical role in social mobility.

The sample is unavailable. The N is unavailable. The relevant property is achieving some upward mobility. The target is all adults. The P% is 75.

This passage has the two step statistical-then-analogical argument (like the Briard puppy case). If you moved immediately from the conclusion of the statistical argument (2) to the conclusion of the author's main argument (5), the passage would commit the Biased Sample Fallacy because the main conclusion isn't limited to men but the only data provided is limited to men. However, the author is drawing an implicit analogy between men and women. The author doesn't list the relevant similarities and dissimilarities between men and women and that is why we've listed the undefined variables F1, F2, F3, etc. Whether the analogical argument passes the proper form test depends on the evaluation of these similarities and dissimilarities. If there're relevant dissimilarities between college-educated men and college educated women, the overall argument fails the proper form test.

8. (1) 100% of the one person observed recalled forgotten memories that seemed to underlie their problems when encouraged to say whatever came to mind.

Therefore,

(2) 100% of all people will recall forgotten memories that seem to underlie their problems when encouraged to say whatever comes to mind.

The sample is one patient. The N is 1. The relevant property is recalled forgotten memories that seemed to underlie their problems when encouraged to say whatever came to mind. The target is all future patients. The P% is 100.

As recounted here, this argument commits the Fallacy of Hasty Generalization and fails the proper form test. It asserts that Freud reached his conclusion from only one case. However, it may well be that the author is using a story to make the passage more lively. It's possible that Freud observed many more cases. The premise can be assumed as an uncontroversial empirical statement by a reliable source.

12. This passage's main conclusion is that Americans read more books in 2007 than they did in the 1950s. To support this conclusion, the author relies on a series of statistical sub-arguments. Sentences (1)–(4) and (7) make statistical arguments. The other numbered sentences are non-statistical premises in support of the main conclusion. None of the statistical arguments appears to commit any fallacy, but it's hard to be sure because the author doesn't provide much information about the data. There isn't enough information provided to put (1)–(4) and (7) into standard form. The premises are all uncontroversial empirical statements, so if there's good reason to think that MacFarquhar is an appropriate expert, these premises may be assumed to pass the true premises test. It's hard to do the proper form test because the author doesn't supply enough information about the surveys. However, if you do research and MacFarquhar turns out to be an appropriate expert, then this would be good reason to think that these statistical arguments have proper form.

Chapter Nine

EXERCISE 9.1 A

4. He's denying that taking the new parkway is a primary cause of getting to the theater. In fact, he thinks that taking the new parkway is a sufficient cause of not getting to the theater on time.

8. *Into the Wild's* being at the Cineplex is a necessary and primary cause of Jack's desire to go there.

12. The use of the word "tendency" suggests that the author sees a positive correlation between the two events being compared (the role of serfdom in the economy and the passage of time in Russia). As time went on, an increasingly large percentage of the economy was dependent on serfs. However, since there's no specific feature about Russia noted, Chamberlain isn't making any clausal claim.

EXERCISE 9.2 A

4. This passage contains a causal argument.
   (1) Stefan's being at his mother's house is correlated with Stefan's texts not getting to Willa.
   [2] Stefan's texts not getting to Willa isn't the cause of Stefan's being at his mother's house.
   [3] There's no third thing that's the cause of Stefan's being at his mother's house and Stefan's texts not getting to Willa.
   [4] Stefan's being at his mother's house and Stefan's texts not getting to Willa aren't coincidentally correlated.
   Therefore,
   (5) Stefan's being at his mother's house is a cause of Stefan's texts not getting to Willa.

8. There's no causal argument in this passage. It makes a series of causal claims about the bad effects of cash-settled contracts, but there're no premises offered in support of these claims.

12. There's no causal argument in this passage. It makes a series of causal claims about the possible effects of global warming, but there're no premises offered in support of these claims. In fact, the passage makes some claims about why causal arguments about global warming can't be made. The main point is that "no one can predict the precise impact of global warming" due to the complexities of the situation. In addition, the author says it would be even more difficult to predict the secondary effects of any potential primary effects of climate changes.

EXERCISE 9.2 B

3. (2) (E2) Economic development in Japan since 1952 didn't cause (E1) the freedom from the burden of supporting a large and costly military establishment.

EXERCISE 9.3 A

4. Binary.

8. Scalar.

12. This passage suggests that friendship and being understood are binary features. It isn't clear that this passage is correct. Friendship and being understood might well be scalar. The degree of friendship might be positively correlated with the degree of being understood.

EXERCISE 9.4 A

4. You wouldn't be able to draw any conclusions. Since Jill never became ill, you'd have a small bit of evidence of a correlation between eating less beans and eating less steak and not getting ill. This is an example of the Method of Scalar Variation. But you'd need to do much more work to check the correlations.

8. No use of Mill's Methods is present. The passage makes the claim that Type 2 diabetes is correlated with developing and developed countries, sex, race, and ethnic group. It also asserts that it's occurring at earlier ages than in the past. In other words, diabetes is positively correlated with virtually all of the categories commonly used to identify public health disorders.

EXERCISE 9.5 A

4. There's a causal claim here. The implied causal argument is here.
    [1] Pouring an acid on litmus paper is correlated with the litmus paper turning red.
    [2] The litmus paper turning red isn't the cause of pouring an acid on litmus paper.
    [3] There's no third thing that's the cause of pouring an acid on litmus paper and the litmus paper turning red.
    [4] Pouring an acid on litmus paper and the litmus paper turning red aren't coincidentally correlated.
    Therefore,
    (5) Pouring an acid on litmus paper is a cause of the litmus paper turning red.

    The sub-arguments:

    Premise (1). To construct a sub-argument for this premise, you'd need to use Mill's Method. The way do to this would be to repeatedly pour (Agreement) and not pour (Difference) acids on litmus paper and see if the paper's turning red is correlated with the pouring of the acid.

    Premise (2). The key point for making a sub-argument in support of this premise is
    (1) The litmus paper turning red came after pouring an acid on litmus paper.
    (2) If the litmus paper turning red came after pouring an acid on litmus paper, then the litmus paper turning red isn't the cause of the pouring an acid on litmus paper.
    Therefore,
    (3) The litmus paper turning red isn't the cause of pouring an acid on litmus paper.

    Premise (3). To make a sub-argument for this premise, you'd need to consider possible third-party causes and then rule each of the out using Mill's Methods.

Premise (4). To make a sub-argument for this premise, you'd need to repeatedly pour an acid on litmus paper to see if the paper repeatedly turned red. If it did, that would be evidence that the correlation isn't a coincidence.

The premises of the implied causal argument can all be assumed to pass the true premise test, as they are all uncontroversial empirical statements.

The implied causal argument can be put into standard form, so it passes the proper form test. It contains no fallacies.

8. There's an argument in this passage, but it isn't a causal argument.
   (1) Emotion is one of the means by which our bodies communicate knowledge to conscious awareness.
   [2] Conscious awareness is included in body intelligence.
   Therefore,
   (3) Emotion must be included in a discussion of body intelligence.

12. There are two possible interpretations of this passage. One interpretation focuses on the particular action, the INS's sending a notice to the Florida flight school. On this view, there's no causal argument. There's only a set of assertions. There's no causal argument because the sending of the notice occurred after the 9/11 attack, so it can't be a cause of the attack.

   The other interpretation takes the passage to be drawing the unstated conclusion that the general incompetence of the INS (as evidenced by the sending of the notice to the flight school) was a cause of the attack.
   (1) The INS' incompetence is correlated with the 9/11 attack.
   [2] The 9/11 attack isn't a cause of the INS' incompetence.
   [3] There's no third thing that's the cause of the INS' incompetence and the 9/11 attack.
   [4] The INS' incompetence and the 9/11 attack aren't coincidentally correlated.
   Therefore,
   (5) The INS' incompetence is a cause of the 9/11 attack.

   Premise (1). Whether the INS was incompetent is a matter of debate. You could make a sub-argument for this premise by pointing to additional examples of the INS's incompetence. It's hard to use Mill's Methods to show correlation with the 9/11 attack because that attack only occurred once.

   Premise (2). To make a sub-argument for this claim, you'd need to show that the incompetence of the INS existed before the 9/11 attack. This is a plausible premise because it's hard to see how the 9/11 attack could have caused a change in the competence of the INS.

   Premise (3). To make a sub-argument for this premise, you'd need to consider possible third-party causes and then rule out each of them using Mill's Methods. This would be hard to do. A number of causes are likely to have been at least contributory causes. One would be the lack of communication between federal agencies. If there'd been better communication between federal agencies, it's possible that both this instance of INS incompetence and the 9/11 attackers obtaining pilot licenses could have been avoided.

Premise (4). Making a sub-argument for this claim would be difficult because it would be hard for you to check for repeated instances of terrorist attacks. Since there's only one 9/11 attack, it's especially hard to prove that the correlation isn't coincidental.

The third and fourth premises of the implied causal argument can't be assumed to pass the true premise test. They are controversial claims that require the support of sub-arguments, and it's unlikely they can be provided. In fact, there's much evidence that Premise (3) is false. This argument doesn't do well on the true premises test.

The implied causal argument can be put in standard form. It passes the proper form test. It contains no fallacies. But it doesn't do well on the true premises test.

EXERCISE 9.5 C

4. There's no causal argument in this passage.

9. There's a causal argument.
  (1) (The Hollywood Ten's) being held in contempt by the HUAC was correlated with their being blacklisted by the movie industry (which effectively ended their careers).
  [2] Being blacklisted wasn't the cause of their being held in contempt by the HUAC.
  [3] There's no third party cause that caused both their being blacklisted and their being held in contempt by the HUAC.
  [4] Their being blacklisted and being held in contempt by the HUAC aren't coincidentally related.
  Therefore,
  (5) Their being held in contempt by the HUAC was a cause of their being blacklisted.

This is a somewhat good particular causal argument. Premise (1) is an uncontroversial historical claim about events. Premise (2) can be shown to be true with a sub-argument because it's an uncontroversial empirical fact that they were blacklisted later in time after their being held in contempt. Premise (3) is more difficult. Some might argue that the anti-communist climate of the Cold War era was sufficient to cause both their being held in contempt and their being blacklisted. That is, it's plausible that they were blacklisted out of fear of further arrests in the movie industry, rather than blacklisted because the movie industry agreed with the contempt charge. Premise (4) is extremely difficult to prove since this is a particular causal argument.

EXERCISE 9.6 A

4. The passage suggests the following causal hypotheses:

Using up its dirt caused Jeri's plant to struggle.

The lower temperatures in Zhouzhou's apartment caused Jeri's plant to struggle.

New potting soil and the shock of transplanting caused Jeri's plant to struggle.

Step One: is to identify the question to be answered: Jeri's initial question is why her plant is struggling.

Step Two: Zhouzhou formulates a tentative theory: that the plant is struggling because it has used up all of its dirt.

Step Three: Zhouzhou checks for correlations by transplanting the plant and giving it new dirt in a bigger pot. At first, Zhouzhou has disconfirming evidence of her tentative theory because the plant didn't cease struggling. So she can't check for reverse causation, third-party causation, or coincidental causation. Zhouzhou returned the plant to its home, after which it began to thrive. This appeared to be some late-developing confirming evidence for the tentative theory, but it also (Step Six) raised new questions about whether the plant began to recover due to its return home or whether the initial theory had been correct but had taken more time to "kick in" than expected. At this point, our passage ends, but ideally, Zhouzhou should now begin checking for reverse, third-party, and coincidental correlation.

8. Jahai is informally using the scientific method. The question to be answered is: why is there water on his floor? He formulates a tentative theory (that he spilled something while cooking) but then rejects it because he finds disconfirming evidence (the water is there when he's sure he hasn't spilled anything). He then formulates a new theory (that the water heater is leaking). However, that theory is also not confirmed when he looks for correlations. The water doesn't come back. He also rejects the theory that the water is caused by rain because that doesn't correlate either. However, the reason he didn't call the staff that day is that he figured the apartment staff, being good scientists, would assume that the rain was a third-party cause. Jahai knew it wasn't a third-party cause because he had the leak when it didn't rain.

11. Step One: Identify the question: What's the best way to treat diabetes?

Step Two: Formulate tentative theory. Diabetes is better treated as a public health disorder rather than treating affected individuals clinically.

Step Three: There's both confirming and disconfirming evidence. Confirming evidence is that prevention strategies are effective. (If something is preventable, it's assumed to be best addressed as a public health issue.) However, there's some disconfirming evidence. (1) Because diabetes is associated "with aging and a possible strong family history, diabetes and its complications may appear inevitable to many. Further, much of the burden associated with diabetes is insidious, coming on gradually only after a considerable number of years." (2) Public concern needed to "galvanize" investigation is only just beginning, so at this point there's no evidence for "the public to demand societal or governmental action." These two facts make it appear that diabetes would be better treated clinically, contrary to the author's tentative theory. The author needs to do more investigative work on checking correlations before knowing whether to come up with a new theory. (See the following exercise.)

12. Since the initial theory, much evidence has been gathered. Scientists have learned more about diabetes, including the fact that it develops from a condition now called prediabetes. So, in line with the scientific method, the scientists come up with a new hypothesis.

Step Four: The new hypothesis is that we should treat prediabetes as a public health disorder instead of treating individuals with diabetes clinically.

Step Five: is checking for confirming or disconfirming evidence. It's now known that the two most important risk factors for prediabetes are obesity and physical inactivity. Both of these factors can easily be addressed to the general public. Both of these factors are things that people can control to some extent. Therefore, prediabetes is much more easily prevented than diabetes. In fact, according to recent findings, "It only takes a 7% to 10% weight loss and sustained moderate physical activity, at least 30 minutes per day."

By contrast, once people have diabetes, they are "devastating health and economic consequences . . . including blindness, kidney disease, . . . and lower-limb amputations." There's little if any chance of recovering from these sorts of consequences, so there's indirect evidence that it would be best to address the risk factors for prediabetes to the entire public, in an effort to ward off development of diabetes. Treating the consequences of diabetes is enormously expensive for patients, insurance companies, hospitals, and the public.

Step Six: New questions raised: How should we best go about addressing the two risk factors of weight loss and increased physical activity so that people are informed? This leads to yet another hypothesis.

Step Four: We should develop "community-based strategies . . . where people live, work, play, and go to school." The passage mentioned several agencies currently engaged in developing such community-based communication and intervention strategies.

Chapter Ten

EXERCISE 10.1 A

4. There's an argument in this passage [Mrs. Long told me that Netherfield Park is let. Therefore, Netherfield Park is let.], but it isn't a moral argument. Mrs. Bennett is relying on the moral presupposition that it's good to know who has rented Netherfield Park, and Mr. Bennett doesn't think it's good to know this.

8. There's no moral argument here. This is an analogical argument. The moral presupposition at work here is the view that it's good to know whether God exists.

12. There's no argument here. It's a series of questions. There's a moral presupposition at work, that it's good to know how markets react when there are only a few firms.

EXERCISE 10.2 A

4. (a) Both. (b) The exclamation points indicate that the author is too emotional for someone concerned to think critically.

8. (a) Cognitivist. (b) The phrasing and terms (such as "idiot") indicate that the author is too emotional for someone concerned to think critically.

10. (a) Noncognitivist. (b) The writer isn't too emotional.

EXERCISE 10.3 A

4. There's no moral argument in this passage.

8. This is a moral argument, but its conclusion is about a person, not an action.

12. There's a moral argument with an unstated conclusion.
(1) Imposing price controls on housing leads to inefficiency.
(2) It's morally bad to do actions that lead to inefficiency.
Therefore,
[3] We shouldn't impose price controls on housing.

EXERCISE 10.6 A

4. This passage contains a moral argument about an action. It's a deontic argument.
(1) Falsely claiming that a book is defective and asking for another is theft.
(2) It's morally bad to do actions that are examples of theft.
Therefore,
(3) People should not falsely claim that a book is defective and ask for another.

8. There's an argument here, but it's not a moral argument.

12. There's no moral argument in this passage. But there's a moral presupposition, that binge drinking is bad.

Reference Guide

Alphabetical List of Fallacies

Alphabetical List of Guides

Alphabetical List of Habits of a Critical Thinker

Index (Including Key Concepts and Technical Terms)

Summary Guide for Finding, Standardizing, and Evaluating Arguments

This Guide is an amplification of the "Guide for Finding, Standardizing, and Evaluating Arguments" that is in Chapter Two. The numbered sentences are merely copies from the Guide in Chapter Two. The paragraphs with "Prop," "Cat," "Analogy," "Statistical," "Causal," and "Moral" in front of them are additional materials that apply only to certain types of arguments.

> Prop = Propositional
> Cat = Categorical
> Analogy = Analogical
> Statistical = Statistical
> Causal = Causal
> Moral = Moral

Finding Arguments

1. Look for an attempt to convince.

Prop.   Look for an attempt to convince that relies on the logical relationships *between* statements.

Cat.   Look for an attempt to convince that relies on the logical relationships *within* statements.

Analogy.   Look to see whether there is an attempt to convince that uses a comparison. Check to see whether the analogy is argumentative or illustrative.

Statistical.   Look to see if there's an attempt to convince that uses observations of a subset of a group to draw a conclusion about the entire group.

Causal.   Look to see if there's an attempt to convince someone that some event or state of affairs is caused by some other event or state of affairs.

Moral.   Look to see whether there's an attempt to convince someone that some person or action is morally good or morally bad.

2. Find the conclusion.

Analogy.   Find the primary subject and the conclusory feature.

Statistical.   Find the target and the relevant property.

Causal.   Determine which kind of causal claim the conclusion is making: particular/general cause, necessary cause, sufficient cause, contributory cause, primary cause, remote/proximate cause.

Moral.   Determine whether the statement makes a moral claim about people or actions.

3. Find the premises.

Analogy.   Find the analogue(s) and the similarities.

Statistical.   Find the sample.

4. Review the following to make sure that you have correctly identified the conclusion and the premises: imperfect indicator words, sentence order, premises and/or conclusion not in declarative form, and unstated premises and/or conclusion.

Causal.   Identify the causes and the effects.

5. Review the following to make sure that you haven't incorrectly identified something as a premise or a conclusion when in fact it isn't part of an argument: assertions, questions, instructions, descriptions, and explanations.

Standardizing Arguments

6. Rewrite the premises and the conclusion as declarative sentences. Make sure that each premise and the conclusion is a grammatically correct declarative sentence. Rewrite the premises and conclusion as necessary to make them clearer, but don't change the meaning of the passage. Remove pronouns from the sentences and replace them with the nouns or noun phrases to which they refer. Remove emotionally charged language.

Cat.   Put all the statements in the argument into one of the standard categorical statement forms (UA, UN, PA, or PN).

7. Review any phrases you have omitted to be sure that they aren't premises or a conclusion.

8. Number the premises and the conclusion. Put brackets [ ] around the number of an unstated premise or conclusion. Place the premises before their conclusion and insert "Therefore," between the premises and the conclusion. Use blank lines to indicate subarguments.

Prop.   Assign the statement letters and formalize the argument.
Cat.   Assign category variables and rewrite the argument using them.
Analogy.   Put the standardization into the standard form of an analogical argument.
Statistical.   Put the standardization in the standard form of a statistical argument.
Causal.   Put the standardization in the standard form of a causal argument
Moral.   Determine whether the argument is a consequentialist, deontic, or aretaic moral argument.

9. Compare your standardization to the original passage to make sure that you haven't omitted any arguments found in the passage and to be sure that you have correctly identified the premises and the conclusion.

Prop and Cat.   Check to be sure that your formalization correctly captures the meaning of the argument as expressed in English.

Evaluating Arguments: The True Premises Test

10. Check to see whether the premises are accurate descriptions of the world.

Analogy.	Check for knowledge about imaginary cases. Evaluate it if it is present.
Analogy.	Check to see whether the analogue and the primary subject have the features that the argument claims they do.
Statistical.	Check to see whether the sample has the relevant property that the argument claims it has.
Causal.	Premise (1). Use Mill's Methods to determine whether the events are correlated.
Causal.	Premise (2). Use information about time to check for reverse causation.
Causal.	Premise (3). Check for third-party causation.
Causal.	Premise (4). Check for coincidental correlation.

11. Consider whether the premises are appropriate for the argument's audience.

12. Review the assumed premises to be sure that the assumptions are reasonable. Make sure that all assumed premises are uncontroversially true empirical statements, uncontroversially true definitional statements, or appropriate statements by experts. Make sure the definitions are good ones

Prop.	If the argument contains a disjunction, check for a False Dichotomy.

Evaluating Arguments: The Proper Form Test

13. Determine whether the argument is a deductive argument or inductive argument.

14. Determine whether the premises are relevant to the conclusion. Look at each premise individually to see whether the truth of the premise provides some evidence for the truth of the conclusion. Look at the premises as a group to see whether the truth of all of them provides some evidence for the truth of the conclusion.

Prop.	Determine the form of the propositional argument. Compare it to the eight propositional argument forms.
Cat.	Determine the form of the categorical argument. Determine whether it has one premises, two premises, or more than two premises.
Cat.	If the argument has one premise, compare it to the sixteen forms of categorical arguments with one premise discussed in this chapter.
Cat.	If the argument has two premises, verify that it meets the criteria for being a categorical syllogism. Use the test method

or the Venn method to determine whether it passes the proper form test.

Analogy. Consider whether the similarities are relevant. Check to see whether there are any relevant dissimilarities. Evaluate the importance of the similarities and the relevant dissimilarities.

Statistical. Evaluate the representativeness of the sample. Determine the sampling technique. Consider whether the sample is sufficiently large and sufficiently varied.

Evaluating Arguments: Checking for Fallacies

15. Compare the argument to the list of fallacies on page 410 to see whether the argument commits any of the fallacies.

Disjunctive Propositional Argument Forms

Denying a Disjunct

1. (1) S1 or S2 (or both).
(2) Not S1.
Therefore,
(3) S2.

2. (1) S1 or S2 (or both).
(2) Not S2.
Therefore,
(3) S1.

3. (1) S1 or S2 (but not both).
(2) Not S1.
Therefore,
(3) S2.

4. (1) S1 or S2 (but not both).
(2) Not S2.
Therefore,
(3) S1.

Fallacy: Affirming an Inclusive Disjunct

1. (1) S1 or S2 (or both).
(2) S1.
Therefore,
(3) Not S2.

2. (1) S1 or S2 (or both).
(2) S2.
Therefore,
(3) Not S1.

Affirming an Exclusive Disjunct

1. (1) S1 or S2 (but not both).
(2) S1.
Therefore,
(3) Not S2.

2. (1) S1 or S2 (but not both).
(2) S2.
Therefore,
(3) Not S1.

Conditional Propositional Argument Forms

Affirming the Antecedent

(1) If S1, then S2.
(2) S1.
Therefore,
(3) S2.

Fallacy: Denying the Antecedent

(1) If S1, then S2.
(2) Not S1.
Therefore,
(3) Not S2.

Denying the Consequent

(1) If S1, then S2.
(2) Not S2.
Therefore,
(3) Not S1.

Fallacy: Affirming the Consequent

(1) If S1, then S2.
(2) S2.
Therefore,
(3) S1.

Tri-Conditional

(1) If S1, then S2.
(2) If S2, then S3.
Therefore,
(3) If S1, then S3.

Some Valid (= Proper) Categorical Argument Forms with One Premise

Contradiction

1. (1) UA
   Therefore,
   (2) It is false that PN
2. (1) It is false that UA
   Therefore,
   (2) PN
3. (1) PN
   Therefore,
   (2) It is false that UA
4. (1) It is false that PN
   Therefore,
   (2) UA
5. UN
   Therefore,
   (2) It is false that PA

6. (1) It is false that UN

Therefore,

(2) PA

7. (1) PA

Therefore,

(2) It is false that UN

8. (1) It is false that PA

Therefore,

(2) UN

Conversion

9. UN (1) All G1 are not G2.

Therefore,

(2) All G2 are not G1.

10. PA (1) Some G1 are G2.

Therefore,

(2) Some G2 are G1.

Contraposition

11. UA (1) All G1 are G2.

Therefore,

(2) All non-G2 are non-G1.

12. PN (1) Some G1 are not G2.

Therefore,

(2) Some non-G2 are not non-G1.

Obversion

13. UA (1) All G1 are G2.

Therefore,

(2) All G1 are not non-G2.

14. UN (1) All G1 are not G2.

Therefore,

(2) All G1 are non-G2.

15. PA (1) Some G1 are G2.

Therefore,

(2) Some G1 are not non-G2.

16. PN (1) Some G1 are not G2.

Therefore,

(2) Some G1 are non-G2.

Validity of Categorical Syllogisms: The Test Method

1. The Equal Negatives Test: The number of negative statements in the conclusion must equal the number of negative statements in the premises.
2. The Quantity Test: If both premises are particulars, then the conclusion can't be a universal and if both premises are universal, then the conclusion can't be a particular.
3. The Distributed Conclusion Test: If a category is distributed in the conclusion, then it must also be distributed in a premise.
4. The Distributed Middle Category Test: The middle category must be distributed at least once.

Validity of Categorical Syllogisms: The Venn Method

1. Draw three overlapping circles. Put the category that is the subject of the conclusion at the top left, the category that is the predicate of the conclusion at the top right, and the category that doesn't appear in the conclusion in the middle under the other two categories.
2. Diagram the premises. Diagram the universal premises, and then diagram the particular premises.
3. Compare the resulting diagram to the conclusion to see whether the diagram of the two premises has diagrammed the conclusion. If it has, the argument has a valid form. If it hasn't, the argument has an invalid form.

The Standard Form of an Analogical Argument

(1) X1s have features F1, F2, F3, ... and feature Fn.

(2) X2s also have features F1, F2, F3, ...

Therefore,

(3) X2s probably have Fn.

The Standard Form of a Statistical Argument

General   (1) P% of the N observed entities in G have F.

Therefore,

(2) P% of all the entities in G have F.

Particular   (1) P% of the N observed entities in G have F.

Therefore,

(2) P% of all the entities in G have F.

(3) X is an entity in G.

Therefore,

(4) There is a P% chance that X has F.

The Standard Form of a Causal Argument

(1) E1 is correlated with E2.

(2) E2 is not the cause of E1.

(3) There is no E3 that is the cause of E1 and E2.

(4) E1 and E2 are not coincidentally correlated.

Therefore,

(5) E1 is a cause of E2.

Standard Moral Argument Forms

Action

(1) Action A has feature F.

(2) It is morally good/bad to do actions that have feature F.

Therefore,

(3) H should/should not do A.

Consequentialist Version of Action

(1) Action A will produce C.

(2) It is morally good/bad to produce C.

Therefore,

(3) H should/should not do A.

Universalistic Maximizing Consequentialist Version of Action

(1) Action A will maximize happiness for everyone in the world.

(2) It is morally good to maximize happiness for everyone in the world.

Therefore,

(3) H ought to do A.

Deontic Version of Action

(1) Action A has intrinsic feature F.

(2) It is morally good/bad to do actions with intrinsic feature F.

Therefore,

(3) H should/should not do A.

Kantian Version of Action

(1) Action A is not universalizable.

(2) It is morally bad to do actions that are not universalizable.

Therefore,

(3) H should not do A.

Cooperation Version of Action

(1) Action A is uncooperative.

(2) It is morally bad to do actions that are not cooperative.

Therefore,

(3) H should not to do A.

Virtue Ethics Version of Action

(1) Action A is an action that would be done by a person with virtue V.

(2) It is morally good to do actions that would be done by a person with virtue V.

Therefore,

(3) H should do A.

List of Citations

Adams, Natalie G. "The Power of the Preps and a Cheerleading Equity Policy." *Sociology of Education* 76, no. 2 (2003): 128–142.

Ainsworth, Penne and Dan Deines. *Introduction to Accounting: An Integrated Approach*. 4th ed. Columbus, OH: McGraw-Hill/Irwin, 2008.

Allen, James. *Thoughts*. New York, NY: Cosimo, 2007.

Allen, Woody. *The Complete Prose of Woody Allen*. New York, NY: Random House, 1991.

Almanac Singers, Their Complete General Recordings, # Label: MCA, ASIN#: B000002P32, Reissued 1996.

Alter, Alexandra. "Reading the Mind of the Body Politic." *The Wall Street Journal*, December 14, 2007: W1&W6.

American Enterprise Institute for Public Policy Research. "AEI's Organization and Purposes." http://www.aei.org/about.

Angelou, Maya. *Wouldn't Take Nothing for My Journey Now*. New York, NY: Bantam, 1994.

Anitei, Stefan. "Once Antarctica Was Tropical and Attached to Europe." Softpedia.com. December 2007 http://news.softpedia.com/news/Once-Antarctica-Was-Tropical-and-Attachhed-to-Europe-51095.shtml.

Anonymous. "A Centipede Was Happy Quite," In *An Anthology of Light Verse*, edited by Louis Kronenberger. New York, NY: Random House, 1935: 161.

Aristotle. *The Nicomachean Ethics*, translated by W.D. Ross. New York, NY: Oxford University Press, 2009.

Aron, Arthur, Elaine Aron and Elliot J. Coups. *Statistics for Psychology*, 4th ed. Upper Saddle River, NJ: Pearson/Prentice Hall, 2006.

Art and the Re-presentation of the Past. *Journal of the Royal Anthropological Institute* 6, no. 1 (2000): 35–62.

Associated Press. "Financial Shares Lead Market Lower." *The New York Times*, December 4, 2007: C13.

Attenborough, David. *Life on Earth*, 4th ed. Upper Saddle River, NJ: Pearson Prentice Hall, 2005.

Atwood, Margaret. *The Handmaid's Tale*. Boston: Houghton Mifflin Co., 1986.

Audesirk, Teresa, Gerald Audesirk and Bruce Byers. *Life on Earth*, 4th ed. Upper Saddle River, NJ: Prentice Hall, 2005.

Austen, Jane. *Pride and Prejudice*. Rockville, MD: Arc Manor LLC, 2008 [1813].

Bakalar, Nicholas. "Fish Oil for Mom May Benefit Her Child." *The New York Times*, January 2, 2007: F6.

Bakeman, Karl. "Reaganomics." In *America: A Narrative History*, 7th ed., edited by George Brown Tindall, and David Emory Shi. New York, NY: Norton & Company, 2007.

Balzac, Honoré de. *Lost Illusions*, translated by Kathleen Raines. New York, NY: Modern Library, 2001 [1843].

Barnes, Harry. "Revisionism and Brainwashing." In *The Right Wing Individualist Tradition in America*, edited by Murray Newton Rothbard and Jerome Tuccille. Manchester, NH: Ayer Company Publishers, 1972.

Barnett, Raymond A., BBC News. "Pluto Loses Status as a Planet." news.bbc.co.uk/2/hi/in depth/5282440.stm.

Basri, Gibor. "What is a Planet?" *Mercury* 32, no. 6 (Nov/Dec 2003): 27–34.

Beehner, Jacinta C., Jane E. Phillips-Conroy and Patricia L. Whitten. "Female Testosterone, Dominance Rank, and Aggression in an Ethiopian Population of Hybrid Baboons." *American Journal of Primatology* 67, no. 1 (2005): 101–119.

Begley, Sharon. "A, My Name is Alice: Moniker Madness." *Newsweek*. November 7, 2007. http://blog.newsweek.com/blogs/labnotes/archive/2007/11/07/a-my-name-is-alice-moniker-madness.aspx.

Bennett, Jeffrey and others. *The Cosmic Perspective*, 4th ed. Old Tappan, NJ: Pearson, 2007.

Bennett, Jeffrey and others. *The Essential Cosmic Perspective Media Update*, 4th ed. San Francisco, CA: Benjamin Cummings, 2007.

Bennett, Mark. "Nexavar Extends Survival in Liver-Cancer Patients." *The Wall Street Journal*, June 4, 2007: D1.

Bentham, Jeremy. *An Introduction to the Principles of Morals and Legislation*. New York, NY: Clarendon Press, 1907 [1789].

Berman, Jane and Charlene Dixon Hutcheson. "Impressions of a Lost Technology: A Study of Lucayan-Taino Basketry." *Journal of Field Archaeology* 27, no. 4 (2000): 417–435.

Besculides, Melanie and others. "Identifying Best Practices for Wisewoman Programs Using a Mixed-methods Evaluation." *Preventing Chronic Disease* 3, no. 1 (2006): 1–9.

Bettelheim, Frederick and others. *Introduction to General, Organic, and Biochemistry*, 8th ed. Belmont, CA: Thomson Higher Education, 2007.

Bettis, Pamela J. and Natalie G. Adams. "The Power of the Preps and a Cheerleading Equity Policy." *Sociology of Education* 76, no. 2 (Apr., 2003): 128–142.

Birtwhistle, Grete and Cayan Tsim. "Consumer Purchasing Behavior: An Investigation of the UK Mature Women's Clothing Market." *Journal of Consumer Behavior* 4 (2005): 453–464.

Blanchette, Patricia. "Frege and Hilbert on Consistency." *The Journal of Philosophy* 93 (1996): 317–336.

Boone, Jan. "Technological Progress, Downsizing and Unemployment." *The Economic Journal* 110, no. 465 (2000): 581–600.

Booth, Wayne C., Joseph M. Williams and Gregory G. Colomb. *The Craft of Research*, 2nd ed. Chicago, IL: University of Chicago Press, 2003.

Borysenko, Joan. "Retrain Your Brain." *Prevention* 58, no. 9 (2006): 117–119.

Bowman, Barbara A. and Frank Vinicor. "Toward Prevention and Control of Type 2 Diabetes: Challenges at the U.S.-Mexico Border and Beyond." *Preventing Chronic Disease* 2, no. 1 (2005).

Bradford, Sarah. *Harriet: the Moses of Her People*. New York, NY: Lockwood & Son, 1897.

BrainyQuote. "Kurt Kobain Quotes," http://www.brainyquote.com/quotes/quotes/k/kurtcobain167113.html.

Breitman, George. *Macolm X Speaks*. New York, NY: Grove Press, 1965.

Brontë, Charlotte. *Jane Eyre*. London: Dent & Sons, 1908 [1847].

Brooks, David. "The Postwar Election." *The New York Times*, December 11, 2007: A33.

Brown v. Board of Education 347 U.S. 483 (1954).

Brown, J. R. *Philosophy of Math: An Introduction to The World of Proofs and Pictures*. London: Routledge, 1999, p. 78.

Brym, Robert J. and John Lie. *Sociology: Your Compass for a New World*, 3rd ed. Florence, KY: Wadsworth Publishing, 2006.

Buxbaum, J. D. and others. Linkage Analysis for Autism in a Subset Families with Obsessive-Compulsive Behaviors: Evidence for an Autism Susceptibility Gene on Chromosome 1 and Further Support for Susceptibility Genes on Chromosome 6 and 19. *Molecular Psychiatry* 9 (2004): 144–150.

Byleen, Karl E. *Calculus For Business, Economics, Life Sciences, and Social Sciences*, 10th ed. Upper Saddle River, NJ: Pearson Prentice Hall, 2005.

Cahoon, Donald R. and others. "Mass Tree Mortality Leads to Mangrove Peat Collapse at Bay Islands, Honduras after Hurricane Mitch." *The Journal of Ecology* 91, no. 6 (2003): 1093–1105.

Campbell, Denise. "Warning Signs." *Black Enterprise*, May 2007: 88–91.

Carlson, Neil R. and others. *Psychology: The Science of Behavior*, 6th ed. Columbus, OH: Allyn & Bacon, 2006.

Carnevale, G. and T.W. Pietsch. "Filling the Gap: A Fossil Frogfish, Genus Antennarius (Teleostei, Lophiiformes, Antennariidae), From the Miocene of Algeria." *Journal of Zoology* 270 (2006): 448–457.

Carroll, Lewis. "Alice's Adventures in Wonderland," In *The Complete Illustrated Works of Lewis Carroll*. London: Chancellor Press, 1982 [1865].

Carroll, Lewis. *Alice's Adventures in Wonderland and Through the Looking-Glass*. New York, NY: Fine Creative Media, Inc., 2004 [1865].

Catling, David C. "Mars: Ancient Fingerprints in the Clay." *Nature* 448, no. 7149 (2007): 31–32.

Centers for Disease Control and Prevention. "National Suicide Statistics at a Glance." 2009. http://www.cdc.gov/violenceprevention/suicide/statistics/rates02.html.

Centers for Disease Control and Prevention. "Peanut Products Recall." http://www.fda.gov/Safety/Recalls/MajorProductRecalls/Peanut/default.htm.

Chaisson, Eric and Steve McMillan. *Astronomy Today*, 5th ed. San Francisco, Calif: Benjamin Cummings, 2005.

Chamberlain, William Henry. *The Russian Revolution*, vol 1. New York, NY: Grosset & Dumlop, 1965.

Chapman, Graham and others. *Monty Python and the Holy Grail*. DVD. Directed by Terry Jones. Sony Pictures, 1999 [1975].

Cherokee Nation v. State of Georgia 30 U.S. 1 (1831).

Churchill, Winston S. *Never Give In! The Best of Winston Churchill's Speeches*. New York, NY: Hyperon, 2003.

Ciulla, Joanne B., Clancy Martin and Robert C. Solomon. *Honest Work: A Business Ethics Reader*. New York, NY: Oxford University Press, 2007.

Concise Oxford English Dictionary, 11th ed. New York, NY: Oxford University Press, 2008.

Cook, Lori A., Sonya A. Dehler and Sandra M. Barr, "Geophysical Modeling of Devonian Plutons in the Southern Gulf of St. Lawrence: Implications for Appalachian Terrane Boundaries in Maritime Canada." *Canadian Journal of Earth Sciences* 44, no. 11 (2007): 1551–1565.

Cornman, James, Keith Lehrer and George Sotiros Pappas. *Philosophical Problems and Arguments: An Introduction*, 4th ed. Indianapolis, IN: Hackett Publishing Company, 1992.

Crawford, Craig. "Seeing a Disinformation Age: Bush and His Public." *The New York Times*, September 22, 2006: E2: E31.

Creedence Clearwater Revival, "Who'll Stop the Rain?" on Chronicle, vol. 1: The 20 Greatest Hits. Fantasy 1976.

Cross, Frank B. and Roger LeRoy Miller. *West's Legal Environment of Business*, 6th ed. Eagan, MN: Thomson West, 2007.

Curry, Jack. "Election 2013 (or Later): Debates Already in Swing." *The New York Times*. December 21, 2007: C12.

Cutnell, John D. and Kenneth W. Johnson. *Physics*, 7th ed. Hoboken, NJ: Wiley, 2007.

Dawson, Philip. *The French Revolution*. Upper Saddle River, NJ: Prentice Hall, 1967.

DeNavas-Walt, Carmen, Bernadette D Proctor and Cheryl Hill Lee. "Income, Poverty, and Health Insurance Coverage in the United States: 2005." In *Current Population Report, Consumer Income*. Washington, DC: Government Printing Office, 2006.

Descartes, Rene. *Descartes' Meditations and Selections from the Principles of Philosophy*, translated by. John Veitch. Chicago, IL: Open Court, 1913 [1644].

Diana Ross and the Supremes. "Stop in the Name of Love." Diana Ross and the Supremes - The Ultimate Collection. CD. Motown, 1997 [1965].

Dickens, Charles. *A Tale of Two Cities*. London: Macmillan & Co., 1922 [1859].

Dickens, Charles. *Bleak House*. London: Adam and Charles Black, 1904 [1852].

Dickens, G. A. *Reformation and Society*. Boston, MA: Harcourt, Brace & World, 1968.

Diener, Paul W. *Religion and Morality: An Introduction*. Louisville, KY: Wesminster John Knox Press, 1997.

Donne, John. *The Works of John Donne*. London: John Parker, 1839.

Dooren, Jennifer Corbett. "Nexavar Extends Survival in Liver-Cancer Patients." *Wall Street Journal*, June 4, 2007: D1.

Doyle, Sir Arthur Conan. *The Sign of the Four*. Charleston, SC: Forgotten Books, 1994 [1890].

Dunch, Ryan. "Beyond Cultural Imperialism: Cultural Theory, Christian Missions, and Global Modernity." *History and Theory*. 41, no. 3 (2002): 301–325.

Durning, Alan B. and Holly B. Brough. *Taking Stock: Animal Farming and the Environment*. Washington, DC: Worldwatch Institute, July 1991.

Einstein, Albert. Cited in Louis L. Snyder. *Encyclopedia of Nationalism*. New York, NY: Paragon House, 1977.

Elizondo-Omaña, Rodrigo E. and Santos Guzmán López. "The Development of Clinical Reasoning Skills: A Major Objective of the Anatomy Course." *Anatomical Sciences Education* 1 (2008): 267–268.

Elizondo-Omaña, Rodrigo E. and others. "Study Pace as a Factor that Influences Achievement in a Human Anatomy Course." The New Anatomist 289, no. 4 (July 2006): 134–138.

Epp, Susanna. *Discrete Mathematics*, 3rd ed. Belmont, CA: Thomson Learning, 2004.

Epstein, Julius J. and Philip G. Epstein. *Casablanca*. DVD. Directed by Michael Curtiz. Los Angeles, Warner Bros. Pictures, 1942.

Fan, Xuesen and others. InCl34H2O-Promoted Green Preparation of Xanthenedione Derivatives in Ionic Liquids. *Canadian Journal of Chemistry* 83, no. 1 (2005): 16–20.

Feinberg, Joel and Russ Shafer-Landau, eds. *Reason and Responsibility*, 11th ed., Belmont, CA: Wadsworth Press, 2002.

Feinberg, Joel. *Harm to Others (Moral Limits for Criminal Law)*, vol 1. New York, NY: Oxford University Press, 1984.

Feynman, Richard. Quoted in: Anonymous. "Conservation News You Can Use." *Journal of Soil and Water Conservation* 61, no.1 (2006): 9A.

Firearms: Definitions. Title 18 U.S. Code, Pt. 921. 2009 ed.

Fountain, Henry. "Arecibo Radio Telescope Is Back in Business After 6-Month Spruce-Up." *The New York Times*, December 25, 2007: D3.

Fredrickson, George. *Racism: A Short History*. Princeton, NJ: Princeton University Press, 2002.

Freeman, R. Edward. "A Stakeholder Theory of the Modern Corporation." In *Business Ethics*, 3rd ed., edited by Milton Snoeyenbos, Robert Almeder and James Humber. Amherst, NY: Prometheus Books, 2001, pp. 101–114.

Freud, Sigmund. *The Interpretation of Dreams*. New York, NY: Basic Books, 1969 [1899].

Fried, Barbara H. "If You Don't Like It, Leave It: The Problem of Exit in Social Contractarian Arguments." *Philosophy & Public Affairs* 31, no. 1 (2003): 40–70.

Frink, Lisa, Brian Hoffman and Robert Shaw. "Ulu Knife Use in Western Alaska: A Comparative Ethnoarchaeological Study." *Current Anthropology* 44, no. 1 (2003): 116–122.

Fritz, Sandy, Kathleen Maison Paholsky and M. James Grosenbach. *Mosby's Basic Science for Soft Tissue and Movement Therapies*. Maryland Heights, MO: Mosby Publications, 1999.

Garrett, Laurie. "The Challenge of Global Health." *Foreign Affairs* 86 (2007): 14–38.

Georgia Secretary of State. "Voting Information." http://sos.georgia.gov/elections/voting_information.htm#Voting%20on%20Election%20Day.

Georgia State University Undergraduate Catalog, 2007–2008. Atlanta, GA: Georgia State University, 2007.

Georgia State University. "Safety Net 2006." http://www2.gsu.edu/~wwwupo/safetynet.pdf.

Giddens, Anthony, Mitchell Duneier and Richard P. Appelbaum. *Introduction to Sociology,* 5th ed. New York, NY: W. W. Norton & Company, 2005.

Gilligan, Carol. *In a Different Voice.* Cambridge, MA: Harvard University Press, 1982.

Goodall, Jane. *The Chimpanzee: The Living Link between 'Man' and 'Beast.'* Edinburgh, UK: Edingburgh University Press, 1992.

Gould, Stephen J. *The Panda's Thumb.* New York, NY: WW. Norton & Company, 1992.

Grundy, Scott M. "Cholesterol-Lowering Clinical Trials: A Historical Perspective." In *Cholesterol-Lowering Therapy: Evaluation of Clinical Trial Evidence,* edited by Scott M. Grundy. New York, NY: Marcel Dekker AC, 2000: 1–44.

Gulick, Danielle and Thomas J. Gould. "Acute Ethanol Has Biphasic Effects on Short- and Long-Term Memory in Both Foreground and Background Contextual Fear Conditioning in C57BL/6 Mice." *Alcoholism, Clinical and Experimental Research* 31, no. 9 (2007): 1528–1537.

Handwerk, Brian. "Upright Walking Started in Trees, Ape Study Suggests." http://news.nationalgeographic.com/news/2007/05/070531-orangutans.html.

Haviland, William A., Harald L. Prins, Dana Walrath. *The Essence of Anthropology.* Florence, KY: Wadsworth Publishing, 2007.

Henderson-King, Donna and Audra Kaleta. "Learning About Social Diversity." *The Journal of Higher Education* 72, no. 2 (2009): 142–143.

Hendrick, Bill. "Superstition Has Its Place on Wall Street." *The Atlanta Journal and Constitution,* March 21, 1999: Business 5.

Henry, Patrick. "Give Me Liberty or Give Me Death!" In *The World's Greatest Speeches,* edited by Lewis Copeland and others. Mineola, NY: Dover Publications, 1999 [1775].

Henry, Patrick. "Give Me Liberty or Give Me Death." In *The World's Best Orations,* vol 7, edited by David Brewer. St. Louis, MO: Fred Kaiser, 1901 [1775].

Herberholz, Jens, Marjorie M. Sen and Donald H. Edwards, "Escape Behavior and Escape Circuit Activation in Juvenile Crayfish During Prey-Predator Interactions." *Journal of Experimental Biology* 207 (2004): 1855–1863.

Hill, Christopher. *The Century of Revolutions: 1603–1714.* New York: W.W. Norton, 1966.

Hippolytus. "Refutation of All Heresies." In *The Hellenistic Philosophers: Translations of the Principal Sources, With Philosophical Commentary,* translated by A.A. Long and D. N. Sedley. Cambridge: Cambridge University Press, 1987.

Human Rights Watch, Hundreds of Chechens Detained in "Filtration Camps." *Human Rights Watch,* February 17, 2000. http://www.hrw.org/en/node/65142

Hume, David. "Dialogues Concerning Natural Religion: And Other Writings." In *Cambridge Texts in the History of Philosophy,* edited by Dorothy Coleman. Cambridge: Cambridge University Press (2007) [1779].

Hume, David. *A Treatise of Human Nature*, Book 1, Part 1, Section 1. Oxford: Clarendon Press, 1896 [1739].

Hume, David. *A Treatise of Human Nature*. London: Penguin Classics, 1985 [1739].

Hurston, Zora Neal. "How It Feels to Be Colored Me." In *The Best American Essays of the Century*, edited by Joyce Carol Oates and Robert Atwan. Geneva, IL: Houghton Mifflin, 2000.

Huston, Aletha C. and others. "Impacts on Children of a Policy to Promote Employment and Reduce Poverty for Low-Income Parents: New Hope After 5 Years." *Developmental Psychology* 41, no. 6 (2005): 902–918.

Hutchinson, John. "What Killed the Dinosaurs?" http://www.ucmp.berkeley.edu/diapsids/extinctheory.html.

Hyde, Henry. *Forfeiting Our Property Rights: Is Your Property Safe From Seizure?* Washington D.C.: Cato Institute, 1995.

Janda, Kenneth, Jeffrey M. Berry and Jerry Goldman. 2008. *The Challenge of Democracy*, 9th ed. Boston: Houghton Mifflin, 2008.

Ji, Quang and others. "The Earliest Known Eutherian Mammal." *Nature* 416, no. 6883 (2002).

Jonahl, Brian A., "Sensation Seeking and Risky Driving: A Review and Synthesis of the Literature." *Accident Analysis & Prevention* 29 (1997): 651–665.

Kaiser, Jocelyn. "Panel Urges Further Study of Biotech Corn." *Science* 290, no. 5498 (2000): 1867.

Kant. *Groundwork of the Metaphysics of Morals*, translated by Mary Gregor. Cambridge: Cambridge University Press, 1997 [1785].

Kaufman, Henry. "Creeping Inflation, Monetary Tactics." *Vital Speeches of the Day* 73.1 (2007): 23–25.

Keller, Edward. *Introduction to Environmental Geology*, 3rd ed. Upper Saddle River, NJ: Pearson Prentice Hall, 2005.

Kelly, Kate. "How Goldman Won Big On Mortgage Meltdown." *The Wall Street Journal* December 14, 2007: A1 & A18.

Kennedy, John F. Presidential Inaugural Address, 1961.

Kim, Hyun Jin and others. "Gain-of-function Mutation in TRPML3 Causes the Mouse Variant-Waddler Phenotype." *Journal of Biological Chemistry* 282, no. 50 (2007): 36138–36142.

Kimbrough v. United States, 552 U.S. 85 (2007).

Kincaid, Peter. *The Rule of the Road: An International Guide to History and Practice*. Santa Barbara, CA: Greenwood Press, 1986.

King, Coretta Scott. Hearings before the Subcommittee on Empoloyment, Poverty, and Migratory Labor of the Committee on Labor and Public Welfare," United States Senate, 94th Congress, second session on S.50 and S.472, May 19, 1976: 636–638.

King, Martin Luther. *A Testament of Hope: The Essential Writings of Martin Luther King*, edited by James Washington. New York, NY: Harper Collins, 1991.

Kingsolver, Barbara. *The Bean Trees*. New York, NY: Harper Collins, 2001.

Kitcher, Philip. *Abusing Science: The Case Against Creationism*. Cambridge, MA: MIT Press, 1983).

Krugman, Paul and Robin Wells. *Economics*. New York, NY: Worth Publishers, 2006.

Lawrence v. Texas 539 U.S. 558 (2003).

Le Meur, G. and others. "Restoration of Vision in RPE65-Deficient Briard Dogs Using an AAV Serotype 4 Vector that Specifically Targets the Retinal Pigmented Epithelium." *Gene Therapy* 14, no. 4 (2007): 292–303.

Lial, Margaret L., John Hornsby and David I. Schneider. *Precalculus*. 3rd ed. Boston: Addison Wesley, 2004.

Liptak, Adam. "Serving Life for Providing Car to Killers." *The New York Times*, December 4, 2007: A1.

Livingstone, Ken. "Clear Up the Congestion-Pricing Gridlock." *The New York Times*, July 2, 2007.

Logan v. United States 552 U.S. 23 (2007).

Lucretius. *Lucretius: De Rerum Natura IV* Bk 4, translated by J. Godwin. Warminster, UK: Aris & Phillips, 1987 [circa 50 CE].

Lucretius. *On The Nature of Things*, translated by Martin Smith Ferguson. Indianapolis, IN: Hackett Publishing, 2001 [cica 50 CE].

Lutgens, Frederick K., Edward J. Tarbuck and Dennis Tasa. *The Atmosphere: An Introduction to Meteorology*, 9th ed. Upper Saddle River, NJ: Pearson/ Prentice Hall, 2004.

Lymon, Frankie and the Teenagers. "Why Do Fools Fall in Love?" Why Do Fools Fall In Love and Other Hits. CD. Rhino Flashback, 2003 [1956].

MacFarquhar, Larissa. "Who Cares if Johnny Can't Read?" In *Reading Rhetorically*, edited by John C. Bean, Virginia A. Chappell and Alice M. Gillam. New York, NY: Pearson/Longman, 2006.

Machan, Tibor R. "Do Animals Have Rights?" *Public Affairs Quarterly*, 5 (1991): 163–173.

Macionis, John J. *Society: The Basics*. Upper Saddle River, NJ: Pearson/ Prentice Hall, 2006.

Mahoney, Christine. "Lobbying Success in the United States and the European Union." *Journal of Public Policy* 27, no. 1 (2007): 35–56.

Martin, Harold. "Homosexuality: A Sinful Way of Life." *BRF Witness*, 28, no. 3 (May/June 1993). http://www.brfwitness.org/Articles/1993v28n3.htm.

McKnight, Tom L. *Physical Geography: A Landscape Appreciation*, 8th ed. Upper Saddle River, NJ: Prentice Hall, 2005.

Melville, Herman. *Moby Dick*. Oxford: Oxford University Press, 2008 [1851].

Mill, John Stuart. "The Subjection of Women." In John Stuart Mill and Harriet Taylor Mill: *Essays on Sex Equality*, edited by Alice Rossi. Chicago, IL: University of Chicago Press, 1970 [1878].

Mill, John Stuart. *On Liberty*, edited by Edward Alexander. Toronto: Broadview Press, 1999 [1859].

Mill, John Stuart. *Utilitarianism*. Chicago, IL: University of Chicago Press, 1906 [1861].

Mill, John Stuart. *Utilitarianism*. Indianapolis, IN: Hackett Publishing Company, 1979 [1861].

Miller-el v. Dretke 544 U.S. 660 (2005).

Minkel, JR. "That's Debatable: Six Debates at the Frontier of Science," http:// www.sciam.com/article.cfm?chanID=sa027&articleID=0005726E-214A-1514-A14A83414B7F013F.

Moore, Kathleen Dean. *Pardons: Justice, Mercy, and the Public Interest*. New York: Oxford University Press, 1989.

Morrison, Toni. *Beloved*. New York, NY: Alfred A. Knopf, 2001 [1987].

Mosher, William and others. "Use of Contraception and Use of Family Planning Services in the United States: 1982–2002." *Advance Data* 350 (2004): 1–14.

National Center for Education Statistics, *Digest of Education Statistics, 1999*. United Nations Educational, Scientific, and Cultural Organization (UNESCO).

Nelson, Willie. *Greatest Hits (& Some That Will Be)*. Sony Music, 2003.

New Yorker Magazine. *The New Yorker Book of Cat Cartoons*. New York, NY: Knopf, 2010.

Nice, Karim. "How Car Steering Works." May 2001. HowStuffWorks.com. http://auto.howstuffworks.com/steering.htm.

Nietzsche, Friedrich. "Beyond Good and Evil," In *Reason & Responsibility*, edited by Joel Feinberg and Russ Shafer-Landau, 11th ed., Belmont, CA: Wadsworth, 2002: 598–604.

Nobel Prize. http://nobelprize.org/nobel_prizes/medicine/articles/cajal/.

Nolen, Joseph and others. *Black's Law Dictionary*, 6th ed. St. Paul, MN: West Publishing Company, 1990.

Norris, Rebecca Sachs. "Embodiment and Community." *Western Folklore*. 60, no. 2/3 (2001): 111–124.

Nussbaum, Martha, "The Future of Feminist Liberalism." In *The Subject of Care*, edited by Eva Feder Kittay and Ellen K. Feder. Lanham, MD: Rowman & Littlefield, 2002, pp. 186–214.

Nussbaum, Martha. "Poverty and Human Functioning: Capabilities as Fundamental Entitlements." In *Poverty and Inequality*, edited by David Grusky and Ravi Kanbar. Stanford, CA: Stanford University Press, 2006, pp. 47–75.

O'Connor, Anahad. "The Claim: Brown Sugar Is Healthier Than White Sugar." *The New York Times*, June 12, 2007: D5.

O'Hanlon, Michael. "Why China Cannot Conquer Taiwan." *International Security* 25, no. 2 (2000): 51–86.

Okin, Susan Moller. "Is Multiculturalism Bad for Women?" *International Herald Tribune*, February 2, 1996, news section.

Palmer, A. Richard. "Evolutionary Biology: Caught Right-Handed." *Nature* 444 (2006): 689–692.

Pascal, Blaise. *Thoughts*. New York, NY: Cosimo, 2007.

Pastan, Linda. "Marks." In *An Introduction to Literature: Fiction/Poetry/Drama*. New York, NY: Harper Collins, 1994.

Pastorino, Ellen E. and Susann M. Doyle-Portillo. *What Is Psychology?* Belmont, CA: Wadsworth Publishing, 2006.

Paul VI. "Response to the Letter of His Grace the Most Reverend Dr. F. D. Coggan, Archbishop of Canterbury, concerning the ordination of Women to the Priesthood" (30 November 1975), *Acta Apostolicae Sedis* 68 (1976), p. 599.

Pennisi, Elizabeth. "Boom Time for Monkey Research." *Science* 316, no. 5822 (2007): 216–218.

People for the American Way. "Our Mission and Vision." http://site.pfaw.org/site/PageServer?pagename=about_mission.

Pepall, Lynne, Daniel Richards and George Norman, *Industrial Organization*, 3rd ed. Mason, OH: Thomson South-Western, 2005.

Perdue, Theda and Michael D. Green, eds. *The Cherokee Removal: A Brief History with Documents*. Bedford, MA: St. Martins, 2005.

Perlez, Jane. "Doubts Engulf an American Aid Plan for Pakistan." *The New York Times*, December 25, 2007: A10.

Petrucci, Ralph and others. *General Chemistry*, 8th ed. Upper Saddle River, NJ: Pearson/Prentice Hall, 2005.

Phillips, Kevin. *Wealth and Democracy: A Political History of the American Rich*. New York, NY: Broadway Books, 2002.

Pirosh, Robert and George Seaton. Groucho Marx in *A Day at the Races*. DVD. Directed by Sam Wood. Buckinghamshire, England: MGM, 1937.

Pirrong, Craig. "Manipulation of Cash-Settled Futures Contracts." *The Journal of Business* 74, no. 2 (2001): 221–244.

Plato. *Apology*, in *Five Dialogues*, translated by GMA Grubes. Indianapolis, IN: Hackett, 1981 [circa 350 BCE].

Plato. *Plato's Apology, Crito, and Phaedo of Socrates*, translated by Henry Cary. Philadelphia, PA: David McKay, 1897 [circa 350 BCE].

Poe, Edgar Allan. *The Tell-Tale Heart and Other Writings*. New York, NY: Bantam Books, 1982 [1843].

Pollock, John. *Contemporary Theories of Knowledge.* Landham, MD: Rowman & Littlefield, 1986.

Porter, Eduardo. "Campaigns Like These Make It Hard to Find a Reason to Believe." *The New York Times*, December 14, 2007: A34.

Posner, Richard A. *Sex and Reason*. Harvard, MA: Harvard University Press, 1992.

Pravda. "Presidential Inaugural Address." http://english.pravda.ru/science/19/94/378/12182_alien.html.

Rawls, John. *A Theory of Justice*. Cambridge, Mass: Harvard University Press, 1971.

Regan, Patrick, ed. *Teachers Jokes Quotes and Anecdotes*. Riverside, NJ: Andrews McMeel Publishing, 2001.

Rieke, Richard D., Malcolm O. Sillars and Tarla Rai Peterson. *Argumentation and Critical Decision Making*. 6th ed. Columbus, OH: Allyn & Bacon, 2005.

Roche, David. "The Global Money Machine," *The Wall Street Journal*, December 14, 2007: A21.

Rohde, David, "U.S. Officials See Waste in Billions Sent to Pakistan." *The New York Times*, December 24, 2007: A1 & A6.

Ross, Catherine and John Mirowsky. "Refining the Association Between Education and Health: The Effects of Quantity, Credential, and Selectivity." *Demography* 36, no. 4 (1999): 445–460.

Rovere, Richard. *Senator Joe McCarthy*. Los Angeles: University of California Press, 1996.

Rowling, J.K. *Harry Potter and the Philosopher's Stone*. London: Bloomsbury Publishing, 1997.

Rupp, E.G., and Benjamin Drewery. *Martin Luther, Documents of Modern History*. London: Edward Arnold, 1970.

Russell, Bertand. *The Problems of Philosophy*. Oxford: Oxford University Press, 1912.

Salkind, Neil. *Exploring Research*, 6th ed. Upper Saddle River, NJ: Pearson/Prentice Hall, 2006.

Salt, Henry S. "Logic of the Larder." Excerpted from *The Humanities of Diet*. Manchester: The Vegetarian Society, 1914. http://www.animal-rights-library.com/texts-c/salt02.htm.

Salzer, James, "Critics: School Tax Cut Flawed." *The Atlanta Journal-Constitution*, December 29, 2007: A1.

Sankar, D. and others. "Effect of Sesame Oil on Diuretics or ß-blockers in the Modulation of Blood Pressure, Anthropometry, Lipid Profile, and Redox Status." *The Yale Journal of Biology and Medicine* 79, no. 1 (2006): 19–26.

Scalia, Antonin. "God's Justice and Ours." *First Thing: The Journal of Religion, Culture and Public Life* 123 (2002): 17–21.

Schaefer, Kayleen. "The Sit-In at the Altar: No 'I do' Till Gays Can Do It, Too." *The New York Times*, December 3, 2006: A20.

Schaefer, Richard T. *Sociology: A Brief Introduction*, 7th ed. New York, NY: McGraw-Hill, 2006.

Schirokauer, Conrad. *A Brief History of Chinese and Japanese Civilizations*, 3rd ed. Boston, MA: Houghton Mifflin, 2005.

Schlafly, Phyllis. "The Media Campaign Against Gun Ownership." *The Phyllis Schlafly Report* 33, no. 11, (2000).

Schmidt, Michael. "Bond's Former Doctor Could Be a Prosecution Witness." *The New York Times*, December 21, 2007: C13.

Schmitt, Carl. *The Concept of the Political*, translated by George Schwab. Chicago: University of Chicago Press, 1996 [1932].

Scopes, John Thomas and William J. Bryan. *The World's Most Famous Court Trial. Tennessee Evolution Case*. Cincinnati, Ohio: National Book Company, 1925.

Scott, Ellen K. "Dangerous Dependencies: The Intersection of Welfare Reform and Domestic Violence." *Gender and Society* 16, no. 6 (2002): 878–897.

Shakespeare, William. *Hamlet* In *The Complete Works of Shakespeare*, edited by David Bevington. New York, NY: Longman, 1997 [1600].

Shakespeare, William. *Pericles. The Complete Works of Shakespeare*, edited by David Bevington. New York, NY: Longman, 1997 [1608].

Shakespeare, William. *Macbeth*. New York, NY: Oxford University Press, 1998 [1611].

Shaw, William H. *Moral Issues in Business*. Florence, KY: Wadsworth, 2003.

Shermer, Michael and Alex Grobman. *Denying History*. Berkeley, CA: University of California Press, 2000.

Sidor, Christian, Molly Miller and John Isbell, "Tetrapod Burrows from the Triassic of Antarctica." *Journal of Vertebrate Paleontology* 28, no. 2 (2008): 277–284.

Singer, Peter. "Famine, Affluence, and Morality." In *Introduction to Philosophy*, 4th ed., edited by John Perry, Michael Bratman and John Fischer. New York, NY: Oxford University Press, 2007.

Smith, Kelley. "NCGA Partners with Retailers in Organic Fraud Detection." *Cooperative Grocer* 133 (Nov/Dec 2007) http://www.cooperativegrocer.coop/articles/index.php?id=762.

Smith, Randolph A. and Stephen F. Davis. *The Psychologist as Detective*, 4th ed. Upper Saddle River, NJ: Pearson Prentice Hall, 2007.

Snyder, LB and others. "Effects of Alcohol Advertising Exposure on Drinking among Youth." *Archives of Pediatrics and Adolescent Medicine* 160, no. 1 (2006): 18–24.

Snyder, Louis L. *Encyclopedia of Nationalism*. New York, NY: Paragon House, 1977.

Sonders, Liz Ann. "The ABCs of CDOs, ABCP, MBSs, SIVs and NAVs." http://www.accessdigital.com/?p=1887

Soter, Steven. "What Is a Planet?" *Scientific American* (January 2007): 34–41.

Stanley, Jason. Review on back cover of *The Elements of Philosophy: Readings from Past and Present*. Tamar Szabo Gendler, Susannan Siegel and Steven M. Cahn, eds. (Oxford: Oxford University Press, 2006).

Steel, Knight and T. Franklin Williams. "It's Time to March." *Journal of the American Geriatric Society* 54, no. 7 (2006): 1142–1143.

Steinberg, Paul, "The Hangover That Lasts," *The New York Times*, December 29, 2007: A17.

Stoll, Matthew and Eugene Tinelli. "The General Effect of Limiting Syringe Availability Within the United States' Intravenous Drug Population, and the Resultant Effect on the Rest of the Heterosexual Community." http://www.reconsider.org/issues/public_health/aids.htm.

Sunstein, Bonnie Stone and Elizabeth Chiseri-Strater. *FieldWorking: Reading and Writing Research*, 3rd ed. New York, NYC: Bedford/St. Martin's, 2006.

Taylor, Travis S and others. *An Introduction to Planetary Defense: A Study of Modern Warfare Applied to Extra-Terrestrial Invasion*. Boca Raton, FL: Brown-Walker Press, 2006.

Temple University. "Addiction Treatment May Benefit From Nicotine-Alcohol Interaction Study," http://www.medicalnewstoday.com/articles/87989.php.

The Beatles. "Lucy in the Sky with Diamonds." Sgt. Pepper's Lonely Hearts Club Band. Parlophone, 1967.

The Boston Globe. "The Cost of No Coverage." *The Boston Globe*, December 29, 2007, http://www.boston.com/bostonglobe/editorial_opinion/editorials/articles/2007/12/29/the_cost_of_no_coverage/.

The New York Times. "Counting Noses in Prison." *The New York Times*, April 18, 2006: A26.

The New York Times. "Junking Fat Foods in Schools." *The New York Times*, December 10, 2007: A22.

The New York Times. "The Poles Get Cold Feet." *The New York Times*, December 30, 2007: C7.

The New York Times. "Time and the Dictator." *The New York Times*, December 29, 2007: A16.

The Rush Limbaugh Show, January 23, 2007. Download from a Web site that is no longer displayed.

Thompson, Bruce. www.cuyamaca.edu/bruce.thompson/Fallacies/amphiboly.asp.

Thomson, Judith Jarvis. "A Defense of Abortion." *Philosophy and Public Affairs*. 1, no. 1 (1971): 47–66.

Thucydides. "Pericles' Last Speech." In *On Justice, Power, and Human Nature: Selections from The History of the Peloponnesian War*, translated by Paul Woodruff. Indianapolis, IN: Hackett Press, 1993 [circa 400 BCE].

Tilley, Christopher and others. "Art and Re-presentation of the Past." *Journal of the Royal Anthropological Institute* 6, no. 1 (March 2000): 35–62.

Tindall, George Brown and David Emory Shi, "Another Red Scare." In *America A Narrative History*, edited by Karl Bakeman. New York, NY: W.W. Norton, 2007.

Todorov, Tzvetan. *The Morals of History*, translated by Alyson Waters. Minneapolis, MN: University of Minnesota, 1995.

Tsang, Gloria. "Benefits of Flax Seed in Heart Disease and Cholesterol Lowering." http://www.healthcastle.com/flax.shtml.

Ture, Kwamel and Charles Hamilton. *Black Power*. New York, NY: Random House: 1967.

Twain, Mark. *The Adventures of Huckleberry Finn*. London: Puffin Books, 2008 [1884].

Twain, Mark. *Mark Twain on Religion*. Charleston, SC: Forgotten Books, 2007.

Twain, Mark. *Mark Twain's Own Autobiography: The Chapters from the North American Review*. Madison, WI: University of Wisconsin Press, 1990.

Twain, Mark. *Pudd'nhead Wilson*. Mineloa, NY: Dover Publications, 1999 [1894].

U.S. Census Bureau, *Statistical Abstract of the United States*, Washington, DC: Bureau of the Census, 2000.

U.S. Census Bureau, *Statistical Abstract of the United States*, Washington, DC: Bureau of the Census, 2010.

Um, Nancy. "Spatial Negotiations in a Commercial City: The Red Sea Port of Mocha, Yemen, during the First Half of the Eighteenth Century." *The Journal of the Society of Architectural Historians* 62, no. 2 (2003): 178–193.

Vinicor, Frank, "Is Diabetes a Public-health Disorder?" *Diabetes Care* 17 Suppl. 1 (1994): 22–27.

Voltaire. *Voltaire: Selections*, translated by Paul Edwards. New York, NY: Macmillan, 1989.

Warrick, Joby and Michael Grunwald. "Investigators Link Levee Failures to Design Flaws: Three Teams of Engineers Find Weakened Soil, Navigation Canal Contributed to La. Collapses," *The Washington Post*, October 24, 2005: A1.

Whelan, Debra Lau. "13,000 Kids Can't Be Wrong." *School Library Journal*, 50, no. 2 (2004): 46–50.

Wikipedia. "Spam (electronic)," http://en.wikipedia.org/wiki/Spam_%28electronic%29.

Winehouse, Amy. *Back To Black*. CD. Republic, 2007.

Wonacott, Peter and Jay Solomon, "Pakistan Violence Threatens Rule Of Musharraf," *The Wall Street Journal*, December 29, 2007: A1.

Yakubinsky, Lev Petrovich. "On Dialogic Speech," translated by Michael Eskin. *PMLA* 112 (1197): 243–256.

Zola, Emile. "J'accuse!," *L'Aurore*, January 13, 1898: 1.

Ziegler, Michael R. and Dana Milbank. "Making Hay Out of Straw Men." *The Washington Post*, June 1, 2004: A21.

Zweigenhaft, Richard L. and Jessica von Ammon. "Birth Order and Civil Disobedience: A Test of Sulloway's 'Born to Rebel' Hypothesis." *The Journal of Social Psychology*. 140, no. 5 (2000): 624–627.